RETHINKING INTERNATIONAL ORGANIZATIONS

RETHINKING INTERNATIONAL ORGANIZATIONS

ORGANIZATIONS

Pathology and Promise

Edited by

Dennis Dijkzeul

and

Yves Beigbeder

Berghahn Books

NEW YORK • OXFORD

Published in 2003 by

Berghahn Books

www.berghahnbooks.com

Library of Congress Cataloging-in-Publication Data

Rethinking international organizations : pathology and promise / edited by
Dennis Dijkzeul and Yves Beigbeder.
    p. cm.
Includes bibliographical references and index.
ISBN 1-57181-380-2 (cl. : alk. paper) – ISBN 1-57181-656-9 (pbk. : alk. paper)
    1. International agencies. I. Dijkzeul, Dennis II. Beigbeder, Yves.

JZ4839 .R48 2002
341.2—dc21   2002018415

British Library Cataloguing in Publication Data

A catalogue record for this book is available from
the British Library.

Printed in the United States on acid-free paper

Cover photo © Victor Mello/United Nations Office for Project Services

CONTENTS

ILLUSTRATIONS

TABLES

PREFACE

This book is born out of frustration. We were unhappy with the way international organizations were treated, or often left untreated, in the social sciences. Nor were we satisfied with the quality of the debates in the press on these organizations. At the same time, international organizations should and could function much better than they often do. We felt that the managerial aspects of these organizations were understudied. Yet the management of these organizations covers broad areas ranging from international diplomacy to specific projects addressing human rights in a developing country to war-related traumas in zones of conflict. It is almost impossible for one person to cover all these subjects. Hence, we decided to bring together an international group of authors with enough practical experience and theoretical background to cover the wide array of possible topics.

Two studies unwittingly functioned as signposts for the state of the art of the management of international organizations. In early 2000, when we were approaching the other contributors to this volume, Yves sent an email: "Just noted that an article has been published in *International Organization* on *The Politics, Power, and Pathologies of International Organization* by Martha Finnemore and Michael Barnett — have they stolen our title?" Of course, Finnemore and Barnett had independently come up with their title, but the article formed a strong indication that the time was ripe for an in-depth investigation into the management of international organizations.

The other study, *Going Global: Transforming Relief and Development NGOs*, was coauthored by Coralie Bryant, a Columbia University colleague, and Marc Lindenberg. It appeared when we were putting the finishing touches on our book. In their preface, Lindenberg and Bryant write that they "look … through a different lens from the socially critical one customarily worn by social scientists. We look through the lens of the actors themselves in the drama rather than through the lens of the social critic" (2001: xii).

These two publications fill the void in the study of the functioning and management of international organizations in a very different manner. Finnemore and Barnett base their work on international relations theory, and with institutional theory they bridge the divide between organizational and international relations theory. They do work as social critics. Bryant and Lindenberg ground their approach in the empirical study of the actual professionals working in these organizations.

Both approaches are necessary, but they are not always easily combined. The contributors to this book also struggled with finding a balance between social critique and an empirically based insider's perspective. They certainly did not always agree with each other, but without their diversity of inquiry the book would have had less value. Ultimately, sound theory building requires both critique and empirical study. We hope that this volume contributes to this end.

This book would not have been possible without the support of several people. At Columbia University, three graduate students from the School of International and Public Affairs, John Hamilton, David Starr, and Shefali Parikh, helped with editing and data collection. The comments of the independent reviewer led to revisions that strengthened several chapters considerably. The interaction with the other authors has been a great learning process for the two of us. Any mistakes remain our responsibility, of course. Finally, the positive and patient cooperation of our publisher, Berghahn Books, is greatly appreciated.

During the final stages of editing, the terrorist attacks of 11 September took place. As a result, the role of international organizations may change considerably. Issues such as multilateralism, cooperation with armed forces, nation building, and human rights have come to the fore in ways previously unexpected. Before 11 September, most observers did not foresee that the US would pay its bills to the UN, nor was the 2001 Nobel Peace Prize expected. And yet, both have come to pass. International organizations will in all likelihood play an important role in the aftermath of the war in Afghanistan. It is a Chinese curse to wish somebody "May you live in interesting times," the point being that boring times are more healthy periods in which to live. When it comes to international organizations, dealing as they do with war, development, human rights, and the environment, the times are always interesting. The problems, relevance, and influence of international organizations cannot be ignored.

We hope that the readers of this book, practitioners and scholars alike, will engage in more vibrant and informed debates about the functioning and possible reforms of international organizations. International organizations need such debate, in terms of both their management and the societal challenges they confront.

Yves Beigbeder   Dennis Dijkzeul
Thonon-les-Bains, France   New York

ABBREVIATIONS

ACABQ	Advisory Committee on Administrative and Budgetary Questions
ACP	Africa, Caribbean, and Pacific states
AI	Amnesty International
ARC	American Refugee Committee
ASEAN	Association of Southeast Asian Nations
BiH	Bosnia and Herzegovina
CEPS	Center for European Policy Studies
CIDA	Canadian International Development Agency
CPC	Committee for Programme and Coordination
CRS	Catholic Relief Services
CUNMA	Centre for United Nations Management Accountability
DAM	Department of Administration and Management (United Nations)
DOS	Dalmatinski Odbor Solidarnosti (Dalmatian Committee for Solidarity)
DPKO	Department of Peacekeeping Operations (United Nations)
ECA	Economic Commission for Africa
ECHO	European Community Humanitarian Office
ECOSOC	Economic and Social Council (United Nations)
ESCAP	Economic and Social Commission for Asia and the Pacific
ESI	European Stability Initiative
EU	European Union
EWI	The EastWest Institute
FAO	Food and Agriculture Organization
FBI	Federal Bureau of Investigation
FDI	Foreign Direct Investment
FICSA	Federation of International Civil Servants' Associations
FRY	Federal Republic of Yugoslavia
G77	Group of 77 (the non-aligned countries)
GATT	General Agreement on Tariffs and Trade

GDP	Gross Domestic Product
Habitat	United Nations Centre for Human Settlements
HDR	*Human Development Report*
HIPC	Heavily Indebted Poor Countries
HRO	Human Rights Organization
IBHI	Independent Bureau for Humanitarian Issues
ICRC	International Committee of the Red Cross
ICSC	International Civil Service Commission
ICVA	International Council of Voluntary Agencies
IDC	Island Developing Countries
IFAD	International Fund for Agricultural Development
IFOR	Implementation Force (NATO)
IFRC	International Federation of Red Cross and Red Crescent Societies
IGO	International Governmental Organization
IHL	International Humanitarian Law
ILO	International Labour Organization
IMF	International Monetary Fund
INGO	International Non-governmental Organization
IOCC	International Orthodox Christian Charities
IPTF	International Police Task Force
IRC	International Rescue Committee
ISNAR	International Service for National Agricultural Research
ITU	International Telecommunication Union
JIU	Joint Inspection Unit
LDC	Least Developed Country
LDLC	Least Developed Landlocked Countries
MERCOSUR	Southern Common Market (Argentina, Brazil, Paraguay, and Uruguay)
MONUA	United Nations Observer Mission in Angola
MSF	Médicins Sans Frontières
NATO	North Atlantic Treaty Organization
NGO	Non-governmental Organization
OCN	Office of the Commissioner in Namibia
ODA	Official Development Assistance
OECD	Organization for Economic Cooperation and Development
OHR	Office of the High Representative (in Bosnia and Herzegovina)
OIOS	Office of Internal Oversight Services
ONUC	United Nations Operation in the Congo
OSCE	Organization for Security and Cooperation in Europe
OSI	Open Society Institute
OTI	Office of Transition Initiatives

PRM	Population, Refugee, and Migration
RRTF	Reconstruction and Return Task Force
RS	Republika Srpska
SEE	Southeast Europe Stability Pact
SFOR	Stabilisation Force (NATO)
SHD	Sustainable Human Development
SRSG	Special Representative of the Secretary-General
TDB	Trade and Development Board
TNC	Transnational Corporation
TOD	Institute for the Transition to Democracy
TRIPS	Trade-Related Intellectual Property Rights
UIA	Union of International Associations
UN	United Nations
UNAMIR	United Nations Assistance Mission for Rwanda
UNAT	United Nations Administrative Tribunal
UNAVEM	United Nations Angola Verification Mission
UNCED	United Nations Conference on Environment and Development
UNCIVPOL	United Nations Civilian Police
UNCLOS	United Nations Conference on the Law of the Sea
UNCTAD	United Nations Conference on Trade and Development
UNDOF	United Nations Disengagement Observer Force
UNDP	United Nations Development Programme
UNEF	United Nations Emergency Force
UNEP	United Nations Environment Programme
UNFICYP	United Nations Forces in Cyprus
UNFPA	United Nations Population Fund
UNHCR	United Nations High Commissioner for Refugees
UNICEF	United Nations Children's Fund
UNIDO	United Nations Industrial Development Organization
UNIKOM	United Nations Iraq-Kuwait Observation Mission
UNJSPF	United Nations Joint Staff Pension Fund
UNMIBH	United Nations Mission in Bosnia and Herzegovina
UNMIH	United Nations Mission in Haiti
UNMIK	United Nations Mission in Kosovo
UNMOGIP	United Nations Military Observer Group in India and Pakistan
UNMOT	United Nations Mission of Observers in Tajikistan
UNOG	United Nations Office at Geneva
UNOSOM	United Nations Operation in Somalia
UNPF	United Nations Peace Forces in the Former Yugoslavia
UNPROFOR	United Nations Protection Force
UNRWA	United Nations Relief and Works Agency for Palestine Refugees in the Near East

UNTAC	United Nations Transitional Authority in Cambodia
UNTSO	United Nations Truce Supervision Organization
US	United States
USAID	United States Agency for International Development
USG	Under-Secretary-General
USSR	Union of Socialist Soviet Republics
WFP	World Food Program
WHO	World Health Organization
WTO	World Trade Organization

INTRODUCTION
Rethinking International Organizations

Dennis Dijkzeul and Yves Beigbeder

International organizations regularly receive fierce criticism. Paradoxically, understanding of these organizations is often limited. The number of studies that shed light on their inner workings is still relatively small, and a satisfactory theory explaining their behavior does not yet exist. Nevertheless, as a field the management of international organizations is attracting increasing attention. This book brings together many disparate strands of criticism regarding international organizations and presents an empirical and theoretical overview of their management issues. The contributors to this book rethink the practice and theory of international organizations.

The book draws attention to the pathologies and promise that are inherent to the concept of international organizations. These organizations operate worldwide on almost all issues imaginable, from peacebuilding to technical standard setting, from promoting literacy to public sanitation. While they influence the lives of many people around the world, these organizations face profound management problems. Some shortcomings persist to such an extent that it is possible to speak about pathologies. Examples include excessive bureaucracy, slow action, humanitarian aid that reignites war, failure to protect refugees, and dependency as a byproduct of development cooperation. Somalia, Rwanda, and Srebrenica have come to symbolize the most horrible failures of international organizations in peacekeeping.

Nevertheless, criticism of international organizations sometimes lacks a sound basis, for example, when it reflects insufficient knowledge of the actual functioning of these organizations, or is based on narrow, sometimes biased political concerns of particular groups. Some countries criticize international organizations because they oppose outside "interference" within their borders. Generally, the national interest of Member States, their tactical alliances, or simply North-South differences determine the degree and nature of the criticism.

This introduction discusses what pathologies and promise mean in the context of international organizations. By studying the scientific and press attention given to these organizations, it also explains the paradox of fierce criticism and limited understanding of their functioning. In particular, this essay looks at the different types of study in the disciplines of international relations and business and public administration to explain why international organizations have not been in the mainstream of research attention. The introduction ends with an overview of the contributions by the different authors of this book.

Pathologies and Promise

Pathology is the science of causes and symptoms of diseases. Of course, a medical concept is not directly applicable to forms of social organization. We use pathology to describe the situation in which the organization's dysfunctional management (causes of disease) results in negative outcomes (symptoms of disease). In management terms, diseases would include inefficiency, waste of funds on petty causes, deviation from mandate, duplication, overstaffing, slow decision-making processes, patronage, and fraud.

The consequences of these diseases range from outright failure to damage to the public image, decreasing interest of donors and other contributors, lessening legitimacy, unfulfilled mandates, unresolved societal problems, and declining organizations (that somehow never really die). However, if one attempts to identify the causes of diseases, one should be careful not to blame the patient too fast. Yes, the patient plays a critical role, but what about the environmental factors? Can the patient influence these factors? In other words, to what extent are international organizations responsible for the outcomes of their activities? Are other actors also responsible for the outcomes of international humanitarian and development work? Traditionally, the state is seen as the main actor in international affairs, which brings up the question of how states and international organizations interact with each other. Are international organizations just passive patients? Another problem is that some supposed remedies do not work well. Reforms of international organizations have often shown disappointing or counterproductive results.

The contributors to this book have attempted to identify explanations and actions that offer promise for a better functioning of these organizations. Ultimately, identifying and proposing promising remedies should be based on a better understanding of these organizations, their shortcomings and strengths, as well as their differences. This will also help to identify promising external trends and internal actions that can foster a stronger functioning of these organizations.

IGOs, NGOs, and Other Distinctions

Knowing that patients differ can assist in providing better remedies. This is important because the definitions of international organizations vary widely.[1] The number and scope of international organizations has been increasing, especially since World War II. NGOs and intergovernmental organizations differ in size, field of interest, financing, mandates, and so on.

TABLE I.1 Types of International Organizations

Characteristics of Intergovernmental Organizations and Non-governmental Organizations

The *Yearbook of International Organizations*, published by the Union of International Associations (UIA), defines IGOs as: (a) being based on a formal instrument of agreement between the governments of states; (b) including three or more states as parties to the agreement; and (c) possessing a permanent secretariat performing ongoing tasks.

The main criteria set up by the UIA for defining international NGOs are the following: The aim must be genuinely international in character, with the intention to be active in at least three countries. The NGO's constitution must provide for a formal structure that allows for periodic elections of a governing body and officers and for a permanent headquarters. No attempt must be made to make profits for distribution to members of the NGO.

Created and financed by Member States, IGOs benefit from governments' support and share some of governments' authority and prestige. The IGOs and their staff members have a legitimate international status, recognized in constitutions, international conventions, and host agreements. National and international NGOs are created under national law: there is no global, international legal regime governing their status and activities.

IGOs are structured, organized bureaucracies, which should ensure permanency and continuity of action to the international organizations. IGO governing bodies formulate, approve, and publicize international policies and strategies, which ideally enjoy global or regional legitimacy and serve as objectives and guidelines for countries and NGOs. While IGOs provide order and continuity, divergences among their Member States, their financial dependency on governments' contributions, and their own diplomatic and bureaucratic nature may slow or stall progress, stifle initiatives, and discourage innovation.

The fact that NGOs are created and managed by private individuals or groups affirms, in principle, their claim to autonomy and independence from governments and IGOs. Their autonomy supports their capacity for

---

TABLE I.1 Types of International Organizations *(cont.)*

innovation and independent advocacy and action. However, this same autonomy has made attempts to coordinate the action of NGOs between themselves, as well as among NGOs and IGOs, difficult. The general public tends to perceive the motivation of NGOs as purely philanthropic, excluding any profit motive. However, critics have challenged their democratic representation; their officials are not elected by the people. The fact that most INGOs have been founded in Western democracies has exposed them to allegations of bias against the interests and "values" of Southern countries.

Source: Union of International Associations, Judge A. "Types of International Organizations" in http://www.uia.org/uiadocs/orgtypeb.htm, and Beigbeder Y. (1991: 19– 21, 80–82).

Sometimes, the term "international organizations" is used to include multinational corporations, bilateral organizations, multilateral organizations, regional bodies, and international NGOs. Other times, only UN organizations are covered by this term. While recognizing that many authors who talk about international organizations actually limit themselves to intergovernmental organizations, we will also include international NGOs that often interface and interact with UN organizations.[2]

These NGOs possess different international legitimacy than IGOs, as they do not represent states. Their growing role in international relations, their independence of spirit and autonomy of action, and their occasionally close or competitive relationships with IGOs make them worthy subjects of study. Since both UN organizations and international NGOs often focus on the same societal issues, we prefer to study them together. In particular, we focus on international organizations active in the areas of development cooperation, human rights, and humanitarian aid. These organizations often originate in the Northern, industrialized countries and are supposed to assist actors in Southern countries. They provide goods or services through which they serve some international public purpose (see Lindenberg and Bryant 2001: 5). They also carry out advocacy tasks and often function as forums for information exchange and debate. In addition, UN organizations are also set up to function as forums to negotiate binding or non-binding international rules and standards (Dijkzeul 1997: 28). Through all these activities, international organizations—both NGOs and IGOs—help to "define shared international tasks (like 'development'), create and define new categories of actors (like 'refugee'), create new interests for actors (like 'promoting human rights'), and transfer models of political organization around the world (like markets and democracy)" (Barnett and Finnemore 1999: 699).

In sum, while international NGOs differ from UN organizations in their relationships with governments, they are rather similar in that they often address comparable societal issues and they are outsiders—often Northern organizations working in Southern countries—who need to establish local roots. In addition, they often interact with each other.

Insufficient Attention and Strong Criticism

The first international organizations originated in Europe, for example, to govern the navigation issues of the Rhine (Archer 1983: 12). Since then, their numbers have exploded. NGOs have always been more numerous than IGOs, and their numbers have continued to increase rapidly. The number of IGOs peaked in 1985 at 378 and has decreased since then.

International Relations

Despite their growth, international organizations have not received much theoretical and empirical attention over the last three to four decades. In earlier decades, the situation was different. During the interbellum, international institution building dominated international relations "to such an extent that international organization was viewed not so much as a subfield but as practically the core of the discipline" (Rochester 1986: 779–780; see also Kratochwil and Ruggie 1986: 776–802). Most studies were of a legal or historical nature.[3]

Hoole has described the period from 1945 to 1960 as an intellectual era in which studies of the UN system dominated (Rochester 1986: 782–797). Yet, in the 1960s, regional integration studies, for example, on the European Economic Community, dominated. In the 1970s, attention shifted to transnational politics, networks of interdependence, and international regimes. In the 1980s, regime theory received considerable notice, and the attention paid to international organizations continued to decline (Kratochwil and Ruggie 1986: 753–755).

By the same token, there was little or no interaction between, on the one hand, international relations theory and, on the other, management and organization theory. However, especially in the 1970s, there have been powerful exceptions to this lack of interaction. Allison's (1971) work on decision making during the Cuban missile crisis showed the explanatory power of an organizational process perspective for international decision making. Jervis (1976) used organizational learning in his book on perception and misperception in international politics. Cox and Jacobson (1973, 1977) also wrote on decision making, which received considerable attention in other social sciences, in particular, in management and organization theory (Simon 1976). However, business and public administration theory moved away from decision-making theory to the study

FIGURE I.1 Growth of International Organizations

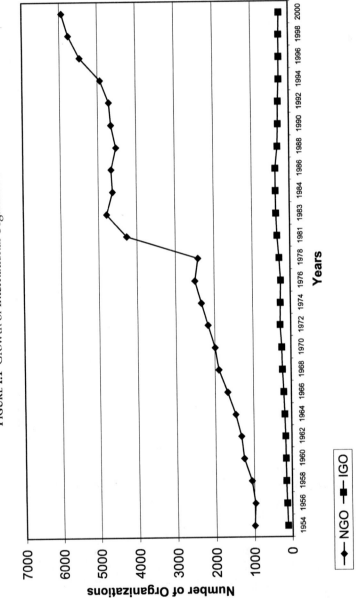

Source: Recent editions of the UIA Yearbook of International Organizations 1909/1999.
International organizations—conventional international bodies—by year and type.

of implementation (Pressman and Wildavsky 1984; see also Dijkzeul 1997: 57–58). Unfortunately, instead of fostering more empirical attention on the actual functioning of international organizations, this move did not make a lasting impact on international relations theory.

In the 1980s, several authors noted the lack of attention to both international organizations and management theory. Jönsson (1986: 39) wrote "the relation between organization theory and the study of international organization ... has largely been one of mutual neglect." Two years later, Ness and Brechin (1988: 246) reached a similar conclusion: "The gap between the study of international organizations and the sociology of organizations is deep and persistent."

Early in the 1990s, this pattern endured. Haas (1990), with his book on learning and adaptation of international organizations, was the exception that proved the rule.[4] Smouts (1993: 443) argued that although "everything seems to have been said about international organizations," an impression of dissatisfaction remained in international relations theory. In a similar vein, de Senarclens (1993: 453) contended that "the study of international organization has made scarcely any progress over the past few decades." Jönsson (1993) again noted the neglect of organization theory and international organizations. Yet he also offered some criticism on the actual study of international organizations. First, he noticed a disproportionate attention to UN organizations.[5] Second, he stated that many studies are monographs that treat "international organizations as self-contained units." In particular, their modus operandi in a heterogeneous and fluid organizational environment received too little attention. Third, he argued that "research on international organizations has by and large been idiographic rather than nomothetic. The weak or altogether lacking theoretical underpinning has ushered in eclecticism and inadequate cumulation of knowledge" (Jönsson 1993: 464).

While the former, European authors were bothered by the lack of attention to international organizations, Ruggie (1993: 6) held a different point of view: "Multilateral formal organizations ... entail no analytical mystery.... These organizations constitute only a small part of a broader universe of international institutional forms."[6] While the latter view explains the lack of attention to international organizations, it is certainly not universally accepted.

Brechin (1997: 18) observed that "for reasons unknown, international organizations, even well-known and influential ones involved in economic development, have not been studied much from a sociological perspective." He applied ideas from institutional and contingency theory as developed in business and public administration to the forestry projects of the World Bank, FAO, and CARE. Finnemore (1993) also used institutional theory on international organizations as teachers of norms. Of course, the concept of norms is linked closely to regime theory (Krasner 1983). According to Klingebiel (1999), the general debate among political scientists on international organizations "must generally be regarded as unsatisfactory ... a convincing and closed theory or conception does not yet exist." He considers the regime approach the most innovative contribution to the debate and also links it to institutionalism. Nevertheless, Klingebiel (1999: 22) also concludes: "The main question as to the effectiveness of international organizations and their impact on international relations has—with a few exceptions—been considered in any depth only in connection with the debate on international regimes, but so far inadequately even in this context."

In addition to institutionalism, two exceptions caught considerable attention in both the international relations and development studies during the 1990s.[7] First, after the end of the Cold War, the number of complex emergencies rose rapidly. Several peacekeeping operations were not able to stop the bloodshed. In some cases, they actually contributed to an increase in the level of violence. The same happened with humanitarian aid. These problems were so horrible and glaring that many (case) studies were written about the role of international organizations in these situations (e.g., Weiss and Pasic 1997; Whitman 1999).[8] Often, more general literature highlighted the failings and counterproductive nature of international organizations (de Waal 1997; Maren 1997). In this context, some authors have indirectly pointed out the operational impact of international organizations (Anderson 1999; Morales Nieto 1996; Uvin 1998). This critical literature has not been fully integrated into international relations theory. Only a few authors have explicitly applied management theory to international organizations in conflict situations (Handler Chayes et al. 1997; Walkup 1997). The transition from case description to theory formulation proves to be difficult. Perhaps this transition does not occur because the linkages between peacekeeping, humanitarian assistance, and development cooperation at the field level and policymaking and norm setting at the intergovernmental level still need to be elaborated.

Second, the non-governmental organizations were studied widely and, initially, often from a positive perspective.[9] They were considered to work better at the grassroots level, and it was often argued that they were more effective than state, bilateral, and multilateral organizations (see Beigbeder 1991; Biekart 1999). Later, they were criticized more strongly.[10] Authors argued that NGOs were not the hoped-for magic bullet (Edwards and Hulme 1996). Biekart (1999: 76) writes: "By the late 1990s, [NGOs] were under fire from various sides: from official donors (demanding measurable results and efficiency), from Southern partner organizations (demanding less paternalism and more 'direct funding' from official donors), from (some) Northern private donors (demanding transparency), and from their own staff which was squeezed between the demands of institutional growth and efficiency (more turnover with less costs at shorter terms) and developmental impact (which had proven to be expensive and rather slow)."

Biekart's description is quite similar to the criticism leveled at UN organizations. The promise that NGOs would do better than UN and other governmental organizations has insufficiently materialized. Both UN organizations and NGOs seem to have fallen upon hard times. Moreover, despite the slowly increasing attention, Keohane still asks why some international institutions—by which he means *both* "the rules that govern elements of world politics and the organizations that help implement rules"—succeed and others fail (1998: 82–96). In addition, Barnett and Finnemore (1999: 699) observe that there are "a variety of [mainly economics-based] theories that explain why [international organizations] have been created.... Research flowing from these theories, however, has paid little attention to how international organizations actually behave after they are created." Paradoxically, these two authors describe the need for empirical research, but rely on case studies by others.

In sum, over the last two to three decades, the debate on international organizations has been characterized by a continuous lament that more and better study is required. Similarly, organizational and management theories have not been used frequently, with the exception of decision-making theory in the 1970s and organizational institutionalism in the 1990s. Nor does an explicit theory exist to explain the behavior of international organizations. However, the attention to complex emergencies and NGOs makes it seem that the consideration granted to international organizations has been rebounding slightly in the course of the 1990s.[11] Nevertheless, we cannot yet speak of a vibrant field with sufficient new empirical studies or adequate theory accumulation.

Business Administration and Public Administration

Could the disciplines of business and public administration offer a way out? After all, examining both the internal functioning and external relationships of organizations belongs to their main activities. Unfortunately, the attention to international organizations from a business administration point of view is minimal. Jönsson has noted that "widely used textbooks on organization theory include no systematic treatment on international organizations" (Jönsson 1993: 464).[12] Similarly, Cooperrider and Pasmore (1991: 765) found that "reports on their functioning lie in undeveloped fragmentary, and anecdotal form, almost entirely outside the leading journals of the organizational sciences" and "despite the rapid proliferation of these organizations during the last 50 years, relatively little is known about [them] or how they operate."[13] With some exceptions (e.g., Van Ruller 1990; Dijkzeul 1997, 2000), the attention to international organizations did not improve much during the 1990s. This is understandable, because the main focus of business administration is on private enterprise, and not-for-profit international organizations fall outside that realm. However, with the growing recognition of the role of private investment in development, interaction between these two types of organizations has received more attention, for example, through UN-business partnerships (Tesner 2000).

In public administration, international organizations do not receive much research attention either, but they are not as marginalized as in business administration. Most attention, however, centers on national not-for-profit and public organizations. This traditional, national focus remains strong in public administration; after all, it is the main market. Fortunately, a mushrooming of attention to topics such as civil society (Carothers 1999) and governance opens the doors for more interest in international organizations as these deal with similar societal issues.

In many ways, this attention implies a shift away from the state, or traditional (top-down) public administration, to other societal actors with their own action potential. Partly, this reflected the ideological trends in the 1980s, which implied more attention to free markets and non-governmental actors (as part of civil society) from a neoliberal or monetarist perspective. Partly, it reflected the practical realization that state planning, or broader political/administrative governing systems, had to deal with implementation problems and policies canceling each others' effects (Kooiman 1993; Van Vliet 1992). In the Anglo-Saxon world, considerable attention was given to (New) Public Management and reinventing government (Osborne and Gaebler 1992; see Dijkzeul 2000: 9–11, 215–218), new policy instruments, and issues such as self-governance (see Grüning 1998). Still, such public administration theory needed to be translated to the international context. At the international level, this resulted in the aforementioned shift in attention from multilateral organizations toward NGOs. In international relations, various authors paid attention to governance, for example, Finkelstein (1995), Knight (1995) Rosenau and Czempiel (1992), Rosenau (1995), Young (1994). The recent interest in (global) public policy networks fits into this trend (see Reinicke 1999).

Public administration, in addition to its attention to civil society, NGOs, and governance, has another obvious benefit that it shares with business administration. Its management and organization theory covers a broad range of topics and allows for a detailed look at organizations and their interactions. In other words, theory from these disciplines facilitates a closer and more balanced look at organizations, which has often been noticed by authors who lament the lack of attention to international organizations. For example, theory about interorganizational relationships can be very useful in understanding coordination dilemmas. On a broader scale, one can also ask what the functioning of international organizations implies about modern societies and the global processes of (differentiation and integration of) human action.[14]

In any case, the specific characteristics of international organizations will require the adaptation of theories and concepts of both disciplines, but as the interest in institutionalism and decision-making theory shows, there is no a priori reason to assume that this is impossible. It just has not occurred often enough (Lindenberg and Bryant 2001: xi, 5).[15] As a result, criticism on the shortcomings of international organizations frequently suffers from empirical and theoretical shortcomings itself.

The Press

The media are another major source of information on international organizations. A number of newspapers report periodically on poor management, financial irregularities, waste, and fraud in UN organizations and large NGOs. Some articles are based on reporters' inquiries, revelations, or indiscretions by UN staff; some contain real facts and/or inaccuracies, or generalizations based on isolated incidents. A few periodicals specialize in exposing "UN corruption" with the obvious intent to debase the image of UN bodies and, more generally, as part of a campaign against multilateralism.[16]

Following the creation of the UN Office of Internal Oversight Services (OIOS) in 1994, the press has often used OIOS reports as a more factual basis for their articles. The title of a *New York Times* article by Crossette, reprinted by the *International Herald Tribune* on 3 November 1997, was "In War on Corruption and Waste, UN Confronts Well-Entrenched Foe." It referred to the 1997 report by OIOS, allegedly containing "ample evidence that the job of cleaning out the corners of the organization is a big one." The same report was the basis for articles in Swiss and French newspapers.[17]

A few British periodicals have been more aggressive. Following an article published in August 1993, "The scandal of the UN 'lost' millions," *The Sunday Times* published an "Insight" on the UN "Runaway Gravy Train" on 2 November 1997, referring to loss, theft, and waste amounting to millions of dollars, mainly in UN peacekeeping operations. The *Financial Times* published in July–August 1998 a series of articles and related letters containing allegations of financial mismanagement by the UNHCR. The agency categorically rejected the newspaper report as "filled with blatant errors and material omissions."[18]

Yet the press has not reported on a recent breakthrough initiated by OIOS: in 1999, OIOS assisted in criminal proceedings initiated by national courts on four continents. These resulted in arrests, trials, jail sentences, and the recovery of funds defrauded by UN or former UN staff. The UN's innovative recourse to national justice was inconceivable for UN legal specialists only a few years ago as a breach of the independence of the international civil service. This new policy is a significant advance in bolstering the principle of accountability of UN managers.

Occasionally, attention to the United Nations borders on the absurd. *De Volkskrant*, a Dutch newspaper, reported how the millennium change, according to some ostensibly deeply religious people in the US, was supposed to lead to destruction and a worldwide dictatorship by the United Nations.[19] A Spanish-language journal of the Jehovah's Witnesses in Guatemala equated the United Nations with the "beast" from the book of Revelations and thus with the coming apocalypse.[20]

UN organizations should reply each time to excessive or ill-founded criticism, and in all cases they should take publicly the required corrective action, including internal disciplinary sanctions or dismissals, recovery of lost or stolen funds, and national judiciary prosecution. The lack of administrative transparency and delays in responsive action only add to the vulnerability of the organizations in view of repeated public attacks. The press, however, should be able to substantiate its claims better. In fact, this concurs with a more general need to measure better the outcomes of the activities of international organizations (see Gordenker 1996). For example, when Paschke, the first head of OIOS, left, the *New York Times* (15 November 1999: A10) wrote that through his work millions had been saved; the article provided some good examples, but no totals.

NGOs used to receive less media attention than UN organizations, perhaps because they were usually seen as a promising alternative to multilateral and state bureaucracies. However, the media has recently become more critical. For example, *The Economist* (29 January 2000) argued that many NGOs have grown very close to governments.[21] Many are dependent on governments for funding and frequently exchange personnel with them. In addition, NGOs often compete fiercely with each other for media attention and funding. In terms of practical results, *The Economist* stated: "NGOs also get involved in situations where their presence may prolong or complicate wars, where they end up feeding armies, sheltering hostages, or serving as cover for warring parties." By their way of operating in the developing world, "they bring in western living standards, personnel, and purchasing power which can transform local markets and generate local resentment." Finally, institutional survival tends to replace original idealism. In other words, despite initial hopes, NGOs have fallen prey to limitations similar to those of many UN and bilateral organizations.

In the press, one also feels that some observers espouse high ideals concerning the UN and international NGOs. They thus hold them to very high standards. However, such standards almost automatically lead to disappointment. Like all other organizations, UN institutions and NGOs are staffed by fallible people who often work under extremely adverse conditions.

The press itself can be further criticized for sensationalism and one-sided attention.[22] Famine victims as shocking images have been overused, but the structural factors underlying famine are less often covered. Moreover, press attention may shame Western governments into action, but prevention and long-term rebuilding are only intermittently covered. In some cases, one can even wonder whether the press has the facts straight or manipulates them (see Girardet 1995). A similarity in these forms of criticism is that press coverage focuses too often on the short term and the dramatic (scandals, victims) and fails to address the deeper roots of societal problems. In addition, the press seldom makes a meaningful effort to understand better the external limitations and internal functioning of these organizations.[23] In the final analysis, the lack of attention paid to international organizations and their problems has not been offset by press coverage.

Perhaps paradoxically, the media and international organizations also share one characteristic that leads to a similar shortcoming. Most media and international organizations originate in industrialized Northern countries, their headquarters are often based there, and in their funding and decision making they are frequently dominated by Northern interests. As a consequence, Southern voices, especially of the poor, are heard only rarely.

Attention and Criticism Revisited

Alger (1996: 335) has argued that "in order to think about the UN, we must escape the narrow perspectives of daily press coverage as well as the mainstream of the scholarly agenda." The same can be said of international NGOs. In his article, Alger takes a historical perspective; our strategy is to empirically assess and critique the functioning of these organizations. But first we need to determine why the attention to international organizations has displayed such shortcomings.

The first reason is an empirical one. During the Cold War, international organizations became paralyzed between the superpowers. In general, the "high" politics of bipolar military security dominated the political and research agendas. Other international relations topics, such as regional integration, deterrence, and regimes, simply explained a larger part of international behavior. This also meant that units of analysis other than international organizations were more relevant, which in turn influenced research questions and outcomes. The end of the Cold War opened up new opportunities for "low" politics in economic and social areas (see Weiss and Gordenker 1996: 24). NGOs benefited from this trend because the international system now allowed non-state actors more leeway. Technological advances in communication and transport also continued to reinforce this trend. Many observers and actors of the UN system thought along similar lines. With the deadlock of the superpowers broken, many hoped, even assumed, that a more effective UN would be feasible (Roberts and Kingsbury 1993: 11). The problems regarding peacekeeping in particular soon dashed these hopes. Still, in "low" politics more is possible than before. In fact, in a more favorable situation, continued pathologies or "broken" promises should receive even more attention as they can point to less noticed or deeper political and organizational problems. It remains to be seen whether the role of international organizations, as well as the delineations of "high" security and "low" socioeconomic policy, will change in the wake of the attacks of 11 September 2001.

The second reason is more conceptual. Like Keohane (1998) above, international relations scholars use the term "institution" freely.[24] International regimes, to give a well-known example of institutions, are defined as "sets of implicit or explicit principles, norms, rules, and decision-making procedures around which actors' expectations converge in a given area of international relations" (Krasner 1983: 2). Hence, they constitute conventions that guide the behavior of international actors. However, a norm, principle, rule, or procedure is just one possible meaning of the concept "institution." It is often used in this way in economics and sociology, but in management and organization theory, "institution" usually means role or organization. The "norm" type of institution is generally diffused among a large number of people. The "role or organization" type is inherent to intentionally constructed human groupings. Goldsmith (1992: 582) states: "Slipping from one definition to the other is easy, for roles and organizations usually need rules and conventions to reinforce them, and vice versa. Moreover, both definitions refer to repetition in the way people act. In either case, an institution is understood to entail stability and persistence."

The main distinction between the two types of meaning is that rules and conventions do not act—people do, in their roles and in their organizations. A greater focus in organizations can help to explain purposive action (and change) better than most regime theory can (see Robles 1995: 114). In organization theory, it is a common observation that organizations take on a life of their own (Brechin 1997: 15). Organizational survival and management interests often supplant the intended goals of their founders. The common observation in international relations that international organizations—in particular, those of the UN system—lack autonomy conflicts with this observation (see Haas 1990: 29). It may be that the end of the Cold War and, currently, a shift to greater international cooperation in the wake of the terrorist attacks of 11 September 2001 have given rise to greater autonomy for international organizations. However, this should be an empirical question, not a theoretical statement. Similar to the choice of the unit of analysis, our concepts also determine the way we carry out research and the findings we obtain. International relations scholars need to be more careful with their use of the concept of institution.

The third reason that international organizations have not received proper study focuses on the theoretical schools in international relations. Just like regime theory, the functionalist and realist schools, and their offspring, often had a simplistic view of international organizations. After World War II, the functionalist school argued that the functioning of international organizations would foster worldwide, peaceful integration. It perceived organizations as pliable instruments in the hands of their masters, which was organizationally naïve (Brechin 1989: 7, 31). The realist school made a similar mistake with its emphasis on (hegemonic) state power, which led to the neglect of international organizations, as well as of organization and management theory. These organizations were simply not seen as independent variables or relevant actors. The assumptions of the functionalist and realist schools led to a simplistic approach toward international organizations. The internal (dys)functioning of international organizations, their implementation problems, and deviations from the mandate could not receive much attention. Instead, organizations became "black boxes, whose internal workings [were] controlled by traditional bureaucratic mechanisms" (de Senarclens 1993: 453). As a consequence, the actual outcomes of the actions of international organizations could be easily criticized, but were much harder to explain.

One of the advantages of governance theory is that it can break away from the state-centric, or government-centered, approach.[25] A governance perspective facilitates the observation of multiactor, interactive process. But still, it does not imply by definition that the internal functioning of organizations receives more attention.

In a similar vein, the application of microeconomic and rational/public choice theory has not led to an extensive study of international organizations. The assumptions behind these theories sometimes fail to do sufficient justice to their rich social and cultural context. Their methodological individualism is hard to generalize to the interplay of different actors from various cultures with different power bases. Economic theories are frequently better at explaining the origins of international organizations than their actual behavior (Barnett and Finnemore 1999).[26]

In conclusion, the international relations discipline has decreased its attention to international organizations over the last half century. This situation has been judged differently from different theoretical perspectives, but from the 1980s on there has been a persistent complaint about the lack of attention. Simultaneously, criticism on the functioning of international organizations has remained constant. The media have not been a countervailing power that could stem the decline in attention. Over the last decade, NGOs, peacekeeping, and humanitarian aid have provided some exceptions to this trend. In addition, it is impossible to find a theory that explains, let alone predicts, why managers in international organizations act the way they do. Four related shortcomings in the study of international organizations recur regularly, namely:

1. A lack of empirical material on, as well as insufficiently appropriate theory about, the actual functioning of international organizations. It is therefore hard to make generalizations about their behavior that would deepen the basis for either positive or negative criticism.

2. A lack of interaction among scholars from the disciplines of international relations, business administration, and public administration. Disciplinary myopia often persists.
3. A choice of units of analysis, concepts, and research methodology that blocks attention to such issues as implementation, internal functioning, and deviations from mandate, but emphasizes instead such issues as decision making and the role of states. This has led to a distorted focus and ultimately an oversimplified view of international organizations.[27]
4. A lack of attention to Southern perspectives and experiences. The ideals of building on local capacities, empowerment, and participation may be strong, but their implementation is not. The organizations, as well as their media and scholarly critics, are often based in and dominated by preferences of the rich, industrialized North. In this respect, these organizations too often are outside intervenors that share a Northern bias that may be subconscious.[28]

In particular, one question stands out. Keohane's question, "Why do international organizations succeed or fail?" should have been preceded by the question "How do these organizations actually function?" (see Biekart 1999: 14). The second question is a precondition for answering the first one.[29]

Overview of Volume

The authors of this volume have attempted to bypass or to surpass the shortcomings described above. We have done this as a group, because addressing these matters requires knowledge of several disciplines. Sound empirical research on international organizations cannot be done within the confines of academia. It is essential to go out into the field and learn from the practitioners and the local participants. Studying these organizations means understanding their organizational processes from the bottom, with action in the field, to the top, starting with funding and multilateral diplomacy. It also requires an understanding of organizational processes and reforms, as well as knowledge of substantive issues in local contexts, be they the application of human rights or the impact of the conceptualization of sustainable human development.

Having already introduced the main theoretical issues, this book follows, to a large extent, the policy and programming process. Each chapter identifies some central pathologies and promises.

The first part examines closely the role of states in the policymaking and decision making of international organizations. In chapter 1, Klaus Hüfner examines the financing of United Nations peacekeeping and "regular" activities. He focuses in particular on the role of the United States.

Dietrich Kappeler then discusses how new technological and social developments change multilateral diplomacy. In chapter 3, Jacques Fomerand studies the conceptualization of sustainable human development and the political struggles surrounding it.

In the second part, the internal functioning of these organizations is examined. This part focuses on the headquarters level and the central problems, such as organizational reform, policymaking, and internal decision making. A common theme in these chapters is the hardship in making these organizations function better. In chapter 4, Dirk Salomons studies the pathologies of human resource management in the United Nations, which have their roots in the League of Nations and which can obstruct efficient, results-oriented management. Matthias Finger and Bérangère Magarinos-Ruchat treat organizational reform in UNCTAD in chapter 5. They study the process from organizational dependency to self-reliance. Is it possible to transform tax-reliant public sector entities into entrepreneurial organizations? What are the pathologies of UNCTAD and its current reform? In chapter 6, Yves Beigbeder focuses on corruption and culture in the UN system and the managerial difficulties in resolving fraud and corruption.

The third part treats the issue of implementation in detail. In chapter 7, Dennis Dijkzeul looks at a central tool of international organizations, the program approach, and assesses one of the main strategies to make this approach work—participation. In chapter 8, Alex de Waal takes a closer look at the counterproductive, if not counterintuitive, aspects of human rights organizations. Dennis Smith, in chapter 9, looks at the implementation problems of CIVPOL as an illustrative case of the challenges of international public management. In chapter 10, Ian Smillie and Kristie Evenson examine how the funding policies of donor organizations actually hamper local NGOs in rebuilding civil society, which is in contradiction to the professed aims of these donors.

In the fourth part, chapter 11 by Dennis Dijkzeul and Leon Gordenker evaluates the contributions of this book in light of the deficiencies in the study of international organizations that have been identified in this introduction. It develops a basic theoretical model for explaining the behavior of international organizations, while emphasizing remaining dilemmas, as well as possible practical cures.

Notes

1. Multinational organizations as a form of (commercial) private enterprise are also international organizations. However, the term is usually reserved for (not-for-profit) multilateral public organizations, as well as civil organizations that carry out activities across borders. Archer (1983: 1–3) describes how the term "international" subsumes three more specific concepts, namely, intergovernmental, transnational, and transgovernmental. NGOs, for example, are actually transnational organizations.

2. We do not include regional (multilateral) organizations, such as the European Union, ASEAN, and MERCOSUR. It would make the scope of this book too broad. Barnett and Finnemore (1999: 700) limit themselves to intergovernmental organizations.

3. In contrast to international relations, legal studies or international law has largely sustained attention on international organizations (predominantly intergovernmental ones) throughout the post–World War II period and has been especially vibrant in the post–Cold War period (e.g., international human rights and humanitarian law).

4. The main shortcomings of Haas's book were its remnants of a state-centered perspective. The learning processes started mainly through international bargaining and decision making. The internal functioning and the extent to which these organizations could act autonomously received far less attention.

5. With the UN system, there actually exists a dichotomy in the type of studies. Legal aspects, top-level decision making, finance, and reform proposals still receive regular attention (e.g., Alger 1998; Malone 2000; Willetts 2000; also Forman and Patrick 2000), while the internal functioning of UN organizations and actual implementation in the field receive far too little scrutiny. In particular, the Security Council, international conferences, and the quintennial celebrations of the founding of the UN system lead to a steady stream of publications, particularly on reform. Many reform studies contain both analysis and recommendations. Examples include the Brandt Commission, the Commission on Global Governance, Bertrand's "Third Generation World Organization," Urquhart and Childers's "Renewing the UN system" and "A World in Need of Leadership," and the Ford Foundation's "Financing an Effective UN." Most scholars studying UN organizations focus on case studies of one or two organizations (Dijkzeul 1997, 2000; Klingebiel 1999; Beigbeder 1998, 2001). The thematic approach is used less often (see Beigbeder 1997; Roberts and Kingsbury 1993). The case study approach centering on only one or two organizations sometimes makes generalization difficult. The thematic approach can hide the interdependence of different issues, as, for example, during organizational change processes. However, in most studies, attention to the hard work of implementation and the inner functioning of these organizations in the follow-up to decision making is still insufficient. In particular, judging from their practical impact, most reform proposals gather dust in drawers.

6. Similarly, Gallarotti (1991) discusses the limitations of International Organization. He points out the possible negative outcomes of actions by international organizations and other international actors (mainly governments), but he does not describe the actual functioning of international organizations.

7. The effort to join international law and politics more firmly in recent years indicates that the legal profession and international law have been among the few areas of study that did not suffer as great a decline of interest in international organizations as did their counterparts in international relations or political science (see also note 3).

8. To a much smaller extent, but in a similar fashion, international organizations addressing AIDS also received attention (e.g., Gordenker et al. 1995).

9. In fact, some of the same authors covered both NGOs and countries in crisis extensively. See, for example, Weiss and Gordenker (1996) *NGOs, the UN, and Global Governance*; Weiss (1998) *Beyond UN Subcontracting: Task-Sharing with Regional Security Arrangements and Service-providing NGOs*. See also Smillie (1996a, 1996b).

10. For his study, Biekart (1999) prefers the more specific term "private aid agencies" to the more general term "NGOs."

11. Two new journals, *Global Governance* (1995) and *International Peacekeeping* (1994), played a pivotal role in this respect. *Disasters*, an older journal, also offers regular articles on international organizations.
12. The opposite is also true. With the exceptions of decision making and institutional theory, international relations textbooks do not use organization and management theory.
13. Their argument mainly applied to non-governmental organizations, but is equally valid for international governmental organizations.
14. This issue will be taken up in the final chapter.
15. The book by Lindenberg and Bryant (2001) is an excellent exception to this trend. It treats the management of relief and development NGOs from the perspective of the people who work for and with them.
16. In the 1980s the Heritage Foundation was very active, but has since grown quieter. Essentially, politically, there are vocal unilateralist US senators and other, quieter Western governments wanting to keep the UN under control.
17. *Tribune de Genève*, 3 October 1997; *Le Monde*, 16 October 1997.
18. The UNHCR detailed response is found in http://www.unhcr.ch/news/media/ft2.htm, 10 August 1998. For example, UNHCR replied that it had not had sufficient opportunity to respond to the journalist before the publication. In addition, practical problems in the work of UNHCR were underestimated, for example, working in emergency situations makes financial control difficult; one even has to move cash physically instead of through electronic transfers. The newspaper mentioned that a report had been sent to the General Assembly, but failed to note that it was a regular annual report.
19. This was also part of a Jewish conspiracy. See Bert Lanting, "Angst voor de Grote Datum," *De Volkskrant*, 21 December 1999, 13.
20. "Use Discernimiento el Lector," *La Atalaya, Anunciado el Reino de Jehová*, 120, no. 9 (1999): 16.
21. *The Economist* "NGOs: Sins of the Secular Missionaries," 29 January 2000, 25–27.
22. In 1998, Alger also argued that "it is not likely that those who have read [newspaper] reports over the past few years have improved their understanding of the United Nations" (1998: 1). Similarly, Alger described how in late December 1994 then Secretary-General Boutros Ghali was interviewed on the *McNeil-Lehrer Report*, a US television news program. He initially received questions only about peacekeeping. Consequently, Boutros Ghali had to remind the interviewer that the UN carried out different types of peacekeeping, as well as other tasks such as facilitating trade, economic well-being, human rights, and ecological balance.
23. In the end, the judgment on the media depends on one's opinion about the role of the media in society. For a more extensive analysis and critique concerning the media, civil war, and humanitarian action—in particular, concerning the impact of the media, especially television, on government decision-making and compassion fatigue, see Girardet (1995), Minear et al. (1996), and Moeller (1999).
24. For another example, see Kratochwil and Ruggie (1986). Similarly, Mearsheimer (1994: 9–10) mentions organizations only once in a lengthy overview essay on international institutions.
25. The state-centric approach also explains the popularity of decision-making theory. In this theory, it is easy to remain at the intergovernmental level, because this is the level where state representatives make decisions. However, the internal functioning, implementation problems, and deviations from mandate then become secondary concerns. With regime theory, something similar happens. Regime theory helps to explain the behavior of state governments and other international actors when there is no central authority. They do this because they adhere to norms and conventions. The state-centric approach and regime theory also tend to ignore the influence or leadership of international secretariats and their executive heads, for example, James Grant at UNICEF and Halfdan Mahler at WHO.
26. For a defense of economic theories, see Nienhaus (1998: 11–13).

27. For example, Mearsheimer (1994: 41) remarks: "Most critical theorists do not see ideas and discourses forming at the grass roots and then percolating up to the elites of society. Rather, theirs is a top-down theory, whereby elites play the key role in transforming language and discourse about international relations. Experts, especially scholars, determine the flow of ideas about world politics. It is especially useful, however, if this intellectual vanguard consists of individuals from different states. These transnational elites, which are sometimes referred to as 'epistemic communities,' are well-suited for formulating and spreading communitarian ideals that critical theorists hope will replace realism." Much like traditional public administration tools, epistemic communities constitute top-down mechanisms.
28. For an early discussion on the activities of outsiders, see Chambers (1983).
29. In other words, measuring effectiveness should be preceded by information on how it is possible to achieve results or failure.

Bibliography

Alger, C.F. "Thinking about the Future of the UN System." *Global Governance*, vol. 2, no. 3 (1996): 335–360.
Alger, C.F., ed. *The Future of the United Nations System: Potential for the Twenty-first Century.* Tokyo: United Nations University Press, 1998.
Allison, G.T. *Essence of Decision Making: Explaining the Cuban Missile Crisis.* New York: HarperCollins Publishers, 1971.
Anderson, M.B. *Do No Harm: How Aid Can Support Peace—Or War.* Boulder: Lynne Rienner Publishers, 1999.
Archer, C. *International Organizations.* London: Unwin Hyman, 1983.
Barnett, M.N., and Finnemore, M. "The Politics, Power, and Pathologies of International Organizations." *International Organization*, vol. 53, no. 4 (1999): 699–732.
Beigbeder, Y. *The Role and Status of International Humanitarian Volunteers and Organizations—The Right and Duty to Humanitarian Assistance.* Dordrecht/Boston/London: Martinus Nijhoff Publishers, 1991.
Beigbeder, Y. *The Internal Management of United Nations Organizations: The Long Quest for Reform.* London/New York: Macmillan Press/St. Martin's Press, 1997.
Beigbeder, Y. (M. Nashat, M.-A. Orsini, and J.-F. Tiercy). *The World Health Organization.* Dordrecht: Martinus Nijhoff Publishers, 1998.
Beigbeder, Y. *Le Haute Commissariat des Nations Unies pour les Réfugiés.* Que sais-je. Paris: PUF, 1999.
Beigbeder, Y. *New Challenges to UNICEF: Children, Women and Human Rights.* London/New York: Palgrave, 2001.
Bertrand, M. *The Third Generation World Organization.* Dordrecht: Martinus Nijhoff Publishers/UNITAR, 1989.
Biekart, K. *The Politics of Civil Society Building: European Private Aid Agencies and Democratic Transitions in Central America.* Utrecht/Amsterdam: International Books/Transnational Institute, 1999.
Boli, J., and Thomas, G.M., eds. *Constructing World Culture: International Nongovernmental Organizations since 1875.* Stanford: Stanford University Press, 1999.
Brechin, S.R. "*Trees for People: An Organizational Analysis of the World Bank, FAO, and Care International.*" Ph.D. diss., University of Michigan, 1989.
Brechin, S.R. *Planting Trees in the Developing World: A Sociology of International Organizations.* Baltimore and London: The John Hopkins University Press, 1997.
Carothers, T. "Civil Society." *Foreign Policy*, no. 117 (1999): 18–29.

Chambers, R. *Rural Development: Putting the Last First*. Harlow: Addison-Wesley Longman Ltd., 1983.

Childers, E., and Urquhart, B. "Renewing the United Nations System." *Development Dialogue*, no. 1, 1994.

Commission on Global Governance. *Our Global Neighbourhood*. Oxford: Oxford University Press, 1995.

Cooperrider, D.L., and Pasmore, W.A. "Global Social Change: A New Agenda for Social Science?" *Human Relations*, no. 10 (1991): 1037–1055.

Cox, R.W., and Jacobson, H.K. *The Anatomy of Influence: Decision-Making in International Organizations*. New Haven: Yale University Press, 1973.

Cox, R.W., and Jacobson, H.K. "Decision Making." *International Social Science Journal*, vol. 29, no. 1 (1977): 115–133.

de Senarclens, P. "Regime Theory and the Study of International Organizations." *International Social Science Journal*, no. 138 (1993): 453–462.

de Waal, A. *Famine Crimes: Politics and the Disaster Relief Industry in Africa*. Oxford/Bloomington: African Rights & The International African Institute, in association with James Currey and Indiana University Press, 1997.

Dijkzeul, D. *The Management of Multilateral Organizations*. The Hague/London/Boston: Kluwer Law International, 1997.

Dijkzeul, D. *Reforming for Results in the UN System: A Study of UNOPS*. London/New York: Macmillan Press/St. Martin's Press, 2000.

Edwards, M., and Hulme, D. *Beyond the Magic Bullet: NGO Performance and Accountability in the Post–Cold War World*. West Hartford: Kumarian Press, 1996.

Finkelstein, L.S. "What is Global Governance?" *Global Governance*, vol. 1, no. 3 (1995): 367–372.

Finnemore, M. "International Organizations as Teachers of Norms: the United Nations Educational, Scientific, and Cultural Organization." *International Organization*, no. 4 (1993): 565–597.

Forman, S., and Patrick, S., eds. *Good Intentions: Pledges of Aid for Postconflict Recovery*. Boulder: Lynne Rienner Publishers, 2000.

Gallarotti, G.M. "The Limits of International Organization: Systematic Failure in the Management of International Relations." *International Organization*, vol. 45, no. 2 (1991): 183–220.

Girardet, E.R., ed. "Somalia, Rwanda, and Beyond: The Role of the International Media in Wars and Humanitarian Crises." *Crosslines Special Report*. Geneva/Dublin, 1995.

Goldsmith, A.A. "Institutions and Planned Socioeconomic Change." *Public Administration Review*, no. 6 (1992): 582–587.

Gordenker, L., Coate, R.A., Jönsson, C., and Söderholm, P. *International Cooperation in Response to Aids*. London and New York: Pinter, 1995.

Gordenker, L. "The UN Tangle: Policy Formation, Reform, and Reorganization." *WPF Reports*, no. 12. Cambridge: The World Peace Foundation, 1996.

Grüning, G. *Origin and Theoretical Basis of the New Public Management* (in mimeo). Draft for the 1998 IPMN Conference, Salem/Oregon, 1998.

Grüning, G. "Grundlagen des New Public Management: Entwicklung, Theoretischen Hintergrund und Wissenschaftlichen Bedeutung des New Public Management aus Sicht der politisch-administrativen Wissenschaften der USA." Ph.D. diss. Hochschule für Wirtschaft und Politik, forthcoming.

Haas, E.B. *When Knowledge Is Power: Three Models of Change in International Organizations*. Berkeley: University of California Press, 1990.

Handler Chayes, A., Chayes, A., and Raach G. "Beyond Reform: Restructuring for More Effective Conflict Intervention." *Global Governance*, vol. 3, no. 2 (1997): 117–145.

Jervis, R. *Perception and Misperception in International Politics*. Princeton: Princeton University Press, 1976.

Jönsson, C. "Interorganizational Theory and International Organization." *International Studies Quarterly*, no. 30 (1986): 39–57.

Jönsson, C. "International Organizations and Cooperation: An Interorganizational Perspective." *International Social Science Journal*, no. 138 (1993): 463–478.

Judge, A. *Types of International Organizations*. Union of International Associations, at http://www.uia.org/uiadocs/orgtypeb.htm, June 2001.

Keohane, R.O. "International Institutions: Can Interdependence Work?" *Foreign Policy*, Frontiers of Knowledge (Spring 1998): 82–96.

Keuning, D., and Eppink, D.J. *Management en Organisatie*. 4th ed. Leiden: Stenfert Kroese Uitgevers, 1990.

Klingebiel, S. *Effectiveness and Reform of the United Nations Development Programme (UNDP)*. London: Frank Cass, 1999.

Knight, W.A. "Beyond the UN System? Critical Perspectives on Global Governance and Multilateral Evolution." *Global Governance*, vol. 1, no. 2 (1995): 229–253.

Kooiman, J., ed. *Modern Governance: New Government-Society Interactions*. London: Sage Publications, 1993.

Kooiman, J., and Van Vliet, L.M. "Riding Tandem: The Case for Co-governance." *Demos Quarterly*, no. 7 (1995): 44–45.

Krasner, S.D., ed. *International Regimes*. Ithaca: Cornell University Press, 1983.

Kratochwil, F., and Ruggie, J.G. "International Organization: A State of the Art on an Art of the State." *International Organization*, no. 4 (1986): 753–775.

Lindenberg, M., and Bryant, C. *Going Global: Transforming Relief and Development NGOs*. Bloomfield, CT: Kumarian Press, 2001.

Malone, D.M. "Eyes on the Prize: The Quest for Nonpermanent Seats on the UN Security Council." *Global Governance*, vol. 6, no. 1 (2000): 3–23.

Maren, M. *The Road to Hell: The Ravaging Effects of Foreign Aid and International Charity*. New York: The Free Press, 1997.

Mearsheimer, J.J. "The False Promise of International Institutions." *International Security*, no. 3 (1994): 5–49.

Minear, L., Scott, C., and Weiss, T.G. *The News Media, Civil War, and Humanitarian Action*. Boulder/London: Lynne Rienner Publishers, 1996.

Moeller, S.D. *Compassion Fatigue: How the Media Sell Disease, Famine, War and Death*. New York and London: Routledge, 1999.

Moore, J. *The UN and Complex Emergencies: Rehabilitation in Third World Transitions*. Geneva: UNRISD and War-Torn Societies Project, 1996.

Morales Nieto, J. *La Politica de Desarrollo Hacia el Futuro: Una Propuesta de Estrategias para Sociedades en Transición: El Caso de Nicaragua*. Managua: Documentos Desarrollo Humano en Acción, PRODERE Centro America, 1996.

Natsios, A.S. *NGOs and the UN System in Complex Humanitarian Emergencies: Conflict or Cooperation?* Pp. 67–82, in Weiss, T.G., and Gordenker, L., eds., *NGOs, the UN & Global Governance*. Boulder/London: Lynne Rienner Publishers, 1996.

Ness, G.D., and Brechin, S.R. "Bridging the Gap: International Organizations as Organizations." *International Organization*, no. 2 (1988): 245–273.

Nienhaus, V. "Principal/Agent Problems." Pp. 11–13, in *Management in Humanitarian Assistance*. 2nd ed. Luxemburg: Network on Humanitarian Assistance/European Commission, 1998.

OECD Development Assistance Committee. *Conflict, Peace and Development Cooperation on the Threshold of the 21st Century*. Paris: Development Co-operation Guidelines Series, OECD, 1988.

Osborne, D., and Gaebler, T. *Reinventing Government: How the Entrepreneurial Spirit is Transforming the Public Sector from Schoolhouse to Statehouse, City Hall to the Pentagon*. Reading, MA: Addison-Wesley, 1992.

Pressman, J.L., and Wildavsky, A., *Implementation: How Great Expectations in Washington Are Dashed in Oakland*. 3rd ed. Berkeley: University of California Press, 1984 [1973].

Reinicke, W.H. "The Other World Wide Web: Global Public Policy Networks." *Foreign Policy*, no. 117 (1999): 44–57.

Roberts, A., and Kingsbury, B., eds. *United Nations, Divided World: The UN's Roles in International Relations*. 2nd ed. Oxford: Clarendon Press, 1993.

Robles, Jr., A.C. "Global Governance and Political Economy: German and French Perspectives." *Global Governance*, vol. 1, no. 1 (1995): 99–117.

Rochester, J.M. "The Rise and Fall of International Organizations as a Field of Study." *International Organization*, no. 4 (1986): 777–813.

Rosenau, J.N., and Czempiel, E., eds. *Governance without Government: Order and Change in World Politics*. Cambridge Studies in International Relations: 20. Cambridge: Cambridge University Press, 1992.

Rosenau, J.N. "Governance in the Twenty-first Century." *Global Governance*, vol. 1, no. 1 (1995): 13–44.

Ruggie, J.G., ed. *Multilateralism Matters: The Theory and Praxis of an Institutional Form*. New York: Columbia University Press, 1993.

Simon, H.A. *Administrative Behavior: A Study of Decision-Making Processes in Administrative Organization*. 3rd ed. New York: Free Press, 1976 [1945].

Smillie, I. "Painting Canadian Roses Red." Pp. 187–197, in Edwards, M., and Hulme, D. *Beyond the Magic Bullet: NGO Performance and Accountability in the Post–Cold War World*. West Hartford: Kumarian Press, 1996a.

Smillie, I. *Service Delivery or Civil Society? Non-governmental Organizations in Bosnia and Herzegovina*. Discussion paper, 1996b.

Smouts, M.C. "Some Thoughts on International Organizations and Theories of Regulation." *International Social Science Journal*, no. 138 (1993): 443–452.

Tesner, S. (with Kell G.). *The United Nations and Business: A Partnership Recovered*. New York: St. Martin's Press, 2000.

Urquhart, B., and Childers, E. *A World in Need of Leadership: Tomorrow's United Nations—A Fresh Appraisal*. Uppsala: Dag Hammerskjöld Foundation, 1996.

Uvin, P. *Aiding Violence: The Development Enterprise in Rwanda*. West Hartford, CT: Kumarian Press, 1998.

Van Ruller, H., ed. *Management van Internationale Organisaties: Een Bedrijfskundige Visie op Internationaal Bestuur*. Alphen a/d Rijn: Samsom H.D. Tjeenk Willink, 1990.

Van Vliet, L.M. "Communicatieve Besturing van het Milieuhandelen van Ondernemingen." Ph.D. diss., Erasmus Universiteit Rotterdam, 1992.

Walkup, M. "Policy Dysfunction in Humanitarian Organizations: The Role of Coping Strategies, Institutions, and Organizational Culture." *Journal of Refugee Studies*, no. 1 (1997): 37–60.

Weiss, T.G., and Gordenker, L., eds. *NGOs, the UN, and Global Governance*. Boulder: Lynne Rienner Publishers, 1996.

Weiss T.G., and Pasic, A. "Reinventing UNHCR: Enterprising Humanitarians in the Former Yugoslavia, 1991–1995." *Global Governance*, vol. 3, no. 1 (1997): 41–57.

Weiss T.G., ed. *Beyond UN Subcontracting: Task-Sharing with Regional Security Arrangements and Service-Providing NGOs*. London/New York: MacMillan Press/St. Martin's Press, 1998.

Whitman, J., ed. *Peacekeeping and the UN Agencies*. London: Frank Cass Publishers, 1999.

Willets, P. "From 'Consultative Arrangements' to 'Partnership': The Changing Status of NGOs in Diplomacy at the UN." *Global Governance*, vol. 6, no. 2 (2000): 191–212.

Young, O.R. *International Governance: Protecting the Environment in a Stateless Society*. Ithaca: Cornell University Press, 1994.

Zijderveld, A.C. "Social Theory, Politics, and Policy: A Theoretical Annotation." In *Between Sociology and Sociological Practice Liber Amoricum dedicated to Mark van de Vall*. Rotterdam: Institute for Applied Social Sciences, 1993.

PART I

DECISION MAKING WITH STATES

One central issue in the management of international governmental organizations is the inherent tension that exists between the organization as an actor and the organization as an instrument in the hands of national governments. International NGOs also have to deal with this tension, but it affects more indirectly their dependence on funding and cooperation of governments. In the end, the actor-instrument tension is an issue of autonomy. Does the international organization determine its own course, or is its course set by governments? Chapters 1 and 2 study two central factors in the behavior of international organizations: funding and decision making in multilateral diplomacy. The third chapter, on sustainable human development, illustrates the regular tensions between Northern and Southern states. The issue of autonomy comes back in such questions as: Do the governments agree or disagree on a substantive policy issue? Is their consensus necessary, and what do international organizations do to achieve consensus? Or can Secretariats and NGOs shape agendas and international outcomes independently? Do governments agree or disagree to grant a degree of autonomy to an international organization? Does governmental control at the strategic level of the organization hamper action in the field?

— *Chapter 1* —

FINANCING THE UNITED NATIONS
The Role of the United States

Klaus Hüfner

Introduction

While the expansion of the tasks entrusted to the United Nations since the 1990s seems to represent a high level of confidence in the capacity of the Organization to meet the needs of the international community, there is a serious imbalance between what is expected from the UN and the financial resources available to translate such responsibilities into reality. Despite the reform measures introduced by Boutros Boutros-Ghali and Kofi Annan, the present financial system of the UN desperately needs to be enhanced or even replaced in order to allow an effective response to the many challenges confronting the UN. These problems become evident with a closer look at the regular budget of the UN for the budget year 2000, which is identical with the calendar year.

- As of 31 January 2000, only 43 of the 189 Member States had met their obligations and paid their contributions to the regular budget in full and on time. These include the Nordic countries, Canada, France, Kuwait, New Zealand, the Netherlands, South Africa, and Sri Lanka.
- As of 31 December 2000, only 117 of the 189 Member States had paid their assessed contributions to the regular UN budget 2000 and for prior years in full; the United States had obligations vis-à-vis the Organization of $165 million (i.e., 74 percent of all arrears).
- In addition, there are missing funds for the peacekeeping operations of the UN that are financed through special accounts outside of the regular UN budget. They amounted at the end of 2000 to

$2,054 million. The United States owed $1,144 million (i.e., 56 percent of all debts).

This troubled financial situation is mainly due to the non-payment of its membership dues by the United States—a Member State that, although having the ability to pay, has demonstrated its unwillingness to pay. It is thus primarily responsible for the bad image of the UN as compared to regional, governmental organizations. This financial crisis has crippled the Organization since the middle of the 1980s and endangered its mandates and programs.[1] Despite the efforts undertaken in connection with the adoption of the assessment scales in 1997 and 2000 and the compromises reached, the requisites for the creation of a stable, sustainable financing mechanism in the service of the goals and principles of the UN are still missing.

In the following discussion, the legal basis and current budgetary process and then the present system and its components of financing the UN will be described. In this context, the UN specialized agencies as well as the UN Funds and Programmes, the latter being financed primarily through voluntary contributions, will be excluded from a detailed assessment. Afterward, a more in-depth analysis of the "dialogue" between the United States and the UN Secretariat, as well as the Member States of the UN, follows. This chapter also considers whether the recent payments by the US in the wake of the 11 September attacks constitute a change in its multilateral policies, and ends with some concluding observations.

Legal Basis and Current Budgetary Procedures

Article 17, paragraphs 1 and 2; Article 18, paragraph 2; and Article 19 of the UN Charter form the financial constitution of the United Nations. Of further importance is Article 97, which declares that the Secretary-General is the chief administrative officer of the UN and, as part of this function, is responsible for the preparation, drafting, and execution of the budget, as well as for the financial behavior of the Organization.

In 1986, the General Assembly approved a two-stage budgetary process based largely upon the recommendations of the Group of High-Level Intergovernmental Experts ("Group of 18"). The new budget process consists of two sequential parts. In off-budget years, the Secretary-General develops a budget outline based upon the past year's budgetary framework. This outline contains the estimate of resources for the biennium and assesses priorities and the (positive or negative) role of growth associated with the activities proposed.

The Committee for Programme and Coordination (CPC) then discusses the proposal and gives a recommendation. Afterwards, a second body, the Advisory Committee on Administrative and Budgetary Questions

TABLE 1.1 Articles 17, 18, and 19 of the UN Charter

According to Article 17, paragraph 1 of the UN Charter, the General Assembly examines and approves the regular budget of the Organization. Article 17, paragraph 2 establishes that Member States cover the Organization's expenditures through an assessment scale approved by the General Assembly.

Article 18, paragraph 2 of the UN Charter stipulates that votes taken on important decisions by the General Assembly, including on budgetary matters, need a two-thirds majority for approval.

Article 19 of the Charter reads as follows: "A Member of the United Nations which is in arrears in the payment of its financial contributions to the Organization shall have no vote in the General Assembly if the amount of its arrears equals or exceeds the amount of the contributions due from it for the preceding two full years. The General Assembly may, nevertheless, permit such a Member to vote if it is satisfied that the failure to pay is due to conditions beyond the control of the Member."

(ACABQ), which is a standing committee of the General Assembly, evaluates the proposal.[2] Its report is guided by the budgetary framework as established by the General Assembly and the recommendations of the CPC. The ACABQ can formulate its own resource allocation suggestions; most often, these are savings measures.

Finally, the Fifth Committee of the General Assembly discusses the outline of the Secretary-General. This discussion is highly influenced by the reports of the CPC and ACABQ. The results of this discussion are presented as a recommendation to the General Assembly, which then has to vote on the budget outline.

In budget years, the Secretary-General returns to the CPC with a fully developed budget, which is also submitted to the ACABQ. Both bodies submit their recommendations to the Fifth Committee of the General Assembly. It is on this basis that the General Assembly makes its final decision.[3]

The growing importance of the CPC during these two stages has to be stressed. Originally a standing committee of the Economic and Social Council (ECOSOC, founded in 1962), the CPC also became a subsidiary organ of the General Assembly in 1976. From 1970 until 1987, its membership included 21 government representatives; in 1987, membership was increased to 34. This coincided with a larger role in the evaluation of the budget proposals and framework, in order to appease the major contributors. The CPC decides by consensus, and although its conclusions are formally only a predecision, in essence it gives the major contributors a veto right in all budgetary matters. Thus, the importance of Article 18, paragraph 2 of the Charter is considerably diminished, which implies a de facto revision of the Charter.

The Three "Pillars" of the UN Financing System

Overview

The system of financing the UN is based on three "pillars." These are:

1. assessed contributions to the regular budget;
2. assessed contributions to the special accounts of the peacekeeping operations; and
3. voluntary contributions.

The three sources of funding differ in their contributions to the UN regular budget, to the special accounts for peacekeeping operations budgets, and to the extraordinary budgets of financing the UN Funds and Programmes such as, for example, UNDP, UNFPA, UNHCR, and UNICEF. As described later, peacekeeping operations are financed almost entirely through assessed contributions. Total UN income for 1999 was about $6.62 billion with obligatory and assessed contributions accounting for $2.32 billion and voluntary contributions for approximately $4.30 billion (see columns 1, 2, and 5 in table 1.2 and figure 1.1).

Assessment Scale and Obligatory Contributions to the
Regular Budget of the UN

As of 2001, the obligatory contributions to the regular budget are based upon an assessment scale with a maximum of 22.00 percent (ceiling) and a minimum of 0.001 percent (floor). The assessments are based primarily upon the capacity to pay, which is calculated with each nation's share of world income—since 1998 measured in terms of GNP (gross national product), thus replacing the national income as the standard. Taking into account changing economic conditions, the assessment scale is reviewed and reset every three years by the Committee on Contributions.

Both the ceiling and the floor rate have changed several times. Originally, in 1946 the ceiling was set at 39.89 percent, although at that time the United States accounted for at least half of the world's income. The United States insisted, however, on a reduction with the understanding that the ceiling would be lowered step by step to the 25 percent level as a result of changing economic conditions and the admission of new members.

· The ceiling drifted progressively downwards, first to 33.33 (1954), then to 30 percent, and then—after the admission of the two German states in 1973—to 25 percent. At this time, the United States spoke about

TABLE 1.2 Total UN System Expenditures, 1986–2001 (*in millions of US Dollars*)

	1 Regular UN Budget	2 Peace- keeping Operations	3 Regular Specialized Agencies	4 Total Assessed	5 Special Organs	6 Specialized Agencies	7 Total Volun- tary	GRAND TOTAL (4+7)
1986	725	242	1,142	2,109	3,075	953	4,028	6,137
1987	725	240	1,178	2,143	3,266	933	4,199	6,342
1988	752	266	1,349	2,367	3,868	1,129	4,997	7,364
1989	765	635	1,359	2,759	4,078	1,183	5,261	8,020
1990	838	464	1,395	2,697	4,436	1,347	5,783	8,480
1991	999	490	1,400	2,889	5,401	1,361	6,762	9,651
1992	1,014	1,767	1,618	4,399	5,888	1,270	7,158	11,557
1993	1,014	3,059	1,594	5,667	6,091	1,217	7,308	12,975
1994	1,088	3,342	1,729	6,159	5,967	1,126	7,093	13,252
1995	1,088	3,364	1,773	6,225	5,778	1,161	6,939	13,164
1996	1,172	1,522	1,902	4,596	5,009	1,045	6,054	10,650
1997	1,172	1,226	1,866	4,264	4,936	1,057	5,993	10,257
1998	1,266	907	1,792	3,965	4,260	1,151	5,411	9,376
1999	1,222	1,100	1,787	4,109	4,300	1,123	5,423	9,532
2000	1,250	1,800*	1,766	4,816	n.a.	n.a.	n.a.	n.a.
2001	1,250	2,500*	1,772	5,522	n.a.	n.a.	n.a.	n.a.

Note: Asterisk indicates estimates.

a final-stage reduction, informing the General Assembly that with the ceiling lowered to 25 percent in fulfillment of the 1946 agreement, the United States would never again seek a further reduction (Laurenti 1998: 4).

Nevertheless, during the second half of the 1990s, the United States began to call insistently for a further reduction in its assessments. One of the conditions for the US payment of back dues, agreed on between the US administration and the Senate Foreign Relations Committee, was a demand for a reduction of the ceiling from 25 to 22 percent in 1998 and to 20 percent in 2000. In December 2000, after long negotiations, a compromise was reached in the General Assembly: as from 2001, the ceiling for the US will be reduced to 22 percent.

The floor was fixed at 0.04 percent in 1946 and lowered in two stages: in 1973 to 0.02 percent and since 1978 to 0.01 percent. For a number of small and poor countries even that level resulted in extremely high per capita assessments. Because the floor imposes its burden on those least able to pay, the United Kingdom (and the European Union) proposed a total abolition of the floor in 1995. In 1997, the United States proposed that the floor be reduced to 0.001 percent, which was adopted by the General Assembly as part of the new assessment scales for 1998–2000 and for 2001–2003.

In sum, it can be said that both the fixing of the ceiling and of the floor caused major distortions to the principle of capacity to pay. This is especially true for the ceiling, which has lowered the assessment of the largest

FIGURE 1.1 Total UN System Expenditures, 1986–1997 *(in millions of US Dollars)*

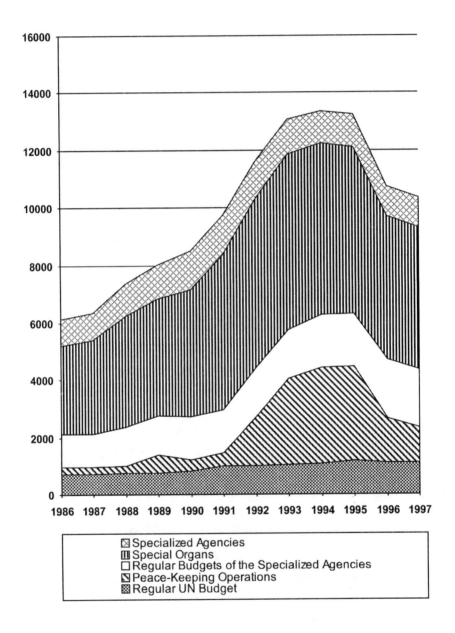

Legend:
- Specialized Agencies
- Special Organs
- Regular Budgets of the Specialized Agencies
- Peace-Keeping Operations
- Regular UN Budget

contributor, the United States, below its proportionate share of world income in the past and will continue to do so in the future (presently, the US share accounts for 28 percent).

The assessment scale is not static; it reflects changing conditions and intends to bring assessments more closely in line with each Member State's actual economic performance. Two additional factors influence the calculations: the base period and low-income effect. Regarding the base period, until 1954, assessments were calculated on the national income data of the prior year; then, the General Assembly decided to apply the prior 3 years' data. In 1977, the base period was extended to 7 years, and in 1981 to 10 years. The application of this formula discriminated against the successor states of the former USSR and other newly created states in Central and Eastern Europe, where official statistics did not exist and were replaced by "guesstimates" of the International Monetary Fund (IMF). Those new Member States protested heavily against their assessments being too high. Therefore, in 1994, the General Assembly approved an averaged 7.5 year base period, which was cut back further to 6 years in 1997 for the assessment scale for the period 1998–2000. For the period 2001–2003, the General Assembly approved two base periods: one of three years and one of six years, the results being averaged to 4.5 years.

The second factor influencing calculations of assessment is the low-income offset, taking into account levels of poverty. The most recent global standard of $4,880 as the average world per capita income is applied as a starting point. The difference between it and the low per capita income countries is expressed as a percentage discount, trimmed slightly by an arbitrary percentage called a "gradient," which was reduced in 1997 from 85 to 80 percent.

In 2000, only one Member State had to pay the maximum of 25 percent, namely, the United States. The US and the next two main contributors, Japan (20.573 percent) and Germany (9.857 percent), made up more than half of the 2000 regular budget (55.43 percent). Fifteen Member States (see table 1.3) contributed around 86.8 percent of the 2000 regular budget. Among those fifteen were eight from the European Union (EU), with a combined share of 33.277 percent.

Figure 1.2 divides the assessment scales into eight groups to show the corresponding number of Member States in each group. The "pyramid" of scale assessments resembles the Eiffel Tower as it reflects the inequality of worldwide income distribution. One hundred thirty-six Member States ranging between 0.001 and 0.059 percent have only a 1.34 percent share of the contributions to the regular budget.

Member States are supposed to pay promptly and fully (i.e., 30 days after notification by the UN Secretary-General) and without conditions. They have no legal right to withhold funds corresponding to the share of expenditures for a specific or controversial activity. However, some Member States do this nonetheless, thereby violating their obligations. As all

TABLE 1.3 The 15 Main Contributors to the Regular UN Budget 2000
(*in percent and in millions of US Dollars*)

Member State	Percent	Absolute Contribution (rounded)
1. United States	25.000	300
2. Japan	20.573	216
3. Germany	9.857	104
4. France	6.545	69
5. Italy	5.437	57
6. United Kingdom	5.092	54
7. Canada	2.732	29
8. Spain	2.591	27
9. Netherlands	1.632	17
10. Australia	1.483	16
11. Brazil	1.471	15
12. Belgium	1.104	12
13. Argentina	1.103	12
14. Sweden	1.079	11
15. Russian Federation	1.077	11
Total	86.776	950

income is pooled and distributed, such practice does not directly affect individual activities but serves to undermine the overall financial and political independence of the UN. This is especially true if done by large contributors such as the United States. The regular budget of the UN, financed by obligatory contributions, is fixed biannually in even years and is denominated in US dollars (in 2000–2001: $2.535 billion).

Assessed Contributions for UN Peacekeeping Operations

The second "pillar" of the UN financing system is based on obligatory contributions as well. However, these contributions are used exclusively for peacekeeping operations. With the exception of two small-scale operations—the United Nations Truce Supervision Organization (UNTSO) in the Middle East and the United Nations Military Observer Group in India and Pakistan (UNMOGIP) in Kashmir—which are included in the regular budget, all other peacekeeping operations are based upon an assessment formula, which in turn is based on the assessment scale for the regular budget. The special peacekeeping assessment scale was initially based on a complex formula adopted by the General Assembly in 1973 (A/Res/3101 [XXVIII]). The underlying rationale for the formula was that

- the permanent members of the Security Council (P-5) should pay more than others to recognize their special responsibilities for world

FIGURE 1.2 Obligatory Contributions of the Member States to the
Regular UN Budget, 2000

Category	Number of Member States	Total per Category
15.001 - 25.000 %	2	45.573 %
6.001 - 15.000 %	2	16.402 %
3.001 - 6.000 %	2	10.529 %
1.001 - 3.000 %	10	15.278 %
0.501 - 1.000 %	8	5.529 %
0.201 - 0.500 %	8	2.682 %
0.060 - 0.200 %	21	2.663 %
0.001 - 0.059 %	136	1.341 %
Total	**189**	**100.001 %**

peace and international security and their veto power over peace-keeping operations;

- the developing countries, especially the least developed ones, should be given some relief.

The following peacekeeping scale, which divided the Member States into four categories, was adopted by the General Assembly in 1973.

1. The economically least developed Member States pay only 10 percent of their share of the regular budget toward the peacekeeping operations. (As this share is only 0.001 percent, they correspondingly are responsible for only 0.0001 percent of the costs of the peacekeeping operations.)
2. All other economically less developed Member States pay 20 percent of their obligatory contributions.
3. Industrialized Member States pay according to their full share of obligatory contributions.
4. The five permanent members of the Security Council (P-5) pay their full obligatory contributions plus the remaining share of the economically less developed countries.

As a result, the United States paid about five to six percentage points above the 25 percent ceiling for the regular UN budget as a proportional share of the reduction allowed for developing countries. However, beginning in October 1995, US legislation limited the amount that the United States should pay to 25 percent, a unilateral decision that threw into question all further decisions on financing UN peacekeeping operations.

This structure showed a built-in rigidity because countries had either to stay at 20 percent (i.e., an 80 percent discount) or else to immediately move to no discount at all in a single step. Therefore, the demand for the creation of intermediate groups from middle-income Member States increased.

In December 2000, the General Assembly agreed to revise the 1973 ad hoc arrangement; it established 10 levels of contributions, depending on Member States' per capita income. On one end of the scale, the least developed countries will receive 90 percent discounts on their contributions (level J), while on the other, the P-5 of the Security Council (level A) will have to pay a premium over their regular budget assessment obligations, sufficient to make up for the discounts resulting from the adjustments to the regular budget assessment rates of Member States in levels C through J. The 10 levels were introduced in order to facilitate an automatic, predictable movement between them on the basis of Member States' per capita GNP.

Although the UN has reported negative year-end cash balances in its regular budget accounts for the past several years, it has been able to cover operating expenses by deferring payments to countries that contribute troops, equipment, and other services to UN peacekeeping operations. In other words, the UN spends cash kept in peacekeeping accounts, thus essentially borrowing from the countries at zero percent interest rate. Sooner or later, funds are reimbursed to the peacekeeping accounts as the Member States pay their regular budget assessments. So far, the availability of peacekeeping cash from which to borrow has sustained the UN. If the number of peacekeeping operations declines, the UN's ability to borrow will diminish because funds flowing in from the assessments for peacekeeping operations will also decline.

The finance system of peacekeeping operations is extremely slow; each peacekeeping mission has to start from scratch. After the approval of the Security Council, the Secretariat prepares a mission budget that must be approved first by the Advisory Committee on Administrative and Budgetary Questions (ACABQ), then by the Fifth Committee of the General Assembly, and finally by the General Assembly. The major problem of the UN's peacekeeping operations is related to the start-up costs. Originally, Boutros Boutros-Ghali asked for $50 million. The 47th General Assembly in 1992 then approved a revolving fund of $150 million dollars; however, only $60 million was immediately available.

Since each peacekeeping mission is financed separately, Member States receive several peacekeeping assessment requests from the Secretary-General each year. These requests are made on an ad hoc basis, coming in the middle of national budgetary cycles, so that the governments of Member States often find it difficult to allocate the necessary funds without seeking special appropriation. Trouble has ensued because of the system's built-in instabilities and the existing uncertainty stemming from both the Member States and the UN Secretariat. This is especially true in periods in which several peacekeeping missions are run by the Secretariat on behalf of the Security Council, which generally approves the missions for a three- or six-month period. The UN is now running 17 peacekeeping missions with 15 separate budgets.

The sudden increase in the number and the scope of peacekeeping missions has raised the expenditure from 1993 to 1995 to over $3 billion per year (see table 1.2 and figure 1.1). This increase in relation to the regular budget has been a growing cause for concern to many Member States, although it is minute compared to national defense budgets. This increase from $1.767 billion in 1992 is largely due to the operations in former Yugoslavia, where the cost of the United Nations Protection Force (UNPROFOR) has come to $1.9 billion, and the operation in Somalia, where the United Nations Operation in Somalia (UNOSOM) has cost more than $1 billion. In comparison, the regular UN budget and the expenditure for peacekeeping operations were less than the annual New York City police and fire department budgets during the same time period. Furthermore, even after the end of the Cold War, global annual weapons and arms expenditure are still over $800 billion. In 1997, for every US dollar spent on military activities, less than a quarter of a cent went to UN peacekeeping. Peacekeeping costs fell in 1996 and 1997, to $1.522 and $1.226 billion, respectively (see table 1.2). It was estimated that the budgetary requirements would increase again to $2.5 billion in 2001.

Peacekeeping soldiers are paid by their own sending governments according to their own domestic salary scale. Those countries volunteering personnel to peacekeeping operations are reimbursed by the UN at a flat rate of about $1,000 per soldier per month. The UN also reimburses countries for equipment. But reimbursements to these countries are often deferred because of cash shortages caused by Member States' failure to pay their dues for peacekeeping operations.

United States vs. the UN: The Debate since the 1980s

After intensive negotiations in the "Geneva Group,"[4] based on the years of the world economic crisis after the second oil shock of 1977–1978 on the one hand, as well as the rapid increase in the US federal budget deficit on the other, the United States demanded considerable reductions in the regular UN budget. For the regular UN budget for 1982–1983, zero real growth was demanded (i.e., the budget should increase only by the amount of the rate of inflation). For the 1984–1985 UN budget, the Reagan administration even demanded nominal zero growth (i.e., the volume of the budget should be frozen at the level of 1982–1983). In the case of non-observance, the United States threatened to reduce or delay its contributions. However, in 1981 the majority of the General Assembly— with the dissent of the United States, the United Kingdom, the Federal Republic of Germany, and Japan—approved the budget for 1982–1983, which provided for an increase of 12 percent (a zero real growth would have amounted to a nominal increase of 1 to 2 percent). The US Congress decided to withhold funding for UN programs that the United States did not support politically. In order to increase the pressure, the US administration announced the postponement of the transfer of its assessed contributions until the fourth quarter of the year by appropriating its UN assessment for each calendar year as part of the US fiscal year, which begins on 1 October.

Starting in 1983, the United States undertook campaigns targeted against the UN system, including the withdrawal of membership in UNESCO on 31 December 1984, and the approval of Nancy L. Kassebaum's first bill to reduce by $500 million the assessed contributions to the UN (and the specialized agencies) for the period 1984–1987. The situation became even more critical when the so-called Kassebaum Amendment of 1985 demanded from 1987–1989 a new ceiling of 20 percent, that is, a reduction of five percentage points, if the UN would not introduce a weighted voting scheme according to the assessment scale for votes in the General Assembly regarding budgetary questions. The Gramm-Rudman-Hollings Amendment, which was approved in 1985, was intended to reduce the US budget deficit and thereby all federal government expenditures.

As a result, the UN, without a strong constituency in the US Congress to intercede on its behalf, started to suffer from sharp budgetary cuts. This meant that the overdue assessed contributions of the United States in the second half of the 1980s rose drastically from 35 percent (1985) to just under 80 percent (1989) of the total overdue assessed contributions (see table 1.4). The operational ability of the UN was thereby extremely jeopardized. The Organization entered into a new financial crisis whereby the UN management specialist, Bertrand, emphasized the political motives for the US behavior: "Above all it was not a question of improving the functioning of the World Organization through a process of management or to increase its efficiency, but solely a matter of regaining control over the United Nations and thereby preventing them from being able to continue serving as a propaganda forum against the United States and against Reagan."[5]

In order to emerge from the crisis, at Japan's instigation a group consisting of 18 high-ranking experts was commissioned in 1985 to examine the administrative and financial efficiency of the UN.[6] The "Group of 18," in view of the grave financial crisis, completed and submitted their report within a few short months. They agreed that the UN would benefit from "budget procedures which would associate with the preparation of the medium-term plan and the programme budget and which would better facilitate a broad agreement among Member States on budgetary matters, while preserving the principle of sovereign equality of States enshrined in the Charter."[7] Moreover, the Group of 18, unable to agree unanimously on one single reform proposal, offered three alternatives. These formed the basis for intensive negotiations in the Fifth Committee of the General Assembly, which then adopted on 19 December 1986, by consensus Resolution 41/213, a new budgetary procedure that enables the main contributors to exercise an effective veto right by increasing the number of members in the Committee for Programme and Coordination (CPC)—a body that operates by consensus. This concession toward the United States and other (western and eastern) main contributors meant a de facto revision of the Charter. By the consensus procedure in the CPC, the plenum of the General Assembly was virtually deprived of an important classical parliamentary function in which, according to Article 18, paragraph 2 of the Charter, decisions about the regular budget are to be made by a two-thirds majority of the present and voting members, whereby every member has one vote.

In the United States, General Assembly Resolution 41/213 was greeted with praise on all sides. The fact that the CPC had been entrusted with the additional task of setting overall budget levels and broad sectoral priorities

TABLE 1.4 The UN Regular Budget: United States Debt to the UN, 1971–2000 *(in million of US dollars as of 31st December and in percent)*

Year	US Dollars (in million)	In Percent of All Debts
1971	0.0	0.0
1972	0.0	0.0
1973	0.0	0.0
1974	0.0	0.0
1975	0.0	0.0
1976	0.0	0.0
1977	0.0	0.0
1978	0.0	0.0
1979	0.0	0.0
1980	0.2	0.0
1981	24.2	16.6
1982	3.4	2.3
1983	27.4	16.1
1984	11.5	6.9
1985	85.5	35.3
1986	147.0	57.0
1987	252.8	71.5
1988	307.7	77.9
1989	365.1	79.2
1990	296.2	73.5
1991	266.4	60.6
1992	239.5	47.8
1993	260.4	54.5
1994	248.0	51.6
1995	414.4	73.5
1996	376.8	73.8
1997	373.2	78.8
1998	315.7	75.7
1999	167.9	68.8
2000	164.6	74.0

was a major concession of the developing countries, which only reluctantly agreed on this compromise solution. President Reagan described the decision of the General Assembly as a "historic step" to adopt sweeping reform of the UN. There was a tacit understanding among all parties involved that the results of Resolution 41/213 would encourage the United States to end its withholdings from the UN regular budget. However, the readiness of the United States to meet its obligations (i.e., to pay at least completely its compulsory contributions to the regular budget within the budget year of the UN) was never fulfilled. Although the US administration was satisfied, and promised that the United States would meet its assessed contributions, there was no way of predicting what the US Congress might do. In fact, the Congress introduced a mechanism of "conditional financing," which included at that stage further demands, such as the reduction of permanent posts in the UN Secretariat by 15 percent and the scaling down to 50 percent of any Member State's nationals who serve at the UN on a seconded basis—the latter demand being primarily addressed against the USSR. Furthermore, the United States has never promised to pay all it owes in back dues, in clear violation of the UN Charter. The United States continued to withhold money that would cover the US share of the costs of activities that it strongly opposes on grounds of principle, such as the work of the Division for Palestinian Rights and the Office for the Law of the Sea.

The second financial crisis of the UN in the 1980s proceeded almost without interruption into a new, third financial crisis in the 1990s. Although the Bush administration early in 1990 unveiled a new plan for full funding of calendar year 1990 assessments and for the payment of arrearages over a five-year period and promised in view of the new challenges facing the UN after the end of the East-West conflict to fully support the work of the Organization, this was not manifested in the financing behavior of the US Congress.

In an addendum to his 1991 Annual Report, Secretary-General Pérez de Cuéllar appealed to Member States to meet their financial obligations. He also submitted a set of specific proposals in order to overcome the financial emergency of the UN:

1. to charge interest on the amounts of assessed contributions that are not paid on time;
2. to suspend the financial regulations of the UN to permit the retention of budgetary surpluses;
3. to increase the Working Capital Fund from $100 million to a level of $250 million as of 1 January 1992;
4. to establish a temporary peacekeeping reserve fund at a level of $50 million;
5. to authorize the Secretary-General to borrow commercially;
6. to establish a Humanitarian Revolving Fund of $50 million through a one-time assessment on Member States; and
7. to establish a UN Peace Endowment Fund, with an initial target level of $1 billion, to be created by a combination of assessed and voluntary contributions.

Although the proposals were on the table for many years, Member States were not eager to reach a consensus—especially those Member States that had been in full compliance with their financial obligations—because they wanted to avoid paying the bills left unpaid by the United States. They argued that, first of all, the crisis caused by enormous unpaid assessments, both to the regular budget and the peacekeeping operations, would need to be resolved before dealing with the problem of the UN having a cash reserve in order to respond immediately when new peacekeeping or humanitarian operations were authorized.

In his "Agenda for Peace" of 1992, the then new Secretary-General, Boutros Boutros-Ghali, repeated the proposals of his predecessor and added others, such as "a levy on arms sales that could be related to maintaining an Arms Register by the United Nations; a levy on international air travel, which is dependent on the maintenance of peace; authorization for the United Nations to borrow from the World Bank and the International Monetary Fund—for peace and development are interdependent; general tax exemption for contributions made to the United Nations by foundations, businesses and individuals; and changes in the formula for calculating the scale of assessments for peacekeeping operations."[8]

In February 1993, the Independent Advisory Group (IAG) on UN Financing, established by the Ford Foundation and cochaired by Shijuro Ogata and Paul Volcker published its report, "Financing an Effective United Nations."[9] Although the IAG reconfirmed the principle that all Member States must pay as a part of their legal obligations their assessed UN dues promptly and fully, thereby stressing the special responsibility of the major contributors, the Group recommended that the dues should be paid in four quarterly installments instead of in a single lump sum at the beginning of the year. In addition, the Group suggested that the UN should be given authority to charge interest on late payments under this new schedule.

The IAG also recommended that the level of the Working Capital Fund should be raised from $100 to $200 million. Although this proposed level was $50 million less than that recommended by Boutros Boutros-Ghali, it would have reduced the UN's cash flow problems significantly and stopped the practice of borrowing funds from peacekeeping accounts to cover regular budget expenditures.[10] In addition, the IAG suggested that the UN should speed replenishment of its depleted reserves by depositing budgetary surpluses owed to those Member States with regular budget arrears into the Working Capital Fund.

The IAG disapproved the proposal put forward by Boutros Boutros-Ghali and his predecessor that the UN be allowed to borrow from commercial institutions or from the World Bank and the IMF in order to meet the UN's obligations when assessed contributions are late. The IAG feared that this kind of authorization could undermine the UN's financial discipline or might even encourage Member States to delay paying their dues. With regard to peacekeeping operations, the IAG recommended treating peacekeeping as an "investment in security," thus considering to finance its future costs from Member States' national defense budgets, which are generally large enough to cover these costs without any major financial problem.[11]

The United States did indeed pay its assessed contribution for the years 1991 and 1992 in full, but still behind schedule—namely, in the last quarter of the calendar year that corresponds to the UN budget year. As a result, it did reduce its "mountain of debts" from over 70 percent to under 50 percent in 1992 (see table 1.4). Added to this came the US arrears amounting to $469 million for peacekeeping operations in 1994. Again, new conditions were formulated by the US Congress: for the US fiscal year 1994, half of the authorized amount would be made available only when the UN had created an independent Office of the Inspector-General.[12] In this critical situation the General Assembly appointed in 1994 a group of experts to check the scale of assessment and make suggestions for alterations. One month later, an open-ended high-level working group was formed to check the financial situation of the UN.[13]

In 1995, the fiftieth anniversary of the United Nations, the financial situation deteriorated even further. At the end of August 1995, the UN was short of a total of $3,800 million of assessed obligatory contributions, including $851 million for the regular budget. The United States owed a total of $1,800 million. Its funds exhausted, the United Nations began to finance itself through the special accounts intended for UN peacekeeping operations. This meant that at the end of 1995, the year of the fiftieth anniversary of the UN, the United States owed the UN a total of 73.5 percent of all outstanding assessed contributions for the regular budget.

The United States took up a line of attack. In July 1995, the US Secretary of State, Warren Christopher, suggested in a letter to all governments a radical reorganization and reduction in the size of the UN as well as the privatization of particular functions, such as public relations. The US payments to the UN would be made dependent upon "UN reforms," which was the equivalent of economic blackmail. Moreover, the United States declared unilaterally that due to a law passed by Congress in 1995,[14] it would, from October 1996 on, contribute a maximum of 25 percent of the costs of UN peacekeeping troops—despite a 1973 agreement according to which the permanent members (P-5) of the Security Council would take on additional obligations, which in the case of the United States corresponded to about six percentage points.

In September 1995, the representative of the European Union declared: "The EU considers that unilateral decisions adopted by any Member State contradicting the fulfillment of its financial obligations with regard to the Organization are not acceptable." The United Kingdom expressed itself in even plainer terms on 26 September 1995 toward the behavior of the United States in the General Assembly: "Perhaps an appropriate policy would best be entitled: 'no representation without taxation!'" The Nordic countries complained that the United States was setting a "deplorable example" for the world. Australia warned that the United States could lose its voting right in the General Assembly. Regarding the financial situation, the UN Secretary-General declared in a speech to the Working Group of the General Assembly at the beginning of 1996:

> The financial crisis has brought the United Nations to the edge of insolvency. The Organization is totally dependent on cash inflows from Member States' assessments to provide liquidity. Unpaid assessments now exceed $ 3.3 billion. We cannot continue to shift funds from the peacekeeping budget to meet shortfalls elsewhere. The United Nations owes about $ 1 billion to countries that contributed troops and equipment for peacekeeping.
>
> I mention these facts not in order to describe once again the magnitude of the crisis, but to point out that the Organization now finds itself trapped in a downward spiral of events in which one problem creates another, and the combination of problems works against the rational solution of any or all.[15]

In March 1996, the Clinton administration announced a five-year plan for paying off $1.5 billion in debt to the UN. But Congress, which had to approve the plan, continued to add new restrictions to some UN funding and to cut funding related to other issues.

In his report "Renewing the UN: A Programme for Reform" of July 1997, the new Secretary-General, Kofi Annan, referred to "the failure of some Member States to discharge their treaty obligations regarding prompt and full payment of assessed financial contributions" and appealed to Member States to resolve the financial crisis speedily and with good will.[16] As an interim measure, he proposed that a revolving credit fund be established, initially capitalized at a level of up to $1 billion, through voluntary contributions or other means that Member States might wish to suggest.[17] Such a fund would allow the Secretary-General to finance, on a recourse basis, newly arising overdue assessment payments of Member States. In addition, the Secretary-General proposed that the General Assembly agree to establish a development account, funded by savings from reduced non-program costs and other management efficiencies. In his opinion, the account could grow to at least $200 million for the biennium beginning 1 January 2002. He also suggested that any unspent funds from the 1996–1997 regular budget be utilized as a "down payment" in order to establish the account. It is highly improbable that both proposals will be accepted by the Member States. They are neither willing to offer additional resources to fill the gap caused by non-payers, especially the United States, nor ready to change the existing provisions and renounce potential surpluses of the budget.

In 1997, the Clinton administration negotiated again with the US Congress, which led to the following "deal": an aggregate amount of $926 million in arrears was acknowledged and the payment of $819 million authorized (this figure resulted from the deduction of a controversial $107 million credit owed to the United States by the UN for outstanding peacekeeping reimbursements). In return, the Clinton administration agreed to the 38 (*sic*) conditions contained in the bill.[18]

Those "Helms-Biden conditions" included, inter alia, the reduction of the US assessment to the UN regular budget from 25 to 20 percent and for peacekeeping operations from about 31 to 25 percent; reimbursement for all US assistance to peacekeeping operations and "full notification and consultation" when new peacekeeping operations are proposed; UN financial records to be made available to both the Congressional Office of Management and Budget and the US General Accounting Office; a prohibition on UN conferences held outside New York, Geneva, Rome, or Vienna; a reduction of 1,000 posts in the UN Secretariat; no "standing army" under Article 43 of the Charter as proposed by Boutros Boutros-Ghali in his "Agenda for Peace"; no tax or fee "on any United States national"; no external borrowing by the UN; no interest fees or other arrears penalties; the establishment of an "independent office of inspector-general" for each of the UN specialized agencies, the FAO, the ILO, and the WHO.

In December 1997, when the General Assembly adopted a resolution establishing the scale of assessments for 1998–2000, it ignored the US demand to lower the ceiling from 25 to 22 percent and stated that the UN would "consider reviewing the scale for the years 1999–2000 during its resumed fifty-second session," depending on whether the US would pay arrears, including disputed amounts. Also, in March 1998, an attempt was made to pass a General Assembly resolution restricting UN procurements to countries that are current in their assessed payments. Finally, in order to gain consensus, the resolution was modified and merely called for a study of this matter, requesting the Secretary-General to explore the practices being implemented by other multilateral organizations (e.g., in 1997, the UN Headquarter Procurement Division procured about two-thirds or $190 million of its goods and services from US vendors).[19]

Although the Clinton administration initially supported the package, it then voiced concerns over some of the conditions and attempted to amend them, but Senator Helms rebuffed these attempts. In April 1998, Congress approved the Helms-Biden package, but delayed sending it to President Clinton, who had threatened to veto it because it also contained an unrelated condition dealing with restrictions on international family planning assistance. When the bill was finally sent to the president in October 1998, he vetoed it, as expected. The Clinton administration and Congress later reached an understanding that permitted the payment of a sum to the UN that was sufficient only to save the United States from losing its voting right in 1999 under Article 19 of the Charter. In November 1999, the US Congress adopted legislation authorizing the payment of $926 million in arrears over a three-year period, subject to the fulfillment of the specific conditions known as the "Helms-Biden agreement," which was now part of federal statute.[20] The first year's installment of $100 million was paid to the UN in December 1999, thus avoiding the loss of the voting right in the General Assembly in 2000.

The "big battle" concerning the negotiations over the assessment scale for 2001–2003 had already started during the middle of 2000. The United States continued to delay paying its dues and insisted on a reduction from 25 to 22 percent, beginning in 2001, as well as on its unilateral decision of 1995 to pay only the maximum of 25 percent for peacekeeping operations as from 1996. Therefore, the other 188 Member States were put under pressure to negotiate the modification of the scales for both the regular as well as the peacekeeping budgets.

In July 2000, France, speaking on behalf of the EU, emphasized the need for revision of the assessment scale for peacekeeping operations, which showed "some anomalies that need to be corrected." The French ambassador mentioned 20 countries—among them Singapore, South Korea, most of the Gulf countries, Argentina, Israel, and Slovenia—as having incomes higher than the world average, but contributing amounts smaller than they are capable of paying. Therefore, the EU proposed that those Member States' total share of peacekeeping contributions be increased from 0.77 to 3.9 percent. On 3 October 2000, the US ambassador, Richard Holbrooke, reported to the Fifth Committee that 18 Member States had stated publicly that they were voluntarily willing to accept a larger burden based on their changed economic situation. This paved the way to find a new formula.

In October 2000, when the French ambassador took the floor in the Fifth Committee on behalf of the EU and 10 other Member States associated with the EU and Iceland, he referred to the EU proposals made five years earlier and stressed that

- each Member State's contribution must reflect its real ability to pay as closely as possible in light of its current economic situation; and
- the method to be used to define its scale of assessment should be simple, equitable, and transparent.

In early December 2000, the EU made its position final: the EU would not pay higher UN dues to offset any reduced payments by the United States.

After long and tough negotiations, the General Assembly reached an agreement on 23 December 2000. The regular budget assessment scale for the period 2001–2003 was to be based on GNP estimates for a base period of three and six years, with a low per capita income adjustment of 0.001 percent, a maximum assessment for least developed countries of 0.01 percent, and a maximum assessment rate of 22 percent. For 2001, part of the 2000–2001 regular budget already adopted in 1999—an amount equal to 3 percent of the amount assessed on Member States—was to be borne by a one-time voluntary donation of $34 million from Ted Turner to help solve the political impasse and to make up the regular budget shortfall that resulted from the reduction of the ceiling. Since the UN cannot accept money from private citizens to pay UN membership dues, Turner made the payment to the United States, which wrote a check to the UN.

In 2002, the five main contributors to the regular UN budget will be the United States (22.000 percent), Japan (19.669 percent), Germany (9.845 percent), France (6.516 percent), and the United Kingdom (5.579 percent). Major increases (in terms of 0.5 percentage points and more) will have to be paid by Brazil (2.093 percent), China (1.545 percent), Korea (1.866 percent), and the United Kingdom (5.579 percent).

The United States vs. the UN: New Developments

In early February 2001, the US Senate agreed to release $582 million to the UN in recognition of the reduction in the US share from 25 to 22 percent for the regular UN budget. While the US House of Representatives was expected to endorse the "deal," at the end of August 2001 the UN had not yet received a penny from the US administration. And then, on 11 September 2001, the political landscape was reshaped beyond recognition by the terrorist attacks on the World Trade Center and the Pentagon. The US suddenly needed the UN in the "war on terrorism." On 24 September 2001, the House responded by unanimously approving legislation that would provide the promised $582 million US dollars to pay back part of the US dues owed to the UN. Does this herald a new era of US multilateralism?

To answer this question fully, it is crucial to look at the signs that previously indicated that the long-standing fight between the United States and the UN was not yet over.

- The Dole Amendment of 1995 still forbids the United States from paying more than 25 percent of the UN costs for peacekeeping operations. But the December 2000 compromise reduces the US obligation only in phases, depending upon the transitional increases paid by other UN Member States. Unless the US Congress does not act to repeal the Dole Amendment soon, the United States will accumulate new arrears that would be contrary to the spirit of the December 2000 agreement.
- Since the early 1980s, the United States continues to pay its dues behind schedule—not before 1 October instead of on 1 January. Since the United States remains the biggest contributor, this continues to make life extremely difficult for the UN.
- The United States and the UN continue to disagree over the amount of money that the United States owes to the Organization. These disagreements include a long-standing dispute between the United States and the UN on the methodology, and hence the amount, of reimbursement to UN staff members of taxes levied by the United States on their UN earnings. Furthermore, there is a cumulative effect of the withholding of the US share as assessments for certain activities to which the United States continues to refuse to contribute—a practice which is incompatible with Article 17, paragraph 2, of the Charter.

But the UN marathon financial crisis, caused primarily by the United States, was only the tip of the iceberg. Since the 1980s, the United States had

> embarked on a deliberate policy of confrontation in the UN. U.S. delegates adopted a "get tough" approach to any criticism of U.S. intentions and challenged the states of Asia, Africa, and Latin America to account for what was construed to be their animosity to the United States, connecting U.S. development assistance to their voting record in the UN.... Supported by a Congress that was traditionally skeptical of international organizations, the United States used its financial position as leverage in forcing administrative reforms on the organization. The issue was not so much that reforms were not needed but rather that unilateral action by the United States ignored its treaty obligations to contribute to the work of the UN and alienated its allies as much as anyone else. (Lyons 1999: 500)

In addition, the unilateralist behavior of the United States was also documented in its voting in the General Assembly. In an analysis of the "U.S. non-multilateralism" between 1968 and 1993, Holloway found a dramatic shift toward unilateralism and an overall increase in total negative votes to over 50 percent for the first time in 1980–1981 during the Reagan administration; it reached 60.5 percent in 1992 during the Bush administration, and dropped only slightly to 57.6 in 1993 under the Clinton administration (Holloway 2000: 369). Also alarming was the fact that the United States trend line was moving in the opposite direction from that of its closest allies. Washburn seemed right when he argued in 1996 that the damage to the United States' relationship with the UN, and to the UN as an institution, would continue: "Clearly, the United States is the only country that can do fundamental damage to the UN—through deliberate neglect or open hostility" (Washburn 1996: 83).

In conclusion, it is simply too early to tell whether the US-UN relationship will change significantly in the wake of the 11 September 2001 terrorist attacks.[21] Changing the relationship will require a profound rethinking of US foreign policy with regard to multilateralism and international cooperation. Changing the above policies will be the signposts for such rethinking.[22] In the meantime, the relationship between the United States and the UN remains full of contradictions. There is no other country in the world in which

- the public, although knowing very little about the UN's activities, broadly supports the UN and its own country's participation in it;
- the academic community analyzes and discusses so intensively UN affairs, but with only very limited impact on official governmental policy;
- private support for and commitment to UN programs and issues articulated through the engagement of national NGOs is so high.

Concluding Observations

The history of the UN could be written in terms of financial crisis management because, since the beginning of its existence, the UN has suffered tremendous problems in financing its activities. The "vicious cycle" in the finance procedures of the UN closes again: although the demands vis-à-vis the UN increased dramatically during the 1990s, the UN remains fully dependent on public means of finance and control through its Member States. Taken together, (1) the real or even nominal zero growth of the UN's regular budget, secured through the consensus procedure of the Committee for Programme and Coordination (CPC); (2) a dismal payment morale of the Member States in light of relatively small assessed contributions to the regular UN budget when compared with national budgets; and, finally, (3) no particular UN financial resources secured independently from Member States, but at the same time the continuation of political declarations of the Member States demanding the strengthening not only of the Office of the Secretary-General, but also of the UN in general, all constitute nothing but a "double standard" in international politics. Governments are spending over $150 per capita on the world's military and still are not willing to spend $2 per capita for the UN and its activities. These governments are the same ones complaining that the UN is unable to handle the sudden increase in peacekeeping operations that they began demanding.

The US-UN relationship has suffered tremendously under the inward-oriented complex political system in the United States and its complicated decision-making procedures. As long as the issues mentioned above are not resolved and decisions by the US Congress continue to be combined with specific conditions concerning the budget size and its components, there will be insufficient reason to believe that the United States is thinking and acting in terms of constructive leadership in the UN.

In order to avoid the League of Nations precedent, UN Member States, especially "like-minded" countries, including Australia, Canada, the Nordic countries, and the EU Member States, are challenged to establish a platform for a new critical-constructive dialogue with the United States about the future of the UN. In that context, financing and management reform measures will have to be treated as "form follows function" issues. For the time being, the pathological lack of effectiveness of the UN was and is, in the final analysis, a pathology fostered by the Member States, particularly by the US government. The continued financing of the UN in the aftermath of the terrorist attacks will become a litmus test for determining whether the renewed interest in multilateralism and international cooperation will bring about a stronger UN, or whether paying the debts was just a temporary deviation from increasing US unilateralism.

Notes

1. These (second and third) financial crises are primarily caused by the United States and affect both the activities financed through the regular budget as well as the peacekeeping operations, whereas the first crisis was solely related to the peacekeeping operation United Nations Emergency Force (UNEF I) after the Suez crisis in 1956 and was aggravated by the much more cost-intensive United Nations Operation in Congo (ONUC) in the early 1960s. It was primarily caused by the non-payments of the USSR, France, and the Arab states.
2. The 16 members of the ACABQ are appointed by the General Assembly on the basis of broad geographical representation, personal qualifications, and experience. They serve for three years, but are eligible for reappointment. At least three of them are recognized financial experts.
3. After the adoption of the new budgetary process, the General Assembly no longer takes a vote on the budget.
4. The "Geneva Group," which met first in October 1964, is an important consultation group of all those "democratic" UN Member States contributing at least 1 percent to the UN regular budget.
5. Bertrand (1988: 5); my own translation.
6. UN doc. A/40/237.
7. UN doc. A/41/49.
8. Chapter IX in UN doc. A/47/277. In 1995, the UN tried to borrow from the World Bank, but the latter refused, arguing that it is only allowed to lend to sovereign states.
9. Ford Foundation (1993); also UN doc. A/48/460.
10. As of this writing, the Working Capital Fund remained at the level of $100 million.
11. Although this proposal is plausible from the economic point of view, it contains a political implication that is much more difficult to be solved, namely, the issue of the distribution of competencies in UN affairs between the Ministries of Foreign Affairs and the Ministries of Defense.
12. Upon this pressure exercised by the United States, the General Assembly established an Office of Internal Oversight Services (OIOS) in July 1994 (Resolution 48/218B).
13. The program of this Working Group included, inter alia, a review of the modalities for the payment of arrears, the introduction of payment schedules, and recommendations for incentives/disincentives to make Member States pay their assessments in full and on time. The Working Group, unable to conclude its work over the years 1995–1997, had to acknowledge its failure to put forward recommendations to resolve the financial crisis of the UN and "interrupted" its work in September 1997.
14. Public Law 103-236.
15. UN doc. SG/SM/5892.
16. UN doc. A/51/950.
17. The 52nd General Assembly took note of this proposal and requested the Secretary-General to submit more detailed proposals relating to the financing, management, and operation of such a fund (see UN document A/Res/52/12B, para. 20). The 53rd General Assembly again took no action and decided to resume consideration of the problem at the 54th session in autumn 1999. It is highly improbable that the General Assembly will reach a consensus on establishing such a fund.
18. Congressional Record-Senate, p. 5785, 17 June 1997.
19. UN doc. A/Res/52/226.
20. Public Law 106-113.
21. While it should be acknowledged that the United States is not alone in rejecting greater financial autonomy for the UN, it should also be noted that an increasing number of Member States fulfill their obligations fully and promptly, and even—as with the Nordic countries—go beyond them in terms of voluntary contributions, which represent a higher share than their assessed rates for the regular UN budget.

22. Similarly, it will be very interesting to see whether the US government will now change its policies regarding such international treaties as, for example, the Kyoto climate treaty, the International Criminal Court statute, the Nuclear Test Ban treaty, the Mine Ban convention, and so on. The abandonment by the Bush administration of the Antiballistic Missile treaty suggests that unilateralists retain the upper hand.

Bibliography

Bertrand, M. *Für eine Weltorganisation der Dritten Generation*. Bonn: UNO-Verlag, 1988.

Ford Foundation. *Financing an Effective United Nations: A Report of the Independent Advisory Group on U.N. Financing*. New York: Ford Foundation, 1993.

Holloway, S. "U.S. Multilateralism at the UN: Why Great Powers Do Not Make Great Multilateralists." *Global Governance*, vol. 6, no. 3 (2000): 361–381.

Hüfner, K. *Die Vereinten Nationen und ihre Sonderorganisationen. Teil 3: Finanzierung des Systems der Vereinten Nationen, 1971–1995. Teil 3A: Vereinte Nationen – Friedensoperationen – Spezialorgane*. Bonn: UNO-Verlag, 1997.

Kull, S., and Destler, I.M. *Misreading the Public: The Myth of a New Isolationism*. Washington, D.C.: Brookings Institution, 1999.

Laurenti, J. *National Taxpayers, International Organization: Sharing the Burden of Financing the United Nations*. New York: UNA-USA, 1995.

Laurenti, J. *The New U.N. Assessment Scale*. New York: UNA-USA, 1998.

Laurenti, J. "US Reluctance and UN Revival." *The International Spectator*, no. 34 (1999): 13–20.

Luck, E.C. *Mixed Messages: American Policies and International Organization*. Washington D.C.: Brookings Institution, 1999.

Lyons, G.M. "Review Essay: The UN and American Politics." *Global Governance*, no. 5 (1999): 497–511.

Maynes, C.W., and Williamson, R.A., eds. *United States Foreign Policy and the United Nations*. New York: Norton, 1996.

Mc Dermott, A. *The New Politics of Financing the UN*. Houndmills/New York: Macmillan Press/St. Martin's Press, 2000.

United States General Accounting Office. *Financial Issues and U.S. Arrears*. Washington, D.C.: GAO, 1998.

United States General Accounting Office. *Reform Initiatives Have Strengthened Operations, but Overall Objectives Have Not Yet Been Achieved*. Washington, D.C.: GAO, 2000.

Washburn, J.L. "United Nations Relations with the United States: The UN Must Look Out for Itself." *Global Governance*, vol. 2, no. 3 (1996): 81–96.

— *Chapter 2* —

DIPLOMACY
Its Place in the Multilateral World

Dietrich Kappeler

Introduction

International governmental organizations would not exist without diplomacy and diplomats. They are themselves created through multilateral diplomacy,[1] and they interact with member countries mainly through the latter's permanent diplomatic missions at the organizational headquarters. Furthermore, their deliberative organs are made up of state representatives who are mostly diplomats. Finally, international governmental organizations are an important venue for bilateral diplomatic interaction by member countries. The role of Non-governmental Organizations (NGOs) in international diplomacy is increasing.

This book is concerned with the pathological aspects of international organizations. With regard to diplomacy, which has always had its shortcomings, speaking of present pathologies would appear somewhat exaggerated.[2] Certainly, there were pathological situations during the first half of the twentieth century,[3] and during the Cold War, diplomacy was greatly hampered and at times twisted by the imperatives of the automatic antagonism between East and West.[4] A similar antagonism also marked, and to some extent continues to mark, the relationship between the Third World and the West—or more accurately, between poor developing countries and rich industrialized ones. The principal victims of this pathological behavior have been international organizations and multilateral negotiations. As these examples show, however, such "pathology" was not necessarily attributable to diplomacy, diplomatic establishments, or the diplomats themselves, but rather to national governments and the political environment created by those governments.

In recent years, diplomacy has been boosted by several developments. First, more effort is now put into training diplomats and keeping them abreast of developments in the later stages of their careers; second, the end of the Cold War has changed behavior in international conference rooms; and third, information technology is providing diplomats and their governments with new tools that are likely to alter profoundly the conduct of international relations.

In order to examine the present situation, this chapter considers who the diplomats are, whom they deal with, and what they do. Subsequently, we shall examine new trends in multilateral negotiations, alternative forums and actors of diplomatic and quasi-diplomatic interaction, and the impact of information technology on diplomacy. Although the general context of this book suggests an emphasis on multilateral diplomacy, the long past of bilateral diplomacy still affects all aspects of international relations and therefore cannot be entirely ignored.

Who Are the Diplomats?

Diplomats of States

Contrary to frequent predictions, diplomats of states still exist and remain rather busy.[5] This also holds true for the traditional diplomats who are officers of the ministries of foreign affairs.[6] States continue to cultivate bilateral relations through resident diplomatic missions, mostly staffed by foreign service diplomats. Foreign ministries are also still active in multilateral diplomacy, in particular with political and legal issues. In other fields, they attempt, with varying success, to coordinate diplomatic action conducted by specialists from other government departments.

Over the last decades, great efforts were made to improve the training of diplomats in foreign ministries before and after they entered their careers.[7] Academic institutions have developed special curricula for persons pursuing careers in diplomacy,[8] and many foreign ministries have created in-house training facilities, both for new entrants and for the purposes of in-service training. Problems still abound, regarding both the proper content of training programs and their attendance by diplomats, especially where in-service training aimed at mid- and higher-level officers is concerned. Such officers find it difficult to get leave or make themselves free to attend even short training courses. Information technology has made new and innovative approaches possible, but their impact will not be felt for a few years. For the moment, such approaches are mostly still at a trial stage, and diplomatic establishments, especially in advanced countries, show great reluctance toward too much innovation. In contrast, among developing countries there is a growing awareness of the possibilities provided by information technology—in particular, for smaller, poor countries.[9]

In addition to foreign ministry diplomats, great numbers of officials of other ministries and government agencies are active in a diplomatic capacity, especially regarding multilateral relations. Negotiations in the fields of international trade and financial relations are mostly handled by specialists from concerned ministries, which tend to have their own external relations departments. This is true for most government agencies as there are few domains left that do not have an international dimension. In many instances, however, diplomatic activities are only a minor part of an officer's job, and there are no services specifically concerned with external affairs.

Unlike foreign service officers, civil servants of other ministries engaged in diplomatic activities are rarely given even elementary diplomatic training. They learn this aspect of their job mainly by engaging in it. Occasionally, training institutions, both outside and inside the foreign ministry, attempt to provide special programs for non-diplomats engaging in diplomatic activities.[10] However, there is again the problem of attendance by persons whose departments find it difficult to dispense with their services even for short periods. As with the case of professional diplomats, information technology can offer innovative ways of providing much needed training.

The United States has a long tradition of using individuals who are not civil servants as diplomats. Best known are the "political appointees"—persons who are close to the president and are rewarded for their support with an ambassadorial position.[11] Some have become quite successful, others less so. In general, embassies led by a political appointee have a seasoned diplomat as deputy head of mission, who is charged with rectifying the sometimes major mishaps of the ambassador. More important, however, are people in high positions in government, such as politicians, or in the private sector who are entrusted with often delicate diplomatic missions. From the private sector, one may remember the legendary Armand Hammer, chairman of Occidental Petroleum, or Henry Ford II. Henry Kissinger, then national security adviser to President Nixon, undertook a number of difficult missions, some of them with considerable success. During his recent career, Richard Holbrooke had one foot in the Clinton administration and another in the private sector. As a negotiator, he became increasingly important—so much so that he was sometimes detached from his position of permanent representative to the United Nations to undertake quite extensive negotiating missions.

In recent years, Russia, too, has relied on well-known personalities from outside the diplomatic service for delicate missions. Memorable among them are the negotiations of former Prime Minister Tchernomyrdin with President Milosevic in late spring 1999, which eventually convinced the latter to give in to the exigencies of NATO.

Diplomats of International Organizations

Although nearly all organizations conduct bilateral relations with states and other entities, and many take part in multilateral diplomacy, none, to our knowledge, has ever attempted to set up anything approaching a diplomatic service. There are individual officers who may engage in what resembles a diplomatic career by being posted repeatedly to permanent missions of their organization abroad, as in the case of representatives of the European Commission. Yet they, too, may at any time be reassigned to a department that does not engage in any external relations at all.

Political organizations tend to call upon professional diplomats from Member States to handle delicate missions. The UN has done so for decades, and the Organization for Security and Cooperation in Europe (OSCE) employs a number of diplomats of member countries in a variety of capacities. At times, these organizations even have recourse to former foreign ministers. Specialized institutions occasionally also rely on experts from member countries for temporary or even long-term assignments.

Non-governmental organizations play a growing role in both national and international affairs. Some become involved in quasi-diplomatic activities.[12] Delegates of the International Committee of the Red Cross (ICRC) deal with governments on temporary missions or head permanent regional delegations enjoying near diplomatic status. The same applies for representatives of the International Federation of Red Cross and Red Crescent Societies (IFRC), who are often provided by national societies. The ICRC trains its delegates, including preparation for dealing with government agencies and international organizations. Its training facilities are also open to officers and temporary envoys of the Federation and of national societies.

Voluntary agencies and charitable organizations have widespread international activities. Frequently, they do not seek interaction with governments and their administrations but prefer to deal with local authorities in the recipient countries. When they are active in regions that lack central governmental structures, they have no choice but to deal with whatever self-appointed leadership they may encounter.[13] Few organizations of this type provide any form of basic diplomatic training to those they send on missions abroad.

There is a growing number of NGOs that specialize in acting as intermediaries in internal conflicts when other types of foreign interference are rejected or impossible. While some of them are rather amateurish, others, such as the Jimmy Carter Center in Atlanta, have well-trained personnel for their missions abroad. In Kenya, a former permanent secretary of the foreign ministry runs a small organization seeking to mediate internal conflicts in neighboring countries.

With Whom Are the Diplomats Dealing?

Their Own Country

Dealing with one's own country is an essential aspect of a diplomat's task that has been given little consideration in the past. Diplomats would report to their superiors and possibly be asked to brief national decision makers, but all this was done with the utmost discretion and without the general public or the media becoming aware of it. The new emphasis on transparent and public diplomacy has changed past procedures, and has given relations with the home country, its authorities, and its media a new importance.

The diplomatic information function implies not only providing data to the authorities at home. More importantly, it is also used to make these officials aware of what is possible and what is not in both the bilateral and multilateral contexts. This becomes particularly relevant when preparing briefs for negotiations, an area in which the diplomatic missions in the field are becoming increasingly involved. Once a negotiation is concluded—or has failed—the diplomats must explain the result to their superiors, the decision-making organs of their country, and, within the framework of public diplomacy, to the media and the population at large. This means that diplomats must expect to be interviewed, give press conferences, and explain complex issues in newspaper articles and specialized publications. This would have been unthinkable a few decades ago, at least in the traditional context of European diplomacy. In multilateral relations, in which alliances and organized groups play an important role, a government depends on its diplomats in the various countries concerned, both to assess the possible courses of action with regard to these countries, and to explore possibilities of joint action at an international conference.

Other Countries

Traditionally, bilateral diplomacy meant representing the sending state in the receiving state in all matters related to their mutual relations. This was done by dealing with domestic government authorities, primarily those in the ministry of foreign affairs. Only consular services dealt with individuals. More recently, diplomatic missions have become involved in cultural relations and also in dealing with the media of the receiving state. One important diplomatic function has always been to cultivate good personal relations with individuals who are able to provide useful background and insider knowledge, and whose influence could help in achieving policy goals. This is done discreetly and without attracting public attention.

Today, public diplomacy requires frequent and open contacts with the media of the receiving country and with such public figures as members of parliament, political party leaders, trade unions, lobbies, and various other interest groups. In bilateral negotiations, this aspect of diplomacy is important as it might influence public opinion toward the point of view of the sending state.

Currently, multilateral diplomacy is very much a matter of the inter-action of groups of states. Some such groups may be ad hoc alliances, oth-ers are geographically based, and yet others are made up of members of regional organizations. Institutionalized groups may have their own organizational setup within whose framework common positions are developed, as is the case of the African, Caribbean, and Pacific (ACP) countries when negotiating with the European Commission.[14] Even then, it may be necessary for an individual country to lobby other member governments in advance. In the case of ad hoc alliances, all of the discus-sions on joint positions are between the delegates of the countries con-cerned, sometimes supported by the direct action of the involved governments' diplomatic missions.

International Organizations

Diplomats have a double function with intergovernmental organizations. They represent their countries within the organs of these organizations (which are made up of representatives of Member States), and they also represent their countries to the organizations' management. The two functions can become rather confused, as shown by the relations between the United States and the UN. The US government strongly insists that the demands of powerful national lobbies regarding the functioning of the Organization are satisfied as a precondition for paying its financial contribution to the budget.[15] This requires US diplomats to become active both regarding the Organization's organs and toward representatives of other member countries with a view to securing support, or at least soft-ening opposition.

In a much broader way, most countries have direct interests to defend when the policies and decisions of international organizations are pre-pared. One very effective way of doing so is to cultivate good relations with the competent services of the secretariat of the organization con-cerned, who can then be influenced to include such concerns in the back-ground papers and drafts being developed for a forthcoming negotiation. For small and weak countries, this is often the only way to make them-selves heard with regard to concerns that are not shared by other mem-bers of the group(s) to which they belong.

States also receive temporary and permanent missions from interna-tional governmental organizations. Relations with such missions may be handled by the foreign ministry, but more often the specialized govern-ment agencies directly concerned are primarily, or exclusively, involved.[16] In some instances, the representation of the international organization is actually set up within the corresponding government department of the receiving country and acts both as representative of the sending organization and as adviser to the department in question. This is frequently the case for permanent missions of the World Health Organization (WHO) in developing countries, which operate from within ministries of health. Sometimes, the representation of the World Bank has its offices at the ministry of finance.

So far, states do not accredit missions to NGOs. However, in places such as Geneva, specific members of permanent missions are entrusted with handling relations with such bodies as the ICRC, the IFRC, and a number of other NGOs established there. Since NGOs and big national and international lobbies tend to maintain permanent or frequent temporary representatives at the headquarters of international organizations, both the officers of such organizations and the diplomats of accredited permanent and temporary missions have to deal with these representatives.

What Do the Diplomats Do?

Gathering and Disseminating Information

Much has been written about the demise of this function in bilateral diplomacy.[17] The media are supposed to have taken over, leaving the diplomat with nothing to do. In fact, this is not true at all. There is information that does not interest the media, and there is background information that they cannot obtain—either because it would take too much time, or because access is denied. Only the resident diplomats can cultivate the kind of interpersonal relations that will allow them to gauge raw news and provide their governments with relevant background evaluation. As for the dissemination of information, we may refer back to what has been said above about public diplomacy. In addition, however, the resident diplomats can feed selected interlocutors confidential information meant for them alone.

In multilateral diplomacy, permanent missions were for a long time the proper and only available channel through which information could be provided by international organizations to member countries. Fortunately, much of this task can now be eliminated since this information is accessible over the Internet.[18] But only diplomats can still provide background information based on their contacts with colleagues and relevant international civil servants. This is critical during the preparatory stages of a negotiation, when good personal relations allow the diplomats to inform their governments of trends in draft documents and approaches already undertaken by colleagues. As to disseminating information, there is still a need to produce data on the diplomat's home country that are not available in computer format. Moreover, diplomats can emphasize certain data that may not arouse much notice otherwise, and can provide confidential information about their governments' attitudes when appropriate.

Preparing Negotiations

In the past, negotiating briefs were prepared by bureaucrats in the foreign ministry or other government agencies and then handed over to negotiators appointed at a relatively late stage. In bilateral negotiations, the views of the diplomatic mission in the target country may have been solicited, while in multilateral negotiations, diplomatic missions in key countries may have been consulted regarding prevailing domestic views.

Information technology has made it possible to associate diplomatic missions with all of the stages of preparing a negotiating brief. The negotiators themselves can be involved. This becomes ever more important because formal negotiations tend to get shorter when crucial agreements have been reached beforehand in the course of informal contacts and discussions. Such preliminary agreements may involve government agencies, para-statal and private sector interest groups, as well as various lobbies, who frequently consult each other separately before the official negotiators meet to hammer out an overall deal. We shall show that these often complex interactions are greatly assisted by information technology.

Conducting Negotiations

In the past, multilateral negotiations were a long process, mostly taking place within the framework of international organizations. An organization would first decide to hold the negotiation and then embark on a preliminary phase by entrusting a standing or ad hoc body with the preparation of an agenda and a draft for the actual conference or collective organ to consider. Even when the negotiation was aimed at dealing with a conflict rather than producing a legal document, drafts regarding the handling of the issues at hand were produced during this preliminary stage. The conference or collective organ would then hold a first round of discussions at committee level under relatively relaxed procedural rules before going over the results in plenary meetings. The plenary might send back all or parts of what the committee had worked out for consideration. This process would take a great deal of time. At least at the plenary stage, politics would also enter the process, and delegations would have to state their positions on issues—and ask for the inclusion of resolutions addressing them in the final document—even if they had nothing to do with the actual subject matter of the negotiation.[19] This manner of negotiating still prevails in parts of the UN system,[20] including the UN General Assembly—particularly when it meets in special sessions.

The disappearance of ideological confrontation[21] following the collapse of communism and the increasing financial constraints under which international bodies have to operate have profoundly changed the methods of multilateral negotiation. Much preliminary work is done in the secretariat of the organization under whose auspices the negotiations take place, where well-informed countries try to inject their views through their permanent missions at the organizational headquarters. The background paper of the secretariat may be circulated to member countries for their comments before being taken by the designated chair for preliminary discussions with key delegations or spokespersons of groups of delegations. The chair is operating under no specific rules and is thus free to arrange its contacts. Once the chair is satisfied that conditions for reaching an agreement exist, it draws its own conclusions, which become the basis of the actual negotiation. The negotiation tends to consist increasingly of informal discussions, with official meetings mainly convened for formalizing a consensus or noting the impossibility of reaching one.

This general pattern tends to prevail in an increasing number of negotiations, with many variations. When highly technical issues (e.g., global warming) are considered, experts will hold a first round of discussions before being replaced by diplomats. These diplomats, in turn, will settle as many points as possible and will then make room in turn for high-powered decision makers, who will attempt to overcome the remaining major political obstacles. An interesting side effect of this new approach is that so much expectation may be generated worldwide or within the region concerned, that political decision makers fall under considerable pressure to reach a consensus. An example is the Rio Conference on the Environment of 1992, when the US president eventually made concessions he would not have authorized his negotiators to consider at earlier stages. If decision makers still fail to agree, this leads to considerable damage to their image, as can be seen in the example of the failure of the effort in Geneva to reach a consensus on a total ban on nuclear tests in 1996.

Following Up on Negotiations

For many years, diplomats would brief their superiors after the conclusion of a negotiation and then move on to other activities. If the negotiation had produced an agreement, the diplomats might be involved in its submission to national decision makers, particularly the parliament. Only in more recent decades have bilateral commissions been set up that meet occasionally or at regular intervals to monitor the implementation and, if necessary, make adjustments to the agreements themselves. They may also suggest negotiating additional agreements.

In the multilateral field, follow-up activities, at least regarding the impact of agreements on the national affairs of contracting parties, are the norm. There may even be national institutions charged with monitoring the implementation and impact of international agreements in such specific fields as trade, financial relations, transport, and communications. In other fields, especially human rights, such monitoring may be undertaken by NGOs specifically set up for the purpose. The follow-up on the impact of multilateral decisions on the institutions or countries concerned is normally left to bodies set up for this purpose when such decisions are adopted. Thus, nearly every major convention on environmental issues has also set up a secretariat in charge of monitoring its implementation. Depending on the subject matter, there may be no foreign ministry diplomats sent to such bodies, as proper monitoring of the implementation and its effects may require specialized knowledge.

New Trends in Multilateral Negotiations

Preparation

As indicated earlier, present-day multilateral negotiations have to be kept short, both because competent delegates have little time and because international organizations are strapped for cash and can no longer finance endless meetings with all of the requisite paraphernalia of simultaneous interpretation and secretarial assistance. This means that much more emphasis is given to preparatory activities.

Complex negotiations in such fields as international trade or disarmament require important preparatory work at the level of international secretariats (e.g., UNCTAD, WTO, or the Disarmament Conference). These secretariats must sound out participating countries regarding possible agendas and then prepare not only background papers, but also complete files containing all of the requisite information. Informal meetings of negotiators are then held to discuss proposed agendas. If they do not produce sufficient consensus at the expert level, high officials or even ministers of all or selected groups of participants may be convened for discussions.[22] These meetings are still informal, so that no major damage is done if they fail. If sufficient consensus is achieved, or if great pressure is exerted to get an agenda and timetable adopted, as was the case for the Millennium Negotiating Round at the WTO, a high-level, formal meeting may be convened to sort matters out. If this fails, as happened in Seattle in late 1999, the proposed negotiation may be derailed or at least sent back to the drawing board.

If an agenda is agreed upon, the chair of the preliminary negotiation, which is normally also the chair of the formal conference, must now actively prepare the latter. For this purpose, the chair may draw up a "non-paper" containing its own views and circulate it—either among all concerned countries or only a selected number. The designated recipients are usually the heads of those countries' delegations or their permanent representatives at the headquarters of the host organization, for example, in Geneva for UNCTAD and WTO. On the basis of their replies, the chair produces an amended paper. This procedure may be repeated several times. For the European Union, this phase is conducted within the framework of meetings of permanent representatives in Brussels. Once the chair feels that it has sufficient clarity on the representatives' various positions, it produces a more formal paper, which will be the basis for the actual negotiation.

Managing the Negotiation

The current trend is to avoid controversy and majority decisions and to seek consensus instead. The reason for this is simple: the participation of some key countries is normally required for the proper implementation of decisions. If attempts are made to force them to take measures they are unwilling to consider, they will simply refuse to ratify the result of the negotiation, which, even if adopted by a large majority of countries, remains, in fact, meaningless.[23] It is therefore preferable to admit the impossibility of reaching a consensus at the moment and allow for further discussions at a later stage. Consensus also makes it easier for a country not to oppose a solution with which it disagrees, whereas in a vote its delegation would be forced to dissent or abstain to prevent adverse reactions at home.

Difficult negotiations therefore begin with a formal meeting during which participating delegations have the opportunity to make official statements. Then the chair suspends the meeting for informal discussions that represent the actual negotiation. Such discussions may group all participating delegations or only some of them, and they may be interrupted time and again for even more informal consultations and efforts by the chair or other delegates to mediate between incompatible positions. Only when a final consensus emerges, or when it becomes clear that no such consensus is currently possible, will the formal meeting be reconvened to register the said consensus or the failure to achieve one. If no consensus is possible, a vote may have to be taken, especially if a majority of participating countries prefer this. But the text thus adopted may not produce the desired results: countries whose participation is essential may refuse to sign and ratify the adopted document. Recent examples of this are the Comprehensive Nuclear Test Ban Treaty[24] and the Statute of a Permanent International Criminal Court.[25]

Managing Outside Interference and Cooperation

Modern multilateral negotiations have to deal with the media, lobbies, and experts. Some of these may assist the secretariat and the chair or even occupy positions of rapporteurs. Yet there are always groups who disagree with the negotiating parties and thus remain outside the ambit of the negotiation proper.

The media are solicited by lobbies and experts, mostly with the aim of influencing the outcome of the negotiation, or, as the example of Seattle shows, of completely derailing it. It is therefore essential for the secretariat and the chair to brief the media properly and maintain as much as possible a friendly cooperation with them. In this manner, hostile interference from lobbies or part of the media may be effectively neutralized. Friendly cooperation means both good personal relations with reporters and editors, and a willingness to allow the media as much insight into the goings-on as is feasible.

Lobbies may either pursue a single issue or set of issues, or aim at orienting or even derailing the negotiation. Supportive lobbies are not very frequent, but they do exist. Sometimes, as shown by the example of the prohibition of contact mines, lobbies may actually be at the origin of a negotiation and provide the principal pressure for its successful completion. Already in the days of the UN Conference on the Law of the Sea (UNCLOS), it was realized that lobbies could provide useful inputs and the chairs of the committees established regular contacts with them. In exchange, lobbies would provide support for clauses and regulations that were elaborated with their cooperation. These days, hostile lobbies, especially national ones, can sabotage the adoption of an agreed text by the national decision makers, in particular, the parliament.

Experts may either be part of the negotiation process or act as outsiders trying to influence it. Insider experts are often used by secretariats preparing background papers and commentary on various items and stages of the negotiation. They may also be appointed as rapporteurs or called upon to assist rapporteurs. During the UNCLOS negotiation, one committee chairman[26] had regular evening discussions with experts to enlighten him in the elaboration of his proposals that would serve as the negotiating basis the next day.

Policymakers as Negotiators

Ministers and heads of state often feel that they are needed to provide the final input or to put their seal on what they consider to be an important negotiation. The UN Charter was discussed at first by experts and only later by diplomats. At a certain stage, the deadlocked discussions had to be unblocked by the top Allied leaders (Churchill, Roosevelt, and Stalin) at Yalta. The plenary meetings in San Francisco finalizing the text were attended by ministers, and the final text was adopted and signed by a number of top leaders. In the following years, it was thought that summit meetings could be used to settle important problems.[27] Such meetings were organized by diplomats and even ministers. If preparatory discussions succeeded in producing generally acceptable drafts, the summit meeting was normally considered a success. If not, the top decision makers might produce a compromise, if only in the shape of directives on how the negotiation was to be continued at a lower level. Lack of previous agreement at lower levels might also lead summits toward failure, and a few such experiences led to considerable restraint in convening top decision makers to conduct actual negotiations, as opposed to simply endorsing draft agreements, possibly while slightly amending them.[28]

Today, the presence of top policymakers is more often required to provide an important negotiation with the necessary glamour in its final stages and also to reassure public opinion at home that nothing harmful to the national interest (which is often equated with the interest of one or several powerful lobbies) will be agreed to. In this latter regard, the participation of a top decision maker in the final stage of a negotiation may actually determine the acceptability of the result at the national level (Evans et al. 1993). This is particularly the case for the US, except when Congress uses presidential support of a draft as the very pretext for not accepting it.

Alternative Forums and Actors of Diplomatic and Quasi-Diplomatic Interaction

Alternative forums have been in existence for quite some time, but have tended to remain discreetly in the background in order to avoid publicity. The term "track two diplomacy" is often used these days to describe discussions of diplomatic issues, often by non-diplomats, in academic or similar contexts. More publicity is given to gatherings at which members of the private economic sector meet politicians. Such meetings are increasingly used by the latter for informal discussions or as platforms for presenting their views in an "unofficial" manner, that is, publicly, but without remaining formally bound to them.

Track Two Diplomacy

Discussion of diplomatic issues by non-diplomats with a view to influencing diplomatic events is relatively old. The most famous of such regular meetings were doubtlessly the Pugwash Conferences, which began in the 1950s and at which scientists discussed important political issues of the day. For a time, this used to be one of the few means whereby scientists from the Eastern and Western blocs could meet. In the 1960s, the Carnegie Endowment for International Peace, a US private foundation, used to convene meetings to discuss issues of the day to which academics, journalists, and diplomats from Western and Eastern countries were invited. These meetings, held mostly under the auspices of the European Centre of the Carnegie Endowment in Geneva, were not open to the public, nor were their discussions reported in the media.

An interesting form of "track two diplomacy" is the bringing together of actual diplomats with academic experts to discuss an important issue about to be submitted to an international negotiation. An early example of this was a seminar convened by the International Relations Institute of Cameroon in 1972 at Yaoundé on issues of the law of the sea. It was attended by African diplomats in charge of their country's law of the sea desk at the foreign ministry and a few international academic experts. It produced a proposal for adding an exclusive economic zone to the territorial waters and contiguous zone to protect the interests of coastal countries in the exploitation of the resources of the sea.[29] This proposal was later submitted by Kenya to the Council of Ministers of the Organisation of African Unity, which endorsed it as its own position and formally presented it to the UN Conference on the Law of the Sea (UNCLOS). Its main findings are now part of the convention adopted in 1982.

Today, many academic institutions, especially those interested in international affairs, convene conferences or seminars dealing with current issues of diplomacy that are attended by a mix of academics and diplomats. The proceedings are often published and may have some influence on diplomatic developments, for example, through the actions participating diplomats take when they are back in their offices.[30]

International Economic Forums

The best known of these forums is the World Economic Forum, which is usually held each winter in Davos, Switzerland. In 2002, the Forum took place in New York to express its solidarity with the city after the terrorist attacks of 11 September 2001. The World Economic Forum also has a summer extension that takes place in Salzburg, Austria. A somewhat similar forum is headquartered in Crans-Montana, also in Switzerland, under the name of Crans-Montana Forum, and convenes in the summer. It also holds meetings in other countries and now has a permanent base in Monaco. Both are private institutions financed by sponsors and by the contributions of participants, who are mostly members of national and international economic enterprises. One attraction is to meet high-ranking invited guests. In the case of Davos, the attendance of top world leaders has now become the custom. These leaders make use of the opportunity to hold private meetings among themselves, besides making statements to plenary sessions.

The presence of top decision makers in Davos has led to a widespread misconception that the World Economic Forum is a kind of international conference. As a result, many NGOs and other lobbies are now clamoring for admission as a matter of right. Should they succeed, the Forum would lose its attraction as a private gathering to be attended by invitation alone. The same misconception has led some groups to attempt to prevent the forum from meeting; they see it as an unacceptable promotion of economic globalization.

Alternative Actors

The last few years have witnessed the emergence of a great number of national and international groups set up as NGOs. In many cases, they are simply one-issue lobbies that have provided themselves with a more official status. Contrary to long-established NGOs, such groups have little knowledge of, or even emphatically reject, diplomatic approaches. Some use all available forms of intimidation, such as street barrages, destructive action, and even physical violence and "cyberterrorism," to achieve their aims, which may simply be to derail an ongoing or planned meeting. Diplomats are not yet prepared for dealing with such groups and prefer to let security forces handle them. It would be useful if contact with even the most disruptive groups could be established—probably through intermediaries—with a view to influencing them toward less disruptive action in exchange for better opportunities to make their views known.

The Impact of Information Technology

Information technology both affects the conduct of traditional diplomacy and opens up possibilities for new techniques and instruments of diplomatic action. The computer has revolutionized the processing of words, first by individuals, and later by offering networking facilities that allow several people to work simultaneously on the same text without actually meeting. Information technology allows for links both with other computers and to any number of texts saved in digital and hypertext formats. For diplomacy, the linking of users is of particular interest.

Internal Networking

Such networking presently exists at the level of most foreign ministries and includes a growing number of missions abroad.[31] If properly exploited, it accelerates the internal flow of data and their proper processing, and creates a storage system that makes the data easily accessible to all concerned. It also allows two or more people situated in different parts of a ministry to work together on a single text. A principal advantage is that overseas missions can work on negotiating briefs that are being developed at the home office.

In a growing number of countries, networking now goes beyond single ministries and tends gradually to encompass the whole apparatus of government. This means that data circulate more easily and can be shared whenever necessary. Moreover, the preparation of negotiations involving more than one government department can now be conducted without the civil servants concerned having to meet all of the time. Preliminary exchanges can take place through email and by working on a single text from several locations. At a later stage, real-time cyberconferences can be held. Selective access to government networks can also be made available to outside entities—in particular, to the private sector. If properly handled, this may allow an official delegation to interact constantly with all interested parties at home and thus ensure that it acts within an acceptable framework.

Building Networks across Borders

During preliminary stages of multilateral negotiations the possibility of interacting with other participants over information technology networks is very useful. It is not just a matter of saving time by avoiding physical displacements. The main point is that the negotiators and those who prepare their briefs can remain in constant contact across borders and thus work out joint positions, especially regarding briefs for negotiating groups.

The importance of preliminary work by international secretariats has already been pointed out. Until recently, government departments had to interact with such secretariats through permanent missions at organizational headquarters. Presently, they can reach such secretariats directly over the Internet. In so doing, they must, however, avoid the confusion resulting from various government departments simultaneously pursuing divergent policies. In other words, interaction with secretariats should first be coordinated at the national level.

It must be realized that governments are not the only institutions able to build up networks across borders. Private sector enterprises already have their own international and even global structures. In order to have a reasonable picture of any given situation, both governmental institutions and international secretariats must also remain in touch with such non-official networks. This is particularly important where lobbies are concerned, as preliminary knowledge of their intentions will help in devising a proper strategy for actual negotiations.

Staying in Touch All of the Time

Negotiators abroad will soon be able to conduct their actions while remaining in online contact with their home base. Thus, much precious time can be saved in comparison to when negotiators had to ask for new instructions and await their arrival, sometimes even by mail. In the case of very small diplomatic establishments, the negotiator is often the person in charge of the relevant desk or division at home and may have to conduct several negotiations at the same time. By remaining in constant contact over international networks, the negotiator can stay ahead of developments, even in such complex situations.

Conducting Virtual Negotiations

In October 1997, the Board of Trade and Development of UNCTAD and the Second Committee of the UN General Assembly held a joint meeting while sitting in Geneva and New York respectively. They were connected audiovisually over the Internet, and delegates could see each other on a screen. The meeting could be directed by a single chair. This type of audiovisual meeting has now become almost commonplace. In June 2001, the World Bank decided to change a July meeting in Barcelona into an audiovisual cybermeeting to escape the disruptive action threatened by violent protest groups.

Even more useful are negotiations conducted at real-time cybermeetings whose participants communicate by typing their messages, which appear on the computer screens of all concerned. While these sessions require a lot of discipline from participants, the great advantage of such meetings is that they leave an immediate record of the proceedings. They also provide more privacy to participants, in that access to the virtual conference room is controlled by passwords. The media and lobbies can be kept out and informed only to the extent desired by the actual participants. The participants can also discuss matters privately outside the main meeting context in separate virtual "rooms" made available to them by the software.

Simulations conducted by DiploProjects at the Mediterranean Academy of Diplomatic Studies in Malta[32] have shown that real-time cybernegotiations can be complemented and even replaced by interaction through email and on hypertext discussion sites, where every participant can intervene at his or her own convenience. This is very important when negotiators live in time zones that are far apart. Real-time interaction may in those cases become difficult, and should be reserved for situations in which the simultaneous presence of all delegations is essential. It is unlikely that cybernegotiations will ever fully replace face-to-face negotiations. Especially where high-level negotiators are concerned, there will remain a mutual desire to have meetings in person. In some cases, they may be satisfied with seeing each other on a screen, but in other situations this may not suffice. It may well be possible that negotiators who have actually met can later meet audiovisually without feeling any inconvenience. In this regard, the Barcelona experience just mentioned may be of considerable relevance. One may hope that in the relatively near future, diplomats and decision makers may have to travel less and can interact more frequently and comfortably over the Internet.

Conclusions

Diplomacy is changing faster and more profoundly than most diplomats themselves probably realize. The number of different international groups and organizations involved in diplomacy has increased, and so have their interactions. Present-day diplomats are generally better trained and better prepared for their tasks, and will increasingly have the capability to brief themselves over information technology facilities for whatever activity is required of them. At the multilateral level, discussions and negotiations are now conducted with much more real desire to reach positive results in an atmosphere of much greater politeness and friendliness and with greater informality than only two decades ago. At the national level, diplomats increasingly become part of an overall network that allows for informal and formal exchanges, constant mutual information, and all sorts of private negotiations. They can stay in touch with this network wherever they are and thus remain at all times trustworthy and fully briefed representatives of their country or organization. This development should ideally also facilitate the monitoring of the implementation of all sorts of agreements. Increasingly, special arrangements, even organizations, are set up either to monitor or to provide follow-up after international negotiations.

At the level of international governmental organizations, interaction with member countries and their representatives will have to be reevaluated. Once the full impact of IT on diplomacy is realized, considerable changes in the way international secretariats are organized and operate can be expected. Recent developments in the behavior of certain NGOs and lobbies will require new approaches in dealing with them, especially on the part of international secretariats and conveners of international conferences.

At the moment, we are living in a period of transition, a time when past attitudes and approaches coexist with new ones. A realistic diplomat must be prepared to encounter old-fashioned colleagues using the language and adopting the archaic attitudes of the past and harboring suspicions of information technology, alongside others who fully exploit the advantages of the new international atmosphere and the facilities provided by the new technology.

In spite of better prepared diplomats and improved facilities and procedures, the success of a diplomatic effort is never guaranteed, and failure always remains a possibility. There will continue to be situations in which diplomats cannot communicate properly, for lack of mutual understanding or empathy. But the main reason for failure, as in the past, does not lie with the diplomats themselves but rather with those who employ and instruct them. A diplomat, after all, is only a representative or a spokesperson of the government or organization he or she represents. If not given sufficient freedom of action, if bound by unrealistic instructions, or if obliged to act in a political, cultural, or mental framework that the other side cannot accept or even understand, then even the best of diplomats is bound to fail. It is not yet possible to evaluate to what extent the intervention of new (quasi) terrorist groups bent only on preventing or derailing a given negotiation will affect the efficacy of diplomacy. This would be the first instance in which failure would not come from those who employ and instruct the diplomats or the diplomats themselves, but from complete outsiders.

Today, governments and international organizations can communicate in many ways and with many groups and organizations without resorting to diplomatic contact. This means that diplomats can better concentrate on their essential role: the creation and cultivation of discreet interpersonal relationships that enable them to communicate with their interlocutors in an atmosphere of mutual confidence and trust. In this way, they can gather knowledge and convey views, feelings, and ideas that are not meant for the public at large. In this way, too, they can explore possible compromises in tense and difficult negotiating situations. But to be able to fully play this role, the diplomat must be allowed to keep out of the limelight when necessary. Openness and transparency that exposes everything to the public are justified and even essential in many instances. But confidentiality—even secrecy—and trust in each other's absolute discretion cannot be dispensed with when delicate issues have to be handled. This is as much the true vocation of the diplomat of today as it was in the past.

Notes

1. To a certain extent, international organizations are the result of the institutionalization of certain types of international conferences in the nineteenth century, such as ITU, UPU, BIRPI (now WIPO).
2. There are a few authors who wrote some years ago in support of this negative view (Cable 1983; Sharp 1998).
3. In the summer of 1914, diplomats were totally sidelined by political and military leaders intent on war. They were in no position to influence the course of events. During the second half of the 1930s, the not very convincing efforts of diplomats on both sides were simply steamrollered by the dictators of the day, especially in the case of Germany and Italy (Craig and Loewenheim 1994; Goldstein 1991; Messick 1987; Walworth 1986).
4. One may remember the hot dispute between the US and the USSR about "automatic majorities" in the UN General Assembly. During the first two decades of the UN's existence, a majority of members favored the US, whereas with the independence of former colonies and their consequent admission to the UN, there were mostly "automatic majorities" voting against the position of the US.
5. States, while handing over competences to international institutions and having to pay more attention to the action of NGOs and other non-state actors, still remain the only actors on the international scene with full international personality. Moreover, as will be shown, they participate in the action of international organizations and provide much of the personnel used by the organizations for their own diplomatic action. This situation is unlikely to change in the near future.
6. See the inaugural lecture for the 1999–2000 academic year at the Graduate Institute of International Studies in Geneva by the Swiss foreign minister, Joseph Deiss. An English version is available on http//diplowizard.diplomacy.edu/tara/GetXdoc.asp?Idconv=2221.

7. An annual International Forum on Diplomatic Training meets alternatively in Vienna and another part of the world to discuss the adjustment of training programs and institutions to the evolution of diplomacy and requirements for diplomats. Its members are deans and directors of diplomatic academies and institutes of international relations, and its secretariat is handled by the Diplomatic Academy in Vienna.

8. Pioneers among academic institutions preparing students for diplomatic careers are the Graduate Institute of International Studies in Geneva and the Fletcher School of Law and Diplomacy in Medford, Massachusetts, US, set up in 1927 and 1933 respectively. These have a long tradition of cooperation and exchanges of students and staff.

9. Much is written about the problems that developing countries are supposed to have with information technology due to lack of funds and specialists. This, and especially the conclusion that a new information technology gap is developing between rich and poor countries, is partly a misconception. Hardware is inexpensive and produces economies that outweigh the cost of its acquisition. The problem is that lack of understanding leads to the acquisition of inadequate (and sometimes unnecessarily expensive) hardware, made worse by gifts from producing countries that do not respond to any serious prior study of actual requirements. As for specialists, there are more of them in developing countries than is generally realized. The main problem is attracting them to the diplomatic establishment.

10. The Institute of Diplomacy and International Studies at the University of Nairobi regularly admits officers from outside the foreign ministries to its yearly diploma course for newly recruited diplomats. The Institute of International Relations in Trinidad offers a diploma course accepting diplomats, ordinary students, and officers from government departments engaged in international activities.

11. The US is not alone in this regard. Many Latin American countries tend to place relatives or supporters of their chief executive into important ambassadorial positions. An even less commendable practice consists of sending embarrassing politicians or dangerous rivals to ambassadorial posts, as far away as possible. One interesting incident happened in 1959 in The Hague (where the author was then posted as a trainee attaché), when the Queen refused an *agrément* to the disgraced Soviet foreign minister Molotov on the grounds that an ambassador should enjoy the confidence of his government. Molotov was then posted to Ulan Baatar.

12. The support of many NGOs for the Campaign to Ban Landmines deeply influenced the governments and diplomats of many countries. In some countries, such as France and Japan, NGOs successfully lobbied their governments to sign the Ottawa Convention on the Prohibition of the Use, Stockpiling, Production and Transfer of Antipersonnel Mines and on Their Destruction. This convention constituted a high mark in the negotiation and advocacy activities of NGOs vis-à-vis governments and intergovernmental organizations (Kirkey forthcoming).

13. Such a situation has prevailed in Somalia for a number of years. Experience gathered by NGOs active there should help them in dealing with similar situations elsewhere. There are also regions that escape control by governments that still operate in other parts of the country, for example in Sudan and Congo-Kinshasa.

14. ACP (African, Caribbean, Pacific) countries used to negotiate conventions at regular intervals with the European Economic Community, now the European Union, represented by its Commission, on trade preferences, stabilization of product prices, financial assistance, and the like. Ministers of component regions and the group as a whole used to meet and work out common positions and strategies. The permanent representatives of these countries in Brussels acted as a sort of standing group, which could negotiate with EC representatives and also work out minor adjustments in the overall ACP strategies. The group also has a standing secretariat. As a result of globalization of international economic relations, mainly within the context of the WTO, the ACP-EC relationship has lost some of its former significance. The round of negotiations concluded in 2000 tried to adjust to these new realities in a more open-ended agreement,

signed at Cotonou, Benin, on 23 June 2000, which shall remain in force for 20 years (consult for details at: http//www.acpsec.org./gb/cotonou/accord1.htm).

15. Non-payment of contributions is used as a means to pressure the Organization to adopt specific strategies and other member countries to vote in the sense desired by the US even when they might not be inclined to do so (Williamson and Maynes 1986).

16. Interestingly, the UN itself maintains no permanent missions with members or other states. All bilateral business is handled through the permanent missions and observer missions of those countries in New York and Geneva. The UN Secretariat only maintains information offices abroad.

17. Such writings are mainly found in the daily or periodical printed press, combined with predictions that diplomats are about to become irrelevant. Occasionally, affirmations of this kind can also be heard at seminars and conferences dealing with diplomacy.

18. Shortly after producing most materials in electronic format, and before waiting for governments to download them from their web sites, the UN ran a program to assist permanent missions in New York in establishing the necessary hardware capacity and personnel resources to download UN documents for the purpose of sending them on to their capitals.

19. For many years, routine condemnation of apartheid was suggested as part of preambles, as was the necessity to recognize and satisfy the needs of the Palestinian people. Another frequently raised issue was the need for a more just international order in all sorts of fields. When such issues came up in technical negotiations, the adoption of the proposed resolutions was resisted by most countries of Europe and by the US, often leading to lengthy and inconclusive debates.

20. Such as in most annual general conferences of such specialized agencies as UNESCO, WHO, FAO and ILO, to mention just a few.

21. This concerns mainly the former East-West confrontation, whereas other antagonisms still prevail, as between North and South. However, one notes a general collapse of monolithic blocs, which are being replaced by more flexible and shifting alliances.

22. In the case of the WTO, such an informal preliminary meeting of selected countries, represented at ministerial level, was convened by Switzerland in Lausanne in November 1999. It did not produce any tangible results, nor was it meant to do so. The intent was rather to gauge positions and the readiness for compromising on them. The impression garnered by participants that it would not be easy to achieve any meaningful results at the forthcoming Seattle conference was fully confirmed.

23. One famous early example of such developments is the UN Law of the Sea Convention. At the beginning of the negotiations, it was agreed that all decisions would be made by consensus and that the convention should be seen as a package to be adopted as a whole. At a relatively late stage, the US government decided no longer to abide by the consensus and package rules, and to insist on decisions being made by vote. When this led to the adoption, with large majorities, of a text that the US government could not agree with, the US and a number of important maritime countries decided either not to sign or at least not to ratify the convention. As a result, large parts of it, especially the one dealing with the exploitation of the seabed beyond the limits of national jurisdictions, remained a dead letter. Only in 1994, when the Convention was about to enter into force, could a solution be found, thanks to the efforts of the UN Secretary-General, under which large parts of the Convention were in fact amended. As a result, many important maritime nations became parties to the Convention.

24. After the breakdown of consensus negotiations in Geneva, the draft treaty was brought directly before the UN General Assembly in September 1996, signed by the five nuclear powers, and formally adopted by a vote on 24 September. However, India and Pakistan, who had opposed the consensus, also refused to sign. Since then, they have become nuclear powers.

25. The statute was adopted on 17 July 1998 at a conference in Rome, against the opposition of the US, which so far has refused to ratify it.

26. Evensen, from Norway, who later became a judge at the International Court of Justice.

27. In 1954, world leaders met in Geneva to find a solution to the conflicts in Indochina. A later conference, again in Geneva, adopted a declaration on the neutrality of Laos in 1962.
28. In recent decades it has become ever more widespread to set up an organ made up of heads of state and government within regional organizations. In order to allow the latter to reach any meaningful decisions at all, a subordinate organ made up of ministers had to be provided for, which normally meets just before the heads of state or government convene to endorse its proposals. The kind of real bargaining conducted at the summits of the European Union twice a year still remains an exception and shows how far the EU has already moved away from the traditional type of intergovernmental organization.
29. The proceedings of this seminar were published in a very limited edition by the International Relations Institute of Cameroon in Yaoundé, P.O. Box 1637, and can be consulted there.
30. The Mediterranean Academy of Diplomatic Studies set up in Malta in 1990 convenes such meetings on a more or less regular basis. Their subject matters normally concern the Mediterranean and deal with political, economic, cultural, and security issues.
31. Initially, networks were simple telephone connections between individual computers. Then computers used the Internet to communicate, but this was found to lack security. At present, most practitioners use intranet, which can be protected against intruding outsiders by a so-called firewall.
32. "DiploEdu" stands for programs for which most of the teaching is done over the internet and in which students are made to discuss issues and attend simulation exercises in virtual chat rooms.

Bibliography

Berridge, G.R., and James, A. *Dictionary of Diplomacy*. New York: Palgrave, 2000.
Berridge, G.R. *Diplomacy, Theory and Practice*. New York: Prentice Hall, 1995.
Bildt, C. "Force and Diplomacy." *Survival*, vol. 42, no. 1 (Spring 2000): 141–148.
Bothe, M. "Compliance Control beyond Diplomacy: The Role of Non-governmental Actors." *Environmental Policy and Law*, vol. 27, no. 4 (1997): 293–297.
Cable, J. "Diplomacy: A Case for Resuscitation." *International Relations* (May 1983): 261–283.
Craig, G.A., and Loewenheim, F.L. *Diplomats 1939–1979*. Princeton: Princeton University Press, 1994.
Diamond, L., and Mc Donald, J.W. *Multi-track Diplomacy: A Systems Approach to Peace*. West Hartford, CT: Kumarian Press, 1996.
Eban, A. *Diplomacy for the Next Century*. New Haven: Yale University Press, 1998.
Evans, P.B., Jacobson, H.K., and Putnam, R.D., eds. *Double-Edged Diplomacy: International Bargaining and Domestic Politics*. Berkeley: University of California Press, 1993.
Ginsberg, R.H. "Conceptualising the European Union as an International Actor: Narrowing the Theoretical Capability-Expectations Gap." *Journal of Common Market Studies*, vol. 37, no. 3 (1999): 429–456.
Goldstein, E. *Winning the Peace: British Diplomatic Strategy 1916–1920*. London, Oxford University Press, 1991.
Hamilton, K., and Longhorne, R. *Practice of Diplomacy*. London/New York: Routledge, 1998.
Hocking, B. *Foreign Ministries: Change and Adaptation*. New York: Palgrave, 1999.
Imai, R. "Diplomacy of Compliance and Modern Arms Control." *International Affairs*, vol. 62, no. 1 (1985–1986): 87–94.
Jakobsen, P.V. *Western Use of Coercive Diplomacy after the Cold War*. New York: Macmillan/St. Martin's Press, 1998.

Jentleson, B.W. *Opportunities Missed, Opportunities Seized: Preventive Diplomacy in the Post–Cold War World.* Lanham, MD: Rowman and Littlefield, 2000.

Kaufmann, J. *Conference Diplomacy: An Introductory Analysis.* Basingstoke: Macmillan, 1996.

Kirkey, C. *Implementing the Ottawa Convention: Explaining the Persistence of State-Nongovernmental Organization Relations.* In mimeo, forthcoming.

Kissinger, H.A. *Diplomacy.* New York: Simon and Schuster, 1994.

Kurbalija, J. *Knowledge and Diplomacy.* Malta, DiploPublishing, 1999.

Kurbalija, J., ed. *Modern Diplomacy.* Malta: DiploPublishing, 1998.

Kurbalija, J., and Baldi, S. *Internet Guide for Diplomats.* 2nd ed. Malta: DiploPublishing, 2000.

Lakos, A. *International Negotiations: A Bibliography.* Boulder: Westview Press, 1989.

Lapointe, E. *Désastres Naturels et Diplomatie*, vol. 59, no. 4 (1994–1995): 1085–1098.

Lavroff, S.V. "On the Ground: Russian Diplomats in Kosovo." *International Affairs*, vol. 45, no. 3 (1999): 15–24.

Martel, G. "Necessity of Negotiation: Diplomacy as a Way of Life." *Behind the Headlines*, vol. 45 no. 4 (1988): 15.

McMillan, J. "Talking to the Enemy: Negotiation in Wartime." *Comparative Strategy*, vol. 11, no. 4 (1992): 447–461.

Melissen, J. *Innovation in Diplomatic Practice.* New York: Palgrave, 1999.

Messick, F.M. *Primary Sources of European Diplomacy 1914–1945: A Bibliography of Published Memoirs and Diaries.* New York: Greenwood Press, 1987.

Newsom, D.D. *Diplomacy and Human Rights.* Georgetown: Georgetown University, 1986.

Newsom, D.D. *Diplomacy under a Foreign Flag: When Nations Break Relations.* New York: St. Martin's Press, 1990.

Owada, H. "Diplomacy Re-considered." *New York University Journal of International Law and Politics*, vol. 27, no. 3 (Spring 1995): 561–570.

Pearce, D.D. *Wary Partners: Diplomats and the Media.* Washington, D.C.: Congressional Quarterly Inc., 1995.

Picco, G. *Man without a Gun: One Diplomat's Struggle to Free the Hostages, Fight Terrorism and End a War.* New York: New York Times Books/Random House, 1999.

Reich, A. "From Diplomacy to Law: The Juridization of International Trade Relations." *North-Western Journal of International Law and Business*, vol. 17, nos. 2–3 (1996/1997): 775–789.

Roberts, W.R. "Media Dimension of Diplomacy in the Information Age." *The World Today*, vol. 47, no. 7 (1991): 112–115.

Seib, P.M. *Headlines and Diplomacy: How Coverage Affects Foreign Policy.* Westport: Praeger, 1997.

Sharp, P. "Who Needs Diplomats? The Problem of Diplomatic Representation." Pp. 59–94, in Kurbalija, J., ed., *Modern Diplomacy.* Malta: Diplopublishing, 1998.

Stearns, M. *Talking to Strangers: Improving American Diplomacy at Home and Abroad.* Princeton: Princeton University Press, 1996.

Strange, S. "States, Firms and Diplomacy." *International Affairs*, vol. 68, no. 1 (1992): 1–15.

Susskind, L.E. *Environmental Diplomacy.* New York: Oxford University Press, 1994.

Talbott, S. "Globalization and Diplomacy: A Practitioner's Perspective." *Foreign Policy*, no. 108 (1997): 68–83.

Tible-Caoyonan, E. *Development Diplomacy.* Quezon City: University of the Philippines, 1994.

Toulemon, R. "Communauté, Union Politique, Confédération: Diplomatie ou Démocratie Plurinationale?" *Revue du Marché Commun*, no. 348 (1991): 428–432.

Walworth, A.C. *Wilson and His Peacemakers: American Diplomacy at the Paris Peace Conference 1919.* New York: W.W. Norton and Co, 1986.

Williamson, R., and Maynes, C.W. *US Foreign Policy and the UN.* New York: W.W. Norton and Co., 1986.

Woods, C.T. *Asia-Pacific Diplomacy: Non-governmental Organizations and International Relations.* Vancouver: UBC Press, 1993.

Wriston, W. "Bits, Bytes and Diplomacy." *Foreign Affairs*, vol. 76, no. 5 (1997): 172–182.

— Chapter 3 —

THE POLITICS OF NORM SETTING AT THE UNITED NATIONS
The Case of Sustainable Human Development

Jacques Fomerand

Introduction

Sustainable Human Development (SHD) has entered the lexicon of the development discourse, and its emphasis on "placing people at the center of development" has been endorsed by all major UN global conferences of the 1990s. Yet SHD's detractors are as numerous and vocal as its advocates. One important criticism is that "the paradigm's abstractness and unfinished nature, coupled with ideological ambiguity and internal tensions, make it extremely difficult to translate into a comprehensive yet concrete development strategy" (Nicholls 1999: 397–398). This chapter seeks to elucidate the role that the United Nations has played, and continues to play, in defining more precisely the concept's policy contours and contents. Because of its fuzziness, the SHD paradigm has lent itself to conflicting interpretations by Northern and Southern countries.[1] In fact, such debates are reflective of the enduring and—some would say—increasing polarization of UN discussions over the nature of the development process, development policies, and the role of the Organization therein. The SHD story suggests that this pattern of dissent—however "pathological" it may be—has not meant disarray, drift, or paralysis for the Organization. Far from being a powerless mirror of the world's divisions or a forum for ritualized exercises in oratory, the United Nations has, in fact, if not restructured, at least contributed to reshape, in no insignificant manner, the SHD discourse and, by the same token, development policies.

The purpose of this chapter is to explore how this course of events unfolded. In brief, the argument presented here is that the United Nations was able to effect changes in development thinking by relying on a variety of legitimizing tools deriving from its universality. First and foremost among them was its advocacy of "Fabian" principles of interpretation of the meaning and directions of development policy.

Conflicting Northern and Southern Views of SHD

At least in theory, SHD pays equal attention to the internal as well as the external parameters of development. In the vernacular of the 1993 *Human Development Report* (*HDR*): "Human development is development of the people for the people by the people. Development of the people means investing in human capabilities, whether in education or health or skills, so that they can work productively and creatively. Development for the people means ensuring that the economic growth they generate is distributed widely and fairly.... [D]evelopment by the people [means] ... giving everyone a chance to participate" (UNDP *HDR* 1993: 3). But the authors of the UNDP flagship report have also been mindful of the international determinants of the development process. Thus, the UNDP administrator prefaced the 1996 *Human Development Report* by pointing out that "all countries must strive to improve the nature and quality of their economic growth.... Of course, policies must be tailored to national circumstances. The global community can, and must, also help countries effect their own strategies of sustainable human development" (UNDP *HDR* 1996: iii–iv).

One of the key policy prescriptions flowing from the SHD approach is the requirement to treat all of the dimensions of human development— internal as well as external—in a "holistic" and "integrated" manner. But the SHD paradigm establishes no a priori directive as to what the most suitable mix and hierarchy of national and international policies should be to achieve these objectives. Understandably, then, SHD has lent itself to very conflicting political interpretations, some leaning toward free market prescriptions, others toward Keynesian policies. Ample ammunition has thus been provided for politically polarized debates between North and South.

SHD has been embraced as the beacon guiding the development discourse of Northern countries, most especially the United States, which sees in it a natural complement to the now conventional wisdom of market-directed capitalist development. This embrace of SHD is hardly surprising, for SHD has much in common with the long-standing US view that development is a process entailing primarily "a fuller utilization" of national resources. From this standpoint, which can be traced back to the immediate postwar years, development hinges primarily on the efforts of individual countries themselves and the mobilization of indigenous, local resources. The purpose of international cooperation is to augment and complement these efforts by advancing "the technical bases of economic development of underdeveloped countries" through studies, surveys, conferences and functional meetings, technical cooperation measures aimed at increasing productivity and fostering capital formation, and a wide array of social and labor measures. National governments need an international economic environment supportive of their efforts. This means the creation of conditions favorable to capital movements and investment, and of an open and free trading system.[2]

The current prevailing thinking embodied in the so-called "Washington Consensus" is an extension of these earlier prescriptions. From that standpoint, the market rather than the state is the best guarantor of efficient resource generation and allocation for development purposes. Rapid trade and capital account liberalization and the privatization of state-owned enterprises are therefore deemed to be the ultimate engines of growth. Public international assistance as well as national government policies should accordingly be designed to create conditions allowing private markets to flourish. Concern for international regime change, which overshadowed development thinking until the late 1970s, has given way to a greater focus on the internal parameters and conditions of development, especially "good governance," a loose term that encompasses a broad range of policy prescriptions from respect for human rights to political pluralism, participation in decision making, and democracy, and from transparent and accountable processes and institutions to effective government.

The present position of the developing countries is also rooted in the past and can be traced back to the "structural" studies that emerged from the United Nations and in particular from its Economic Commission for Latin America in the early 1950s. The underlying premise was that developing countries would never overcome their "backwardness" as long as the structural problems facing them at the international level were not dealt with. A sine qua non condition of economic development was accordingly the establishment of regulatory regimes in international trade and financial markets that would shelter national economies and their infant industries from the vicissitudes of global markets while at the same time providing them with "fairer" playing field opportunities (Emmerij et al. 2001).

Import substitution at home and international regime change as a dominant development model are now things of the past. But by and large, developing countries continue to adhere to that conceptual paradigm that singles out the primacy of the external over the internal determinants of development. This much emerges from the studies emanating from the South Centre—essentially a think tank for the Group of 77 (G77). For the South Centre, the current "international development agenda has been radically 'pruned' and become unbalanced" by a new, liberalizing world order that is unleashing "new forms of colonization."[3] International issues of ongoing concern to developing countries—commodities, development finance, transfer of technology, market access, external debt—have been taken off the multilateral agenda and superseded by Northern concerns regarding matters such as human rights, the environment, poverty alleviation, governance, and corruption. To achieve this objective, the North has relied on the Bretton Woods institutions and their capacity to impose policy prescriptions for structural adjustment and setting external debt relief conditionalities. The end result of the process has been a net loss of sovereignty by developing countries.

Yet the development challenges facing developing countries remain the same. Primary commodities-related issues continue to play a significant economic role for numerous developing countries, and questions of terms of trade and programs enabling them to secure adequate benefits from the production and export of commodities should be reintroduced in the agenda of international organizations. The new WTO trade regime does not acknowledge that developing countries are still unequal trade partners and can potentially prevent their growth and development. Special support and exemptions thus remain necessary, and new forms of protectionism emerging in the North that are related to environmental and social considerations should be rolled back.

Notwithstanding the prevailing mood of "aid fatigue," the South still needs external capital and Official Development Assistance (ODA). New sources of concessional flows (e.g., a tax on speculative global financial transactions) are essential, especially for those developing countries bypassed by commercial capital flows. UN studies should be undertaken to facilitate a "sustained and serious process of negotiations" about the debt question in a comprehensive manner. New arrangements to govern international capital flows as well as a review of the functions and governance of the Bretton Woods institutions should be considered in the wake of the financial crises that rocked the world economy throughout the 1990s. The emergence of new forms of technological protections (the so-called TRIPS, Trade-Related Intellectual Property Rights) would amply justify the resumption of a North-South dialogue on science and technology questions. The characteristics and behavior of TNCs (Trans-National Corporations) that would make them suitable partners for development should be brought back on the international agenda as "it is hardly prudent to allow monopoly control of vital areas of human activity by a handful of private actors from a few countries in the North, and to refrain from introducing some sort of oversight by the international community in the public interest." Finally, in regard to environmental questions, developing countries should come to an understanding with the North on the underlying tradeoffs between the environment and development: "Policies to effect changes in patterns of development and lifestyles, the development and transfer of environmentally sound technologies, and automatic means of financing global environmental actions still hold the key to a sustainable future" (South Centre 1998: 3–21).

Against this background, the prime objective of the South should be to "work towards universal recognition of the pivotal role of the UN" and of its Charter-mandated functions in the UN system "for global macro-economic management and strategy formulation and guidance." The Organization should be "fully democratic and pluralist." Its overarching goal should be to "seek improvements in international economic and political relations and to create an external environment that is conducive to the development of the countries of the South." This would involve significant changes in the relationship between the UN and the Bretton Woods institutions. The IMF should be "subjected to full multilateral control and revamped in ways to ensure that it focuses on providing a proper framework for international monetary policy which ensures that the burden of adjustment is shared between deficit and surplus countries and that surveillance and discipline apply to all countries." As to the World Bank, it should reduce "substantially" its development policy role, which "properly belong to the UN," and focus on the provision of concessional flows of resources "in adequate volumes and on manageable terms to developing countries" (South Centre 1996: 9, 157, 165–167, 197, 201–219).

Discord at the United Nations: The Rocky Rio Process

Not surprisingly, Northern and Southern countries have clashed repeatedly in United Nations forums. In brief, the North has sought to focus political action primarily on the internal parameters of SHD that it views as conducive to development, such as good governance, democracy, social progress, and human rights, while pressing for market-based policy prescriptions. In contrast, developing countries have used United Nations forums, especially the "plus five" events sponsored by the Organization in follow-up to its global conferences of the 1990s, to cast doubt on the market development paradigm and to refocus policy debates on international governance issues and the design of international regulatory and redistributive regimes in finance, trade, science, and technology.

The slow grinding to a halt of the "UNCED process" set in motion by the Rio conference provides a stark illustration of the contrasting démarches of Northern and Southern countries. One of the central ideas laboriously crafted in Rio was that both rich and poor nations could contribute to the preservation of the global environment, albeit in different ways. This meant that developing countries would have to factor environmental issues into their national development policies. Concurrently, Northern countries would help them to defray the higher costs of sustainable development by increasing their ODA. This was the meaning of the principle of "common but differentiated responsibilities." For Northern countries, especially the

United States, these core ideas were to be understood in the context of national development policies that developing countries should be adopting in order to share in the global responsibilities for the protection of the environment. In contrast, developing countries repeatedly and without success sought to make the principle a part of bilateral and multilateral efforts to foster what they called "an enabling environment," a code word for the creation of international structures and policies supportive of their development efforts.

The Rio summit did succeed in avoiding a showdown over development finance by eschewing the question of whether or not genuine commitments had been entered into. But the subsequent "Rio process" has stumbled over the reluctance of developing countries to proceed with serious discussions of cross-sectoral issues due to what they perceive as the failure of developed countries to fulfill their Rio "commitments" in regard to poverty eradication, the provision of new and additional financial resources, the transfer of technology, and the initiation of bold steps to alleviate unsustainable levels of debt servicing. Major policy differences over targets and quantified goals and timetables, increases in alternative energy investments, changes in consumption patterns in developed countries, reductions in fishing subsidies, and the phasing out of lead gasoline have also plagued the ill-fated UNCED process. Not surprisingly, the 1997 General Assembly special session assessing the state of implementation of Agenda 21 and the April 2000 session of the Commission on Sustainable Development devoted to financial resources and mechanisms for the implementation of Agenda 21 were both jolted by renewed disputes over interpretations of the principle of common but differentiated responsibilities and insistent calls by developing countries upon donor countries to "recommit" themselves to the ODA target of 0.7 percent of their GNP. The latter once again countered by reiterating the importance of focusing efforts on the effectiveness and quality of aid, the policies of recipient countries in domestic resource mobilization, and the role of private sector resources.

Discontent is thus brewing among developing countries and has surfaced repeatedly in international meetings. At the end of the Tenth Session of the United Nations Conference on Trade and Development (UNCTAD), the president of Algeria sourly pointed out that in "this new order of international economic relations and its proclaimed advantages, how can one refrain from recalling the fable of the fox offering the stork delicious meals on dinner plates, but making the food out of reach" (*New York Times* 16 December 2000: 16). Two months later, the foreign ministers of the Group of 77 issued a ringing statement prior to their April 2000 summit meeting in Havana, which, in words reminiscent of their 1963 founding manifesto, reiterated their determination to launch "an unrelenting struggle against the forces of poverty and marginalization, which atrophy the vigor of our countries and peoples" through "a viable, equitable and results oriented

North-South dialogue for a just and sustained partnership in the interest and well-being of the greater human family" (*Earth Times* 2000: 5).

A New United Nations?

Decades-old lines of cleavage between developed and developing countries persist over

1. the definition of the development process;
2. the prioritization of international or internal considerations in the promotion of development; and
3. the role of the United Nations therein.

The intensity of these differences belies the notion that the SHD concept encapsulates a novel commonality of political views. What does this mean for the United Nations? One school of thought takes the view that with the ascendance of neoliberalism, the entire UN multilateral machinery has shifted gear and is now being guided by a liberal, market-oriented conception of SHD.

Striking changes have indeed taken place in the activities of the Organization. The Bretton Woods institutions, of course, lead the pack as their stated language is now cast in the vernacular of SHD. Thus, according to its 2000 annual report, the World Bank spends close to one-fourth of its total lending on "human development" (i.e., anti-HIV/AIDS and malaria strategies, basic health services, non-traditional approaches to delivering education services to poor people, and social protection). But the UN General Assembly also now gives its imprimatur to "sound" national macro-economic policies with their cohort of old developmental prescriptions, ranging from entrepreneurship promotion to access to land to education and general health conditions as investments in human productivity and well-being. Organizational mandates have been reformulated: populist entities created to effect international regime and structural change such as UNCTAD and UNIDO have jettisoned their original charters and now concentrate on achieving "global partnerships" with governments, civil society, and the private sector (Finger and Ruchat 1999).[4]

Poverty eradication through sustainable human development has become UNDP's overriding programmatic objective. The main tool to achieve this objective is "good governance," which takes almost one-third of UNDP's budgetary allocations (UNDP 1998). The agency's country programs are now designed to strengthen institutional transformations for "democratic governance" and "decentralized development," and to increase "equity of opportunities through access to productive assets" (that is, housing, safe water and sanitation, health, education, sustainable energy, and social services). Such programs, especially in "transition countries," also seek to contribute to the "development of the market economy."[5]

Critics also draw attention to the entanglement of the United Nations with the corporate world after decades of antagonistic relations. They point to the jargon of business organizations that has crept into the culture of the Organization, as UN officials now feverishly craft "business plans" and "mission statements," and devise new "partnerships" and "new structures of cooperation" in support of the development process that ascribe to the UN the modest role of "facilitator, catalyst, adviser and partner."[6] More disquieting to these observers is the joint initiative of the Secretary-General with leaders from the business community, labor, and civil society to enter into a "global compact" in support of "universal values."[7] This Faustian embrace of the private sector, the argument goes on, simply underlines the continuation of a process set in motion in 1992, with the abolition of the Commission on Transnational Corporations and the quiet dismantling of its Secretariat-servicing structures. Both moves effectively put an end to international efforts to make transnational corporations accountable through binding "codes of conduct."[8]

Internationally Managed Capitalism

Does this mean that the United Nations has turned into an unconditional advocate of the free market version of the SHD model of development? Appearances notwithstanding, there is no evidence that the Organization has cast away the developmental norms of universality, justice, equity, and equality that provided the foundations of its earliest developmental concerns (Therien 1999). These values derive from the broad injunctions of Article 55 of the Charter and have been reaffirmed by the global conferences of the 1990s. To these, the 2000 Millennium Summit has added another layer of "fundamental values"—solidarity, respect for nature, and shared responsibility—all now deemed "essential to international relations in the twenty-first century."

With these moral beacons as policy guideposts, the UN's desirable order of things takes it as axiomatic that social systems should be inclusive and that all groups in society should enjoy the fruits of development. The notion that greater income inequality could be a necessary condition for faster growth and therefore temporarily tolerated while the country establishes itself on a self-sustained high-growth path is clearly more at home in Bretton Woods than at Turtle Bay. As the 1996 *Human Development Report* tersely noted: "We now know ... the limits of trickle-down economics" (UNDP *HDR* 1996: iii). The underlying reasoning is that by eliminating deprivation and strengthening democratic institutions and processes, social and economic relations will be more harmonious and provide firm foundations for long-term development as well as for civil peace. The same logic applies to the international society in which the moral imperative of "inclusiveness" makes inequalities among nations no less acceptable than inequalities within them. Hence, the insistence of UN discourse on the need for policies designed to reduce disparities between have and have-not nations, to promote "equality of opportunity," to remove factors conducive to "dependency," and, more generally, to protect the global commons for the "benefit of mankind." The "development decades" launched by the United Nations since 1961 have all been grounded on these assumptions.[9] The same value system pervades the "declarations" and "programmes of action" produced by UN global conferences.[10] Indeed, it was not fortuitous for the UN Secretary-General to label the 2000 Havana Declaration of the G77 as "a message of pain— the pain felt by so many of the world's peoples at the injustice of the world we live in and the needless misery to which so many of our fellow human beings are condemned."[11]

Against this background, a typical UN report would frame a particular development issue or group of issues into a virtually identical pattern of dialectical reasoning: "yes," "but," and "thou shalt." Such reports would recognize the immense developmental progress of the South, stress the continuing prevalence of deprivation in terms of empirical indicators, and conclude with a set of remedial policy recommendations addressed to individual Member States and the "international community."

Twenty-five years or so ago, the remedial policy measures proposed in the name of the Secretary-General would have focused on the central role of the state in the macroeconomic management of national economies to achieve employment growth, poverty alleviation, and overall development. At the international level, such reports would have proposed structural and regime changes, such as the establishment of an integrated commodity program, a common fund, and the development of codes of conducts for multinational corporations.

Nowadays, the normative work of the United Nations has shifted to winning acknowledgment that if development is to be both sustainable and human, what must be done encompasses more than merely achieving macroeconomic stability, deregulating and privatizing large chunks of national economies, and liberalizing international trade. It also entails public corrective interventions in the operation of national and international markets. For the United Nations, capitalism is a necessary safeguard to personal liberty as well as an essential condition of economic efficiency. But laissez-faire policies alone will not suffice to achieve social justice, stability, and inclusion, or to promote rapid and large-scale improvements in living conditions in developing countries. Markets cannot by themselves reduce inequalities, correct their own imperfections, and promote social convergence and integration. The very first *HDR* had already stressed that "peoples must be free to exercise their choices in *properly functioning markets*" (emphasis added) (UNDP *HDR* 1990: 1). The current efforts of the UN to giving a "human face" to globalization stem from the same concerns: "[I]f globalization is properly managed it can produce beneficial effects for the eradication of poverty; but for this to happen, certain measures both at the national and at the international levels must be in place."[12]

What is the ultimate objective of these "measures"? In a nutshell, to pave the way toward an internal and external "enabling environment," that is, at the national level, strengthening macroeconomic institutions, reforming the financial and banking sectors, developing progressive and effective taxation systems, formulating pro-poor and employment creation public policies, promoting civil society and the private sector, strengthening government capacities for economic management, delivering of antipoverty strategies, and coping with the risks and opportunities of globalization. At the international level, the term carries with it injunctions aimed at allowing access to globalization opportunities in foreign investment and in trade and technology transfers; a level playing field in international economic relations (especially for the poorest among developing countries); coordinated and intensified development assistance and support for the development of healthy commodity sectors to reduce commodity dependence; technology adaptation; debt management, relief, and reduction; improved terms of trade and market access; and improved access to development finance.[13]

Norm Setting as a Process: Summitry, Targeting, and Expertise

Global conferences have been the privileged setting for harnessing the UN system to these essentially Keynesian normative developmental principles.[14] Persisting Southern political pressure has prevailed over Northern "conference fatigue," and the conference cycle of the 1990s is continuing under new clothes in the form of "special events," special sessions of the General Assembly, or simply "high-level forums." Slated for 2001 in the wake of the Millennium Assembly were meetings on the least developed countries, habitat, HIV/AIDS, racism, and children. Other subjects to be debated in subsequent years include aging, financing for development, telecommunications and information, and Africa. Each of these conferences can be expected to have the same global agenda and norm-setting function as the "megaconferences" of the 1990s. How to make globalization an inclusive process was the main focus of the Millennium Assembly Declaration. Citing the "resolve" of governments, the Declaration states the determination of the UN members to create a national and global environment conducive to development and the elimination of poverty through good governance within each country and at the international level, and to transparency in the financial, monetary, and trading systems.[15] The 2002 Conference on Financing for Development in Monterrey,

Mexico, planned to address "in a holistic manner" development issues through the perspective of finance and the mobilization of financial resources for the implementation of the action plans agreed to at major UN conferences in the 1990s.[16]

The 2003 ITU-led World Summit on the Information Society will endeavor "to develop a common vision and understanding of the information society and to draw up a strategic plan for concerted development towards realizing that vision" with particular attention to bridging the "digital divide," promoting "universal and equitable access to the information society and meeting the needs of the developing world."[17]

"Summitry" has also crept into the Economic and Social Council. Heads of states, ministers, and UN agencies' executive heads now mingle with CEOs from the private sector and representatives of civil society in the Council's annual "policy dialogues." These proceedings lead to "Ministerial Declarations"—in effect, manifestoes deemed to reflect the "general will" of the international community on such North-South issues as information technology (2000), employment and work in poverty eradication (1999), market access (1998), and "fostering an enabling environment for development and financial flows" (1997). For example, the declaration adopted regarding the "role of information technology in the context of a knowledge-based economy" warned that the ICT revolution "can lead to further disparities between and within countries ... [and that its] huge potential for advancing development has not been fully captured...." This is why there was a "need to address the major impediments to the participation of the majority of the people in the developing countries in the revolution of ICT, such as the lack of infrastructure, education, capacity building, and investment connectivity."[18]

Global conferences are not only "town meetings" for the exchange of ideas, but also instruments of international monitoring and accountability. Generally taking place at five-year intervals, each conference serves as a benchmark against which "progress" (or the lack thereof) can be measured in the intervening five years. Global conferences are thus, in effect, mechanisms for singling out those who have "performed" from those who did not, for allotting praise or blame, and, ultimately, for setting new benchmarks to be achieved in a given time frame. A powerful tool for such purposes is the extensive use of targeting, that is, the identification of goals and objectives to be reached at the national or international level within a set time frame. This practice has a long history in the United Nations going back to the December 1961 General Assembly proclamation of a United Nations Development Decade, which called for an average annual growth rate of 5 percent by developing countries in the course of the decade. It has become a recurring feature of UN global conferences, as indicated in table 3.1.

These figures, however "political" they may be, are not purely arbitrary. The 5 percent growth target of the first UN Development Decade did

TABLE **3.1** International Development Goals (IDGs)

Conference	Policy Objective	Time Frame
1997 Kyoto Protocol	5.2% average emission cuts by industrial countries	between 1990 and 2010
2000 Copenhagen "Plus Five"	Reduce the incidence of HIV/AIDS among young Africans by 25%	by 2005
	Halve the proportion of people living in extreme poverty	by 2015
	50% improvement in adult literacy	by 2015
	Universal access to high-quality primary health care	not later than 2015
2000 Beijing "Plus Five"	Equal access for boys and girls to primary and secondary schooling	by 2005
	Free and compulsory universal education for both boys and girls	by 2015
	50% improvement in literacy rates, especially for women	by 2015
	Universal access to high-quality primary health care throughout the life cycle	not later than 2015
2000 Millennium Declaration	Achieve universal primary education	by 2015
	Reduce overall mortality rates by three-fourths, and under-five mortality by two-thirds	by 2015
	Halve and reverse the spread of HIV/AIDS	by 2015
	Significant improvement in the lives of at least 100 million slum dwellers	by 2020

rest on a number of assumptions about rates of growth in the agricultural sector, domestic savings, and earnings from international trade and lending, which had emerged from years of research and policy analyses undertaken within the UN Secretariat. The quantified target, which eventually found its way into the Decade, was both a product of the political process and the result of extensive research work. Policy-oriented studies in support of UN intergovernmental processes thus constitute a critical foundation to the normative functions of the United Nations. Insofar as they provide an empirical basis to policy demands and claims, they can lend greater weight to prescriptive political exhortations. The current debate over globalization and human rights provides an arresting illustration of the mix of political, empirical, and normative processes involved in the

UN endeavor to make the national and international environments of SHD as safe as "humanly" possible.

Globalization and Human Rights

The basic message emerging from the analytical work of the United Nations is that globalization is, under the best of circumstances, a mixed blessing. Globalization does open new opportunities for development through the integration of world markets of goods, services, capital technology, and labor. But it can also lead to increased marginalization and poverty. UN reports and studies document a globalizing world perpetuating an increasing wealth inequality within states and between rich and poor countries. Various states have also become more vulnerable with the liberalization of capital flows. They provide evidence that globalization contributes to the delocalization of production, trade tensions, and the desynchronization of economic cycles in the various regions of the world, thus increasing the potential for conflict over goals and policies.[19]

Policy research recently undertaken by the UNCTAD Secretariat recalls in this respect that early UN trade discussions had recognized the need for trade liberalization to be integrated with economic domestic policies as well as suitable social policies, such as income distribution and appropriate labor standards within the context of an economy's level of development. Today's integration of money and capital markets is proceeding in widely different domestic cyclical and structural conditions, and "asymmetries" have arisen in the treatment of nations because they are at different levels of development or in different stages in the economic cycle. Such is the case with natural resources, technology goods, and intellectual property rights. Natural resources, the predominant export of developing countries, have been subject to relatively low levels of protection. Generalized tariff reductions applied across the board to all countries and low levels of protection in developing countries have provided greater relative benefits to developed countries, insofar as their exports were more highly protected manufactured goods. At the same time, developed countries continue to protect sectors that they consider "strategic" or "socially sensitive," while developing countries are asked to promptly liberalize their trade of manufactured goods.[20]

Against this background, it is not surprising that the UN Secretary-General should have raised the question of the compatibility of globalization with sustainable human development and, more specifically, with the extension of democracy and the promotion of human rights.[21] Linking human rights to development is not new and could, in fact, be traced back to the Declaration on the Right to Development adopted by the General Assembly in 1986.[22] Originally embedded in the discourse on the "New International Economic Order," the rights approach to development is now framed in a policy agenda linking human rights, development, and globalization. As in the SHD paradigm, the focus is on the promotion of freedom, well-being, and the dignity of individuals and the centrality of the human person as a subject of the development process. But the area of human rights also brings in principles of accountability. Additionally, "When human development and human rights advance together, they reinforce one another—expanding people's capabilities and protecting their rights and fundamental freedoms." Accordingly, achieving "all rights for all" should be a normative goal and guiding principle of the international community. States as well as international bodies such as the Bretton Woods institutions and global corporations should be guided by human rights principles so that their combined actions can pave the way toward the creation of an inclusive and just international economic system (UNDP *HDR* 2000: 1–13, 89–111).

Among the "follow-up mechanisms" established by the UN political organs to look into the implementation of the Declaration on the Right to Development was the appointment of an independent expert who was asked to submit "comprehensive reports" on the effects of poverty, structural adjustment, globalization, financial and trade liberalization, and deregulation on the prospects of the enjoyment of the right to development in developing countries.[23] The independent expert has so far produced a report on poverty focusing on how poverty-related issues affect the prospects of realizing the right to development and how the elimination of poverty could contribute to its realization.[24] Invoking arguments developed by Amartya Sen (1999) that poverty must be seen as a deprivation of basic capabilities rather than merely as low income levels, the report elaborates on the idea that capabilities are essentially related to human rights insofar as they give individuals expanded choice or freedom to be and do things that they value. From this vantage point, the right to development is not merely a set of discrete rights "to have a claim to something of value on other people, institutions, the state, or the international community, who in turn have the obligation of providing or helping to provide that something of value." It is also the right to a process "that expands the capabilities or freedom of individuals to improve their well-being and to realize what they value." The right to development is thus construed as a "vector" of different elements, including the rights to food, health, education, housing, and civil and political rights, as well as "the rates of growth of representative resources such as per capita consumption, output, and employment."

The right-to-development approach accordingly "focuses attention on those who lag behind others in enjoying their rights and requires positive actions to be taken on their behalf." At the national level, the realization of the right to development would entail programs of coordinated action in the form of development plans that strive for growth of Gross Domestic Product (GDP) and other resources, as well as sustained improvements in the social indicators related to different rights. At the international level, a compact should bind both the developing countries concerned and the representatives of the "international community." The latter would accept the corollary obligation of providing all of the necessary support for implementing these plans, such as making every effort to ensure equality of treatment in the decision making and operations of the international financial and trading system, reducing commodity and export earning fluctuations, lightening up the debt burden of developing countries, and improving capital flows into developing countries.[25] Similarly inspired "Rawlesian" reports are in the making as the General Assembly has reaffirmed that the right to food, clean water, and shelter are basic human rights and that health and education are essential for development.[26]

A Human Face for SHD

To what extent have the UN's advocacy of "managed capitalism" and insistent demands "that the affluent do not leave the less fortunate behind" steered the concept of sustainable human development away from the market-dominant ethos of the "Washington Consensus"?[27] The record is mixed, but a number of changes are unmistakably pointing to greater political sensitivity to the "human" dimension of SHD.

To begin with, poverty eradication, an essential condition for the achievement of SHD, has become the overriding programmatic objective of the United Nations. In the wake of the 1995 Copenhagen Summit for Social Development, the General Assembly launched a Decade for the Eradication of Poverty, and requested the Secretary-General to mobilize the whole UN system to take action to eradicate poverty worldwide.[28] Copenhagen "Plus Five" reaffirmed the "commitments" agreed upon five years earlier, and produced a global target for poverty reduction that was endorsed in 2000 by the G8 Summit in Okinawa and the 2000 Millennium Summit. The UN is now developing an Action Strategy for Halving Extreme Poverty involving normative work, policy guidance, program development, and monitoring at the global level, as well as advocacy, policy dialogue, and direct support for national poverty eradication initiatives.[29]

The attention generated by the Copenhagen Social Summit on the close interrelationships between economic, environmental, and social policies, and the concerns arising from the financial turmoil that rocked several Asian economies in the late 1990s, have given a new lease on life to the old notion that stable economies cannot be built on unstable societies, and that the quality of growth rather than growth itself is a determining factor of progress. Prodded since Copenhagen to integrate social considerations into the design of structural adjustment and reform programs, the Bretton Woods institutions have introduced new processes (notably, the preparation of Poverty Reduction Strategy Papers by recipient low-income countries) to sharpen their focus on poverty reduction and take into account more fully the views of all "relevant stakeholders."

The IMF has broadened its original mandate by including the "structural and social aspects of fiscal policy" in the programs that it supports and in its general policy advice. A major element of this advice is to facilitate "high-quality growth," meaning growth that can be sustained by "appropriate domestic and external balances as well as by adequate investment, including human capital, so as to lay the foundation for future growth … [and] policies that protect the environment … and attempt to reduce poverty and improve equality of opportunity."[30] A recent issue of the World Bank's *World Development Report* seems to jettison some of the key tenets of the "Washington Consensus." Citing "more recent thinking" as well as "empirical evidence," the authors of the report acknowledge that inequality may not necessarily translate into growth and development. They also recognize the need for "much more emphasis on laying the institutional and social foundations for the development process and on managing vulnerability and encouraging participation to ensure inclusive growth." In a nod to demands that could bear a UN imprimatur, they also underline the importance of "global action" designed to open the markets of rich countries to the agricultural goods, manufactured products, and services of poor countries; bridge the digital divide; provide debt relief to poor countries; reduce the risks of economic crises through international systemic financial reform; produce "pro-poor public goods"; and strengthen the capacities of poor developing countries to be represented in global forums, such as the WTO (World Bank 2001: v–vii).

The impact of the UN advocacy of an "enabling" international environment for SHD is also noticeable in debt-related matters. For a long time now—going back to the launching of the Brady and Baker plans—the UN has taken the position that some measures of debt relief are necessary. The 1996 Heavily Indebted Poor Countries (HIPC) initiative of the World Bank and the IMF was a response to growing pressures from the United Nations and other sources to address the difficult situation of a number of low-income countries (mostly in Africa) for whom traditional rescheduling mechanisms were not sufficient to attain sustainable external debt levels. Under continuing criticism, the Bretton Woods institutions approved in September 1999 further changes in the HIPC with the promise of deeper and faster debt relief for more countries and a greater focus on poverty reduction.

More important, perhaps, is the increasingly accepted idea that there should be a linkage between debt relief and poverty alleviation. Again, for a long time extending back to UNICEF advocacy in the 1980s of structural adjustment programs "with a human face," the United Nations has taken aim at IMF policies for their focus on macroeconomic aggregates and alleged neutrality in respect to their impact on sectors and industries. Different sectors of the economy, UN researchers argued, are differentially affected by "neutral" policies related to interest rates, money and credit, taxation, exchange rates, and import restrictions. To forestall such adverse consequences, the economic and social components of the Fund's and Bank's reform packages and structural adjustment programs should be mutually supportive and consistent with one another, as indeed the 1995 Social Summit "encouraged" (commitment 8).

As seen earlier, both the World Bank and the IMF have agreed that the prime objective of development is not only the acceleration of growth in developing countries, but also the eradication of poverty and the recognition of the necessity of social safety nets. The new policy was further highlighted by the September 1999 agreement reached in the Interim and Development Committee to incorporate "poverty reduction strategies" into IMF programs supported by the Enhanced Structural Adjustment Facility, the Fund's concessional lending arm for low-income countries, now rechristened as the Poverty Reduction and Growth Facility. These developments, coupled with the acceptance by multilateral donors to increase the relief of repayment obligations of HIPC debt in exchange for a closer link of debt-relief and poverty-reduction expenditures, thus appear to vindicate the so-called 20/20 initiative that the UNDP launched in the wake of the Copenhagen Summit. The initiative was designed to promote a reciprocal commitment by participating aid-receiving and donor countries to increase their investment in basic social services from current levels to an indicative level of 20 percent of their budgetary expenditures and other ODA.

Continued Disjointed Incrementalism

Many see the movement of the Bretton Woods institutions to address poverty reduction as a mere tactical move intended to silence increasingly noisy critics. Be that as it may, the wall of the temples of neoliberal orthodoxy have certainly not crumbled, and the international environment of sustainable human development is not by any means as "enabling" as some might wish. Without much regard for internal consistency, the Bank's *World Development Report* still portrays the freeing of trade, the privatizing of government companies, and the limiting of government spending as key ingredients of a sound development strategy. It would therefore be premature to conclude that the battle of ideas hovering over SHD has unambiguously evolved in favor of one of the possible political interpretations of it. It is clear, though, that the meaning and contents of SHD remain ultimately a function of the political process. From this vantage point, the realities of political power combined with the persistence of developmental issues and North-South polarization are likely to produce incremental patterns of doctrinal change, with the United Nations continuing to promote a Keynesian approach to SHD.

Persisting Development Challenges

More and more Southern countries may one day achieve developed status, or at least escape from their poverty traps. For the foreseeable future, however, the data simply underscore the immensity of the unfinished development tasks facing the majority of Third World countries. The proportion of population below the poverty line declined from 28.3 percent in 1987 to 24 percent in 1998. However, the number of people living on less than $1 a day changed little, and has remained at about 1.2 billion. The number of undernourished people has decreased slightly to 791 million in 1995–1997, but one-third of the total population in sub-Saharan Africa and more than one-fifth in South Asia still face shortages of food. Improvements in education and health are essential aspects of human resource development, and have been "slow" or "elusive." Eight hundred eighty million people lack access to health services, and an estimated 2.6 billion people lack access to basic sanitation.[31]

Globally, inequality between countries and concentrations of income and wealth appear to be an increasingly prevailing pattern. By the late 1990s, 20 percent of the world's people living in the highest-income countries accounted for 86 percent of the world GDP, 82 percent of the world export markets, 68 percent of FDI, and 74 percent of the world telephone lines. In sharp contrast, the respective shares of the bottom 20 percent were no higher than 1.5 percent (UNDP *HDR* 1999: 3). International trade questions still represent a potent rallying point for the South insofar as developing countries either continue to have an access problem or are hampered by a supply constraint. The latter group includes the poorest countries among developing countries. Plagued by endemic civil wars, they produce only a few commodities for export earnings, are heavily vulnerable to the vagaries of international markets, and face a crippling long-term debt and an increasingly pronounced deterioration in world market prices.[32] Countries with an access problem could link up with international markets, but high tariffs, quotas, and antidumping and unfair competitive practices such as subsidies thwart their competitiveness in the agriculture, textile, and clothing sectors where they could have a competitive advantage.[33]

Debt-relief policies of donor countries did not prevent the volume of the total debt stock of net-debtor developing countries to climb from $1.4 trillion in 1990 to $2.5 trillion in 1999. In marked contrast to the handling of the debt of mainly middle-income countries, the debt problem of low-income developing countries is dragging on despite improvements in debt rescheduling terms. Africa's external debt alone now exceeds $300 billion, and the continent spent no less that an average of $12 billion a year on debt repayment between 1990 and 1995. More than two dozen countries—poor, of course—share the unenviable distinction of an external debt that is greater than their GDP.[34] Meanwhile, "aid fatigue" has translated into declining levels of ODA, which remains far below the 0.7 percent normative target set by the United Nations. Perhaps more alarming is the fact that the share of aid to the Least Developed Countries (LDCs) in the DAC donors' GDP fell from 0.09 percent in 1990 to 0.05 percent in 1998. In fact, in real per capita terms, net ODA to the LDCs dropped 45 percent since 1990, that is, to the level that it was in the early 1970s. ODA to Africa has been falling by about 24 percent in real terms since the 1990s, and about 70 percent of the ODA flows to sub-Saharan Africa were offset by terms of trade losses in the period 1970–1997.[35]

Continuing Political Polarization

Whether market-based economic policies can resolve these daunting challenges remains the subject of lively controversies. Under the circumstances, developing countries are unlikely to slacken their efforts to affect international regime change. From their standpoint the governance of the international economy suffers from a fundamental "legitimacy deficit," and their attention will remain primarily focused not on their internal political and economic systems but on the "injustices" engendered by an international system that, they feel, cancels out their internal efforts. Initially skeptical about the whole notion of a "Millennium Assembly," they have embraced the exhortations that the Secretary-General directed at developed countries, inviting them in the name of "global solidarity" to further open their markets, provide deeper and faster debt relief, and give more and better-focused development assistance.[36] The lofty language of the Millennium Declaration, which developed countries subscribed to, could soon haunt them, as developing countries have made clear their determination to use it as a normative ram to batter the wall of Northern indifference. The implementation of the Declaration will be monitored through an elaborate procedure laid down by the General Assembly that will provide the South with multiple opportunities to press for its demands while at the same time putting the North in the box of the accused. The Secretary-General was asked to prepare a long-term "road map" for the implementation of the Declaration, which the Assembly discussed in the fall of 2001. The head of the Organization was also required to submit quinquennial "comprehensive reports" supplemented by annual updates assessing progress made in the implementation of the Millenium Declaration.[37]

Preparations for a number of UN global conferences give additional clues about the developing countries' resolve to legitimize their quest for an international "New Deal." Education—especially girls' education—access to basic health services, clean water, safe sanitation, and proper nutrition were major subjects of debate at the 2001 World Summit for Children. But globalization, the importance of ODA, external debt reduction, and the need to focus aid flows on neediest countries as instruments to promote children's rights and welfare are paramount in the agenda of developing countries. They provide less than subtle hints about their views of what they consider the proper focus of such conferences and their desirable outcomes.[38]

In a preview of future debates likely to be far more contentious, preparatory documents for the 10-year review of UNCED in 2002 state that it will dwell with the "identification of accomplishments and areas where further efforts are needed to implement Agenda 21." The review should result in "action-oriented decisions," "renewed political commitment, and support for sustainable development consistent inter alia with the principle of common but differentiated responsibilities." It should also identify constraints that hinder the implementation of Agenda 21, propose specific time-bound measures to be taken, and identify institutional and financial requirements, as well as the sources for such support.[39] The preparations for the 2002 International Conference on Financing for Development were even more explosive in light of the mindset of developing countries' governments. The foreign ministers of the Non-Aligned Movement who met in Colombia in early April 2000 signaled that this event should "offer a good opportunity for developing countries to discuss with the different financial institutions and developed countries what our development needs really are and how we want them to help us solve them." A few days later, the chairman of the Group of 77 stressed the paramount importance of international systemic issues. He warned:

> The countries of the South must be suitably represented in any forum for deliberating and deciding on social, economic or political matters which can have effects on our countries, adversely or otherwise, whether individually, severally, or as a group. The Group of 77 will not consider any social, economic, financial or political architecture decided without equitable representation. Notwithstanding such representation, such fora have no authority under international law to take binding decisions that affect us.[40]

In the meantime, through their numerical majority, developing countries are driving the Organization into uncharted and controversial fields. They have pressed UN human rights bodies to monitor the Bretton Woods institutions and the WTO. The linkage between human rights and globalization issues has already been noted but is spilling into new areas. The preliminary reports of the special rapporteurs are providing ammunition to the argument that the current rules and policies developed by multilateral trade and financial institutions promote a form of economic globalization that reinforces existing inequalities within and between countries. And the Commission on Human Rights has recommended that the Bretton Woods institutions should accordingly integrate human rights into their rule-making processes from the outset on the assumption that "the primacy of human rights law over all other regimes of international law is a basic and fundamental principle that should not be departed from."[41] In the same vein, the UN Sub-Commission on the Promotion and Protection of Human Rights, at its August 2000 meeting, adopted a resolution on intellectual property rights and human rights emphasizing that "actual or potential conflicts exist between the two." The WTO TRIPS Agreement does not adequately reflect "the fundamental nature and indivisibility of all human rights, including the right of everyone to enjoy the benefits of scientific progress and its applications, the right to health, the right to food, and the right to self determination...." In the same stride, the Commission requested the WTO in its ongoing review of the TRIPS Agreement to "take fully into account the existing State obligations under the international human rights instrument."[42]

Power and Incrementalism

Numerical majorities at the United Nations, however, do not necessarily translate into actual power. In fact, a number of Southern demands collide head on with the economic and financial clout of industrial countries and are thus likely to remain political nonstarters. For example, "aid fatigue" dims the prospects of a world solidarity fund for poverty eradication that was endorsed by the General Assembly in the context of its discussions on the UN Decade for the Eradication of Poverty (1997–2006).[43] Problematic to say the least are the prospects for the "democratic and equitable international order" called for in a resolution adopted at the same session by the General Assembly by a lopsided recorded vote of 91 to 50 with 13 abstentions and over the objections of all developed countries.[44] The relationship between the United Nations, the Bretton Woods institutions, and the WTO also falls into the category of probable "dead on arrival" proposals. The initial American response to the G77-stated views of the objectives of the finance-for-development "event" was to underline the sanctity of present international financial arrangements and to remind everyone of the limited role of the United Nations. The IMF and the World Bank were "uniquely placed and uniquely empowered" to deal with financial crises such as the Asian crisis. Nor was it the business of the General Assembly, the UN Secretariat, or UNCTAD to "supplant" the Bretton Woods institutions. The proper role of the United Nations was to "air ideas, provide for open debate, and put some of the technical issues into a political context."[45]

The unwavering pressures of Northern countries to link trade, environmental, and labor issues with the spread of democratic institutions at the country level—while rejecting the Southern claim that structural change and democratization should be the top priorities of the international agenda—continue the pattern of incremental and disjointed doctrinal change that has prevailed in the last two decades of North-South relations. A typical instance of this process is the "dialogue" that has flourished in the past few years between the Economic and Social Council

(ECOSOC) and the Bretton Woods institutions. In these "high-level special meetings," coinciding with the semiannual meetings of the World Bank's and the IMF's governing bodies, there is no room for demands for international structural change. Rather, the focus is on each institution endeavoring to gently coax the other toward its viewpoint within existing institutional arrangements. In April 1998, following the IMF-World Bank annual meeting, finance ministers, in an unprecedented move, went to the Economic and Social Council in New York to discuss financial global integration questions and root causes of financial instability. The following month, it was the turn of the ECOSOC delegations to meet formally for the first time with the World Bank Executive Board in Washington. At the ECOSOC regular session in New York in July, the heads of the Bank, the IMF, and UNCTAD participated in discussions that led to the issuance of a communiqué urging governments to keep world markets open in the face of financial instability and economic slowdowns. In 1999, the World Bank Board members met with ECOSOC delegations in New York. Two months later, in April, a second ECOSOC-Bretton Woods institutions meeting was held, ending with calls for greater recognition of the need to have social support measures to alleviate the impact of financial crises and recessions. The UN Secretary-General was invited for the first time to address a ministerial-level trade negotiations meeting and called for better market access for developing countries and a "fair as well as free" international trade regime. The third special high-level meeting of the Economic and Social Council and the Bretton Woods institutions in 2000 addressed the theme of strengthening international financial arrangements and poverty eradication. The process is still unfolding along the same lines.

SHD and the Role of the United Nations: Prodding and Needling

In this politically polarized setting, what is the role of the United Nations? Enough evidence has been presented here contradicting the widely held view that it is "a disabled body, with diminishing authority" (*The Economist* 22 November 1997: 50). The rope on which the Organization treads is indeed tight, and the United Nations needs to constantly strike a balance between the compelling realities of Northern political and economic clout and Southern deep suspicions of the SHD agenda. But the United Nations is clearly not "disabled." As a "town meeting of the world," where public opinion is focused as an effective force" (Dulles 1945: 165), the United Nations has a normative agenda for building capacity that should not be underestimated. As was pointed out long ago, the United Nations "authorizes and endorses in compensation for its inability to effectuate commands, and it condemns and deplores in compensation for its inability to prohibit and prevent" (Claude 1968: 88). "[C]ustodian of the seals of international approval and disapproval," the United Nations is an approximation of a "global version of the general will" (ibid: 86). Its influence stems from the fact that "statesmen take collective legitimization seriously as a factor in international politics" (ibid: 93). More generally, in the vernacular of a recent public relations document, the United Nations acquires a political role because "of the values it represents, its role in helping to set and sustain global norms, its ability to stimulate global concern and action, and the trust inspired by its practical work to improve people's lives (DPI/2107A, March 2000).

In the ever shifting grounds of development thinking, one may expect the United Nations to endeavor to give a more human face to SHD through the advocacy of the same "Fabian" global norms and principles that helped the Organization, in the immediate postwar years, to place the concept of development on the international agenda as one of the key desirable objectives of the international community. It was undoubtedly in that spirit that the Organization issued in 1998 a ringing manifesto, proclaiming that "poverty is a denial of choices and opportunity, a violation of human dignity" and calling upon the UN system to mobilize "the energies and resources of all human development actors in the campaign against poverty."[46]

The Global Compact initiative of the Secretary-General springs from the same concern. As Secretary-General Kofi Annan stated on 26 July 2000: "What we must do ... is to ensure that the global market is embedded in broadly shared values and practices that reflect global social needs, and that all the world's people share the benefits of globalization."[47] The same could be said about Annan's proposal to initiate an international "campaign for the millennium development goals" that would track countries' progress toward these goals, assess the costs implications at each stage, and identify resource requirements.[48]

Undoubtedly, the production of "information and evidence," as a recent *HDR* put it—"that can break down barriers of disbelief and mobilize changes in policy and behavior" (UNDP *HDR* 2000: 10)—will remain a hallmark of UN research and policy analysis. The question is whether the economic prescriptions of the Bretton Woods institutions are sufficient or even necessary to SHD.[49] Early warning and prevention for poverty eradication[50] and cost benefit analyses[51] will be privileged targets of UN research on SHD-related issues. Through the provision of policy advice outlining "shared bases for action," the United Nations may also become part of the policy process. For example, a recent report issued on behalf of the Secretary-General prescribed methods to attract more private investment and promote trade to offset declines in foreign aid. An outgrowth of the Millennium Assembly, which had expressed concern about "the obstacles developing countries face in mobilizing resources needed to finance their sustained development," the report's recommendations include "significant and immediate" debt relief for the poorest countries, the reduction or removal of duties and market quotas on exports from developing countries, and mechanisms to reduce the risk of fluctuating markets and commodity prices. The report also broke new ground by calling for a study of the potential for international cooperation in tax matters, including tax evasion. Clearly, the Secretary-General hoped that the report would trigger discussions capable of shaping the outcome of the March 2002 conference on finance for development.[52] The head of the Organization may have entertained the same objective when he set up a high-level advisory panel of international financial experts to recommend "achievable actions" by governments, business, civil society, and international institutions that would help developing countries fulfill their financial needs.[53]

It is difficult to determine the degree to which the Secretary-General may have influenced the policy process leading up to the conference. Earlier, there had been no enthusiastic response to his proposal for an "objective and comprehensive" study of the debt problems of developing countries by an independent panel of experts "not unduly influenced by creditor interests."[54] Likewise unheeded was his call "to critically rethink the basis for development finance with a view to fashioning innovative approaches that, among other things, guarantee the flow of aid to deserving countries ... and in an amount that bears a relationship to the countries' state of development."[55] In fact, it is not difficult to anticipate that the road to a more human sustainable human development concept will be littered with rejects deemed to be unduly "radical." Active candidates for benign neglect include proposals such as the enactment of multilateral codes of conduct for MNCs, the creation of a world antimonopoly authority, the establishment of a global central bank and lender of last resort, a world environment agency, a world investment trust with redistributive functions, and mechanisms for a broader participation of civil society within the United Nations.[56]

Yet incremental changes are still possible, and, as was seen earlier, the UN's relentless reaffirmation of the legitimacy of the notion of "equality of opportunity" for the weak throughout its empirical and normative work has had a noticeable impact on the understanding of the internal and external parameters of SHD.[57] It is increasingly acknowledged that social protection and the reduction of vulnerability are legitimate developmental goals, that debt relief must come faster and be more generous, and that international trade is a two-way street. Words still need to be matched by deeds. But there is a growing convergence of views that poor nations have done more than their fair share to free up trade and that the pressure is decidedly on the rich countries.

In this context, greater attention should be paid in the UN to the fact that North-South policy perspectives are often more complementary than contradictory. Continued antagonism also hides that both Northern and

Southern governments often blame each other to avoid criticism on their own individual performance. At the same time, the UN should bring home the message that the abstract and unfinished nature of SHD, coupled with ideological ambiguity and internal tensions, hampers its implementation, which weakens all actors involved.

Of course, the United Nations is not the only actor involved in these processes. As the Secretary-General has recognized on numerous occasions, the UN is part of those "global policy networks" and other informal "coalitions for change"—transcending both geographical and political boundaries—that have emerged to pursue cooperative solutions to common problems, as was the case in the campaigns to reduce global warming, ban landmines, and provide debt relief for developing countries.[58] From "trade plus aid" and "industrialization" to "redistribution with growth" and "basic needs" to "sustainable human development," development thinking has been anything but static over time (Rapley 1996). The crises of the 1990s and the documented sharp declines in economic and social well-being have mobilized worldwide movements that the information and communication technology revolutions have brought to the fore in the streets of Seattle, Prague, Quebec, Genoa, and Washington. Indeed, globalization is not just merely a North-South problematic. It has triggered fierce debates within industrial states involving labor unions, environmental groups, and human rights activities.

Intellectual debates and a renewed interest in alternative development schemes have thus been rekindled, and the tragic 11 September 2001 events may herald a renewed emphasis on or at least attention to multilateral and development cooperation.[59] Still, the $5 billion increase in US foreign aid over three years that President Bush announced at the Monterrey Summit, while welcomed by all actors involved, draws more from a security perspective than an SHD approach. The increase pales when compared to the expenditures of $1 billion a month for the war against terrorism. In contrast, SHD advocates would argue that the war against poverty would be the best anti-terrorism approach. It is not yet clear whether security and SHD will coexist, conflict, or reinforce each other. In short, we have not yet seen the latest act in the global political drama shaping the contents of sustainable human development.

Notes

Jacques Fomerand is Director of the UN University Office in New York. These are his personal views and notes.

1. I am fully aware that there are significant differences—political, economic, and cultural—among "Northern" and "Southern" nations. I use the terms here in a generic sense to convey the idea that the "South" is essentially a low-income, low-productivity group of nations where deprivation prevails, whereas the "North" is basically at the other end of the spectrum.
2. These views are articulated in the earliest issues of the annual reports of the president to the US Congress, *US Participation in the UN*, published by the State Department.
3. See also the closing address of the Chairman of the Group of 77 at Havana, http://www.g77.org/summit/obasanjo_closing.htm).
4. See, for instance, http://www.unctad.org/en/aboutorg/aboutorg.htm; http://www.unido.org/doc/7.htmls "Business Plan on the Future Role and Functions of UNIDO."
5. http://www.undp.org/rbap/country_operations.htm. For a sample of such country programs, see the program for Vietnam (DP/CCF/VIE/1 of 8 July 1996), South Africa (DP/CCF/SAF/q of 29 June 1997), Nigeria (DP/CCF/NIR/1 of 29 July 1997), Ukraine (DP/CCF/UKR/1 of 3 July 1997), Azerbaijan (DP/CCF/AZE/1 of 30 June 1997), and Jordan (http://www.undp-jordan.org/programmes_countries.html).
6. "The Way Forward: The Administrator's Business Plans, 2000–2003," DP/2000/8, 15 December 1999.
7. http://www.org/partners/business/gcevent/press/summary.html
8. http://www.villagevoice.com/issues/0036/todaro/shtml
9. See UN General Assembly resolutions 1710 (XVI) of 19 December 1961, 2626 (XXV) of 24 October 1970, and 35/56 of 5 December 1980.
10. (Report 1979: para. 1) (ILO 1977: 189; WHO 1978: 2) (Aging 1983: 12) (Copenhagen Declaration: 3) (Agenda 21: 14).
11. UN press release SG/SM/7549 of 15 September 2000.
12. "Implementation of the First United Nations Decade for the Eradication of Poverty (1997–2006)," A/55/407 of 21 September 2000, para. 28–46.
13. Report of the ECOSOC for the year 1997, GAOR 52nd session, Supplement no. 3 (A/52/3/Rev.1), pp. 9, 12–15, and A/AC.257/12 of 18 December 2000.
14. "International Years" and "Decades" have also been used by the UN to mobilize the Organization and generate support and commitment at the grassroots and community leadership levels.
15. UN General Assembly Resolution A/55/187.
16. UN General Assembly Resolution A/54/196 of 22 December 1999.
17. http://www.itu.int/wsis/action-plan.htm
18. E/2000/L.9 of 11 July 2000.
19. A/55/350 of 15 September 2000.
20. See A/55/381 of 13 September 2000.
21. As the Secretary-General put it in one of his latest reports to the Assembly: "The challenge of article 28 of the Universal Declaration of Human Rights, to ensure the entitlement of everyone to a social and international order supportive of the realization of human rights, remains. At the heart of the challenge is the need to examine the social, political, cultural and economic dimensions of globalization and the impact they have on the rights of every human being" (A/55/342 of 31 August 2000).
22. In language strikingly foreshadowing SHD, the Declaration had already proclaimed: "The right to development is an inalienable human right by virtue of which every human person and all peoples are entitled to participate in, contribute to, and enjoy economic, social, cultural and political development.... The human person is the central subject of development [and] should be the active participant and beneficiary of

the right to development.... [This is why] ... States have the duty to cooperate with each other in ensuring development and eliminating obstacles to development" (Articles 1.1, 2 and 3.3). The text of the Declaration can be found in UNGA Resolution 41/128, annex of 4 December 1986.

23. ECOSOC Decision 1998/269 of 30 July 1998.
24. A/55/306 of 17 August 2000.
25. The report of the independent expert is summarized in A/55/306 of 17 August 2000.
26. GA Resolution 54/175 of 17 December 1999.
27. Statement of the Secretary-General at the Tenth Annual Ministerial Meeting of the LLDCs (press release SG/SM/7553 of 18 September 2000).
28. GA resolution 53/198 of December 1998.
29. ACC/2000/POQ/CRP. 16 of 14 September 2000.
30. "The IMF and the Poor," pamphlet series no. 52, Fiscal Affairs Department, IMF, DC 1998, p. 1.
31. A/55/209 of 31 July 2000, and ACC/2000/POQ/CRP.16 of 14 September 2000.
32. A/55/332 of 24 August 2000.
33. Support for farm production in OECD countries reached $361 billion in 1999, the equivalent to 1.4 percent of their combined GDP and slightly exceeding Africa's GDP. See "OECD Warns over High Level of Farm Subsidies," 9 June 2000, and "Chance of Economic Revival Beckons Marginalized Africa," *Financial Times*, 1 June 2000. The 1992 *Human Development Report* had already estimated that tariff and non tariff trade barriers imposed by industrial countries cost developing countries about $40 billion a year in lost revenues (p. iii). More recent figures suggest combined losses in the range of $100 billion and $150 billion annually (A/AC.275/12).
34. "Finding Solutions to the Debt Problems of Developing Countries," Report of the Executive Committee on Economic and Social Affairs of the United Nations, in mimeo, New York: United Nations Department for Economic and Social Affairs, 2001.
35. A/55/350/Add. 1 of 15 September 2000.
36. A/54/2000 of 3 April 2000.
37. Follow-up to Millennium Assembly Declaration, A/55/L/56/Rev.1 of 12 December 2000.
38. "State of the Preparations for the Special Session of the General Assembly in 2001 for Follow-up to the World Summit for Children," Document A/55/429 of 28 September 2000.
39. Report of the Second Committee, A/55/582/Add1, of 12 December 2000.
40. Document A/54/917-S/2000/580 of 16 June 2000, "Final Document of the Thirteenth Ministerial Conference of the Movement of Non-Aligned Countries," p. 35. The Statement of the Chair of the G77 can be found at http://www.g77.org/summit/obasanjo_closing.htm.
41. E/CN.4/Sub.2/2000/13 Commission on Human Rights.
42. Resolution 2000/7of 17 August 2000.
43. A/55/210 of 20 December 2000.
44. Report of the Third Committee, A/55/602/Add.2. The resolution drew from "A Strategy for the Promotion of a New Global Human Order" floated by the Chair of the Group of 77, which was designed to serve as "a framework for action on the growing recognition of the importance of human development in the realization of the values and principles of the United Nations." Following immediately this nod to SHD came the politically divisive assertion that there was an imperative need for such a "framework" because many developing countries in the global economy had only narrow choices and that "greater efforts [were] required from the multilateral institutions to modify the system of global governance in order to provide a greater voice and ensure a more equitable distribution of the benefits of globalization" (A/55/496 of 19 October 2000).
45. See the statements of the Deputy US Representative to ECOSOC of 23 July 1998 and of Ambassador Betty King to the Second Committee of the General Assembly on 6 October 1998. USUN Press release #135 (98) of 24 July 1998 and USUN press release #165 (98) of 6 October 1998.

46. ACC Statement of Commitment for Action to Eradicate Poverty, adopted by the ACC in May 1998.
47. http://www.un.org/partners/business/gcevent/press/opening_remarks.htm
48. "Selected Aspects of International Cooperation in Strengthening Financing for Development," note by the Secretary-General, E/2001/45 of 18 April 2001, p. 3.
49. For example, the critiques of the Bank's education and health policies by a number of UN bodies in *World Economic and Social Survey*, 1997, pp. 99–100 and 162-3 UN Publication Sales No. E.97.II.C.1.
50. See, for instance, the warnings of the FAO about the persistence of hunger (*State of the Food Insecurity in the World*, www.fao.org) and IFAD about the grinding to a halt of poverty reduction in the countryside because of a two-thirds reduction in the absolute value of agricultural aid between 1987 and 1998 (*Rural Poverty Report of the International Fund for Agricultural Development*, http://www.IFAD.org).
51. See, for instance, UNICEF, *The State of the World's Children 2001*, New York: UNICEF, 2001, pp. 52–57.
52. "The UN Offers 87 Remedies to Help Poor Nations Develop," *New York Times*, 4 February 2001.
53. "UN Economic Panel to Study Ways to Help World's Have-Nots," *New York Times*, 16 December 2000.
54. A/55/422 of 26 September 2000.
55. A/55/350/Add.1 of 15 September 2000.
56. These proposals were made in the 1999 *Human Development Report*, pp. 8–13.
57. For a broader and exhaustive analysis of the economic and social ideas that have "nurtured" the development work of the United Nations, see the first volume of the United Nations Intellectual History Project by Louis Emmerij, Richard Jolly, and Thomas Weiss, *Ahead of the Curve? UN Ideas and Global Challenges*, Bloomington and Indianapolis: Indiana University Press, 2001.
58. Press release SG/2067 GA/9762 of 1 September 2000. For a useful discussion of the new aspects of multilateral diplomacy, see James P. Muldoon, Jr., et al., eds., *Multilateral Diplomacy and the United Nations Today*. Boulder: Westview Press, 1999.
59. In essence, the reactions to the terrorist attacks of 11 September 2001 lie between two extremes: (1) a military approach alone, based on Cold War habits and perceptions, possibly resembling a "Clash of Civilizations" conflict, which will strengthen antagonism and can make SHD implementation very difficult; (2) a reconsideration of the role of the rich Western countries—in particular, the US—in the world, emphasizing multilateralism, and development cooperation in order to address global differences in equity. The near future will tell which position in between these extremes will be taken.

Bibliography

Claude, Jr., I.L. "Peace and Security: Prospective Roles for the Two United Nations." *Global Governance*, vol. 2, no. 3 (1996): 289–298.
Claude, Jr., I.L. *Swords into Plowshares: The Problems and Progress of International Organization*. 4th ed. New York: Random House, 1971.
Claude, Jr. I.L., *The Changing United Nations*. New York: Random House, 1968.
Dell, S., "Contributions of the United Nations to Economic Thinking and Action." *Journal of Development Planning*, no. 17 (1987): 113–123.
Dulles, J.F. "The General Assembly." *Foreign Affairs*, vol. 24 (1945): 165–175.
Earth Summit +5. *Programme for the Further Implementation of Agenda 21*. New York: United Nations Department of Public Information. DPI/1953-97.36773 (March 1998).

Emmerij, L., Jolly, R., and Weiss Th.G. (with a foreword by Kofi A. Annan). *Ahead of the Curve? UN Ideas and Global Challenges*. Bloomington and Indianapolis: Indiana University Press, 2001.

Finger, M., and Ruchat, B. "Transforming Public Organizations: The Case of UNCTAD." Paper presented at the 1999 meeting of the ISA. Washington, D.C.: 16–20 February 1999.

Finnemore, M. "Redefining Development at the World Bank." Pp. 220 in F. Cooper and R. Packard, eds. *International Development and the Social Sciences: Essays on the History and Politics of Knowledge*. Berkeley, CA: University of California Press, 1997.

Food and Agriculture Organization. *The State of the Food Insecurity in the World 2000*. Rome: FAO, 2000.

International Labour Office. *World Employment Report 1998–99. Employability in the Global Economy: How Training Matters*. Geneva: ILO, 1998.

International Labour Office. *World Employment Report 2001: Life at Work in the Information Economy*. Geneva: ILO, 2001.

International Labour Organisation (with an introduction by James P. Grant). *Employment, Growth and Basic Needs: A One World Problem*. Published by the Overseas Development Council in cooperation with the ILO. New York: Praeger Publishers, 1977.

Muldoon, Jr., J.P., et al., eds. *Multilateral Diplomacy and the United Nations Today*. Boulder: Westview Press, 1999.

Nicholls, L. "Birds of a Feather? UNDP and Action Aid Implementation of Sustainable Human Development." *Development in Practice*, vol. 9, no. 4 (1999): 396–409.

Rapley, J. *Understanding Development: Theory and Practice in the Third World*. Boulder: Lynne Rienner Publishers, 1996.

Sen, A. *Development as Freedom*. New York: Alfred Knopf, 1999.

South Centre. *For a Strong and Democratic United Nations: A South Perspective on UN Reform*. Geneva: South Centre, 1996.

South Centre, *Towards an Economic Platform for the South*. Geneva: South Centre, 1998.

Therien, J-P. "Beyond the North South Divide: The Two Tales of World Poverty." Prepared for delivery at the 1999 Convention of the ISA. Washington, D.C.: 16–20 February 1999.

UNCTAD. *The Least Developed Countries 2000 Report*. Geneva: United Nations, 2000.

UNDP. *Human Development Report*. Oxford/New York: Oxford University Press (annual series).

UNDP. *Overcoming Human Poverty: Poverty Report 2000*. New York: UNDP, 2000.

UNDP. *UNDP Today: Introducing the Organization*. New York: UNDP, 1998.

UNICEF. *The Progress of Nations 1999*. New York: UNICEF, 1999.

UNICEF. *The State of the World's Children 2001*. New York: UNICEF, 2001.

United Nations. *Report of the United Nations Conference on Science and Technology*. Vienna, 20–31 August 1979 (A/CONF.81./16).

United Nations. *Report of the United Nations Conference on the Least Developed Countries*. Paris: 1–14 September 1981. New York: United Nations, 1982

United Nations. *International Plan of Action on Aging*. New York: United Nations, 1983.

United Nations. *Report of the United Nations Conference on Environment and Development*. Rio de Janeiro: 3–14 June 1992. Vol. 1. Resolutions adopted by the Conference. New York: United Nations, 1993 (United Nations Publication Sales No. E.93.I.8).

United Nations. *The Copenhagen Declaration and Programme of Action: World Summit for Social Development*. New York: United Nations, 1995.

United Nations. *1999 World Survey on the Role of Women in Development: Globalization, Gender and Work*. New York: United Nations, 1999.

United Nations. "Review and Appraisal of the Implementation of the Beijing Platform of Action." *Report of the Secretary-General*. E/CN.6/2000/PC/2 of 19 January 2000.

United Nations. "Towards a Stable International Financial System, Responsive to the Challenges of Development, Especially in the Developing Countries." *Report of the Secretary-General*. A/55/187 of 27 July 2000.

United Nations. "Update on the Implementation of the Declaration on International Economic Cooperation, in Particular the Revitalization of Economic Growth and Development of the

Developing Countries and Implementation of the International Development Strategy for the Fourth United Nations Development Decade." A/55/209 of 31 July 2000.

United Nations. "Globalization and Its Impact on the Full Enjoyment of All Human Rights." *Report of the Secretary-General.* A/55/342 of 31 August 2000.

United Nations. "The Role of the United Nations in Promoting Development in the Context of Globalization and Interdependence." *Report of the Secretary-General.* A/55/381 of 13 September 2000.

United Nations. "Halving Extreme Poverty: An Action Strategy for the United Nations." ACC/2000/POQ/CRP.16 of 14 September 2000.

United Nations. "Implementation of the United Nations New Agenda for the Development of Africa in the 1990s." *Report of the Secretary-General.* A/55/350 of 15 September 2000.

United Nations. "Implementation of the United Nations New Agenda for the Development Africa in the 1990s." Addendum, "Mobilization of Additional Resources for African Development: A Study on Overall Resource Flows to Africa." *Report of the Secretary-General.* A/55/350/Add. of 15 September 2000.

United Nations. "Implementation of the First United Nations Decade for the Eradication of Poverty (1997–2006)." *Report of the Secretary-General.* A/55/507 of 21 September 2000.

United Nations. "Recent Developments in the Debt Situation of Developing Countries." *Report of the Secretary-General.* A/55/422 of 26 September 2000.

United Nations. *Report of the Secretary-General to the Preparatory Committee for the High-level International Event on Financing for Development.* A/AC.257/12 of 18 December 2000.

United Nations Association of the United States of America. *A Global Agenda. Issues before the 55th General Assembly of the United Nations. 2000–2001 Edition.* New York: Rowman and Littlefield Publishers, Inc., 2000.

WHO. *Report of the International Conference on Primary Health Care.* Alma Ata, USSR, 6–12 September 1978. Geneva: WHO, 1978.

World Bank. *2000 Annual Report.* Washington, D.C.: World Bank, 2000.

World Bank. *World Development Report 2000/2001: Attacking Poverty.* New York: Oxford University Press, 2001.

PART II

DECISION MAKING IN INTERNATIONAL ORGANIZATIONS

Part I shows that international organizations are largely, but certainly not fully, dependent on government support. Funding and multilateral diplomacy pose strategic design issues in which the top management of the organization can be intimately involved in both following and shaping government decisions. Decision making is also crucial within the organization, for example, when effecting organizational change. This part looks more closely at decision-making issues in which the balance between external government control and internal managerial control shifts toward internal decision making and action. Human resource management, strategic reorientation, and organizational change, as well as fraud and corruption, are areas in which the organization can take action that is, in principle, more autonomous when compared to funding and multilateral diplomacy. The increasing importation of management techniques from private enterprise also reflects that the role of the state is changing, which implies shifting roles for governmental institutions, private enterprise, NGOs, and international governmental organizations.

— *Chapter 4* —

GOOD INTENTIONS TO NAUGHT
The Pathology of Human Rescoures
Management at the United Nations

Dirk Salomons

Introduction

When the Preparatory Commission sat down in 1945 to draw up a framework for the establishment of the United Nations, it paid particular attention to the staffing of its Secretariat. In doing so, the Commission was guided by the staff regulations that governed the Secretariat of the League of Nations. These, in turn, had been inspired by the British concept of an independent civil service, based on merit, first formulated in the Trevelyan-Northcote Report of 1853, which meant to bring an end to a pattern of patronage and incompetence that the British Empire could no longer afford as it rapidly expanded its grip on its colonies.

If there were such a discipline as "administrative archeology," the current staff regulations of the United Nations, with their venerable roots in the nineteenth-century management reform movement, would present a prime site for digging, and a museum of memorabilia would easily be filled. Where in the modern world (other than the Salvation Army) are staff members still called "officers," are business trips called "missions," and do remnants of the colonial era, such as "home leave," remain in such a well-preserved state? Yet the influence of these strong historical traditions is felt in more than just a few comical administrative relics. It has permeated the culture of the United Nations to the extent that the reforms of the Victorian era have now become the stumbling blocks of the present.

In this chapter, we will examine how the very principles that created a strong British civil service in the days of the empire—command-and-control, seniority, independence, and merit—have become fetishes standing in the way of true human resources reform at the United Nations. In doing so, we also hope to point at possible avenues that may lead to effective change.

The starting point for this review of UN staffing policies and practices is the assumption that there are no "good" or "bad" human resources strategies in absolute terms; their effectiveness is determined by their context. While, for example, the concept of "career service" may be functional for a post office, where experience contributes to quality performance, this vision of long-term employment would be totally inappropriate for a football team, where youth and physical prowess are everything. We should therefore begin by asking: What are the current functions of the United Nations Secretariat, its funds and its programs, and what staff competencies and characteristics would best match these functions? What conditions would attract and retain the most suitable staff? Which human resources strategies and policies are most likely to create such conditions? How do these compare to the current human resources framework? In what ways does the past thwart the future?

That leads to other questions: How are human resources strategies at the United Nations shaped? What is the role of Member States? How have they helped or hindered reforms? Did the results of their efforts match their intentions?

Vision of the Founding Fathers

The Preparatory Commission, in recommending staff regulations and rules to the UN General Assembly (Preparatory Commission 1945), followed closely in the tracks of the League of Nations. A comparison of the League's 1945 Staff Regulations with the draft text submitted by the Commission shows remarkable similarities, and many parts are identical. Both stress that the responsibilities of international civil servants are "not national, but exclusively international." Both prescribe the same oath of office, mutatis mutandis. Both grant the same functional immunities and privileges. Both restrict staff's participation in public activities. Men and women are equally eligible for posts in the UN Secretariat, as they were in the League. And both the League's and its successor's Regulations stress that appointments shall be made on a competitive basis.

Characteristic for both organizations' design is the emphasis on seniority and on promotions from within in preference to appointments from outside (LoN Staff Regulations, Article 16; Preparatory Commission, Section D, para. 47). This trait is still as dominant in the UN today as it was 50 years ago. The structure of oversight committees for appointments and promotions emphasizes broad and high-level participation, so that no single department can decide on staffing issues; these decisions are made for, and by, the Organization as a whole. While the

League of Nations had a seven-year term limit on the service of Directors and Under-Secretaries-General (and a limit of 10 years for the Secretary-General), the Preparatory Commission did not recommend such restrictions for the United Nations, and proposed that Assistant Secretaries-General, Directors, and "other principal higher officers" serve for five years, but subject to the possibility of renewal (Preparatory Commission: Chapter VIII, Section 2, E, para. 61). This further strengthened the concept of a career service.

The Preparatory Commission had strong views on the importance of career prospects:

> Unless members of the staff can be offered some assurance of being able to make their careers in the Secretariat, many of the best candidates from all countries will inevitably be kept away. Nor can members of the staff be expected fully to subordinate the special interests of their countries to the international interest if they are merely detached temporarily from their national administrations and remain dependent upon them for their future. Finally, it is important that the advantages of experience should be secured and sound administrative traditions established within the Secretariat.
>
> For these reasons, it is essential that the bulk of the staff should consist of persons who will make their career in the Secretariat. They should be given contracts for an indeterminate period subject to review every five years on the basis of reports by their superior officers. (Preparatory Commission: Section 2, E, paras. 59–60)

From the perspective of those early days, this vision was fully functional. The Secretariat's main role at the time was to support a set of intergovernmental committees: the Security Council, the Economic and Social Council, and the Trusteeship Council. In addition, there would be staff versed in public information, legal issues, conference services, and administration.

Once a candidate had the basic academic qualifications, most of the specific skills required for these types of functions could be acquired through on-the-job training, and the necessary further experience could best be gained in-house. The Organization's mandate, and hence its functions, were limited. The emphasis in all of this was on the servicing of the UN's deliberative bodies. Operational activities were not foreseen. Most posts were funded from the regular budget, and extrabudgetary activities were few and far between.

All the secondary characteristics, therefore, of the UN personnel system as it emerged were linked to the concept of lifelong employment in a stable and static bureaucracy. Pension benefits accrued slowly over time and had value only if one endured until retirement age; premature departure carried a heavy penalty. Benefits such as home leave, children's allowances, education grants, and generous annual leave mimicked the pattern of the major powers' foreign services.

What's Needed Now: Staffing for the New UN

To what extent does this static staffing model still apply? The needs of the UN have changed dramatically since its inception. It is required to display expertise in a far broader range of specializations, so that it tends to recruit people who have gained experience elsewhere: in national government, academia, NGOs, or the private sector. It employs far more people in activities funded from extrabudgetary resources, which tend to be limited in time, as trust funds and donor-funded projects make up an increasing part of the UN's budget. UNDP, UNICEF, and UNHCR together, as of 30 June 2000, had far more staff than the UN Secretariat (16,993 compared to 13,164), and of those UN Secretariat posts, only 2,389 are subject to geographical distribution.[1] In the UN's Funds and Programmes, such as UNDP, UNICEF, and UNHCR, all funding is voluntary, and much of this now is "tied aid" in the form of trust funds earmarked for specific purposes as designated by the donors. The programs and activities implemented by these actors tend to be complex, decentralized, and often highly specialized—thus requiring higher-level, experienced staff with a track record acquired outside of the UN system. The obsessive focus of the General Assembly on the relatively small "political" group "subject to geographical distribution," which has remained constant throughout the years, is thus becoming increasingly marginal in relation to the real issue: how to recruit and retain a multi-faceted and mobile staff in this changing and demanding environment. The fact that "geographical distribution" itself, as defined by the UN General Assembly, has become highly politicized (as we will see later) does not help matters.

The Secretariat's regular budget shows another reason why the old career-based staffing model no longer holds up: in the biennium 2000–2001, there were only 436 entry level posts (P-1/P-2), compared to 2,244 midlevel posts (P-3/P-4).[2] The average age of professional staff members is 46.1; they have a relatively high average age even at the entry grades (37.9 years at the P-2 level).[3] In the Funds and Programmes, staffing patterns are very similar; UNFPA, for example, has no P-2 posts in its Headquarters staffing table. Training resources are limited everywhere, and are mainly allocated to language training, information technology, and management—leaving little for occupational training or professional development. Posts for young professionals under extrabudgetary programs are even scarcer, and special programs, such as the donor-financed Junior Professional Officer program, are not large enough to change the picture. Posts funded from extrabudgetary resources, moreover, tend to be short term.[4]

The lack of resources (and career path models) to create entry-level positions for young professionals makes it far more difficult to build a common culture, and the energy and critical enthusiasm that characterize young staff are now scarce. At the same time, the emphasis on hiring people who have already been "molded" by careers outside the UN is now a fact on the ground, and adjustments have to be made to serve at least this group well. This means that the UN should be able to offer terms of employment that are appealing for people entering in midcareer, and for people who plan to spend only a few years at the UN as part of a career path that may include alternatives such as academia or national institutions.

As so many government functions have been privatized over the past 10 to 15 years, the skills and knowledge associated with them have also wandered over to the private sector. Gone are the days when cutting-edge knowledge in fields such as tropical medicine, telecommunications, or remote sensing could be found in the Member States' ministries. Competencies that are key to the UN's mandate in the fields of international finance, trade, and economic development are now most easily found in the banking sector. A suitable human resources framework for the United Nations should therefore be geared to facilitate recruitment of talent and expertise from the private sector. This, in turn, should have implications for the manner in which salaries are set.

Given the UN's wide mandate, which encompasses a bewildering range of activities, the Organization will have to rely on staff who show a high level of initiative and autonomy, and provide them with the tools to work independently in the context of teams, rather than in a top-down and controlled environment. This will require a change not just of culture but also of financial regulations and of audit practices.

The rapid ascent of Southern countries in academic and professional terms has created a vast pool of talent that would allow the UN to reach a truly "equitable geographic distribution" of staff. Current recruitment policies and practices, however, cut off access to UN positions for the vast majority of this deserving group of potential "players," and until the UN Secretariat reconsiders its definition of "equitable geographical distribution" (i.e., who pays the most gets the largest number of posts), it will remain a postcolonial museum. The UN Funds and Programmes, likewise, should be less inclined to link their staffing to their funding, as this creates undue dependence on a few wealthy donors as the core recruitment source.

If the UN intends to remain relevant, therefore, and staffed with people "of the highest competence," in accordance with the Charter, it must ensure that its human resources policies and its terms of employment will enable it to recruit and retain staff who meet this new profile: truly multinational, specialized, mobile, midcareer, entrepreneurial, and independent. Will it be able to do so? A review of the UN's past efforts to adapt the organization to the reality of its environment may shed some light on its capacity to handle internal reforms, and help us identify some of the key policy issues that will affect its prospects of meeting future challenges.

Implementing the Vision:
Pathological Problems Emerge (1946–1974)

Article 101 of the UN Charter states that "the paramount consideration in the employment of staff and in the determination of conditions of service is the necessity of securing the highest standards of efficiency, competence, and integrity. Due regard is also to be paid to the importance of recruiting the staff on as wide a geographical basis as possible." The Preparatory Commission understood that there was a potential conflict between these two objectives, but it believed that they could "in large measure be reconciled."[5] While it recommended the use of tests, especially for higher-level positions, the Commission argued for flexibility. It also noted that the examination system would "be inapplicable to many candidates of high character and ability who, owing to war service, underground activities in enemy-occupied territories, internment in concentration camps, etc., would not have the desired academic qualifications and will be at a disadvantage in formal examinations. For such candidates other processes of selection—the interview, and the analysis of personal records, for example—would be useful."[6] This illustrates the strong faith that the Preparatory Commission had in the value of character and life experience as indicators of success—a hallmark of the British civil service tradition. Implicitly, this approach would also make it easier to recruit candidates from underrepresented countries.

When the General Assembly met in 1946 to discuss the report of the Preparatory Commission, it found very little that was controversial, and the Commission's recommendations were adopted virtually unchanged. Thus, a framework was put into place that defined the organization of the Secretariat, adopted an information policy, set out staff regulations, and defined key personnel policies (including taxation, types of appointments, options for termination, and retirement benefits). Within a year, however, the General Assembly began to express misgivings about the manner in which the personnel system was put into place, and it asked the Secretary-General "to examine the recruitment policy that has been followed to date with a view to improving the present geographical distribution of posts within the various Departments," and to review "the qualifications, background and experience of the present members of the staff, with a view to replacing those who do not reach the high standards fixed by the Charter."[7] Clearly, the flexibility advocated by the Preparatory Commission had led to some undesirable results.

This was hardly surprising, as the United Nations had started in 1946 with some 300 persons, most of them belonging to the Secretariat of the Preparatory Commission or to the now defunct League of Nations. The first Secretary-General had to improvise the recruitment of about 2,900 staff members in a few months, and the demobilization of US troops provided a ready recruitment source. Soon, half of the staff subject to geographical distribution were US nationals. The British army also was an attractive pool for the hiring of candidates with logistics and management experience. The resulting lack of balance in the composition of the staff took years to redress, and was then compounded by the onset of the Cold War, which made it difficult to recruit candidates from the Soviet bloc (Langrod 1968: 175).

In the fall of 1952, the General Assembly adopted a set of expanded staff regulations based on the work of the International Civil Service Advisory Board (ICSAB). These regulations addressed issues related to social security, staff relations, and disciplinary measures and appeals, and established a detailed pay system for the professional and director categories, including mechanisms for salary differentials to reflect relative costs of living across the globe, as well as children's allowances, repatriation grants, and education grants. This system has remained virtually unchanged ever since.

During the first 25 years of its existence, the UN Secretariat maintained a very simple system of career development based on the principle that staff had priority over outsiders when it came to filling vacancies (in this way, recruitment would focus on the lower ranks, and a UN career would span several decades). Staff who had reached a certain level of seniority within their grade became eligible for promotion. The most deserving staff members (selected by an appointment and promotion board) would be placed on a promotion register, and vacancies would be filled from the register as they occurred. While merit played a role, seniority was the key determinant. There was a strong sense that careers should develop slowly, like fine wine, and that no one should be left behind. While the promotion register has made way for a system of managed competition, the underlying emphasis on seniority has not changed; to this day, vacancy announcements for senior-level UN posts stress the need for decades of experience.

Under the influence of the major contributors to the United Nations, a formal system was put into place to regulate geographical distribution, whereby each Member State received a basic post allocation, and the remaining posts were allocated in proportion to a country's assessed contribution. This system has remained virtually unchanged over the past 50 years (although the emergence of so many new countries has led to a very different staffing pattern), and it has led to a highly questionable situation, whereby India, for example, has an allotment of 27 to 36 posts, while the United States has a desirable range of 314 to 424, and Japan, 257 to 348. The Netherlands, with a range of 24 to 34, has a right to nearly as many posts as China, which can claim between 40 and 55. It is hard to argue that this pattern represents the "wide geographical distribution" envisaged by the Preparatory Commission, and it is harder to argue that wealth, not talent, should be the basis on which countries may compete for representation in the Secretariat.

The First Malignancy: The Unresolved Tension between Merit and Patronage

As the Secretariat became operational, it quickly became apparent that the British model of the civil service as an independent meritocracy was by no means a commonly accepted standard. The basic underlying assumption that a cast of permanent civil servants will be able to serve neutrally and loyally under varying ideological regimes, executing faithfully whatever the legislature decides, is shared by only very few national administrations. In the United States, for example, a party change in the presidency leads to a virtual exodus in Washington, as thousands of civil service appointments linked to the losing party are terminated, and new staff are selected, taking into account their party loyalty as much as their competence. Similar massive turnovers occur at the state and local level when party control shifts. Only in this manner, advocates of patronage systems believe, can one make sure that the ideological convictions of the victors will be translated into political action—"independent" civil servants could never be trusted to implement change. Many Western countries, such as Canada, Italy, Ireland and Iceland, follow a similar pattern (Kristinsson 1996: 438). As Nikita Krushchev, the premier of the USSR, put it in an interview with Walter Lippman of the *New York Herald Tribune* in 1962: "While there are neutral countries, there are no neutral men. There can be no such thing as an impartial civil servant in this deeply divided world, and the kind of political celibacy which the British theory of the civil servant calls for is in international affairs a fiction" (quoted in Langrod 1968: 320).

In many other administrative cultures, the quid pro quo is even more direct: power brings with it an obligation to share the spoils. When people have learned from experience that loyalty to the family, clan, or tribe is the most reliable strategy for survival, this awareness is carried over into governance models. When one has finally gained a position in which one controls resources, it is time to honor the many obligations that have accrued on the way up. Associates have to be rewarded, and favors have to be returned. At the same time, security is paramount—jobs can be given only to people who can be fully trusted, and again, the family, clan, or tribe is the most reliable recruitment source. This, in the eyes of those who have grown up with this type of patronage, is not corruption but rather realism.

Many developing countries have relied on this model for governance since their early days, as it often had its roots in tribal systems and usually also in the social control mechanisms of the colonial era. While efforts are made to introduce the rule of law, court systems, procedural protections, and other elements of a framework that shifts trust from kin to codes, it will take a long time before these new notions have been fully assimilated.

When people nurtured on patronage, be they from the North of from the South, are brought into the UN, either as government representatives or as staff, they experience a total cognitive disconnect: the UN and its Member States in the General Assembly volubly endorse a merit-based system, behave as if it did not exist, and then censor themselves in resolution after resolution denouncing the evils of political deal making. If the United Nations were able to acknowledge openly that patronage is an important and valuable element of the way in which it operates, much could be gained, because then the boundaries of the patronage system could be drawn, and the space for the inclusion of merit could be demarcated.

The vaguest outlines of such a system already exist. Appointments at the senior Director level (D-2) and above, for example, are the prerogative of the Secretary-General, and are not subject to review by the regular Appointment and Promotion Board. But this does not mean, unfortunately, that therefore appointments at lower levels are made purely on merit, as the review process itself has ample room for political influence. It is only when a Department, Programme, or Fund has a clear mandate with concrete outputs—and when the results of its work are immediately visible to the public eye—that merit, by necessity, becomes an issue. UNHCR, for example, cannot afford to let "first cousins" run its refugee programs. The World Food Programme must be able to rely on each and every logistician on its staff in order to get food to the needy. One could therefore formulate a law: the amount of patronage in the management of the UN's human resources is directly inverse to the level of public accountability of the entity affected.

This also means that the end of the Cold War, and the increased emphasis on good governance as a prerequisite for continued development assistance, has brought about a renewed effort at the UN to make accountability and responsibility central to its own management. These attempts at reform, which started with the appointment of Kofi Annan as Secretary-General in 1996, have had a certain measure of success, although the underlying sources of managerial disarray (i.e., the tension between central control and individual empowerment, between patronage and merit, and between political and management values) have not disappeared.

The Second Malignancy: Control Crushes Empowerment

The staffing structure of the United Nations, with its strict hierarchy and top-down, quasi-military command structure, as well as the control mechanisms embedded in its financial regulations, create an environment in which decisions are not easily made. The UN Standards of Conduct, promulgated in 1954 by the International Civil Service Advisory Board, stipulate obedience: while a staff member "has the right, which should be safeguarded, to record his views in the official files, it is his duty to accept, carry out, and even defend decisions of his superiors once they are taken, whether or not they accord with his own opinions."[8]

When it comes to the control of financial resources, managers have to face a series of hurdles. They must deal with a budgetary process whereby the use of program funds is planned on a biennial basis. The process of budget formulation, review, and approval takes about one year. This means that managers must be able to look as far as three years ahead in planning their work. Since there are restrictions on their ability to move money across budget lines, and since money not spent reverts to the Member States, managers have little room left for flexible responses to external changes or unforeseen developments.

An extensive system of internal controls further ensures that no official can authorize any expenditure without third-party approval and certification.[9] This makes a lot of sense in a static environment, but it can create embarrassing delays in relief operations or other situations in which rapid action is required. Managers have responsibility, but not the corresponding authority. While this has been common knowledge for the past 50 years, the system seems immutable, notwithstanding external criticism. Recently, for example, this created major problems when UNHCR was called upon in 1999 to respond at very short notice to a large flow of refugees from Kosovo to adjacent countries. UNHCR encountered major delays in mobilizing staff and resources, and ultimately it accommodated only 12 percent of the refugee population that sought shelter in camps (and two-thirds of the refugees went directly to private homes, particularly in neighboring Albania). NATO and some large NGOs took up the slack. There were obviously many factors that affected UNHCR's performance, but the lack of autonomy at the level of senior managers played a big role. An independent evaluation of UNHCR's emergency preparedness and response in the Kosovo crisis came to the following conclusion:

> For the emergency manager in the field, it is essential that staff, computer and vehicle resources have been addressed administratively in order for them to deal with substantive issues such as distribution of relief materials. Neither the Former Yugoslavia Liaison Unit nor the Special Envoy, however, had control of the required resources or the authority to direct support. More generally, the same applied to the decision-making structure relevant to the emergency. The authority over UNHCR's resources to support the emergency operation was vested in the Directors of the "four pillars" [the four major Divisions], but they were not responsible for the substantive decisions regarding policy implementation through operations. (Suhrke et al. 2000)

The Third Malignancy: A Punitive Audit Culture

These constraints on managers have contributed to a climate of "passing the buck," a feeling that initiatives are rarely rewarded but frequently punished, and a belief that a low profile is the best survival strategy. This attitude is compounded by a very aggressive audit culture, whereby staff members are regarded as guilty unless proven innocent.

A telling case that illustrates this harsh attitude of the UN's senior oversight staff is the so-called "Skylink Affair," which made headlines in all of the major US and European media during the summer of 1993. In May 1993, the president of Evergreen Helicopters, Inc., a US corporation, wrote to the chairman of the US House of Representatives Subcommittee on Commerce expressing his concerns at "irregularities in the procurement of UNTAC [UN Transitional Authority in Cambodia] helicopter contracts." He claimed that, because of these irregularities, "the contracts went principally to one Canadian helicopter broker," although Evergreen "was the lowest bidder." A similar letter went to the US permanent representative to the UN and to Melissa Wells, the Under-Secretary-General for Administration at the UN, a US national. Allegedly, "through a secret process, a company named Skylink ... has been able to obtain a virtual monopoly on UN procurement."[10]

This letter arrived at the UN just as the US administration was making a major effort to have an independent oversight mechanism established at the UN, similar to the General Accounting Office of the US Congress. This would create a new post at the Assistant Secretary-General level, and the Director of Audit (a compatriot of the then Secretary-General, Boutros-Ghali) was one of the candidates. Thus, Audit was keen to show its mettle. A preliminary investigation of the awards process for air support contracts was undertaken, and, in June 1993, an audit report concluded that "practically all of the fifty-two cases reviewed showed non-compliance with established procurement procedures."[11] Five staff members were unceremoniously escorted from their offices and suspended, a press conference was called to expose the alleged culprits, and, in December 1993, the case finally was referred to the internal Joint Disciplinary Committee (JDC), which advises the Secretary-General.

It took the UN Administration several months to prepare its case, and then the JDC, supported by a lawyer specializing in contracts law, spent nearly three months examining voluminous reams of contracts, transcripts, depositions, and correspondence. A lengthy report ensued, and the JDC unanimously advised the Secretary-General that it "did not find any evidence of misconduct on the part of the [applicants] in connection with the charges. No instance was found in which the UN paid more than it would otherwise have had to pay for air transportation services because of any improper conduct by the staff members." In fact the JDC, of which this author was a member, found that the auditors had bent over backwards to construct a case against the five staff members that should never have been brought in the first place, as the cases presented lacked "a thorough, exhaustive examination of the available documentation," a polite way of saying that the allegations were based on sloppy and biased audit work.[12]

The UN Administration acknowledged that in fact its charges were unfounded, and that no improprieties had occurred, but because the JDC had noted a few instances where the staff members had cut corners to speed things up, they were disciplined by a salary reduction. This then led the staff members to appeal to the Administrative Tribunal (AT), the highest judiciary body at the UN (composed of internationally respected specialists in labor law, and elected by the General Assembly), which was established to adjudicate differences between the staff and the Secretary-General.

The AT, in its judgment, noted that the staff members, under great pressure to respond speedily, had in fact performed extremely well, and that the disciplinary measures taken against them on grounds of poor performance were not justified. In this context, the AT cited a memorandum dated late August 1994 from the Assistant Secretary-General for the Office of Internal Oversight Services (who had been appointed after Audit made its allegations) to Joseph Connor, the Under-Secretary-General for Administration and Management (who had replaced Miss Wells, and had thus inherited the case). The relevant portion, as cited by the AT, read as follows: "In this regard I would like to advise that regardless of the outcome of the JDC proceedings, the former PTS officials [the accused] must not be permitted to resume their previous positions, *even if they are exonerated*. To do otherwise will surely result in widespread negative repercussions, including a further deterioration of morale and motivation among the existing staff members" (emphasis added by the AT).[13]

The AT then noted that it was "dismayed, not only by the proposed prejudgment and denial of due process rights contained therein, but also by the apparent illogic of the reason advanced for it. The suggestion by the ASG for the Office of Internal Oversight Services that even if the investigation then under way were to exonerate the Applicant, it should be decided in advance to treat them as if they had been found guilty, is abhorrent to the most basic concepts of justice and fair play." Thus, the AT concluded: "[T]he Tribunal finds that the Applicants were unfairly and improperly treated by the Respondent [i.e., the UN Administration] when he penalized them, despite the findings of their innocence by the JDC and his own acceptance of this finding. The Applicants were deprived of the due process to which they were entitled, and were subject to a serious irregularity of procedure."[14]

It goes without saying that the ASG, who so seriously violated the UN standards of conduct, was never reprimanded. Morale, especially among the staff involved in servicing the peacekeeping operations, reached an all-time low, and from then on, procurement staff worked in a purely defensive mode. The fact that one of the staff members involved in the disciplinary proceedings had died of heart failure in preparing his appeal, and that the UN Administration never acknowledged to his family how poorly he had been treated, was the final straw. Five years later, the Organization has still not quite recovered from this (and similar) incidents; thus, all references to accountability and empowerment are met with considerable cynicism. The fact that the Office of Internal Oversight Services has in other instances proven its mettle in uncovering fraud (see Yves Beigbeder's chapter in this book) has not done much so far to improve its image.

The Fourth Malignancy: Poor Governance—Reforms Abandoned (1974–1994)

In 1974, the UN General Assembly, inspired by several studies submitted by the International Civil Service Advisory Board, the Advisory Committee on Administrative and Budgetary questions (ACABQ), as well as the Joint Inspection Unit, expressed its support for a program of major reforms in the area of human resources, which consisted of the following elements:

- defining a staff structure for the Secretariat, based on specialized occupational qualifications and on the need for job classification;
- introducing a modern and efficient recruitment system, paying more attention to the principle of geographic distribution (as defined by the UN General Assembly) while adopting long-term forecasting and competitive selection methods; and
- introducing a new promotion, career planning, and training system, based on occupational groups.[15]

Two years later, the Joint Inspection Unit (JIU) carried out an evaluation of the results achieved.[16] This effort was led by Maurice Bertrand, a French public administration specialist who had spearheaded the JIU's efforts to guide personnel reform at the UN since the late 1960s, and who had consistently argued for a system that included the elements of a French *cheminement de carrière* (career path). In this model, staff compete for entry into an organization through exams held on the basis of occupational groups, and their career develops strictly along an occupational career path. This contrasts starkly with the British civil service concept, whereby a "good man" with a general broad academic background can be expected to succeed in virtually any occupation; character, gender, and networks define the career path. (The topic of gender at the UN deserves separate treatment; it took several decades before women became visible at the UN's top levels.) For the UN Administration, which in the late 1960s and early 1970s was still very much influenced by the same British culture that had created the UN staff regulations in the first place, the approach of the JIU reeked of heresy. Lip service was paid to reform, but resistance was strong.

In their report to the General Assembly, the inspectors criticized both the pace of the implementation of the approved reforms, and the methods used. They cited the Secretary-General's progress report, which recognized that "much further action is needed," and listed as goals "the division of the staff into occupations and occupational groups, the completion of the job classification system, the development of career patterns, the organization of staff assignments, the restructuring of the General Service category and the completion of the review of the appointment and promotion procedures."[17] Thus, the inspectors concluded: "[F]ive years after submission of the report[18] we are still, as regards the most important fields, in the preliminary study and experiment phase."[19] The inspectors recalled that a long-term recruitment plan had been published in 1972, but that no system had been developed for the regular updating of such a plan. While a roster had been instituted, only 7 percent of the recruitment in 1974 had been drawn from that roster, and less than 0.3 percent of the staff recruited over a three-year period (1973 through 1975) had participated in special recruitment examinations. The inspectors noted a similar lack of progress in the area of job classification: "Basically, as regards the problem of structure, there seems to be no real reason why most of the remaining measures needed to institute reform could not be carried out in the course of 1977, since the job classification system for professional posts begun in 1975 was to be ready in two years and since there are no real obstacles remaining to the immediate drafting of comprehensive and detailed rules on occupational groups."[20]

The UN Secretariat began to draw increasingly sharp criticism during the 1970s. In addition to the reports of the JIU, various external observers raised words of warning (James 1970; Finger 1975). Their studies emphasized the need to raise the quality of the staff through improved recruitment, training, and career development practices. In doing so, they pointed at the underlying cause: political pressures and interference by Member States. In a follow-up study conducted in 1980, Finger found that the situation had deteriorated (Finger and Hanan 1981). He noted that officials were accused of taking payoffs from individuals seeking jobs, and that, as a result of preliminary investigations, the Assistant Secretary-General for Personnel had left the employment of the Secretariat in the fall of 1980. Employees felt alienated, high-ranking officials engaged in political give-and-take, and interest groups lobbied for their country's advantage. There was a growing rift between management and staff, and a class system had emerged whereby movement from the support staff levels to the professional ranks had become nearly impossible.

To some extent, this general malaise was a direct corollary to the overall impact of the Cold War on world affairs. The United Nations was largely paralyzed in the exercise of its core functions under the Charter—certainly in the areas of peace and security, as well as human rights—and the General Assembly had become a forum for recriminations and ideological sparring. Most of the positive results coming out of the UN system could be attributed to the specialized agencies and to the UN Funds and Programmes, such as UNDP and UNICEF, rather than to the Secretariat. Where there was no real work to do, and where no measurable results could be expected, posts became chips in a global poker game. The poor leadership of Secretaries-General U Thant and Kurt Waldheim further demoralized staff and Member States alike.

The rapid growth in the number of Member States during the decolonization process also created pressures to allocate high-level posts to nationals of newly emerging countries, and in the 1960s, 1970s, and 1980s merit was often secondary to geographic distribution in the recruitment process, even at the lower levels. In Resolution 33/143 of 20 December 1978, the General Assembly reaffirmed that the chief considerations in the employment of staff were high standards of efficiency and competence, together with the principle of equitable geographical distribution. At the same time, the Assembly expressed concern about the urgent need to improve the representation of developing countries at senior policymaking levels—sending a double message to the Administration. Robert Jordan, former Director of Research at UNITAR and the Dag Hammarskjold Professor of International Relations at the University of South Carolina at the time, concluded: "The pendulum may have swung too far in favor of [so-called] equitable geographical distribution, and it is time to focus more on efficiency, competence and integrity. Since the organization, in its economic and social activities, exists more to serve the needs of development rather than, for instance, advancing greater industrialization in the advanced industrial states, it stands to reason that the more efficiently the organization's activities are carried out, the greater the benefits for the newer Member States" (Jordan 1981). The United States, meanwhile, resisted any pressures to redefine the formula for the allocation of posts in favor of the financially less endowed nations. "It [the US] was determined to resist efforts to reduce the weight assigned to the value of contributions in establishing targets to reflect the geographical considerations laid down in the Charter."[21] The battle lines were clearly drawn.

As the UN Secretariat did not manage to develop a coherent human resources policy, and as the long-awaited job classification standards failed to materialize even several years after the JIU had derided their slow development, the General Assembly began to look to the International Civil Service Commission (ICSC) for guidance. The establishment of this body had been part of the Preparatory Commission's recommendations in 1945, but it did not come about until 1974, as part of the overall reform process.

The ICSC consists of 15 experts, appointed in a personal capacity by the General Assembly. It makes recommendations to the General Assembly and other governing bodies on personnel policies and on conditions of service, including salaries, and it has limited decision-making powers in the area of job classification and certain allowances, such as cost-of-living adjustments and compensation for hardship. Its statute has been accepted by all of the specialized agencies, thus creating a "common system" of salaries and benefits that facilitates mobility across the UN organizations. The Bretton Woods institutions, however, while part of the UN system, are not part of this arrangement, and salaries in the World Bank and the IMF are therefore much higher than those of their UN counterparts. Hence the subtle difference between "the UN system" and "the UN common system."

As the reforms proposed by the JIU had never taken hold in the UN Secretariat, the General Assembly asked the ICSC to develop common job classification standards for all professional posts throughout the UN organizations in order to ensure that the concept of "equal pay for equal work" would permeate the entire "common system" network. It also asked the ICSC to develop a broad framework for the concept of careers and to prepare guidelines for recruitment, training, promotion policy, human resources planning, and performance evaluation. In 1982, the ICSC promulgated a comprehensive job classification system, based on a points factor analysis model supported by occupational standards and a fully developed occupational coding system. This made it possible to prepare an inventory of all common system jobs grouped by occupation, and to develop career paths across organizations within common fields of work. To some extent, the reform process had moved from the UN Secretariat to the "common system," and some progress became visible. Once the job classification standards had been implemented by all of the organizations, some three years after their promulgation, a framework for mobility had been created that moved the discussion about careers from the level of individual organizations to that of the UN common system as a whole. The ICSC's numerous recommendations made between 1982 and 1986 on personnel policies, furthermore, shaped the thinking about a common approach, while respecting the individual characteristics of the participating organizations (Goossen 1990).

While these systemwide changes had some impact on the UN Secretariat, they did not resolve its problems. In 1985, the General Assembly created an advisory "Group of 18," composed of high-level intergovernmental experts called upon to reform the UN's structure. This occurred at a time of severe financial constraints. The UN faced major unpaid balances, exacerbated by US withholdings linked to legislation seeking weighted voting on budgetary questions in the UN.[22] A recruitment freeze played havoc with the ability of the Organization to deliver key program elements, and staffing patterns were severely disrupted as the freeze continued for several years. The "Group of 18" recommended 15 percent staff cuts across the board, with additional cuts at senior levels. Pension benefits were reduced, and cost of living adjustments were frozen, further reducing the purchasing power of salaries, which had themselves been frozen since 1975. Promotions were deferred. In this climate, "reform" became a synonym for "cost cutting," and concerns about career structures or the development of a learning culture were subjugated to a relentless quest for savings. Staff representatives were highly critical of these developments, and suspended their participation in most consultative mechanisms in which staff welfare matters are discussed.

During all of these years—before and during the financial crisis—the General Assembly time and again expressed its disappointment about the state of human resources management in the Secretariat, and the Secretary-General, year after year, submitted ambitious plans for systemic reforms—but they never materialized. In 1976, the General Assembly, "concerned about the slow pace of the implementation of those reforms [i.e., the JIU proposals]," invited the Secretary-General "to accelerate the implementation of the above-mentioned reforms."[23] In 1977, the Assembly urged the Secretary-General to intensify his efforts for the effective implementation of its previous resolutions on personnel reform, and requested detailed information on staff demographics as well as on recruiting missions, including "publicity, groups contacted, meetings held, the number interviewed by age and sex, the number of candidates added to the roster, and the number of candidates appointed, and thereafter to report on this matter annually."[24] Needless to say, given the rapid turnover of diplomats in the Fifth Committee, these data were produced only once.

In 1980, the General Assembly expressed its concern "about the limited progress achieved in the establishment of a coherent personnel policy," and stressed the need to improve geographical distribution and to increase the representation of developing countries in senior and policy-making post. It then set out the most detailed recruitment procedures ever devised by any governing body: a convoluted scheme whereby vacancies were to be grouped by those "for which it is reasonable to expect several vacancies each year," and those "for which recruitment will be open only at widely spaced intervals." On the basis of this distinction, work plans would be developed for the recruitment process, and a program of competitive exams was introduced for levels P-1 and P-2, later to be extended to level P-3.[25] Movement of General Service staff to these entry-level posts was limited to 30 percent of the available vacancies, and "a given number of vacancies should be defined and offered to each [underrepresented] country in advance." Examinations were to be conducted on a national basis, in consultation with the government concerned (an idea first proposed by inspector Bertrand of the Joint Inspection Unit).[26]

The impact of this decision can be felt up to this day, and its unintended consequences continue to hamper the Organization's recruitment efforts. While there is merit in the concept of competitive examinations, and while the Charter emphasizes geographical diversity, the combination of these two mandates into one program has created some odd anomalies. The General Assembly, in insisting on examinations on a national basis, created a situation whereby the UN Administration conducts competitive exams only in countries that are underrepresented in the Secretariat. This means that young people from countries within range, such as the United States, have no access to entry-level "core" posts.

In 1999, for example, examinations were held in 19 countries (Albania, Bahrain, Belize, Brunei, Comoros, Germany, Indonesia, Italy, Japan, Kazakhstan, Mozambique, Norway, Samoa, São Tomé and Principe, Saudi Arabia, Slovenia, Tajikistan, United Arab Emirates, and Vanauatu). This massive effort led to 60 placements.[27] It follows that young people from 160 other countries were blocked from competing for P-1 to P-3 posts that year. Nationals of the selected countries who could not make it to their capitals or to a major UN Headquarters office could not sit for the exam. Nationals of designated countries who will graduate a year after the competition may have to wait several years before the caravan passes by again. Promising young people who graduated a few years earlier may have found other work or left the country, thus also reducing the eligible pool. Thus the competitive exams in fact diminish the UN's access to good candidates, and they frustrate numerous young people whose countries happen to be in range—nationals from these countries enter only at P-4 and above.

Around the same time, the UN Secretariat abandoned the practice of an annual promotion review, and adopted a "vacancy management" process, whereby all posts are advertised, staff as well as external candidates compete (with preference still given to staff), and the candidate selected automatically gets the grade of the post. Seniority requirements to be eligible for selection at a higher level, however, remained intact.

Two years later, the General Assembly stressed, among other concerns, the importance of having the largest possible number of Member States represented at the higher levels of the Secretariat, and welcomed the Secretary-General's intention to develop medium-term plans for recruitment and career development.[28] These plans never materialized, and in 1984 the General Assembly, in what had become something of a ritual, deplored "the lack of progress toward meeting the goals and objectives established" with respect to recruitment and career development, especially for women.[29]

By 1986, a medium-term recruitment plan had been completed, but since a recruitment freeze had gone into effect a year earlier, this had little practical effect. Under the circumstances, the General Assembly could only ask the Secretary-General to explore alternatives to the recruitment freeze—not a promising undertaking. At the same time, the Assembly maintained its special concern for equitable geographical distribution at the highest levels, particularly for Under-Secretaries-General and Assistant Secretaries-General. The problems facing staff, such as the salary cuts and the drastic reduction in posts, were ignored in that year's resolutions.[30] The fact that a relatively large number of posts was cut at the most senior levels caused the General Assembly in 1987 to deplore "the negative effect" on geographical distribution, and in 1988, another resolution was passed that focused exclusively on geographical distribution at the top.[31]

This obsession with geographical distribution—to the detriment of all other aspects of personnel policy—continued to characterize the considerations of the General Assembly at the beginning of the next decade as well. As the Soviet Union fell apart, a new problem emerged: what to do with the Soviet nationals who happened to be on secondment to the Secretariat when the game of musical chairs came to a sudden halt. For 50 years, the Soviet Union had selected and placed its own candidates, who were rotated regularly, and kept on a very short leash (with salaries confiscated by the Soviets and mandatory housing in Soviet compounds.) Now these staff members clamored for regular appointments, while the new post-Soviet regimes hoped to fill their allotment of posts with their own protégés. The Administrative Tribunal ruled in favor of the incumbents, notwithstanding the General Assembly's protestations. Thus, many former Soviet Union "apparatchniks" found a safe haven in the UN's career service while their empire crumbled. This left the Secretariat, at the end of the Cold War, with a legacy of political wounds created by relentless jockeying for posts by players exerting patronage, by staff cuts and reductions in terms of employment advocated by governments that wanted to gain budgetary control and weighted voting, and by anemic personnel policies and management practices brought about by the benign neglect of a series of weak or unconcerned Secretaries-General.

In Remission: Reforms Revisited, Hope Renewed (1994–2001)

At the 49th session of the General Assembly, in the fall of 1994, the UN Secretariat stepped forward with a full-blown proposal for an integrated human resources management strategy based on the development "of a culture supportive of having staff members contribute to their maximum potential, effectiveness, and efficiency."[32] This included the establishment of a planning unit within the Office of Human Resources Management, the introduction of a goal-oriented performance appraisal system (moving away from the traits-based system used earlier), more flexibility in recruitment procedures, improvements in career counseling and training, and renewed efforts to achieve gender balance and equity. Links were made between the overall strategic plans of the organization, the program budget, and the development of skills profiles. This would coincide with an "enhanced attrition program" (euphemism for voluntary separations induced by financial incentives) and a new emphasis on mobility across the offices of the UN.[33]

In the following years, particular efforts were made to introduce a performance evaluation system that would create direct links between the achievement of individual performance plans and the overall objectives of the Organization.[34] In 1997, the Secretary-General came forward with an ambitious proposal to introduce a system of performance awards or bonuses, reflecting recommendations made earlier by the International Civil Service Commission (ICSC).[35] The debate about reform further deepened as Secretary-General Annan, who once had been Assistant Secretary-General for Human Resources Management, took a personal interest in the development of a comprehensive human resources management program. This led to a broad process of internal and external consultations (including the private sector), culminating in the most far-reaching and comprehensive proposal for change and renewal thus far.[36] As a companion to his personnel reform proposals, the Secretary-General issued a report on accountability and responsibility in the Organization, based on the premise that "giving managers more authority and responsibility for decision-making is essential to the improvement of delivery of programme objectives."[37]

This most recent set of reform proposals for human resources management covers the entire gamut: planning, recruitment, placement, promotion, mobility, contractual arrangements, competencies and continuous learning, performance management, career development, and conditions of service. But it remains to be seen whether these reforms will ever be implemented, and, if they are, whether they will represent an improvement over the previous systems.

The proposals for the streamlining of the recruitment process, to begin with, aim at reducing the overall time to fill a vacancy from 275 to 120 days.[38] This is still an excruciatingly long period by any standard. The General Assembly's decision that all external vacancies must be posted for 60 days contributes to the length of this process—as if the age of information technology and rapid data flow had completely escaped it. While in principle managers now have the decisive say on selection, their discretion is tempered by the oversight of a review body that is supposed to ensure gender equity and geographical balance, and a recourse process involving the Department of Management. Across the street, the UN Office of Project Services, a self-financing entity with performance standards linked to the private sector, is able to hire professional staff members within 10 days (Tesner 2000: 135). The dazzling complexity of the recruitment process, both before and after reform, is best understood from the comparative charts prepared by the UN's Advisory Committee on Administrative and Budgetary questions, which are reproduced here as figures 4.1 and 4.2.

The UN's capacity to develop a credible human resources planning function is equally doubtful. It has been struggling with this challenge for over 30 years, and, according to the Office of Internal Oversight, most of

FIGURE 4.1 The Current Recruitment and Placement Process *(taking on average 275 days)*

Pre-recruitment

Recruitment process

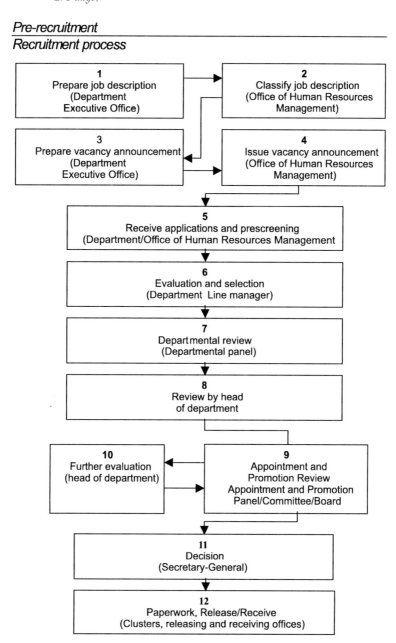

Source: A/55/499, Annex III: 10.

FIGURE 4.2 The Proposed, Accelerated, and Simplified Recruitment and Placement Process *(which can be completed in as "little" as 120 days)*

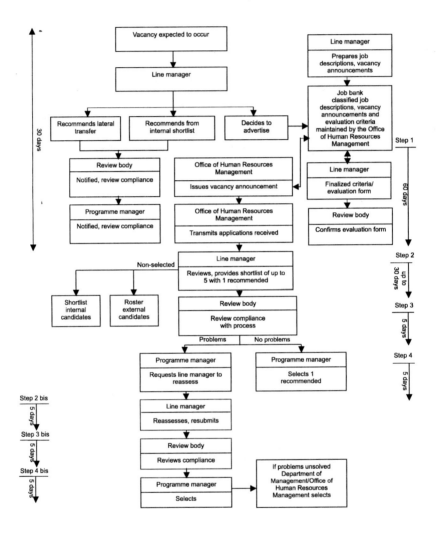

Source: A/55/499 Annex III: 11.

the Human Resources Planning and Management Information Systems Service's resources "are committed to IMIS [integrated management information system] support activities, such as data cleansing and statistics production, and file maintenance, rather than to planning. Only two temporary junior professional staff are assigned to the planning function, which mainly involves preparing materials for departmental human resources planning meetings."[39]

When it comes to promotions, mobility, and placement, two conflicting approaches clash. Since the mid-1980s, the UN has moved toward a system of "vacancy management," whereby each post would be advertised, the selection would be done on a basis of open competition (more often than not including external candidates), and appointments would be made at the grade level of the post. Thus, a promotion required the identification and successful acquisition of a higher level post. No active placement on the part of the UN's Administration was needed, as the competitive process was self-guiding. Staff either remained where they were and saw their careers stagnate, or they ventured into the internal job market. Often, the best opportunities existed in the field, and thus the choice became stagnation or mobility.

Under the latest round of reforms, this faith in the markets has been replaced by faith in central planning. Rosters of qualified candidates are created as an alternative to vacancy announcements, allowing managers to pick directly from a prescreened set of candidates, and a mobility policy has been announced that signifies "movement from a voluntary to a managed approach."[40] Post occupancy will be time limited, lateral moves are required before upward moves toward a promotion are permitted, and junior professional staff will be assigned to posts across the entire range of UN offices on a rotating basis.[41]

These reform proposals include a drastic and much-needed simplification of the current broad array of contractual instruments. The so-called "permanent" contract will be abolished, and only three types of contracts will remain: (1) short-term, up to six months; (2) fixed-term, with extensions of up to a maximum total of five years; and (3) continuing, open-ended contracts whereby service continues as long as organizational requirements are met, and performance is satisfactory. This in itself is eminently sensible, but at the same time it hints at a further erosion of the career service model that was at the base of the UN's early staffing models.

At the end of a lengthy and costly consultative process, supported by external consultants, the UN has arrived at a competency model that includes three core values, eight core competencies, and six managerial competencies, as follows:

1. Core values: integrity, professionalism and respect for diversity;
2. Core competencies: communication, teamwork, planning and organizing, accountability, creativity, client orientation, commitment to continuous learning, and technological awareness;
3. Managerial competencies: leadership, vision, empowering others, building trust, managing performance, and judgment/decision-making.[42]

Here, notwithstanding the consultants' guidance, the UN has fallen into a classical trap—confusing traits, values, and competencies. These competencies are meant to be applied to the areas of recruitment, staff development, career support, and performance management. But most of these so-called competencies are traits or skills, rather than competencies proper, which are defined as "a cluster of related knowledge, attitudes and skills that affects a major part of one's job, *that correlates with performance on the job, that can be measured against well-accepted standards, and that can be improved via training and development*" (Parry 1998; emphasis added). Integrity and respect for diversity are impossible to measure, and usually only become manifest by default (and rarely in interviews). Creativity and commitment are equally nebulous. Professionalism is in the eye of the beholder and cannot be imparted in a training course. Vision and leadership are elusive and come in many shapes and colors. It is hard to imagine how these "feel good" concepts can contribute to better human resources management and create "a culture of continuous learning in the Organization."[43]

Particularly complex is the issue of reforms in conditions of service. Here the Secretary-General has little leeway, as these are common to all organizations of the UN common system, and are subject to the regulatory powers of the International Civil Service Commission and the General Assembly. The reform proposals call for "a competitive compensation package that is able to attract and retain high-quality staff and a good working environment."[44] It is hard to see how a compensation package can attract a good working environment, but apart from its editorial infelicities, the proposal has little to offer beyond a pious genuflection in the direction of the staff. The political climate in the General Assembly has been hostile to any fundamental improvements in the compensation package of UN staff for the past three decades. In relative terms, service in the field and frequent reassignments are recognized more fairly in financial terms, thanks to strong advocacy on the part of the ICSC, but the overall compensation package has deteriorated over time.

As the purchasing power of the comparator civil service, the US government, slowly eroded over the years (ever since President Jimmy Carter decided to reject the recommendations of the independent "Pay Agent," who was to advise on ways to keep the US civil service competitive with the private sector), the standard of living of UN staff has slowly declined as well. The ICSC's efforts to remedy this situation hit a brick wall in the General Assembly, and now the ICSC has basically given up. Meanwhile, some Member States, such as Germany and Japan, subsidize their nationals, in violation of the UN Charter, and the ICSC has failed to take action against them. While the US has taken recourse to so-called "occupational rates" for some fields of work in which it is hard to compete with the private sector, the UN has not done so, relying instead on staff from lower-income countries when the required skills are hard to get.

One area where reforms would not be amiss, but that does not figure into the Secretary-General's reform package, is social security—in particular, the pension system. The system is designed to benefit the "survivors."

Staff who leave before the designated retirement age are penalized, and staff who serve for only a few years subsidize the ones who manage to stay in the system. The entire system, moreover, has been caught up in a series of benefit cuts and rate increases to maintain the actuarial balance of the Fund. Originally, staff accrued an entitlement of 2 percent of their final pay for every year of service. So in principle, 30 years of service would lead to a pension equivalent to some 60 percent of one's most recent salary (averaged out on the last three years). The General Assembly adjusted this benefit downward in the 1980s by lowering the rate of accrual during the first 10 years of service, bringing it down to 1.5 percent for the first five years, then 1.75 percent for the next five years. Now 30 years of service render only 56.25 percent of final remuneration.

Originally, also, staff members who left their UN organization in mid-career and who had five or more years of service could take a deferred retirement benefit whereby they would receive the actuarial value of their pension fund assets at the age of 60, with adjustments for inflation for the period between their departure and the beginning of their entitlement. This feature was also amended so that this benefit is no longer indexed, except for staff aged 55 or over. Thus, a deferred benefit of $10,000 accrued in 1990 will be paid out in 2010 as $10,000—and by that time, it will have lost half of its original purchasing power, if not more. Staff members who leave in midcareer now do better by taking their own contribution out (7.9 percent of pensionable pay). The pension contribution paid out by the employing agency (15.80 percent) is split: half goes back to the employer, and the Fund keeps the other half—thus subsidizing the pension of the "survivors." All in all, this is a powerful disincentive for people to join the UN as part of a career that leads across various sectors. The UN has reciprocal arrangements with only a handful of national governments, and there is no possibility to move the UN pension benefits into a portable instrument such as a US Individual Retirement Account (IRA).

The Fund also places special hurdles in front of staff members who want to retire early, that is, at age 55 or above, but before the mandatory retirement age (60 for the UN and 62 for some specialized agencies and for project personnel). Benefits are reduced by 6 percent for every year that they fall short of the normal retirement age, but again the long-term players have an edge: after 25 years of service, the deduction is only 2 percent (for service before 1985) or 3 percent (pro rata for the years after 1985), and staff with 30 years of service who retire early get a 1 percent deduction.

All this shows how the Fund is structured to benefit career staff who have put in 25 years or more, and who retire at the mandatory age. Staff who have served less than five years or who leave in midcareer are left out in the cold. They get their own money back, but the 15.80 percent paid in by the employer (and intended to benefit the staff member) reverts to the Organization and is split with the Fund.

The Legacy of Reform: Unresolved Dilemmas and Self-Inflicted Wounds

Thus, after all these years, the United Nations is still struggling to adjust its human resources policies and practices to the reality that surrounds it. At the beginning of this chapter, we noted how the profile of the typical international civil servant has changed over the years. To function effectively, the UN must be able to attract and retain people with a prominent professional track record, recruit them swiftly while they are still interested and available, compete with the private sector for their skills, give them control over the resources for which they are accountable, create an environment that favors learning and welcomes an honest mistake, give them opportunities to compete for advancement, and, in so doing, demonstrate that the Charter's insistence on staff of the highest caliber is no hollow phrase.

This is no time to stand by idly. In the area of development, the Bretton Woods institutions threaten to marginalize the UN system. In the area of global trade, the WTO overshadows UNCTAD. In peacekeeping and peace building, large regional organizations such as NATO move in when their interests are at stake (as in the Balkans) and play dead when there is nothing to be gained (as in Rwanda). In the delivery of humanitarian assistance, NGOs and bilateral agencies are becoming the agents of choice (as became manifest in Kosovo). In this highly competitive environment, the UN will have to reform its reforms, or go down reforming.

Several dilemmas that have crippled the UN for generations, however, remain unresolved, and this organizational pathology stands in the way of the UN's efforts to remain meaningful as the competition mounts. When it comes to managing human resources, the following are the obstacles that the UN must overcome:

- its addiction to the trappings of a careers-for-life staffing model, with its emphasis on seniority, managed careers, and slow accrual of material benefits such as pensions;
- its adherence to a compensation system that uses a poorly paid national government, that of the United States, as its sole comparator—ignoring its competitors;
- its affection for a "winner-takes-all" pension system that penalizes all but the hardy lifers by depreciating accrued benefits for early leavers;
- its fear of offending Member States that exert political pressure—by not insisting on merit in staffing, even at the highest levels;
- its reliance on patronage as a survival strategy, especially where outputs are nebulous;
- its obsession with central control mechanisms, at the expense of individual initiative and efficiency;

- its tolerance of an audit culture that looks for crooks instead of heroes;
- its tacit understanding that equitable geographical distribution is defined by the financial clout of wealthy donors, rather than the intellectual acumen of individual candidates;
- the persistent gap between its perennial promises to improve human resources management and its capacity to deliver; and
- its obsession with cosmetic reforms, hiding the root causes of dysfunctionality.

For most pathologies, there is a cure. For the UN, faith healing will not suffice. Surgery may be called for. The decision to take up the scalpel, however, can only come from Member States. They have allowed most of the symptoms to fester, and they alone have the power to reverse decades of poor governance at the UN.

Notes

1. A/55/427, para. 13.
2. Annex II to GA Resolution 54/249.
3. A/55/427, para. 48.
4. While the UN Funds and Programmes do not release data on staffing patterns under extrabudgetary activities, a comparable report about WHO, in the 1 February 2000 issue of *UN Special*, indicates that 30 percent of the workforce is on contracts of three months, and 75 percent of this group has been working at WHO for over a year on these terms (communication to author dated 24 March 2001 from Jon Ebersole, WHO Geneva).
5. Ibid., Section 2, A, para. 7.
6. Ibid., Section 2, D, para. 54.
7. GA Resolution 153 (III) of 15 November 1947.
8. International Civil Service Advisory Board, *Report on Standards of Conduct in the International Civil Service*, COORD/CIVIL SERVICE/1986 EDITION, Section II, para. 15.
9. Financial Regulations and Rules of the United Nations, ST/GB/Financial Rules/1/Rev.3 (1985), Article X.
10. Quoted in UN Administrative Tribunal Judgement No. 744.
11. Ibid.
12. JDC report, para. 47, cited in AT Judgement No. 744.
13. AT Judgement No. 744, Section XXI.
14. AT Judgement No. 744, Section XXIII.
15. GA resolution 29/24.
16. JIU/REP/76/8, annexed to A/31/264 of 13 October 1976.
17. A/C.5/31/9.
18. *Report of the Joint Inspection Unit on Personnel Problems in the U.N.*, A/8454, 5 October 1971.
19. JIU/REP/76/8, para. 7.
20. Ibid., para. 16.
21. Doc. A/C/.5/34/SR.33, 13 November 1979, p. 3.
22. For a detailed discussion of UN reforms, see Beigbeder (1990). Some of the underlying issues are further examined in Beigbeder (1997).
23. GA Resolution 31/27, 29 November 1976.
24. GA Resolution 32/17, 11 November 1977.

25. GA Resolution 40/258, 18 December 1983.
26. GA Resolution 35/211, 17 December 1980.
27. A/55/427, para. 27.
28. GA Resolution 37/235, 21 December 1982.
29. GA Resolution 39/245, 18 December 1984.
30. GA Resolution 41/206, 11 December 1986.
31. GA Resolution 42/220, 21 December 1987; Resolution 43/224, 21 December 1988.
32. A/C.5/49/5, para. 5.
33. GA Resolution 49/222, 18 December 1994.
34. A/C.5/51/55.
35. A/52/30, chap. VI, sect. B.; A/51/950.
36. A/55/253.
37. A/55/270, Summary.
38. A/55/253, annex II, para. 5. The estimate of 275 days as the current timeline is contested as being too low.
39. A/55/397, para. 25.
40. A/55.253, para. 40.
41. A/55/253, Sections C and D; annex III.
42. A/55/253, para. 58.
43. A/55/253, para. 59.
44. A/55/253, para. 71.

Bibliography

Beigbeder, Y. "Administrative and Structural Reform in the Organisations of the UN Family." In Chris de Cooker, ed., *International Administration*. Dordrecht: Martinus Nijhoff Publishers, 1990.

Beigbeder, Y. *The Internal Management of United Nations Organizations: The Long Quest for Reform*. New York: St. Martin's Press, 1997.

Finger, S.M. "The Politics of Staffing the United Nations Secretariat. *ORBIS* (Spring 1975).

Finger, S.M., and Hanan, N. "The United Nations Secretariat Revisited." *ORBIS* (Spring 1981).

Goossen, D.J. "The International Civil Service Commission." In Chris De Cooker, ed., *International Administration*. Dordrecht: Martinus Nijhoff Publishers, 1990.

Jordan, R.S. "What Has Happened to Our International Civil Service? The Case of the United Nations." *Public Administration Review* (March/April 1981): 236–245.

James, R.R. *Staffing in the U.N. Secretariat*. Sussex: Institute for the Study of International Organizations, 1970.

Kristinsson, G.H. "Parties, States and Patronage." *West European Politics* (July 1996): 433–458.

Langrod, G. *The International Civil Service*. Leiden: A.W. Sijthoff, 1968.

Parry, S.B. "Just What Is a Competency?" *Training* (June 1998).

Suhrke, A., Barutciski, M., Sandison, P., and Garlock, R. *The Kosovo Refugee Crisis: An Independent Evaluation of UNHCR's Emergency Preparedness and Response*. Geneva: UNHCR Evaluation and Policy Analysis Unit, 2000 (EPAU/2000/001).

Tesner, S. *The United Nations and Business*. New York: St. Martin's Press, 2000.

PUBLIC DOCUMENTS, LEAGUE OF NATIONS
Secretariat of the League of Nations. *Staff Regulations*. Geneva, 1946.

PUBLIC DOCUMENTS, UNITED NATIONS

Preparatory Commission of the United Nations. *Report of the Preparatory Commission of the United Nations.* New York: 1945.

Joint Inspection Unit. *Report of the Joint Inspection Unit on Personnel Problems in the U.N.* A/8454, 1971.

Joint Inspection Unit. *Report of the Joint Inspection Unit on the Implementation of the Personnel Policy Reforms Approved by the General Assembly in 1974 (JIU/REP/76/8).* A/31/264, 1976.

Financial Regulations and Rules of the United Nations. ST/GB/Financial Rules/1/ Rev.3, 1985.

International Civil Service Advisory Board. *Report on Standards of Conduct in the International Civil Service.* COORD/CIVIL SERVICE/1986 EDITION. New York: 1986.

United Nations. *A Strategy for the Management of the Human Resources of the Organization: Report of the Secretary-General.* A/C.5/49/5, 1994.

United Nations. *Regulations, Rules and Pension Adjustment System of the United Nations Joint Staff Pension Fund.* JSPB/G.4/Rev.15, 1998.

United Nations. *Human Resources Management Reform: Report of the Secretary-General.* General Assembly A/55/253, 2000.

United Nations. *Accountability and Responsibility: Report of the Secretary-General.* A/55/ 270, 2000.

United Nations. *Follow-Up Audit of the Recruitment Process in the Office of Human Resources Management: Note by the Secretary-General.* A/55/397, 2000.

United Nations. *Composition of the Secretariat: Report of the Secretary-General.* A/55/427, 2000.

United Nations. *Human Resources Management Reform, Accountability and Responsibility, Personnel Practices and Policies and Management Irregularities: Report of the Advisory Committee on Administrative and Budgetary Questions.* A/55/499, 2000.

— *Chapter 5* —

THE TRANSFORMATION OF INTERNATIONAL PUBLIC ORGANIZATIONS
The Case of UNCTAD

Matthias Finger and Bérangère Magarinos-Ruchat

Introduction

The goal of this chapter is to understand better and ultimately facilitate the transformation process of international and intergovernmental organizations. Evolving in a constantly changing environment, such organizations have to adapt in order to remain legitimate and relevant in the global governance system. Consequently, this chapter emphasizes the specificities of the transformation of international and intergovernmental organizations, the obstacles and the nature of their transformation, as well as the newly emerging power relationships and actors. Organizational pathologies particularly reveal themselves in situations of transformation and change. As such, this empirical study of the United Nations Conference in Trade and Development's (UNCTAD) transformation offers a concrete opportunity to crystallize the problems faced by international public organizations in today's changing environment.

The focus of this chapter is thus on the transformation of international public organizations in light of their currently evolving environment. There exists already some literature on the pathologies of international organizations from a static perspective (e.g., Barnett and Finnemore 1999). Building on this literature, we see intergovernmental organizations as being relatively autonomous and purposive entities. Thus, they are not simply instruments through which states act. They are also agents pursuing their own strategies. Such organizational autonomy warrants the study of international organizations and their transformation in their own right.[1] As a result, we consider international public organizations as being a particularly challenging object of study, as they are not only part of a complex system of intergovernmental governance, but also, and above all, independent structures with their own histories and cultures.

The research underlying this chapter follows, consequently, an internal approach toward the organization in order to understand better its staff, history, symbols, culture, and especially the problems related to its transformation. For over a year, we have conducted a case study on UNCTAD based in Geneva.[2] We found UNCTAD to be a particularly relevant case, as UNCTAD is a highly complex organization, being simultaneously active in policy advice as a result of its analytical work; in consensus building, especially between the North and the South, but also among developing countries; and in technical cooperation. As such, UNCTAD as an organization is quite similar to a university. During the last 10 years, many observers have said that UNCTAD was no longer useful and relevant, putting particular pressure on UNCTAD. Moreover, the United States, along with some other governments, wanted the organization to be shut down. However, as will be shown below, since 1996 UNCTAD has been "reinventing" itself and is finding a new role in the system of global governance as it essentially helps developing countries to better integrate and take advantage of the WTO's negotiations.

This chapter is thus divided into four main sections. In the first section, an organizational transformation model will be presented. This is a model we have developed in order to analyze the transformation processes of public organizations at the national level. It will structure the analysis of UNCTAD and its pathologies that follows. In the second and third sections, we will describe our case study, that is, the origins and earlier evolution of UNCTAD, as well as its recent transformations. In the last section, we will analyze the UNCTAD case against the background of the transformation model and, by doing so, highlight particular pathologies of international organizations.

Conceptual Background: A Transformation Model of Public Organizations

The purpose of this first section is to present a transformation model of public sector organizations, which we have developed inductively from studying and working with public organizations at the national level, especially public enterprises and other semiautonomous public entities. More precisely, these are public organizations that have undergone a process of commercialization of some of their services, of corporatization, and, in some cases, even of privatization (e.g., Finger and Ruchat 1997; Finger and Bürgin 1999). In this section, the overall transformation model—its origins as well as its intellectual roots—will be presented, and then some of the key dimensions of the model will be discussed in more detail.

Overall Transformation Model

The transformation presented here is the inductive result of our empirical research on public enterprises, which have been, or still are, undergoing profound transformations, changing from public administrations into businesses thriving in an international and competitive market. Grounded in participatory action research with the Swiss Postal Service (Finger and Rey 1994), the model has been empirically tested with five other public enterprises in the aviation, the audiovisual, the telecommunications, the railway, and the electricity sectors (Finger et al. 1997). The model stresses the fact that there are several interrelated dimensions to this organizational transformation process and that this transformation takes place over time and in different stages. While it is important to stress that such organizational transformation is a process, its exact duration, however, can vary from two to eight years or even more, depending on the size of the organization, the degree of pressure, and the complexity of its relationships with the environment.

Intellectually, our approach is basically rooted in organizational sociology; an approach that stresses the complex interplay between actors and their strategies on the one hand, and institutional norms and rules on the other (e.g., Clegg 1989; Crozier 1963; Crozier and Friedberg 1977; Etzioni 1964; Mintzberg 1983). There exist, indeed, many organizational change models, developed mainly by management professors and consultants (e.g., Adizes 1988; Gouillart and Kelly 1995; Kottler 1996; Miles 1997). However, as they all generally refer to private sector organizations, the two main problems of these models are (1) that they are basically interventionist and not transformational in nature, and (2) that they tend to ignore power and power relationships, which are particularly prevalent in public organizations (Mercier et al. 2000). New public management literature also addresses some of these aspects of organizational change and transformation (e.g., Pollitt 1993). Yet, again, most of this literature is weak on transformation processes and contains recipes mainly for financial and other efficiencies, or for various sorts of managerialism, including managerial leadership.

We thus see organizational transformation as the result of a complex interaction between internal dynamics and external pressures. Such pressures generally stem from the various stakeholders, the customers, and/or the owner(s). The goal of such organizational transformation is to bring organizational structure, culture, and purpose in line with perceived environmental requirements. Such transformation can therefore be either adaptive or anticipatory, as it can be either incremental or systemic. The proposed model, however, does not conceptualize the transformation of the stakeholders or the changes in environment. Nevertheless, it does take into account the changes in the relationship between the organization and its key environmental actors. Graphically, this model can be summarized as illustrated in figure 5.1.

FIGURE 5.1 The Organizational Transformation Model

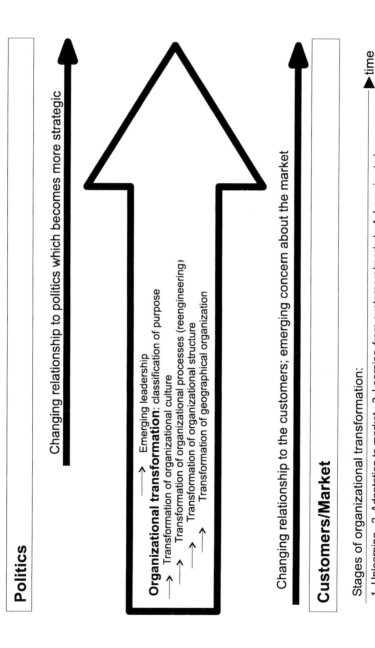

Politics

Changing relationship to politics which becomes more strategic

→ Emerging leadership
Organizational transformation: classification of purpose
→ Transformation of organizational culture
→ Transformation of organizational processes (reengineering)
→ Transformation of organizational structure
→ Transformation of geographical organization

Changing relationship to the customers; emerging concern about the market

Customers/Market

Stages of organizational transformation:

1. Unlearning 2. Adaptation to market 3. Learning from customers/market 4. Learning to learn

▲ time

Key Dimensions of the Model

In essence, this model describes how a public organization transforms from a basically bureaucratic one (a monopoly) into an organization concerned with efficiency, transparency, and competitiveness, that is, an entrepreneurial organization in the sociological sense of the word, not necessarily in the economic sense. Indeed, for many public organizations, the "market" will always remain an artificial construct, rather than an economic reality. Nevertheless, this transformation does affect the very purpose and identity of a public organization. If the original, overall purpose of such organizations can be summarized by the relatively vague term "public service provision"—actually, a combination of multiple and often conflicting objectives, many of them self-assigned—the transformation process generally also leads to a clarification of purpose and of services rendered to the public. Such a clarification occurs along with cultural change, structural transformation, and more efficient processes, as well as a more transparent relationship with the citizens who turn into customers, and a more contractual relationship with politics. More concretely, during this transformation process, the organization changes its culture from a bureaucratic to a more "entrepreneurial" one. It also rearranges its processes along customer demands and production processes, and transforms its structure from a functional one to one that is more suitable to its changing processes. Moreover, during this process a more coherent (corporate) identity emerges, along with a growing sensitivity to better communication and marketing. Some strategic thinking, or at least the need for it, also emerges as the transformation unfolds. Indeed, in the beginning, strategy is seen as being a political prerogative, whereas at the end of the process, the transformed organization will have a strategy of its own. Generally, this process is driven by a leader, who gradually reveals him- or herself as the process unfolds.

All of these organizational changes correspond to a changing relationship with the customer, who is increasingly taken into account, in terms of both customer feedback and customer demands. This changing relationship with the customer can also lead to some geographical reorganization. At some point later in the organizational transformation process, the relationship with politics changes as well; the organization will increasingly feel the need to make this relationship more transparent, while putting it onto a more contractual basis. Indeed, mainly for purposes of internal management, the organization will increasingly seek to clearly define what politics wants from it and what the organization can deliver. This changing relationship might go so far as to propose new organizational governance structures, or even to suggest changes in the legal framework that governs and legitimizes the organization. Overall, this transformation process takes place in four distinct stages, which can be different in length, but which must occur in this sequence. We have conceptualized these changes in cultural terms, meaning that, in a first step, the organization has to unlearn its old habits; in a second step, it has to turn outward and adapt to the new (more commercial environment); in a third step, it has to start learning from its customers; and, finally, it has to become a self-learning organization.

This transformation process reveals numerous pathologies, that are further highlighted by the transformation model, along cultural, structural, process, political, and transformational dimensions. For example, note the paradox between a strong culture and a weak identity, between a hierarchical and authoritarian structure and significant freedom of behavior inside the organization, between precise rules and multiple norms and fuzzy and incoherent processes, between strong strategizing vis-à-vis politics and the refusal to take any political responsibility, between a powerful discourse on public service and the absence of any clear definition of such service, and, finally, between elaborate planning and the inability to learn.

The next two sections describe UNCTAD's transformation process based on the above model, distinguishing, in particular, between a first phase leading up to the Midrand Conference, and a second phase since then.

UNCTAD and Its Evolution from Geneva to Midrand (1964–1996)

This section presents a long-term perspective of UNCTAD's evolution from its creation in 1964 to the 1996 Midrand conference. Such a historical perspective is necessary in order to understand the nature of the transformation process. As noted in the conceptual framework, a transformation model has a time dimension—it is not a one-shot exercise. Moreover, the transformation is deeply influenced by the historical heritage of the organization. In this particular case, important parts of the staff have worked with UNCTAD for more than 20 years. They are carrying with them a lively institutional memory, which strongly influences UNCTAD's capacity or willingness to transform. Indeed, in order to understand the culture, the obstacles to change, and the complex debate about UNCTAD's future work, it is necessary to understand where the organization comes from. In this respect, one cannot limit oneself to the description of the organizational changes, since in the specific case of UNCTAD, the changes in the organization's ideology are closely related to the organizational changes. Let us describe the organization's history in three parts: first, the motivation for its creation; second, the sequence of its first nine conferences; and, third, the content of the organizational issues, including the Secretariat's analytical work and technical assistance programs.

Origin and Mandate

UNCTAD was created as an organ of the UN General Assembly in 1964. With the emergence and increased participation of a large number of developing countries as members of the United Nations, there was a growing focus within the UN on development problems. The important factor that sparked these efforts was the progressively deteriorating position of developing countries in world trade in the 1950s and early 1960s. It was at this point in time that Raul Prebisch's[3] analysis of the center-periphery relationships, the commodity problems, and the unequal terms of trade of developing countries in the context of economic development focused attention on the inherent defects of the international economy and of the trading system (UNCTAD 1985). Indeed, at its creation, UNCTAD's goal was to transform the rules of the game of the international system of trade. More precisely, its mission was to ensure equity among developed and developing countries so that every country could benefit from economic development, technological progress, and investments.

To recall, UNCTAD emerged in an environment in which the General Agreement on Tariffs and Trade (GATT) and other agencies dealing with international trade were considered inadequate to meet the development needs of the developing countries. In that respect, UNCTAD became the "voice of the South," the "consciousness" of international development. In the final act of its first conference, which took place in Geneva in 1964, UNCTAD received the following mandate: "To seek a better and more effective system of international economic co-operation ... and lay the foundations of a better world economic order." UNCTAD's principal functions were thus described as follows:[4]

- to promote international trade;
- to formulate principles and policies on international trade;
- to review and facilitate the coordination of activities of other institutions within the UN system in the field of international trade;
- to initiate action, where appropriate, in cooperation with the competent organs of the UN; and
- to be available as a center for harmonizing the trade and related development policies of governments and regional economic groupings.

The description of these original UNCTAD functions shows the complexity of the organization, which is active in three different yet interrelated areas: research and analysis, technical cooperation, and consensus building. The concrete agenda and mandates in these three areas are elaborated by the UNCTAD Secretariat to the intergovernmental machinery. After negotiations on the substance of UNCTAD's work plan, the Secretariat then executes the analytical work and technical assistance projects. The intergovernmental machinery, in turn, takes the form of the Trade and Development Board (TDB), composed of 188 Member States; various commissions on specific issues; and various experts groups. The TDB gives its mandate to UNCTAD every four years during an intergovernmental conference.

Functioning and Impact of the Intergovernmental Machinery

Since its inception in 1964, the UNCTAD intergovernmental machinery has grown to impressive dimensions. Indeed, setting up experts groups, session committees, and ad hoc intergovernmental working groups over time represented a complex process of negotiation. But the critique of this machinery actually stems from the very beginning of UNCTAD, when it was said not to be satisfactory for either developed or developing countries. Early on, an UNCTAD document noted: "It is conventional wisdom either to put these Conferences down as failures in terms of the results attained or to fault them for raising undue and unrealistic hopes and expectations" (UNCTAD 1985: 26). Yet one can say that these periodic conferences should be seen not as isolated events but rather as important stages in the ongoing process of dialogue and negotiation on trade and development.

Roughly, one can consider that the first five conferences were organized around very similar ideas, which unfolded in an environment particularly conducive for North-South debate. The 1970s were, without any doubt, the "golden years" of UNCTAD. Thanks to the introduction of new negotiation techniques—in particular, negotiations in small groups—developing countries took a critical stand on international trade and were often promised radical changes. A staff member relates that the 1970s were the "period of UNCTAD's institutional fortune," when developing countries took the driver's seat, discussing their problems and bonding together. Indeed, through UNCTAD, and until the mid-1980s, the Third World countries did set the development agenda.

However, most of those conferences essentially ended in a compromise between the positions of industrialized and developing countries. Consequently, results were generally modest because, instead of negotiations aiming at international cooperation, there had been mainly confrontation and political compromise. Indeed, UNCTAD followed an agenda defined around the notions of interdependence,[5] of problems of trade, of development, and of finance. The principal objective was the establishment of a "New International Economic Order," which became UNCTAD's leading ideological tenet. In addition, UNCTAD strongly supported the governments of developing countries in their fight against poverty. However, UNCTAD, at that time, never really questioned the power exercised by those governments. As a result, it suffered from the power bargain over the oil crisis in the 1970s, when developing countries started to block any type of negotiations.

This approach entered into a crisis in the 1980s. The 1983 Belgrade conference had been a deep disappointment with meager results achieved, at least according to the Group of 77.[6] Indeed, the resolutions adopted showed only little progress as compared to the positions agreed upon at earlier UNCTAD sessions. In fact, the United States opposed propositions for a "Generalized System of Preferences" for developing countries and applied strong pressure, condemning UNCTAD for being too ideological.

After Belgrade, UNCTAD was confronted with the emergence of a new engine of development, namely, the private sector—more particularly, the multinational companies. At the seventh UNCTAD conference in Geneva (1987), Secretary-General Dadzie introduced, for the first time in UNCTAD history, the idea that the market could play an important role in development. As a result, the priorities of UNCTAD were redefined, and more resources were allocated to issues of investment and privatization. However, Southern countries resisted this new approach, leading to the fact that the working group on privatization did not produce results until four years later, that is, at the eighth UNCTAD conference in Cartagena. Already back in 1987 in Geneva, the United States had threatened to "kill" UNCTAD, as one observer put it, saying that the survival of UNCTAD was at the price of becoming a global OECD.

UNCTAD VIII in Cartagena in 1992 was an important step in the process of transformation of the organization. Over the previous years, UNCTAD had become more and more involved in technical work, even though this work had remained ideologically solidly anchored in dependency theory. This more technical orientation did not, however, reduce UNCTAD's emerging "identity crisis." Rather, this crisis grew deeper as a result of several factors: the emerging "Washington consensus" (World Bank-IMF), the neoliberal criticism articulated by Thatcher and Reagan, the crisis of multilateralism as a means for action, and the growing concerns regarding the economic and social capacity of the UN. In spite of this difficult context, UNCTAD VIII was considered a relative success, as it opened the door to the ideological and organizational transformation of UNCTAD. In order to overcome the gridlock of the various groups' bargaining positions in the intergovernmental machinery, UNCTAD VIII proposed the notion of a "New Partnership for Development." The goal was to create a partnership among Member States and to engage in a constructive dialogue that should overcome confrontation. In fact, in Cartagena UNCTAD moved from a negotiation forum to a consensus-building forum, constituting one of the major transformations of the organization. UNCTAD staff describes it as the transition from a political to a pragmatic organization. At the same time, UNCTAD lost considerable power, which was transferred to a new trade negotiation forum—the World Trade Organization (WTO). Also, at Cartagena hopes for the future of the organization were still constrained by the continued pressures of the United States and the European Union.

Before the nomination in 1996 of Rubens Ricupero, a former Brazilian finance minister, UNCTAD had remained without a Secretary-General for 14 months, putting it in a very unstable position. Upon his nomination, Ricupero inherited the challenge to re-create UNCTAD's political legitimacy, credibility, and utility. In 1996 in Midrand, South Africa, UNCTAD IX thus marked a complete ideological shift. If Cartagena had announced a transformation of the North-South relations into a more uniform global system, Midrand continued this trend to create a totally new approach to North-South relations. The idea of a "New Partnership for Development," launched in Cartagena, was now given a much more comprehensive meaning. It included partnerships with non-state actors, and particularly with the business sector. This global partnership meant mobilization of resources through dialogue and common action between governments and civil society, along with partnerships between the public and the private sectors.

Moreover, at Midrand UNCTAD updated its approach to development by giving a clear priority to the Least Developed Countries (LDC). Liberalization and globalization were the twin themes of the conference, and UNCTAD entirely abandoned its opposition to the international system and redefined its objectives in the context of globalization. As Ricupero noted in his keynote address to the conference: "UNCTAD must offer practical advice and tangible support to developing countries, carefully calibrated in accordance with their differing stages of development and of integration in the world economy" (Midrand Declaration 1996). Indeed, UNCTAD's new task now is to help developing countries and economies in transition to integrate better and more fully into the international trading and economic system. According to one observer, Midrand followed the agenda of the United States by reducing UNCTAD's mandate on commodities and shipping, and finally killed the "common fund," a fund into which the richest countries paid.

In short, with Midrand, but starting already in Cartagena, a complete ideological shift of UNCTAD took place, moving from dependency theory to emphasizing the need of developing countries to be integrated into the global trading and financial system. In this respect, UNCTAD has been capable of changing the very nature of its policy advice to governments, and of adapting to the transformation of the world economy.

Reforms

UNCTAD has tried to undertake many reforms since the 1970s. Early on, in a resolution adopted in Manila in 1979, governments asked UNCTAD to restructure and rationalize its machinery (UNCTAD 1985: 34). By the end of the 1970s, it had become increasingly evident that what was required was a more extensive and purposeful adaptation of the UNCTAD structure and operating procedures. The growth in numbers and variety of UNCTAD bodies had given rise to several problems, and had exceeded the substantive, technical, and logistical resources of the Secretariat and strained budgets, leading to the proliferation and overlapping of activities within UNCTAD bodies themselves. Propositions for reforms were suggested but had no effect before the mid-1980s. UNCTAD justified its incapacity to reform in twenty years as follow: "To conclude, every UNCTAD mandate has been a major effort in overcoming the resistance of developed countries. These gains could be lost by hasty and ill-considered measures put forward in the name of efficiency and rationalization" (UNCTAD 1985: 37). As a result, it was considered that UNCTAD needed a gradual, step-by-step approach to the restructuring of its organization. In fact, UNCTAD's transformation process always strongly depended upon the capacity of politics to find a consensus on change. In the environment of confrontation between North and South, such a consensus was obviously not possible, as rationalizing UNCTAD implied weakening the position of the governments of developing countries on the international scene.

However, changes in international relations—especially North-South relations—during the 1990s allowed for a transformation process to emerge slowly. Indeed, the 1992 Cartagena conference was the starting point of a spirit of reform, which evolved further in Midrand, and which probably saved UNCTAD from closing down. The Cartagena reform touched upon practically all aspects of the institution, that is, its intergovernmental machinery and working methods, as well as its mandate and program orientations. Among other decisions, the mandate in the area of services was broadened, and new areas of work were introduced, especially in the areas of privatization. The Board decided to introduce new working methods that required streamlining, in particular, due to resource constraints.[7] However, Cartagena still focused only on the transformation process of the governmental meetings; the functioning of the Secretariat was left unaddressed.

As mentioned, at Midrand UNCTAD found itself in a very critical situation. Both the Report on Global Governance (1990) and Maurice Bertrand's (1989) suggestions for UN reform had already introduced the idea of an Economic Security Council, which would have made UNCTAD totally irrelevant. Against this and other pressures facing UNCTAD, fundamental proposals for the transformation of its ideology, its work priorities, and the functioning of its Secretariat were made. As we will show below, the transformation process initiated at Midrand is both radical and difficult. For example, 25 work programs and subprograms were replaced by one program consisting of five subprograms, nine divisions were reduced to four, and the number of intergovernmental bodies was cut in half.[8] Midrand also stressed the need to improve accountability and assessment in the Secretariat. To summarize, Midrand aimed at turning UNCTAD from a critique of the global economy into an instrument of the global economy, in other words, an instrument of global economic governance. The next section shows that since Midrand, UNCTAD has taken on the role of facilitating global trade.

UNCTAD between Midrand and Bangkok (1996–2000): The Dimensions of Change

The second part of this case study focuses on UNCTAD's Secretariat after the resolutions for reforms were endorsed in Midrand. It offers a comprehensive picture of UNCTAD's current transformation process. Through six different aspects, all of which refer to the model presented in the first section of this chapter, this section will discuss the changes UNCTAD is undergoing and the challenges and problems that still remain to be addressed. It thus will present the transformations in UNCTAD's structure, staff, leadership, ideology, partnership strategy, and culture.

The Structure

Upon the initiative of Rubens Ricupero, the overall structure of UNCTAD was considerably simplified at Midrand: four divisions were created, which correspond to UNCTAD's new priority of work and especially to its new role of integrating developing countries into the economic globalization process. In doing so, UNCTAD sees itself as being complementary to the WTO. If the WTO's role is to remove barriers to global trade, UNCTAD's role is then to assist developing countries to participate in and take advantage of global trade. As a result, UNCTAD is now restructured into the following divisions: Globalization and Development Strategies; International Trade; Investment, Technology, and Enterprise Development; Services Infrastructure; and a subdivision dedicated to the coordination of the work done for the Least Developed Landlocked Countries (LDLC) and Island Developing Countries (IDC). Besides these divisions, UNCTAD has also reorganized into three services for administrative support: Executive Direction and Management Services (including external relations), Administrative Services, and Intergovernmental Support Services.

Implementing the new structure after Midrand, the UNCTAD Secretariat identified several complex problems related to this restructuring exercise.[9] Among these, the question of the redeployment of staff and of the competencies available to address the new challenges before UNCTAD is a major concern, which will be discussed below. The most difficult issue, according to the efficiency review team, is the capacity of the new divisions to create coordination mechanisms among themselves. The question is how to reconcile the need to decentralize, to delegate, and to empower program managers, while at the same time ensuring central and effective coordination, which has been profoundly lacking in the past. This is a problem that UNCTAD has not been able to solve in the past few years since this research started. As a result, information still does not flow well among and even within divisions, which are operating like

FIGURE 5.2 The New UNCTAD Organizational Structure

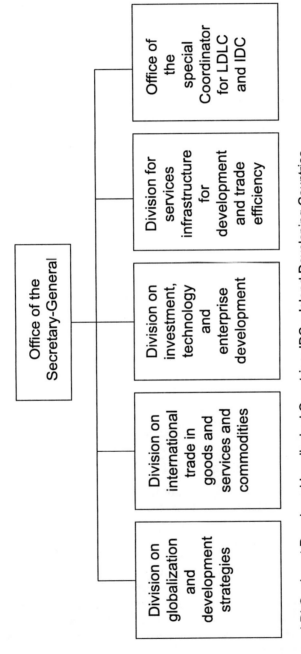

LDLC = Least Developed Landlocked Countries; IDC = Island Developing Countries

independent organizations. Some divisions even follow conflicting approaches to economic development.

On paper, the new structure of UNCTAD might indeed appear to be simplified and to work smoothly. The reality, however, is different. In our study, over 50 percent of the interviewed staff considered the new structure to be inefficient. Some of them considered the divisions[10] and the branches too big and too difficult to manage, since each branch is working on very specific projects not directly linked to the work of the division. Some staff even considered that many projects are totally disconnected from UNCTAD and could be carried out somewhere else. Two divisions are said to be problematic: Globalization and Development Strategies, and International Trade. The Globalization division, it is said, is in charge of too broad a variety of activities, ranging from the development of computer programs, to managing the debt of developing countries, to the publication services, to the analytical work on the effects of globalization. In the International Trade division, the problem is the comparatively slow transfer of trade issues in comparison to the WTO, leading to staff demotivation. A senior staff member even said that if there is no more room for trade in UNCTAD, the division should be closed because the priority is to remain relevant and especially complementary with the WTO.

In that respect, some interviewees argued that the new structure (1) does not totally reflect the mandate, (2) still has problems setting priorities, and (3) reflects too many compromises in order to keep small programs, rather than redefining divisions around clear topics. Staff members said that they expected a much flatter structure, which they consider to be better for delegating responsibility. In this respect, a director said that he has little power to manage a division, not just because of the political constraints of the UN system, but also because of the difficulty of letting staff go. Overall, staff members were more or less indifferent to the structure of the organization. They continue to do their work, which has not changed much, and for some of them the transformation of the organization does not seem to be fundamental. One staff member said: "They invented the branches, sections and division without consulting the staff. I could not tell you for which branch I am working and actually I do not care. I continue doing my work, since the mandate gives us an important flexibility of interpretation." Another person, explaining the obstacles to changing the functioning of the Secretariat, said that staff basically has an interest in perpetuating the traditional way of working. As a result, underneath the new formal structure, there continues to exist an informal structure made of small and strong entities, which have been working together for a long time. These informal structures resist change because they want to continue to do what they like and what they have an interest in. Such a structure is definitely chaotic and difficult to manage. According to one staff member, this is also a strength, because it allows for diversity of opinion.

Nevertheless, it creates incoherence and considerable impatience in the international community.

In conclusion, it appears that even with a new structure, the internal functioning of the organization remains very traditional in various parts of the Secretariat. Indeed, alliances among individuals freeze the transformation process. Some staff also view the drive to change management practices as a fad decided by the political environment, arguing, for example, that a concept such as "efficiency" is primarily tied to the political agenda, implicitly suggesting that the political agenda is not a noble one, and that it is almost the duty of the staff to resist such change. The literature on changing such relatively politicized organizations is actually quite clear (Crozier and Friedberg 1977): such an organization, it is said, cannot be changed by decree. If it is to be successfully transformed, the concerned actors of and within the organization must be involved in a complex bargaining process, which will ultimately redefine their power.

The Staff

One way to effect change in an organization is through the transformation of the mentality of its staff. After Midrand, the UNCTAD Secretariat had to face important issues concerning its human resources. The new mandate's emphasis on consensus building outside of formal negotiations, reinforcing technical cooperation, and opening new areas of work—especially in the domain of investment, technology, and enterprise—revealed an important lack of competencies among UNCTAD staff. Overall, UNCTAD needs staff with more and better communications and management skills. An interviewee explained that at Midrand the Secretariat had received an innovative mandate, but had not received the necessary human resources to implement it. He added that UNCTAD needs to recruit people with stronger personal skills, rather than with specialized economic competencies. But because of the UN context of reform and corresponding budget cuts, UNCTAD has not had much flexibility to hire new staff, and consequently has had to struggle between new needs and demands and the limited capacity of its staff to fill those needs. Significantly, the Midrand midterm review, which took place in the summer of 1998, pointed out "the growing gap between the level of requirement and the level of resources available. This refers both to the quantity and the quality of resources."[11]

This situation, among others, is creating a feeling of demotivation among staff. There is indeed no system to reward them, and at that level no visible change is taking place. To illustrate this point, we have come across staff members who have been in the same rank for over 15 years. In the 1970s, staff used to come to UNCTAD because of idealism and because it was a new, attractive institution for young economists eager to criticize mainstream ideology. A senior staff also remarked that, before the 1990s, staff were mainly recruited because of their strong academic records and because they were prominent in their discipline. Starting in the 1990s, staff members have more often been recruited through the official UN examination process. While this process may be more transparent, it appears that less bright and less intellectually original people are joining UNCTAD.

From our personal experience of working often with groups of UNCTAD staff, we are struck by their incapacity to communicate with each other. While they are usually high-level professionals in their domain, they do not know how to work as a team. Moreover, they are often divided into cliques and do not really appreciate input from each other. They are able to argue for hours on the relevance of their individual points without listening to the others' critical comments. Moreover, there seems to be a very strong division between the "new" and the "old" UNCTAD. New UNCTAD staff certainly are less formal and more entrepreneurial. But they remain a strongly criticized minority, even though they appear to be supported by the Secretary-General. In short, UNCTAD faces various serious problems of staff competence and motivation, as well as of respect and cooperation. Only some of these issues have been addressed since 1998 by means of group training and team building.

The Leadership

Indeed, the Secretary-General took rapid initiatives in favor of staff development after Midrand. In a "Memorandum of Understanding" with the UN Staff College in Turin, he decided to offer to 75 staff members (one-third of UNCTAD's employees) three training and learning workshops that were aimed at creating team spirit and a shared vision, and at identifying possible change projects. During the activities, most of the staff were enthusiastic to be put into new environments and new situations. Most of them had never spoken with each other, which made the human dimension of this event of great importance. However, one year after those workshops, staff were more or less disappointed, as senior management had never systematically implemented the change projects that were developed in Turin. Staff members said that they were frustrated that they were never able to reproduce the newly learned ways of interacting with each other back in their traditional environment. While these workshops provided relaxation and created discussion among staff, they did not transform the organization as was expected.

Conducting these workshops exemplifies the new UNCTAD leadership, which actively seeks to provoke its staff and to put them into new situations. Ricupero sees this as an essential part of the organizational change process. Nevertheless, his main contribution to changing UNCTAD is on the political and ideological, rather than the managerial, side. Indeed, he repositioned UNCTAD in the context of economic globalization, outlining a new vision for the organization. In doing so, he is certainly a visionary and a very charismatic leader, well respected by his entire staff, whatever their divergences. He is viewed as "the engine of change," the person who saved UNCTAD in Midrand. Whenever he is introducing a new line of thought, his staff generally builds on his ideas. Ricupero has a clear vision for UNCTAD, and has various ideas as to how to implement them and to make their impact more relevant. Also, among UN agencies he has been an early advocate of the notion of partnership with the private sector, supporting many individual initiatives within his Secretariat for private sector partnerships. Even more importantly, he has succeeded in creating a relative consensus on UNCTAD's new approach, that is, now working with—instead of against—the global system. This leads directly to UNCTAD's new ideology.

The Ideology

The concept of ideology, and especially of changing ideology, is particularly relevant when presenting UNCTAD's various dimensions of change. Indeed, unlike many other organizations, which are transforming their structures, processes, and perhaps even their culture, UNCTAD has, at least in the past, had a strong ideological dimension, which cannot be neglected in any analysis of its transformation. The dominant ideology of the past may be characterized by dependency theory and criticism of transnational corporations. In fact, one could probably argue that UNCTAD is replacing its past ideology with a new one, but we prefer to explore the idea of UNCTAD "abandoning ideology" in favor of a more pragmatic approach. The majority of the interviewees are saying that UNCTAD is increasingly grounding itself in pragmatism instead of ideology. It is obvious that UNCTAD is no longer searching for a new development paradigm or a new global economic order, but rather for policy guidelines, which will help developing countries to adapt to the liberalization of world trade. If one wants to use the concept of ideology, one might call UNCTAD's new approach one of capacity building, that is, empowering developing countries to participate in and to take advantage of economic globalization. Such capacity building is being developed in UNCTAD's research work and implemented through technical assistance programs. For example, capacity building can take the form of training sessions on international trade to electronic-commerce or small- and medium-sized enterprises of developing countries. On the other hand, UNCTAD does not want to be criticized for blindly supporting liberalization and economic globalization. In a brainstorming seminar prior to the Bangkok conference in 2000, staff members strongly stressed the necessity to promote the notions of equity and social justice in global trade. It appears that UNCTAD wants to keep its advocacy role and remain the "development conscience" of the world, even though it no longer criticizes the capitalist system per se. This combination might be tricky to maintain in the long run.

In parallel to UNCTAD's organizational transformation, its strategic options are also changing from a philosophical approach of politically acceptable and equitable development to a more market-oriented approach to global trade, while optimizing Third World participation in it. In this respect, UNCTAD's leadership is constantly arguing that priorities have to be redefined along the demands of the international economic community. In other words, while changing from an ideological to a pragmatic organization, UNCTAD is also becoming more proactive, rather than reactive. It is precisely this new approach that allows for new types of strategic alliances—in particular, alliances with the business sector. It is probably in this sector that the UNCTAD Secretariat has experienced the most important changes to date, as far as its culture, its staff, and its processes are concerned. Indeed, thanks to the Lyon summit "Partners for Development," a new type of staff has emerged, promoting a new image of UNCTAD worldwide. Since Lyon, UNCTAD has become particularly active in the areas of e-commerce and investment. It is especially in the area of investment that UNCTAD has occasionally become part of the UN Secretary-General's "Global Compact," even though historically there is no direct relationship between the UNCTAD transformation and the Global Compact.

The Partnership Strategy

Affirming in Midrand the key role of business leaders in the development process, UNCTAD sought a way to create dynamic links with them. But because of its political nature, UNCTAD's intergovernmental machinery was not the right place to start with the integration of business actors. As a consequence, UNCTAD began building a partnership strategy with business actors linked to its technical assistance programs and based on a project-by-project type of integration. The objective was to select a few sectors where private partners might be interested in working with UNCTAD. The selected topics were e-commerce, biotrade, microfinance, global movement of goods, and risk management. The culminating event marking the official starting point of UNCTAD's partnerships with business took place in November 1998 in Lyon, France.

During four days, 2,200 representatives from business associations, corporations, NGOs, academia, governments, and the media, coming from 164 countries, met in Lyon for the UNCTAD summit "Partners for Development." The key aim of the gathering was to focus on ways of mobilizing the huge amounts of potential investment capital available in the developed world to help the poorest nations to catch up. In his keynote address, the Secretary-General spoke of civil society and the private sector as the real actors of development. He added that by working with the private sector, UNCTAD will demonstrate that profit and development, as well as market and solidarity, are no longer in opposition to each other but rather are complementary. The central premise of the conference was that strategic partnerships between governments and the private sector can play a significant role in promoting development. The summit was indeed a dynamic forum showing a new media-conscious image of UNCTAD. Debates resembled television shows more than classical UN debates. Beside the various conferences and working groups' meetings, a commercial fair was organized for businesses investing in development projects, among them global consulting firms working on risk management.

Officially, eighteen partnership agreements were launched in Lyon. For instance, the International Association of Ports and Harbors and UNCTAD will work together to develop and implement information systems that respond to the particular requirements of ports in developing countries. Another partnership is aimed at linking the UNCTAD Secretariat with a regional development bank, Banco do Nordeste, and a private investment bank, Banco Axial[12] S.A., in order to improve the living conditions in the poor, underdeveloped northeast and Amazon regions of Brazil. Jean Gurunlian, the executive director of the Lyon summit, noted at one of the seminars that there are two types of partnerships: "Thinking together and acting together through operational partnerships; we focused on the latter, where UNCTAD is a catalyst for change." Indeed, UNCTAD's first strategy works at the project level where partnerships are being developed case by case. As the Secretary-General commented in the Partners for Development report: "In Lyon there will be no attempt at following a uniform approach to the concept of partnership between UNCTAD and civil society, but different modalities will be considered according to the various goals to be reached."[13]

The second level of partnership strategy is the development of strong and active networks between UNCTAD's leadership and business leaders. UNCTAD has participated in all recent gatherings that the UN's Secretary-General Kofi Annan has organized for business leaders, at which CEOs from the biggest oil, chemical, food, and computer companies are defining social action plans for the field, together with UN agencies, and by doing so are taking on social responsibility.

UNCTAD is expanding the boundaries of traditional private-public relationships, while changing the rules of the game for governments, for businesses, for NGOs, and for itself. This change process creates considerable contradictions and instabilities within the Secretariat. The question now is whether UNCTAD can sustain such partnerships in the future. The Trade and Development Board, which during the summer of 1998 reviewed the work carried out by the Secretariat since Midrand, found among other things: "The partnership for development envisaged in the Midrand Declaration should be the hallmark of UNCTAD. This will require further changes in the way business is conducted. UNCTAD should strengthen its links with civil society, in particular the private sector, and international organizations. Links with the private sector should be aimed at tapping its innovative capacity, engaging in joint activities and supplementing funding, and in this connection clear guidelines should be adopted for private sector funding."[14]

Considering such a recommendation, it is only logical that UNCTAD prepared the UNCTAD X conference in Bangkok, held in February 2000, along these lines. If, at the political level, partnerships are certainly viewed as a very positive evolution, at the Secretariat level, however, this desire of governments is seen with some perplexity. Moreover, the concrete application of this spirit of change, announced in Lyon and elsewhere by UNCTAD's leadership, still requires deep changes within the organization before being fully integrated and adopted. Knowing the history of the organization and its internal culture, we will now discuss the cultural obstacles to making partnerships a long-term and sustainable strategy for UNCTAD.

The Culture

As noted, UNCTAD is not a homogeneous organization but rather a conglomerate of individuals and ideas that contradict each other. In this respect, UNCTAD has diverse cultures. If we may, we will separate the old UNCTAD from the new. It is not surprising that the old UNCTAD still refers to a bureaucratic culture based on loyalty more than on openness. The loyalty is mainly to ideas (the "UNCTAD ideology"), and has as its goal maintaining the stability of the structure. Since results are not rewarded, individuals become absorbed within the organization's habits. Most of the time, papers and research work are not signed by authors. UNCTAD, like any other public administration, does not like leaders and personalities. Moreover, UNCTAD is made up of economists and has a profoundly academic culture, in which people work by themselves and do not like to interact. Historically, UNCTAD has had a very individualistic culture, at least in the old part of the organization. This is slowly changing in the new part of UNCTAD, which is working more in teams. But the new teams still do not share their work with the skeptical old UNCTAD. There remains a willingness to avoid conflict.

In short, UNCTAD, in its majority, is still a self-reproductive or closed-loop organization. One of the interviewees quite self-critically explained: "We should stop looking and talking about ourselves and talk more about concrete problems of development." And we have also noticed in UNCTAD seminars the difficulty of being critical about oneself. Above all, it seems difficult to accept critiques pertaining to the functioning of the organization. It looks like each staff has in its mind another perception of what the organization is or should be. This situation is probably due to the fact that UNCTAD has no strong shared culture and shared vision. On top of that, the mission is not a shared one, but is rather defined by governments. As a consequence, organizational culture remains the main obstacle to transformation.

Conclusion

In order to understand better UNCTAD's pathologies, this section briefly compares UNCTAD's transformation process to the transformation model as presented earlier in this chapter. This will put UNCTAD's pathologies into relationship with the pathologies that emerge from public organizations' transformations more generally.

Confrontation with the Transformation Model

The model systematizes the transformation of public organizations in the context of current pressures toward competition, efficiency, and marketization. It helps identify the main pathologies, which emerge along the transformation process in the areas of organizational culture, structure, processes, relationship to politics, public service, and learning. It appears that the case of UNCTAD highlights four different areas where our initial model seems to be particularly challenged, namely, the areas of organizational culture, the relationship with the clients, politics, and leadership.

1. UNCTAD's organizational culture seems to be significantly more blocked than bureaucratic cultures at national levels. In our view, this blockage can be explained by the more complex and more politicized environment of international organizations, which considerably impedes organizational change. As a result, UNCTAD's organizational culture is stronger than is generally the case in national bureaucracies, and its identity is weaker. This paradox continues to exacerbate UNCTAD's organizational fragmentation.
2. UNCTAD's relationship with its clients appears to be more complex than in the case of national public organizations, which is certainly related to the fact that, at an international level, clients are much more difficult to define and, in any case, are not homogeneous. The difficulty of defining the clients of an international organization also results from the growing importance the private sector is taking in the newly emerging partnerships. Indeed, the private sector, by becoming a partner, certainly influences the very definition of a customer, as well as of the products and the services of the organization. This, in turn, changes the relationship between UNCTAD and its historical "clients": the governments. This certainly further exacerbates the growing tension between UNCTAD and traditional politics.

3. Politics is particularly present in the case of UNCTAD. This presence manifests itself, among other places, in the intergovernmental machinery, and also in the organization's ideology (development versus trade, South versus North), culture, and even structure (a special crosscutting unit on least developed countries, for example). An international organization such as UNCTAD reminds us especially that politics, in our model, has probably been conceptualized in a too simplistic way so far. While all public organizations are caught in a tension between striving for autonomy from politics and needing political backing, this tension seems to take a particularly pathological turn in the case of UNCTAD, where the potential for tensions between the organization and politics is high.

4. Leadership, at least in the case of UNCTAD, seems to be a particularly important element, a fact that our model so far does not adequately reflect. This leadership, of course, is actively supported by friendly Member States, who give it the necessary backing to be effective. In light of the above, we can also better understand the particularly paradoxical functions such leadership has—to promote transformation while simultaneously preventing the organization from breaking up because of fragmentation, to encourage partnerships while simultaneously keeping up the dialogue with politics, and to more generally hold the organization together at an ideological level.

Critical Observations: UNCTAD's Three Pathologies

The case study presented in this chapter has clearly shown that UNCTAD is still in the midst of a profound transformation process. As a result, the traditional bureaucracy coexists along with a more entrepreneurial and market-oriented organization in such areas as ideology, culture, structure, and staff. While the future direction of the transformation is clearly indicated, the traditional UNCTAD still exists, especially when it comes to certain world-views held by certain staff members. In addition, the new idea of partnership clearly is not as strong a belief system as was UNCTAD's original "social development ideology." This tension between the old and the new UNCTAD, which is likely to continue for some time, also defines UNCTAD's three main organizational pathologies, as we see them, namely, in the areas of organization, relationship to politics, and ideology.

On an organizational level, UNCTAD can be compared to a university with its specialized research institutes, which neither talk to one another nor know exactly who their "clients" are. It is moreover a "university" that reports to a board of 180 members from as many different countries. As stated earlier, UNCTAD's activities encompass three different levels: analysis (policy advice), consensus building, and technical assistance. If the work of analysis can best be compared to the work of a university, technical assistance is more like the work of a public enterprise, while consensus building is quite similar to the work of a traditional public administration. In terms of management, this means that at least three different kinds of organizational processes apply—transformation of a classic administration, transformation of a public enterprise, and transformation of a university—meaning different transformation speeds and different cultures. Therefore, as UNCTAD's transformation progresses, this is likely to exacerbate the currently existing fragmentation of the organization. In other words, fragmentation of the organization defines UNCTAD's first pathology.

The case of UNCTAD also highlights a profound change in international governance. This change can be seen in the growing number of actors from civil society and the private sector now interacting with international organizations such as UNCTAD. In the case of UNCTAD, such new governance mechanisms emerge essentially at the interface with the private sector, especially through UNCTAD's partnership strategy, while the intergovernmental machinery does not yet seem to be affected by this transformation in governance. However, it is easy to predict that if the intergovernmental machinery will not follow suit, a growing discrepancy between UNCTAD and its political environment will arise, which will inevitably lead to problems with the governments. The tension between (the new) UNCTAD and (traditional) politics thus defines the second pathology.

Finally, this evolution toward new governance mechanisms is paralleled by a change in global ideology, a change clearly reflected in the case of UNCTAD. Indeed, the world in general, and UNCTAD in particular, seems to be moving from an ideology of development—which was particularly embraced by UNCTAD from a Southern perspective—to an ideology of free trade. If Midrand and especially Secretary-General Ricupero seem to have made this transition, furthering it by organizational changes and partnerships, neither UNCTAD as an organization nor the United Nations as a whole system has yet followed suit. Therefore, in the long term, this not only creates tension within UNCTAD, but is likely to put UNCTAD at odds with the UN system more generally. Ideological tensions and inconsistencies thus make up UNCTAD's third pathology.

Organizational fragmentation, growing tensions with politics, and ideological inconsistencies thus define, in our view, the three main pathologies as they emerge from our case study. All three are particularly exacerbated by UNCTAD's recent transformation process, especially by its partnership strategy. In light of this analysis, UNCTAD needs to pay much stronger attention to its organizational transformation than is currently the case, if it again wants to play a significant role in the international development arena.

Notes

1. Both of us have a background in political science, public administration, and organizational behavior. Moreover, Matthias Finger is engaged in both the academic and the consulting world, while Bérangère Magarinos-Ruchat currently works within the UN system, which means that we are particularly concerned with the concrete questions of advising international organizations along their transformation process.
2. In order to conduct our case study, we have used different methods. We had the opportunity to facilitate five workshops for UNCTAD staff between 1998 and 1999. Three of them focused on staff growth and development, introducing team building and reflection about UNCTAD's vision, mission, and change processes. The two other seminars were the first step of UNCTAD's preparatory work for its next conference, UNCTAD X, which took place in 2000 in Bangkok. We consequently mainly used methods of participatory observation, but we also conducted more than 40 interviews among UNCTAD staff during the summer of 1998. We met with people from all divisions and services with a balance of senior and junior staff. Finally, we also collected and analyzed various UNCTAD reports and documents.
3. Prebisch was a famous political economist. Central thinker of the so-called "dependency theory," he was also one of the founders of UNCTAD, and subsequently became its first Secretary-General.
4. "General Assembly Establishes New Institutional Machinery for International Trade," *UN Chronicle*, 1965.
5. Interdependence implies that both the North and the South have an interest in negotiating trade and finance. However, UNCTAD has always had difficulty convincing the North of the benefits of negotiating with Third World countries.
6. *UN Chronicle*, 1984.
7. Homero L. Hernandez, *UNCTAD: Review of Institutional and Programme Issues.* Geneva: Joint Inspection Unit, 1996.
8. *UNCTAD in Brief.* Geneva: UNCTAD, 1998.
9. UNCTAD Efficiency Review, *Final Report of the Efficiency Review Team*, July 1996.
10. For instance the globalization division has 180 people and some branches have 40 people.
11. UNCTAD, TDR 18th Executive Session, Geneva, July 1998.
12. The bank was set up last year by Pierre Landolt, president of the Sandoz Family Foundation, one of the biggest Swiss chemical companies.
13. UNCTAD and City of Lyon, "Partners for Development: The First Meeting," *The Business Community, Governments and NGOs Join Forces with the UN for Development*, November, 1998.
14. Mid-term Review Outcomes, Chairman's draft, TDB, Geneva, 10 July 1998.

Bibliography

Adizes, I. *Corporate Lifecycles.* Englewood Cliffs, NJ: Prentice-Hall, 1988.
Barnett, M., and Finnemore, M. "The Politics, Power, and Pathologies of International Organizations." *International Organizations*, vol. 53, no. 4 (1999): 699–732.
Bertrand, M. *The Third Generation World Organization.* Dordrecht: Martinus Nijhoff Publishers/UNITAR, 1989.
Clegg, S. *Frameworks of Power.* London: Sage Publications, 1989.
Crozier, M. *Le Phénomène Bureaucratique.* Paris: Seuil, 1963.
Crozier, M., and Friedberg, E. *L'acteur et le Système.* Paris: Seuil, 1977.
Etzioni, A. *Modern Organizations.* Englewood Cliffs, NJ; Prentice-Hall, 1964.
Finger, M., and Rey, J-N. *Le Défis de la Poste.* Lausanne: L.E.P., 1994.

Finger, M., et al., eds. *Du Monopole à la Concurrence: Analyse Critique de L'évolution de Six Entreprises Suisses*. Lausanne: L.E.P., 1997.

Finger, M., and Ruchat, B., eds. *Pour Une Nouvelle Approche du Management Public: Réflexions Autour de Michel Crozier*. Paris: Seli Arslan, 1997.

Finger, M., and Bürgin, S. "The Concept of the 'Learning Organization' Applied to the Public Sector." Pp. 130–156, in Easterby-Smith, M., ed. *Learning Around Organizations: Developments in Theory and Practice*. London: Sage Publications, 1999.

Gouillart, F., and Kelly, J. *Transforming the Organization*. New York: McGraw-Hill, 1995.

Haas, E.B. *When Knowledge Is Power: Three Models of Change in International Organizations*. Berkeley: University of California Press, 1999.

Homero, L.H. *UNCTAD: Review of Institutional and Programme Issues*. Geneva: Joint Inspection Unit, 1996.

Jazairy I. *UNCTAD 1997 Report on Least Developed Countries: A Critique*. South Letter, vol. 1, 1998.

Kottler, J.P. *Leading Change*. Boston: Harvard Business School Press, 1996.

Lawson, C. "The Future of East-South Trade After UNCTAD VI." *Third World Quarterly* (1984).

Logan, D. "Corporate Citizenship in a Global Age." *RSA Journal*, nos. 3/4 (1998).

Logan, D. *Companies in Communities: Getting the Measure*. London: The London Benchmarking Group, 1997.

Mercier, J.-Y., Bürgin, S., and Finger, M. *A Critical Analysis of Power in Organizational Learning*. Paper presented at the Second Connecting Learning and Critique Conference, Lancaster University, UK, 19–21 July 2000.

Miles, R. *Leading Corporate Transformation*. San Francisco: Jossey-Bass, 1997.

Mintzberg, H. *Power in and around Organizations*. Englewood-Cliffs, NJ: Prentice-Hall, 1983.

Morgan, G. *Image of Organizations*. London: Sage Publications, 1997.

Murphy, C. *International Organisation and Industrial Change: Global Governance since 1850*. Oxford: Oxford University Press, 1994.

Nelson, J. *Social Responsibility and Corporate Competitiveness in the Global Economy*. London: The Prince of Wales Business Leaders Forum, 1998.

Pollitt, C. *Managerialism and the Public Services: Cuts or Cultural Change in the 1990s*. Cambridge: Basil Blackwell, 1993.

Ramsey, R. "UNCTAD's Failures: the Rich Get Richer." *International Organization*, no. 38 (Spring 1984).

Rothstein, R. *Global Bargaining: UNCTAD and the Quest for a New International Economic Order*. Princeton: PaperBack, 1979.

Scholte, J.A. "The Globalization of World Politics." In Baylis, J., and Smith, S., eds. *The Globalization of World Politics: An Introduction to International Relations*. Oxford: Oxford University Press, 1997.

Sinan, J.M. "UNCTAD and Flags of Convenience." *Journal of World Trade Law* (April, 1984).

Strange, S. *The Retreat of the State: The Diffusion of Power in the World Economy*. Cambridge: Cambridge University Press, 1996.

Therien, J-P. "La CNUCED et La Dynamique des Rapports Nord-Sud." *Etudes Internationales*, vol. 21, no. 2 (1990).

UNCTAD. *The History of UNCTAD 1964–1984*. New York: United Nations, 1985.

UNCTAD. *The Development Dialogue in the 1980s—Continuing Paralysis or New Consensus*. New York: United Nations, 1985.

UNCTAD. *Meeting the Development Challenge: Technical Cooperation Programmes of UNCTAD*. New York: United Nations, 1995.

UNCTAD. *Technological Capacity-Building and Technology Partnership: Field Findings, Country Experiences and Programmes*. New York: United Nations, 1995.

UNCTAD. *Exchanging Experiences of Technology Partnership: The Helsinki Meeting of Experts*. New York: United Nations, 1996.

UNCTAD. *Report of the Working Party on the Medium-Term Plan and the Programmme Budget on Its 27th Session*. Geneva: UNCTAD, 17–29 June 1996.

UNCTAD. *TradePoint Review*. Geneva: UNCTAD, September 1997.

UNCTAD. *The Uruguay Round and Its Follow-Up: Building a Positive Agenda for Development*. New York: United Nations, 1997.

UNCTAD. *Selected Policy Issues, Measures, and Programmes on Inter-firm Partnerships*. Expert Meeting on Inter-firm Cooperation, April 1998.

UNCTAD. *Electronic Commerce: Legal Consideration*. 15 May 1998

UNCTAD and City of Lyon. "Partners for Development: The First Meeting." *The Business Community, Governments and NGOs Join Forces with the UN for Development*. November, 1998.

UNCTAD, TDB. *Review of Technical Cooperation Activities of UNCTAD*. Report by the Secretary-General, August 1997.

UNCTAD, TDB. *Review of Technical Cooperation Plan for 1998–2000*. 16 February 1998.

United Nations. *Proposed Programme Budget for the Biennium: 1998–1999*. Vol. 1, General Assembly, Section 11A: Trade and development, Programme 9 of the Medium-Term Plan for the Period 1998–2001. New York: United Nations.

Weiss, T. *Multilateral Development Diplomacy in UNCTAD: The Lessons of Group Negotiations, 1964–84*. New York: St. Martin's Press, 1986.

— *Chapter 6* —

FRAUD, CORRUPTION, AND UNITED NATIONS CULTURE

Yves Beigbeder

Introduction

United Nations (UN) organizations have periodically been accused of
widespread fraud and corruption. Fraud or poor management have
caused financial losses to the organizations concerned and damaged their
public image and credibility. The revelation that public funds provided by
governments and other contributors had been defrauded by staff members or outsiders, or wasted through incompetence or negligence was
made even more damaging by the high expectations created by the worthy UN ideals—world peace and security, development of poor nations,
protection of the environment, promotion of human rights, and humanitarian assistance—and the assumption that UN staff should be less subject
to human frailties than national bureaucrats or staff of non-governmental
organizations (NGOs) or profit-making organizations. In fact, in spite of
their involvement in high-minded global programs, UN staff as a whole
cannot be expected to deviate from the standard norms of human and
bureaucratic behavior found in other organizations.

Corruption is generally defined as an abuse of power or a deviant behavior by employees for personal gain, which can be financial in the case
of fraud or non-material as in the case of favoritism. This chapter will
deal only with cases of personal financial gain. Investigations of alleged
corruption and fraud must be carried out by independent bodies, either
internal or external to the organization. Their recommendations must be
dealt with promptly and effectively by top management. Employees
found guilty of fraud must be sanctioned by disciplinary action, or dismissed. They must be required to return misappropriated funds, and

they may be prosecuted in civil or criminal courts for their misuse of funds. An effective oversight body is an essential requirement for good management. It is also a credit to an organization. Inversely, an organization's obfuscation of corruption and fraud and a lack of corrective action make it an easy target for criticism. For intergovernmental organizations mainly dependent on public and private contributions, hidden and untreated corruption may affect performance levels and discourage Member States and other potential donors from continuing to contribute to the organization.

Why do public employees commit fraudulent acts? Some of the varied reasons and factors include lack of moral fiber, greed for personal or family gain, financial problems and pressures, lack of supervisory and financial control, connivance with other employees and/or outsiders, and the belief that they will not be caught, that "everybody does it," or that "the organization can pay." This chapter will first recall cases of fraud and corruption recorded in recent years, in an attempt to assess their extent and impact in relation to the organizations' budgets and staffing. Second, the probable causes of these abuses in the context of a "UN culture" will be examined. Third, the discussion then focuses on finding and applying effective remedies in terms of prevention and sanctions.

The present study is limited to problems found in the UN Secretariat, the UN Funds and Programmes, and the UN Peacekeeping Operations, the main targets for criticism. It deals with corruption in the sense of the misuse or abuse of UN funds or privileges by UN staff for their personal gain. For instance, staff corruption can involve embezzlement of UN funds or theft of UN property, the submission of false documents as a basis for undue allowances or grants, the acceptance of undue excess payments, bid rigging, the search for or acceptance of bribes, unauthorized outside financial activities, or other unethical conduct. This study also examines fraud and theft committed by outsiders (non-staff members) as a result of the incompetence or negligence of UN staff at various levels.[1]

Recent Cases of Fraud or Corruption

Until 1994, cases of financial irregularities and fraud were included in the UN External Auditor's annual reports,[2] which were submitted to the General Assembly through the Advisory Committee on Administrative and Budgetary Questions (ACABQ)[3] and the Fifth Committee. Following the creation of the Office of Internal Oversight Services (OIOS) in 1994, any such cases are included in the Office's annual reports submitted to the General Assembly through the Secretary-General. Complementary information on cases of fraud or other misconduct allegedly committed by UN staff members is found in judgments of the UN Administrative

Tribunal (UNAT). However, these judgments concern only those cases that have been submitted to the Tribunal by applicants who have decided to avail themselves of this judicial process. They do not constitute an exhaustive list of all such cases.

A number of cases have been reported in the media, in order to inform the general public about the management conditions under which abuses occur and the obstacles to the effective prevention and sanctioning of such abuses. A few periodicals specialize in exposing "UN corruption" with the obvious intent to debase the image of the Organization and, more generally, to oppose multilateralism. The reports in periodicals usually name the perpetrators of abuses,[4] a practice that is avoided in UN reports, giving the impression that the UN wants to hide these abuses and protect its staff members, including the guilty ones. The UN is indeed shy about giving names, in some cases so as not to upset government representatives who have lent senior officials to UN missions, or to protect the accused until inquiries are completed. Furthermore, the UN has rarely replied to charges published in periodicals nor has it explained publicly, in cases of established fraud, what sanctions have been applied and what further preventive or corrective action has been taken—again, a self-defeating position. Finally, the Centre for UN Management Accountability (CUNMA), created in 1998, has publicized cases on an email list, including cases already published in the media.[5]

Between 1980 and 1998, the most significant financial losses were incurred during peacekeeping operations and in field operations of the UN Children's Fund (UNICEF) and the UN High Commissioner for Refugees (UNHCR). Others involved UN Headquarters, the UN Office in Geneva, the UN Conference on Trade and Development (UNCTAD), the UN Relief and Works Agency for Palestine Refugees in the Near East (UNRWA), Habitat, the UN Environment Programme (UNEP), the Economic Commission for Africa (ECA), the Economic and Social Commission for Asia and the Pacific (ESCAP), and the UN Development Programme (UNDP).

Fraud and Financial Losses in Peacekeeping Operations

The theft of $3.9 million was discovered on 17 April 1994 at the headquarters of the UN Operation in Somalia (UNOSOM II). The sum had been kept in the bottom drawer of a reinforced filing cabinet. The budget for the operation was approximately $242 million for the period 1 June–30 September 1994. An investigation was carried out by a UN Headquarters team, under the direction of OIOS. At the UN's request, an investigation team was sent by Scotland Yard to Mogadishu to complement the UN team's inquiry. The stolen funds were not recovered, nor were the thieves identified. The Scotland Yard report, dated 30 September 1994, stated in part: "Long-term ineffective local management was the major contributing factor to this offence. Mr. D. (the former Chief Financial Officer) is identified as the person most culpable for mismanaging the security." Mr. D., who had left UNOSOM on 26 March 1994, was informed of the Administration's conclusion that he had been grossly negligent. His repatriation grant and annual leave balance were withheld, though his pension rights could not be withdrawn. The Chief Cashier received a written reprimand, a mild sanction.

The Director of Administration (Mr. M.) resigned on 12 May 1994, a resignation that was treated as a "summary dismissal." However, the UN Tribunal rejected the qualification that his resignation was tantamount to a summary dismissal for serious misconduct.[6] There was no suggestion that Mr. M. had been involved in or had benefited in any way from the theft. He contended that the UN decision was a reaction to political pressure and was aimed at deflecting criticism of the Organization by pinning the blame on a scapegoat. There was evidence that UN Headquarters had a large share of responsibility in rejecting Mr. M.'s several proposals for banking arrangements that would have averted or minimized cash security problems. Furthermore, UN Headquarters is responsible for the recruitment of all professional posts in peacekeeping operations; many administrative posts had remained unfilled in UNOSOM II. The Tribunal considered that the theft was primarily "due to wrong-headed decisions by others [than Mr. D.], coupled by the fact that the Organization was attempting a very difficult mission in an extraordinarily adverse environment, without the number or the types of persons required, the equipment required, and without ... essential infrastructure support."

In its report for the period from 1 July 1995 to 30 June 1996 (Doc. A/51/432), the OIOS gave several instances of mismanagement that caused financial losses. The lack of guidance to field personnel in the UN Peace Forces in the Former Yugoslavia (UNPF) led to the transfer of UN-owned equipment worth over $35 million to the non-UN (NATO) Implementation Force (IFOR) without a proper accounting. UNPF had also purchased approximately 650 generators valued at $7.2 million that were either not used or sent to other missions. Avoidable delays in establishing ration and service contracts by the UN Mission in Haiti (UNMIH) cost the UN $12.4 million. The UN Mission of Observers in Tajikistan (UNMOT) made overpayments of allowances to military and civilian staff of about $400,000 between January and August 1995: only about $100,000 was recovered due to delayed action by the Mission. The UN Iraq-Kuwait Observation Mission (UNIKOM) identified overpayments of Mission subsistence allowances estimated at $844,000, which were to be recovered. In 1996, an investigation was conducted into allegations that two senior staff members of the UN Disengagement Observer Force between Israeli and Syrian Forces (UNDOF) were interfering with the bidding process on contracts with a view to favoring one of the local fresh-ration suppliers. Charges were to be brought against these staff members for breaching procurement rules and the provisions of the OIOS mandate.

In its third report (Doc. A/52/426), the OIOS identified serious breaches of financial regulations and rules as well as improprieties and irregularities in the procurement process of the UN Angola Verification Mission III (UNAVEM III), resulting in significant losses to the UN. For instance, acceptance of delayed, defective, and short supplies from a vendor resulted in excess payments of $288,000 and losses of $980,000. Administrative lapses also led to irrecoverable losses of $241,000 for the rental of buses.

The Chief Financial Officer of the UN Forces in Cyprus (UNFICYP) was involved in an ongoing scheme to defraud the Organization by siphoning funds from the mission's account for fresh rations—fresh fruits and vegetables—provided to the peacekeeping troops. His account showed a balance of $100,000 when, in fact, it had a deficit of $400,000. The Chief Financial Officer was dismissed, and the fresh-ration contractor was removed.

OIOS's fourth report (Doc. A/53/428) found recurring abuses in a few of the same peacekeeping forces. Incorrect payments of mission subsistence allowances to UNIKOM personnel had continued in spite of recommendations made by the auditors. The resulting overpayments now amounted to $6.3 million. The payments were finally halted, and recovery was started in 1996.

Following an inquiry conducted from 1996 to 1997 by OIOS, evidence of the theft of UN-owned equipment by a UN contractor was obtained. The contractor had supplied catering services to two peacekeeping missions, the UN Transitional Authority in Cambodia (UNTAC) and the UN Operation in Somalia. The firm's owners and officials had stolen a total of approximately $400,000 in UN equipment, located in Mombassa, from both missions. In consultation with the Kenyan attorney general, the Kenyan police filed criminal charges of theft and possession of UN-owned equipment against four of the contractor's officials in mid-1997. Two were arrested, then released on bond; the trial has been suspended in the absence of the defendants.

In a case submitted to the UN Administrative Tribunal, a Procurement Assistant assigned to UNTAC was summarily dismissed for serious misconduct in 1993—for having accepted bribes from a UN contractor. The decision was maintained by the Tribunal, but because of various extenuating circumstances, the applicant was granted a year's salary as compensation.[7] In another case, a staff member assigned to UNDOF was dismissed for submitting a fraudulent claim for education grant benefits. The Tribunal agreed with this sanction: "[T]he element of fraudulent intent warrants the imposition of the sanction of dismissal."[8] In yet another case, a Field Service Officer assigned to the UN Truce Supervision Organization (UNTSO) as Finance Clerk was summarily dismissed for serious misconduct in 1992. He had borrowed $8,800 from a fund-in-trust (a non-UN fund) held by him on behalf of the UN community in Gaza. Although he had admitted his guilt and repaid this sum, the Tribunal agreed with the sanction.[9] In a case not involving fraud or financial losses but rather a breach of standards of conduct, the Chief Administrative Officer of UNAVEM II in Angola was found to have condoned racial discrimination in the allocation of housing. His demotion from grade P.5 to P.4 for one year was confirmed by the Tribunal.[10]

In a cause célèbre well publicized by the media, the Tribunal found in favor of four applicants dealing at UN Headquarters with the procurement of air transportation services for peacekeeping operations. A US company, Evergreen Helicopters Inc., had alleged that irregularities in UN procurement practices had resulted in contracts being awarded principally to one Canadian helicopter broker. In 1993, the applicants were suspended from duty and charged with misconduct. However, the applicants were exonerated by the UN Joint Disciplinary Committee in respect of all charges. While Secretary-General Boutros Boutros-Ghali accepted the Committee's findings, he still imposed disciplinary measures on the applicants, which the Tribunal then rescinded. In their applications to the Tribunal, the applicants had stated, in part, that "the harsh measures of suspension inflicted on [them] were motivated by extraneous factors including media rumors of corruption in the UN, [and] a US proposal for the appointment of an Inspector-General...."[11]

OIOS's fifth annual report (Doc. A/54/393) produced evidence that the former Chief of the Traffic and Travel Unit of the UN Mission in Bosnia and Herzegovina (UNMIBH) had defrauded the Organization to an amount of approximately $800,000. Following a complaint by the UN, when it was discovered that he had left the Mission without authorization, the former Chief was arrested in December 1998 by the Federal Bureau of Investigation in New York and then charged with crimes under US law. In September 1999, a jury found him guilty of five counts of international wire fraud and conspiracy to commit international wire fraud. He was sentenced to 41 months in US federal prison and ordered to make restitution to the Organization. By October 2000, the Chief, while serving his prison sentence, had made one payment in the amount of $110,000 to the UN. OIOS was cooperating with Croatian authorities to secure the prosecution of accomplices and restitution of the money they had obtained through fraud.[12]

In its sixth annual report, for the period 1 July 1999 to 30 June 2000, the OIOS reported on a fraud concerning four faxes received by the UN Federal Credit Union in June and July 1999, requesting it to perform wire transfers of funds from the private bank accounts of two former staff members of the UN Observer Mission in Angola to bank accounts established by others at financial institutions in the Netherlands and Angola. The evidence obtained during the investigation revealed that the faxes were not issued by or on behalf of those staff members; a locally recruited former staff member of the Mission was responsible. OIOS recommended that the investigation report be made available to national law enforcement authorities for further inquiry. The UN office in Angola was also notified not to offer employment to this individual.

Fraud and Financial Losses at UNICEF

Out of its $37 million budget for its Kenya operation in 1993 and 1994, UNICEF lost approximately $10 million, to serious fraud and mismanagement in its Nairobi office. A UNICEF auditor uncovered the first irregularities during an unannounced visit to Nairobi in November 1994. More auditors were brought in. They found $500,000 in unpaid bills, and identified more than $1 million lost through fraud. The fraud included payments for non-existent services, double billing, bogus contractors, and insurance claims for non-existent medical treatment. An additional $8 to $9 million was lost due to mismanagement, including spending beyond the authorized budget, failing to oversee contract services, and using UNICEF vehicles for personal purposes. By June 1995, 24 staff members had been suspended or dismissed, and 23 more were under investigation. The main responsibility appeared to lie with the two successive Directors of the Kenya Office, who were suspended without pay. The fraud was probably facilitated by the doubling of the Office's budget in that period, caused by the drought and an influx of refugees from the war in Somalia. The Office's staffing then increased from 71 to 300.[13]

During the period 1996–1997, 54 cases of fraud and presumptive fraud were reported to the UNICEF Executive Board. Forty-two of the reported cases involved staff members. In 11 cases, the perpetrators could not be identified, and one case involved a staff member from another UN organization. In 30 cases, the organization suffered losses totaling $777,342. No losses to UNICEF were found in 16 cases. The Administration had not yet established responsibility in a fraud case in a field office involving falsification of records that resulted in an estimated loss of $445,000. The Board expressed concern about the low recovery rate of the amounts involved in the fraud cases: only $6,833 had been recovered by 31 December 1997, and $213,930 had not been recovered from staff members no longer employed by the agency.[14]

Other individual cases of fraud can be found in UNAT judgments:

- In May 1989, a Supply Assistant/Senior Secretary in the UNICEF Office in Islamabad, Pakistan, was dismissed for misconduct. He had participated with suppliers to defraud the agency by manipulating the bidding process.[15]
- The Secretary of the Administration and Finance Unit and a driver employed at the UNICEF Kaduna Office (Nigeria) were both dismissed for misconduct for the theft of six cartons of vehicle spare parts and medicine tablets from the UNICEF store.[16]

- An Accounts Clerk employed at UNICEF headquarters was summarily dismissed in November 1996 for serious misconduct for his unauthorized use of official telephone codes for personal reasons.[17]

The Tribunal confirmed the dismissal decisions in all of these cases.

Fraud and Financial Losses at UNHCR

The Sunday Times reported on 15 August 1993 that the former UNHCR Special Representative to Uganda and Djibouti, Mr. S.-V.L., was forced to resign after financial irregularities were discovered by an internal UN audit. The auditors found more than £2 million (approximately $3.2 million) in losses from his relief operations. After his transfer to Djibouti, an additional £450,000 (approximately $726,000) in UN funds went missing, apparently paid to companies that did not exist. On his forced resignation, Mr. L. was denied his severance pay, but his pension rights could not be terminated by the Administration. The newspaper alleged that Mr. L. had "powerful friends in the UN's African hierarchy" and that the UN tried to cover up this scandal. Rather than being "forced to resign," one wonders why Mr. L. was not summarily dismissed for serious misconduct.

According to an article in a Swiss newspaper, *Le Temps*, dated 28 October 1998, UNHCR lost almost 2.5 million Swiss Francs ($1.6 million) in six years by purchasing tons of rice to feed refugees from only one firm in Guinea at twice the market price. The article blames the UNHCR Representative in Conakry, Mr. A.S. who was transferred from Guinea shortly before his retirement, allegedly at the demand of donor governments. Locally, he was considered to be autocratic and incompetent. The only official comment from the agency, clearly an understatement, was: "The management of Mr. A.S. and of his team did not correspond any longer to the level expected by us." Was any internal investigation initiated by the agency concerning the allegations of overpayment and on the possible responsibility of the Representative? No questions appear to have been raised as to whether such overpayment was connected with bribes.

In its second annual report (Doc. A/51/432), the OIOS disclosed that major amounts were due from UNHCR's main implementing partner in one country, going back to 1984. It was agreed that $323,000 should be recovered from this partner.

From 29 July to August 1998, the *Financial Times* published a series of articles charging UNHCR with financial and other mismanagement and claiming that the agency has been wasting millions. UNHCR rejected all allegations in a Briefing Note dated 10 August 1998. However, the Under-Secretary-General Karl Paschke, head of OIOS, told a news conference in October 1998 that his office was probing possible fraud in the UNHCR's West and East African operations, including Guinea and Congo (formerly Zaire).[18]

In a case submitted to the UNAT, a UNHCR Senior Protection Officer was dismissed in 1994 for misconduct. He was found not to have met the moral standards or to have exercised adequate judgment as required by his functions. His conduct had been negligent and irresponsible, casting suspicion on his integrity and on the agency's public image. The Tribunal confirmed the sanction.[19]

The sixth report of OIOS mentioned, without further precision, that its Investigation Section "worked on two matters involving senior UNHCR staff members, in which the evidence obtained indicated that these individuals had violated UN regulations and rules." The Office recommended that appropriate action be taken against the individuals.

Related or unrelated to these "matters," *Newsweek* published in 26 February 2001 a disturbing report according to which UNHCR had recently begun investigating "myriad cases" of abuses carried out by UNHCR resettlement and protection officers through a network of middlemen in Kenya and other stations. The article alleged that half of the thousands of refugees resettled by the agency over the past five years had paid bribes totaling hundreds of thousands, if not millions, of dollars to UNHCR staff members in order to be resettled. UNHCR would need to come out publicly on these allegations, explain why these abuses were not detected and stopped earlier, and advise as to what action had been taken to sanction the offenders.

Fraud and Financial Losses at UN Offices and in Other UN Funds and Programmes

Data based on UN Internal Audit statistics on recovery against fraud were obtained by the JIU Inspectors when they prepared their 1993 report "Accountability and Oversight in the UN Secretariat."[20] Between 1988 and mid-1993, the internal auditors recommended $3.5 million for the recovery of misappropriated funds, while only $85,000, 2 percent of the total, had actually been recovered.

An OIOS investigation established that three documents circulated in late 1997 among the representatives of Member States at UN Headquarters had been forged by two staff members in order to advance their careers. Their action had had a negative effect on the Secretary-General's planning and decisions in respect to the decolonization program. No information was yet available as to the possible sanctions applied to these staff members (Doc. A/53/428).

The Director of the Office of the Commissioner for Namibia at UN Headquarters (OCN) was summarily dismissed for serious misconduct in 1982. He was, among other functions, in charge of the distribution of scholarship assistance and social welfare payments to Namibians in the US from UN funds specifically established for this purpose. He misappropriated $207,582 during 1980 and 1981, by obtaining over 400 checks payable to non-existent persons, whose names he falsely endorsed on the checks and for which he received payment. The theft was found by a UN audit carried out in 1982. The UN Administration made clear to the Director, without apparent results, that he was expected to reimburse the UN for the funds he had misappropriated.[21] As another issue, the fact that this case, which occurred in 1980–1982, was not judged by the Tribunal until eight years later in 1990 shows that the UN internal justice system may need reform. Delayed justice is often justice denied.

In 1995, OIOS received a complaint that a former senior staff member of Printing Services at the UN Office at Geneva (UNOG) had engaged in "private" printing by using UN resources for his own purpose. It was then found that this practice was accepted and had become entrenched. The former staff member was (belatedly) reprimanded for mismanagement, abuse of authority, and waste of resources. A general warning was issued that such practices would not be tolerated (Doc. A/51/432).

In a case submitted to the UNAT, another staff member assigned to UNOG was dismissed for having breached the standards of conduct required of international civil servants. He had assumed outside financial activities during his employment with the UN. He also was guilty of absenteeism, did not observe working hours, and showed aggressiveness toward and lack of respect for his superiors. The Tribunal confirmed the sanction.[22]

UNRWA auditors found that a former staff member of the UNRWA West Bank Field Office in East Jerusalem had used false refugee registration numbers, with a mix of names from his extended family, to defraud the agency of approximately $355,000 over the period from 1992 to 1995. He had forged medical reports and hospital invoices so as to submit false claims for reimbursement of medical expenses incurred by theoretically eligible Palestinian refugees. The investigation found 209 individual cases of fraud, including 191 cases that involved his extended family. UNRWA passed this criminal case to both the Israeli and the Palestinian authorities for prosecution.

In a case submitted to the UNAT, a teacher employed by UNRWA was summarily dismissed for serious misconduct in May 1992 for having altered a check issued to him by the Agency, which he subsequently cashed, receiving $10,000 in excess of the amount for which the check was issued. The Tribunal confirmed this decision.[23] In another UNRWA case, an Assistant Claims Examination Officer was terminated in the interest of the Agency on the grounds of "strong suspicion" of forging signatures and cashing outstanding amounts. The Tribunal found that no cogent evidence had been presented and ordered the rescission of the termination decision.[24] In a case of ethical conduct not involving loss of funds, a staff nurse was demoted from grade 08 to grade 06. She had registered "imaginary and incorrect numbers of children vaccinated against hepatitis," which gave false data to the Agency, to donor countries and to the host governments about the coverage of the Agency's vaccination program.

Her breach of professional norms could have undermined the Agency's credibility. The Tribunal confirmed the demotion decision.[25]

An OIOS investigation found in 1996 that a senior staff member at UNCTAD had been submitting false obligation documents and payment vouchers for several years, embezzling more than $600,000. Using his delegated powers, he submitted additional false documents to hide the thefts. In July 1996, the UN Office at Geneva made a criminal complaint to the Swiss authorities, who arrested the staff member pending investigation. He was summarily dismissed from UNCTAD. In April 1997, in a written *convention de remboursement,* the staff member formally admitted to owing the UN a total amount of $609,704, and agreed to liquidate his entire assets, including the lump sum of his pension entitlements, in order to make restitution to the UN to the extent that his assets allowed. The UN recovered approximately $350,000. The Swiss Court ruled the defendant guilty of the thefts, condemned him to a suspended sentence of 18 months in jail (he had already served nine months), directed that he pay the balance due to the UN, and prohibited him from entering Switzerland for ten years (Doc. A/52/426).

According to the OIOS report for 1995–1996, audits of rental subsidies on the UN Centre for Human Settlements (Habitat) and UNEP revealed large overpayments to staff as a result of serious flaws in internal controls. The next report identified significant shortcomings in the management of the programs and resources of Habitat, both human and financial. It also referred to a conflict of interest centered on actions during 1991–1993 by a staff member whose spouse was an external consultant to Habitat (Doc. A/51/432 and A/52/426). According to the OIOS's fourth report (Doc. A/53/428), the audit of the second UN Conference on Human Settlements (Habitat II) found that a breakdown of internal controls left Habitat with an uncovered deficit in the range of $2 million. Its Secretariat resorted to extensive hiring of consultants at a total cost of $2.5 million without competitive bidding, with little value received in return. The former Habitat II Secretary-General traveled more than 80 percent of the time while employed, incurring travel costs of $370,000, while his assistant spent more than 50 percent of his time traveling.[26]

In a case submitted to the UNAT, a staff member employed by UNDP in Bangladesh as summarily dismissed for serious misconduct in 1991. He allegedly obtained bribes from government officials by threatening them with withdrawal or suspension of projects, which, by implication, could affect their continued employment. The Tribunal was satisfied that UNDP's use of discretion in dismissing the applicant could be upheld.[27] In another case, the Senior Security Officer of Habitat in Nairobi, Kenya, was dismissed for misconduct in 1992 for having stolen a Panasonic Notebook computer from the UNICEF/WFP Office in the UN complex in Gigiri, Kenya. The Tribunal agreed with the sanction, but granted the applicant two months' salary as compensation for a procedural irregularity.[28] In yet another case, a Senior Officer at ESCAP was separated from service in 1996 for misconduct on the grounds that she had altered a certificate as a basis for payment of a dependency allowance. The Tribunal maintained the sanction.[29]

A Reuters release dated 25 September 1998 reported that the former chief of the UNDP housing section was arrested by FBI agents and charged with bid rigging for his role in overseeing UNDP-sponsored housing in Africa. Mr. K.G. was charged by the US attorney for Manhattan with defrauding the UN out of more than $1.5 million between 1989 and late 1995 in a scheme to inflate costs and misappropriate UN funds.[30]

In a case not involving fraud or financial losses but a horrendous breach of standards of conduct, a staff member of the Economic Commission for Africa was summarily dismissed for serious misconduct. He had supported one of the parties during the Rwanda conflict in violation of his duty of impartiality, denounced a colleague and other persons to the authorities, and lied in denying that he had been the author of the denunciation *note au préfet*. The Tribunal confirmed this decision.[31]

The OIOS's sixth report refers to the misdirection of the contributions made by several Member States to the UN Environment Programme (UNEP) Trust Fund at the Chase Manhattan Bank. Although the UN Office at Nairobi had provided the correct bank account number to the Member States, 13 contributions—totaling over $700,000—made by nine Member States was deposited in error into the account of another customer. The recipient of the misdirected funds refused to comply with the request of Chase to transfer the money to the UNEP account and claimed that the money belonged to her. The UNEP account was later credited with the entire amount misdirected, while the recipient of the funds faced criminal proceedings in the US for her actions. OIOS found no evidence of wrongdoing on the part of UN staff members but noted deficiencies on the part of the UN Office at Nairobi and Chase.

During the same reporting period, OIOS looked into the abuse of entitlement benefits, such as medical insurance claims, sick leave claims, security grants, education grants, and rental subsidies. The Office then issued reports of entitlement frauds to program managers to make them more sensitive to the possibility of abuse.

OIOS also submitted reports to the Department of Peacekeeping Operations on procurement (multiple reports), fraud in the Travel Unit, wire fraud, and medical insurance fraud. The UN Office at Nairobi received reports on false dental claims, false security grant claims (multiple reports), procurement (multiple reports), and the trafficking of duty-free items.

Assessment

While a degree of financial irregularity and occasional fraud may be expected in large organizations, some of the instances given above can only be labeled as scandalous. The fact that some of the financial losses—with the notorious exceptions of the UNICEF losses in Kenya and the UNOSOM losses in Somalia—are relatively small in relation to the total budgets or expenditures of the organizations concerned does not excuse fraud in any amount.[32]

The lack of professionalism and effective control in a few peacekeeping operations and in UNICEF, UNHCR, UNRWA, and UNCTAD, as well as the lack of work ethic and proper staff supervision at UNOG and in Habitat, are not acceptable. In most of the reviewed cases, the organizations and agencies concerned have not openly acknowledged their failings nor have they announced publicly the sanctions taken against those staff members responsible for fraud or other misdeeds, or the measures adopted to prevent the recurrence of such grave incidents. Any of these events should have been taken as an alarm signal by the executive heads concerned and should have triggered prompt and public administrative action.

The "UN Culture"

The cases referred to above include major financial losses—$10 million lost by UNICEF in Kenya in 1993–1994, and $3.9 million stolen in Somalia by UNOSOM in 1994—and lesser amounts. Fraud and theft were committed in some cases by outsiders—with or without insiders' support—in others, by staff members at senior or lower levels. Some cases involved fraud in bidding, bribery, submission of fraudulent certificates, the use of altered checks, and the theft of minor items of UN property. Some cases did not result in financial losses but were breaches of standards of conduct: false vaccination statistics, unauthorized outside financial activities, racial discrimination. In some cases, allegations of misconduct were rejected by the UNAT on the grounds that reliable evidence was lacking or that the requirements of due process had not been followed.

Those who condemn or criticize the UN on account of these serious or minor misdeeds believe that the cause lies in the "UN culture," generally described as set in an overstaffed, permissive, loose, and politicized bureaucracy. One element of the UN culture, common to other intergovernmental organizations, is that the staff is multinational and therefore heterogeneous. It is composed of persons of different nationalities; with different education and professional backgrounds; brought up in different cultural situations; with experience in different countries, administrations, or firms; and with varied personal and work ethics. Conflicts arise because of different values—the Max Weber bureaucratic ethos of public service versus loyalty and obligations toward regional, ethnic, or family groups, as well as the constant debate over promotion based on merit or on long service. Working for the UN under UN staff rules and regulations does not guarantee that all of the staff will understand, agree, and comply with required personal and professional standards of conduct. They need to be properly briefed and trained as international civil servants, and their performance and conduct must be periodically and effectively supervised.

One problem specific to the UN is that the heads of the Secretariats—the Secretaries-General—have traditionally been more concerned with their political and diplomatic functions than with ensuring the effective management of their staff. This lack of interest on the part of top management, together with weak resistance to Member States' pressures or even blackmail, has resulted in too many cases in which the political appointment of unqualified candidates is unopposed. Political appointees are often thought by supervisors and other staff to enjoy immunity from sanctions. In addition, mismanagement and poor morale are often caused by uneven workloads in parts of the UN. This results in dynamic, hard-working units contrasting with idle workers who lack motivation and spend months without tasks. Mismanagement often results from uneven leadership skills down the line; lack of management qualifications and training of directors, supervisors, and other responsible officials; lack of on-hand supervision and control; lack of accountability; reluctance to take disciplinary action; collusion and mutual protection among staff of regional or ethnic groups or of the same nationality; and the impunity of political appointees. Lack of transparency is often due to a top-heavy bureaucratic hierarchy of many levels in which initiatives and whistle-blowing are discouraged.

Secondly, the UN is not, as was the Secretariat of the League of Nations, a small group of elitist bureaucrats assigned to one comfortable and safe duty station, Geneva. Most of the staff of UN Funds and Programmes and of Peacekeeping Operations are not only assigned to New York and Geneva, but to many hardship duty stations around the world. Many have arduous operational tasks that include, for some, diplomatic and management functions.[33]

Peacekeeping missions, another specificity of the UN, have generally been organized in haste, following political approval given by the Security Council and financial authorization given by the General Assembly. By definition, they have been run in conflictual or even adverse environments, while being exposed to strong political pressures and critical media observation. The administration of these missions is the responsibility of the Department of Peacekeeping Operations at UN Headquarters, but missions have often suffered locally from the lack of adequate financial and personnel resources; the lack of basic equipment and reliable communications; the lack of adequate administrative leadership, staff supervision, and regular financial control by headquarters; and mismanagement at the local level.

In a memorandum dated 5 October 1994 and addressed to all Assistant Secretaries-General, Directors, and Section Chiefs, the Under-Secretary-General for Administration and Management emphasized the need to respond speedily to emergencies and to the humanitarian needs of peace-keeping missions and other similar operations. He urged rapid decision making and the use of verbal communications rather than memoranda "whenever possible." He noted that "rules are developed to provide safe-guards, which cannot be strictly followed in emergency situations such as the ones we have in human rights, humanitarian affairs and peacekeeping."[34] Although these new, sensible instructions may have caused administrative or financial irregularities or opened the door to fraud, they did not obviate the need for inspection, control, and sanctions.

Finally, corruption is not UN-specific. It is due to human greed and dishonesty and can be found in many organizations—national and international administrations, non-governmental organizations and profit-making organizations, and local associations. To a degree, corruption is related to the presence or absence of effective controls and sanctions.[35]

As only one instance of problems faced by other IGOs, allegations of mismanagement and fraud have been addressed by the European Union Commission. According to an internal memorandum submitted by its Budget Commission in January 1995, the European Commission's services are not organized to guarantee effective financial management, and little heed is paid to the advice of the European Union's Court of Auditors. Following a series of critical audit reports, pressure from members of the European Parliament, and press reports, the European Commission decided, in June 1995, to improve financial safeguards in its management of the Union's 80 billion ECU ($60 million) to ensure better value for taxpayers' money and to cut down on the opportunities for fraud. Following an investigation by the now defunct weekly *The European*, a British member of the European Parliament lodged a formal complaint with the Brussels fraud squad. In February 1995, the Commission's Secretary-General lifted the immunity of three officials charged with financial irregularities, and allowed the police to investigate a department of the Commission for alleged fraud and corruption. The police had access to all documents, and all officials were instructed to cooperate.[36]

Following a report by a team of independent experts, the 20-member European Commission resigned as a group in March 1999. The experts had found considerable evidence of corruption and nepotism. Individual commissioners had not enriched themselves, but, as a body, the Commission had lost political control. One of its members, Martin Bangemann was placed on "operational leave" on 1 July 1999 after his decision to take a consulting job with a Spanish telecommunications company. As he had been in charge of industry and telecommunications at the Commission, he was accused of a conflict of interest, which he denied. The President-designate of the Commission, Romano Prodi, then called for new ethics rules, in order to avoid such a situation in the future.

A later report found that the system of financial controls had an "antediluvian feel" and that the number of staff dedicated to internal audits was "derisory." These institutional and management issues will need to be looked into.[37] As illustrated, even an organization such as the European Commission, which works with more resources and in a more conducive and homogeneous environment—as compared with global peacekeeping and development cooperation—is not immune to corruption and nepotism.

What Remedies?

Preventing fraud and corruption, or at least limiting it, demands strong leadership, visible discipline, clear rules on what constitutes misconduct, and the assurance that misconduct will not be tolerated. In the UN system, the UN Secretary-General and his close assistants and the executive heads of UN Funds and Programmes should show their determination to carry out a "clean hands" program by issuing statements of policy, tightening controls, carrying out prompt investigations, and applying stern sanctions without exceptions, even for political appointees, at all levels of the hierarchy. Member States cannot abdicate their own primary responsibility, insofar as money lost or stolen has been mainly provided by governments, that is, taxpayers, and in part by other donors, while allegations of corruption discredit organizations and discourage donors. Member States' representatives should therefore make the organizations' managers fully accountable for their financial management. They should demand periodic reports on all financial irregularities, their causes, and the individual sanctions applied, and that further preventive and corrective actions are taken.

The Rules

Article 101, paragraph 3, of the UN Charter defines the qualities required from candidates for UN employment as the highest standards of efficiency, competence, and integrity. Detailed provisions on the rights and obligations of staff members are contained in the UN Staff Rules, complemented from time to time by information circulars. As shown below, Staff Regulations and Rules were revised as of 1 January 1999. Former Staff Rule 112.3 stated: "Any staff member may be required to reimburse the United Nations either partially or in full for any financial loss suffered by the United Nations as a result of the staff member's negligence or his or her having violated any regulation, rule or administrative instruction." Financial Rule 114.1 confirms that "[a]ny official who takes any action contrary to these Financial Rules, or to the administrative instructions issued in connection therewith, may be held personally responsible and financially liable for the consequence of such action." Former Staff Rule 110.1 provided that disciplinary proceedings and the imposition of disciplinary measures may be initiated in cases of misconduct. However, these texts did not refer specifically to willful fraud.

A Code of Conduct

The "Report on Standards of Conduct in the International Civil Service" was issued in 1954 by the International Civil Service Advisory Board. The Board was replaced in 1975 by the International Civil Service Commission, and the Report was reissued in 1982 by the UN Administrative Committee on Coordination. The Report includes in the definition of "integrity" "such elementary personal or private qualities as honesty, truthfulness, fidelity, probity, and freedom from corrupting influences." Staff members must scrupulously comply with the laws of the host country and honor their financial obligations. In the 1950s, the notion of "integrity" had been misused by several UN organizations in order to terminate allegedly disloyal UN staff of US nationality, under US pressure, during the McCarthy witch-hunt.[38]

For the Commission, high standards of conduct are best attained by a universal understanding among staff members of the relation between their conduct and the success of the international organizations, and by the development of a strong tradition among men and women who are jealous of the reputation of the organization they serve and are anxious to safeguard it. Applicable throughout the UN system, the standards have no legal force unless incorporated in personnel rules, but they are guidelines often cited in Administrative Tribunals' judgments as being fundamental to the rules and regulations of the organizations.

In 1953, Secretary-General Dag Hammarskjöld defined his approach regarding violations of the law as follows:

> The standard of conduct applicable to staff members is more exacting than ordinary legal standards. A conviction by a national court will usually be persuasive evidence of the commission of the act for which the defendant was prosecuted. And acts which are generally recognized as offences by national criminal laws normally will be violations also of the independent standard of integrity developed by, and proper to, the United Nations. However, the Organization must remain free to take no account of convictions of staff members for trivial offences or for offences which are generally held not to reflect on integrity, or of convictions made without observation to the generally recognized requirements of due process of law.[39]

In his 1994 report on the efficiency of the administrative and financial functioning of the UN (Doc. A/C.5/49/1), Secretary-General Boutros Boutros-Ghali announced that he would promulgate a code of conduct. This was a direct response to one of several demands made by the US Senate under the direction of Jesse Helms as prerequisites for the payment of US arrears to the UN regular and peacekeeping budgets, although the quid pro quo was not honored by the US.

Following difficult consultations with staff representatives, the Secretary-General submitted the proposed Code of Conduct to the General Assembly in 1997 and 1998.[40] The Code was integrated into Article 1 of the UN Staff Regulations and Chapter 1 of the Staff Rules. The Assembly approved its text, with a few changes, by Resolution 52/252 of 8 September 1998, to be effective on 1 January 1999.[41] The new rules apply to all staff, including the separately funded organs. Additional rules were to be issued for finance officers and procurement officers. The new regulations and rules are more detailed and specific with regard to financial issues. Regulation 1.2 (b) includes "honesty" in the concept of integrity, one of the standards to be upheld by staff members. Regulation 1.2 (g) prohibits staff from using their office or knowledge acquired from their official functions for private gain, financial or otherwise, or for the private gain of any third party. Under Staff Regulation 1.2 (m), staff cannot be actively associated or hold a financial interest in any profit making, business, or other concern if either the concern or the staff member is to profit by the association with the UN. Staff Regulation 1.2 (r) requires staff to respond fully to requests for information from staff members and other UN officials authorized to investigate possible misuse of funds, waste, or abuse.

Finally, a new financial disclosure obligation was created in order to prevent any financial conflict of interest. All staff at the Assistant Secretary-General level and above are required to file financial disclosure statements upon appointment and at periodic intervals in regard to themselves and their dependent children. These statements remain confidential.

The Code received harsh criticism from the staff representatives. For instance, according to the UN staff union, the Code was "draconian, antediluvian and archaic in nature ... only officials with plenty of time on their hands could have spent their working hours dreaming up rules relating to the conduct of staff." Representatives of the Federation of International Civil Servants' Associations (FICSA) asked rhetorically: "Can this repressive Code of Conduct, which violates freedom of expression and association and the right to privacy, be called progress?" FICSA was "outraged" that the Code is worded in such a way as to imply that international civil servants and their families are potentially capable of wrongdoing.[42]

These criticisms are excessive: most large organizations define norms of conduct for their staff as well as disciplinary rules and sanctions. Even if the UN Code was initiated under strong US pressure and some of its rules (on collective staff rights) may be questionable, its creation by the UN Secretariat, in consultation with the staff, and its adoption by the General Assembly followed a legitimate process. It will help the UN Administration in assessing cases and making decisions, and should enable staff members to know the extent of their rights and obligations.

However, setting rules and sanctions does not end the matter. Supervisors need to exercise leadership, instill motivation, control the performance and conduct of their staff, and apply sanctions as required. In large organizations, there is a need for an effective internal and external financial control system.[43]

The UN Financial Oversight System

The UN financial oversight system includes an internal mechanism—internal auditors—and external mechanisms—the UN Board of External Auditors, the Joint Inspection Unit (JIU), an interagency body. Intergovernmental or expert bodies—the Advisory Committee on Administrative and Budgetary Questions (ACABQ) and the Committee for Programme and Coordination (CPC)—provide the General Assembly with additional assessments and recommendations on administrative and financial questions.[44] Among these bodies, only internal and external auditors have hands-on functions of financial inspection and investigation, among other duties, and in particular the detection of management and financial irregularities, including fraud, that result in financial losses to the UN. UNDP, UNFPA, UNHCR, UNICEF, and UNRWA rely on their own Internal Audit Units to provide for investigations, in consultation with the UN Office of Internal Oversight Services (OIOS) as required.

In the UN Secretariat, prior to 1994, the Internal Audit Division was responsible for the compliance by the UN Administration of financial transactions with General Assembly resolutions, financial and staff regulations and rules, and administrative instructions. Since 1993, the Division has been located within the Department of Administration and Management (DAM) and has reported to the Under-Secretary-General for Administration and Management at UN Headquarters. Even though the Division was formally independent, its location in DAM and its hierarchical supervision by the USG for Administration and Management could not but restrain its autonomy, its freedom of investigation, and its influence or authority. Furthermore, its reports were confidential; they could easily result in no effective follow-up action.

The General Assembly expressed its "concern" in 1990, 1991, and 1992 about cases of deficiencies in program and financial management and inappropriate or fraudulent use of resources as reported by the UN Board of Auditors (Res. 45/235, 46/183, 47/211). Under pressure from the Assembly and in response to another specific US demand, Secretary-General Boutros Boutros-Ghali appointed Mohamed Aly Niazi (Egypt) as Assistant Secretary-General for Inspections and Investigations as of 1 September 1993. As another instance of financial blackmail and as a unilateral decision, the US Congress withheld 10 percent of the US contribution to the UN budget for 1993, then 20 percent for 1994, until the US Secretary of State had certified that an independent Inspector-General had been appointed.

The General Assembly finally established, by Resolution 48/218 B of 29 July 1994, the Office of Internal Oversight Services (OIOS). The Office is placed directly under the Secretary-General. Its head exercises operational independence, and the Office maintains expertise in the fields of accounting, auditing, financial analysis and investigations, management, and law or public administration. The new USG is appointed by the Secretary-General, following consultations with Member States, and is approved by the General Assembly with due regard to geographical rotation. On 24 August 1994, the Assembly approved the nomination of Karl Th. Paschke (Germany) as Under-Secretary-General (USG) for Internal Oversight Services. He assumed his duties on 15 November 1995 for a non-renewable five-year term.

The purpose of the OIOS is to assist the Secretary-General in fulfilling his internal oversight responsibilities in respect of the resources of the staff of the Organization through the exercise of the functions of monitoring, internal audit, inspection and evaluation, investigations, implementation of recommendations and reporting procedures, and support and advice to management. Any relevant reports are submitted to the Secretary-General, who submits them to the General Assembly together with any comments he might consider appropriate. Reports are also provided to the Board of Auditors and the Joint Inspection Unit.

The Secretary-General was requested to ensure that the Office had procedures in place that provided for "direct confidential access of staff members to the Office and for protection against repercussions, for the purpose of ... reporting perceived cases of misconduct." He was also requested to ensure that individual rights and the anonymity of staff members be preserved, that due process be observed, that falsely accused staff members be fully cleared, and that disciplinary and/or jurisdictional proceedings be initiated if justified. The functions and reporting procedures of the Office were to be evaluated and reviewed at the General Assembly's 53rd Session.[45]

In its third annual report to the General Assembly, for the period 1 July 1996 to 30 June 1997, the OIOS congratulated the Assembly for its own creation. The institution of independent oversight in the UN was, in its view, a most meaningful and effective reform step. The Office felt that its impact on the UN management culture was significant: "It has heightened fiscal awareness among staff, contributed to streamlining many administrative and other UN activities, watched over the strict observance of rules and regulations, promoted economic solutions and battled irregularities and wrongdoing against the Organization. OIOS recommendations have aimed at structural change, better management, more accountability and increased transparency." Much work was needed to substantially change the prevailing UN culture. In its second annual report, OIOS had noted that it had been confronted with some attempts to slow down, stall, or discredit its work. It observed that an organization that had lived without independent and effective internal oversight for decades still had to adjust to outspoken criticisms, all the more so in documents that reach the General Assembly.

The Office's own performance improved between 1995 and 1997. From July 1995 to June 1996, with an implementation rate of its audit recommendations at 61 percent on 30 June 1996, OIOS saved the UN $15.8 million. The implementation rate increased to 71 percent on 30 June 1997, and the savings amounted to $17.8 million. The rate went up to 73 percent on 30 June 1998, with savings and recoveries amounting to $10.3 million. OIOS's budget for 1996–1997 was $14.6 million (Res. 52/213).

The "Conference on Financial Oversight and Accountability in the UN System," organized by the UN Association of the US, took place in Princeton from 30 October to 1 November 1998.[46] Among other comments, the discussants found ambiguous the innovative hybrid of internal oversight functions with external reporting lines: the work of the Office is addressed to managers and the Secretary-General, while the political bodies are informed. Discussants echoed complaints in various quarters of the Secretariat about the "overzealousness" of the Office in investigating alleged fraud and abuse. On the other hand, OIOS champions stressed that the investigative function has had a bracing and wholesome effect, "deterring" abuse and fraud. It may be argued that being labeled "overzealous" can be taken as a compliment within the UN environment and administrative culture. The fact that OIOS reports are sent to the General Assembly, and not retained as confidential internal documents, should be an incentive to UN managers to prevent fraud and to apply sanctions in cases of proved misconduct.

The role and mandate of the Office were reaffirmed by the General Assembly in its Resolution 54/244 of 23 December 1999. Reflecting the concerns of developing countries, the resolution oddly reaffirmed the General Assembly's role as the principal oversight organ of the Organization—as if there could be a competition between OIOS and the Assembly—and stressed that OIOS should not propose any change in the legislative decisions and mandates approved by intergovernmental organs. These warnings were no doubt a response to Paschke's reference in the preface of his last annual report, dated 31 July 1999, to "[t]he constantly growing number of mandates where their reduction and a new definition of UN priorities would be desirable."

Paschke's non-renewable term of five years ended in November 1999. The General Assembly approved the appointment of Dileep Nair (Singapore) as Under-Secretary-General for Internal Oversight Services by decision 54/320 of 2 March 2000. He took up his duties on 24 April 2000.

Nair's first report—the sixth OIOS annual report—on the period 1 July 1999 to 30 June 2000, noted that the Investigations Section had investigated 38 cases that were presented for administrative or disciplinary action. Of these cases, 22 were recommended for criminal prosecution by national law enforcement authorities. As UN organizations have no criminal justice system (the UN Administrative Tribunal deals only with non-observance of contracts of employment or terms of appointment), this was a significant concrete advance in confirming the principle of the accountability of UN managers for their deeds and misdeeds.

The Applicable Disciplinary Sanctions

Instances of fraud may be discovered by a supervisor, colleagues, a department, a mission, internal or external auditors or the OIOS through audits, management inspections, or other forms of disclosure.[47] Upon determination of sufficient prima facie of wrongdoing, if the fraud has been committed by a staff member, it should be reported to the Controller and referred to the Assistant Secretary-General for Human Resources Management for appropriate disciplinary action. In cases when the evidence is patent and leaves no doubt that serious misconduct or fraud has occurred (e.g., when the staff member admits to the fraud), the staff member is summarily dismissed. He or she then loses the termination indemnity and repatriation grant to which he or she would otherwise have been eligible on separation.

In other cases, the matter is referred to the Joint Disciplinary Committee. If the Committee establishes that misconduct has occurred, any of the following disciplinary measures may be recommended: written censure; loss of one or more steps-in-grade; deferment, for a specified period, of eligibility for within-grade increment; suspension without pay; fine; demotion; separation from service, with or without compensation; summary dismissal. The Under-Secretary-General for Management may then decide, on behalf of the Secretary-General, what disciplinary measure to impose.

As seen before, disciplinary measures may be appealed to the UN Administrative Tribunal; however, the institution of proceedings to the Tribunal does not suspend the decision made by the UN Administration, although the Tribunal's later judgment may rescind or amend it. In a few recent cases (Kenya, Switzerland), the UN has sought and obtained the assistance of national law enforcement authorities such as police and courts to complement internal administrative sanctions with national criminal prosecution and possible sentences involving incarceration and fines. Already in 1992, the General Assembly had requested the Secretary-General to make proposals on seeking criminal prosecution of those who have committed fraud against the Organization (Res. 47/211). This finally followed the approach taken earlier by the European Union in Belgium. However, the UN has warned that a staff member's misconduct may not necessarily correspond to the definitions of criminal offenses found in different national legal systems. Furthermore, the evidence considered by the UN may not satisfy the standard of proof applicable in criminal matters by national courts. Finally, criminal prosecution is a matter within the discretion of national criminal authorities.

If non-staff members are responsible for acts of fraud or theft, the UN's only effective recourse is to call on national authorities to investigate the case and identify, arrest, and judge those alleged to have carried out the wrongdoing.

Recovery Procedures

In the same 1992 resolution (47/211), the General Assembly requested the Secretary-General to make proposals for establishing legal and effective mechanisms to recover misappropriated funds, as recommended by ACABQ. In its report,[48] the Committee noted that, in quite a few cases, efforts toward recovery of misappropriated funds or other losses to the Organization had been negligible or unsuccessful, due in some cases to the individual having left the jurisdiction of the UN.

When losses incurred by the Organization are recoverable from the staff member, deductions may be effected from the staff member's salary and other emoluments, including termination payments. However, this is only feasible when the staff member is still employed by the UN and when the sums involved do not exceed the staff member's credits.

Recovery of indebtedness cannot, however, be obtained directly from the pension entitlements of staff members. While the Administrative Tribunal noted with regret this state of affairs,[49] it rejected previous attempts by the Administration to obtain such direct recovery, as this was precluded by the Regulations of the UN Joint Staff Pension Fund. It would therefore be desirable that the Administration submit to the General Assembly a proposal to amend the Pension Fund Regulations to permit such recovery. This change would constitute another deterrent to misconduct and a more significant compensation for fraud and theft.

In addition to recovery action taken internally, cases may be referred to national authorities with a view to recovering the full amount of indebtedness to the UN or obtaining compensation for damages. However, the Organization would consider whether the amounts that it could reasonably expect to recover are commensurate with the costs to be incurred as a result of the Organization's involvement in national legal proceedings. The UN Administration appears to remain skeptical about the effectiveness and economic value of such referrals.

Conclusion

The accusations of widespread fraud and corruption in the UN system are excessive as a broad judgment, and too often linked to anti-UN campaigns. While specific charges have been shown to be true, only a small minority of staff members are potential or actual offenders, a proportion likely to be found in other national and international organizations.

Thanks to the creation of OIOS, a degree of transparency and accountability has been imposed on the UN Administration, on some of the UN Funds and Programmes, and, mainly, on UN Peacekeeping Operations. OIOS investigations into financial irregularities and fraud and their results are now released publicly. OIOS has revealed management and administrative weaknesses and has prodded the UN Administration into taking preventive and corrective action. In particular, prompt and effective action should be taken to prevent the recurrence of financial irregularities and fraud that had been found earlier. The UN has had to sanction offenders more severely, and, in a few cases, referral to national police and judiciary authorities has usefully complemented and added teeth to the UN internal processes. Recovery of lost or stolen funds has remained difficult and, in some cases, is impossible. In any case, it is not acceptable to have allowed bureaucratic delays in effecting recovery that have caused avoidable losses.

In 1993, the General Assembly had requested the Secretary-General "to include in the system of accountability and responsibility the following elements, taking into account relevant experience within and outside the United Nations system":

1. the establishment of clear responsibility for program delivery, including performance indicators as a measure of quality control;
2. a mechanism ensuring that program managers are accountable for the effective management of the personnel and financial resources allocated to them;
3. performance evaluation for all officials, including senior officials, with objectives and performance indicators; and
4. effective training of staff members in financial and management responsibilities.[50]

Many public administrations and the UN itself have been deficient in defining performance indicators, which in turn depend on setting clear and measurable objectives—a difficult task for many non-profit organizations. In particular, the expected achievements of most UN organizations—that is, the results obtained, not the activities performed—are dependent on the action or inaction of governments and on many political, economic, and social factors over which the Organization has no direct influence. However, the introduction of better information systems may prove beneficial to performance measurement and evaluation.

Training is an obvious requirement for improving staff performance, but governments are loath to authorize its financing. To the excellent recommendations of the General Assembly, one should add that the effectiveness of financial control systems depends first on the recruitment and assignment of experienced, competent, and honest managers; on their guidance and supervision; and on the periodic assessment of their performance and conduct. It also depends on the qualifications and independence of internal and external auditors, on the quality and honesty of their reports, and on the capacity and will of senior management to respond promptly to audit criticisms and recommendations and to consider sanctions and to impose management reform when and where needed. In other words, there is a need to create and maintain a new "financial culture" among the staff of UN organizations.

However, as noted in the Princeton report, "oversight is but a tool, not a substitute, for effective management. Even the most lavish investment in oversight bodies may yield only modest results if officials and Member State representatives are complacent about deficient performance." Behind and beyond the issues of management reform and oversight mechanisms lie larger questions concerning the lack of agreement of Member States on program and budget priorities, or, more generally, on the extent of the mandate of UN organizations.

Do Member States really want to "clean up" the UN bureaucracies? Do they really want a more effective UN? One cannot generalize about the motivation of 189 Member States. However, serious doubts about their collective will are justified as the creation of a new UN culture is facing many obstacles, some of which are being created by the Member States themselves. UN staff may remain skeptical when they see Member States delaying or reducing payment of their contributions to the UN. They also remain skeptical when they see Member States pushing political appointees, especially those who lack essential qualifications and managerial skills. In addition, staff members can also become demotivated when they see the UN being used as an easy scapegoat or when they receive politically motivated criticism. Similarly, some calls for staff reduction lead at best to insecurity and at worst to an emaciated workforce, with the best people leaving in frustration. Finally, UN employees also have to cope with corruption, fraud, and nepotism in the use of UN funds by some governments.

In the end, the role of Member States is pivotal in fighting corruption and changing the financial culture of the UN. These States could do much more themselves. In conclusion, the Secretary-General faces formidable hurdles both externally and internally in his fight for the administrative reform of the UN.

Notes

1. For more comments from a different perspective on the UN audit culture, see Dirk Salomons's chapter in this book.
2. On external auditors, see Beigbeder (1997): 115. Chapter 7 is titled "The Extent of Fraud and Losses."
3. ACABQ is a 16-member expert committee, which reviews the budget initially submitted by the Secretary-General. Its report is submitted to the General Assembly's Fifth Committee.
4. For instance, see *The Sunday Times*, "UN Officials Exposed in Sleaze Scandal," 2 November 1997.
5. CUNMA is a non-profit, non-partisan, public interest law firm/NGO. Its primary goals are "to drive the process of reform throughout the UN system through the use of internal judicial action and external journalistic exposure, and … to highlight and expose corrupt, wasteful, or inefficient practices, as well as incompetent and rogue managers throughout the UN system."
6. UNAT Judgment no. 742, 22 November 1995, in re *Manson*.
7. The Tribunal cited the organizational weaknesses at UNTAC, the frequent absence of a supervisor, prevailing local business and bribery practices, threats to his personal safety, willingness to return the $1,000 bribe to its author, his otherwise unblemished 17 years of service, and his positive attitude, which saved $4 million to the UN. UNAT Judgment no. 755, 17 July 1996, in re *Chen*.
8. UNAT Judgment no. 898, 20 November 1998, in re *Uggla*.
9. UNAT Judgment no. 721, 21 November 1995, in re *Hevi*.
10. UNAT Judgment no. 785, 21 November 1996, in re *White*.
11. UNAT Judgment no. 744, 22 November 1995, in re *Eren, Robertson, Sellberg, Thompson*.
12. UN Doc. A/54/683.
13. *International Herald Tribune*, 27–28 May 1995; *Le Monde*, 15 June 1995.
14. UNICEF Doc. A/53/5/Add.2, Report of the Board of Auditors.
15. UNAT Judgment no. 515, 27 May 1991, in re *Khan*.
16. UNAT Judgments no. 756, 16 July 1996, in re *Obinba*, and no. 830, 1 August 1997, in re *Anih*.
17. UNAT Judgment no. 890, 7 August 1998, in re *Augustine*.
18. Elif Kaban, "UN Sleuth Probing Possible Refugee Agency Fraud," 19 October 1998 (Reuters).
19. There were suspicions that the applicant might have improperly granted refugee status to two Iraqi asylum seekers: UNAT Judgment no. 849, 25 November 1997, in re *Von Seth*.
20. Doc. JIU/REP/93/5, 1993, pars. 76–77.
21. UNAT Judgment no. 479, 18 May 1990, in re *Caine*.
22. UNAT Judgment no. 797, 21 November 1996, in re *Bouras*.
23. UNAT Judgment no. 714, 28 July 1995, in re *Saleh*.
24. UNAT Judgment no. 877, 31 July 1998, in re *Abdulhadi*.
25. UNAT Judgment no. 908, 20 November 1998, in re *Baghoud*.
26. See also *The Sunday Times*, 2 November 1997.
27. UNAT Judgment no. 698, 28 July 1995, in re *Huda*.
28. UNAT Judgment no. 897, 20 November 1998, in re *Jhuthi*.
29. UNAT Judgment no. 850, 26 November 1997, in re *Patel*.
30. Communicated by CUNMA.
31. UNAT Judgment no. 738, 21 November 1995, in re *Nkubana*.
32. For instance, the total expenditures under the UN regular budget for 1998–1999 were $2.5 billion, and the cost of peacekeeping operations from August 1997 to July 1998 was $992 million; UNICEF expenditures for 1996–1997 were $1.8 billion; the UNHCR budget for 1997 was $1.2 billion: Res. 53/215 A, UNICEF and UNHCR docs.
33. For instance, 41 percent of UNHCR's 274 field offices are in "hazardous" locations. See "UNHCR Response to Issues Raised by the *Financial Times*," 10 August 1998.

34. Quoted in UNAT Judgment no. 744, par. 19.
35. Among recent examples: losses due to corruption in Bosnia have been estimated at $1 billion, mostly stolen from Bosnian public funds or lost through the failure of officials in Bosnia to collect taxes, either through corruption or mismanagement (*International Herald Tribune*, 21–22 August 1999); a former military accountant in the Swiss federal secret information services is alleged to have embezzled $5.8 million from the Defense Ministry through the submission of false invoices between 1994 to 1999 (*Le Point*, 27 August 1999). Even the Vatican bureaucracy was recently alleged to suffer from intrigue and corruption in the book *Shroud of Secrecy: The Story of Corruption within the Vatican* by Father Luigi Marinelli (2000). One problem with assessing the corruption of NGOs lies in their huge diversity. Some are highly professional, while others are poorly organized. In some cases, NGOs may be a deceptive front for fraudulent activities.
36. *The European*, 24 February–2 March, 17–23 March, 23–29 June 1995.
37. *International Herald Tribune*, 2, 3–4, 23 July and 11–12 September 1999. For a discussion of political and administrative corruption in public administration, see the report with the same title from a seminar in Ankara, in 1997, organized by the International Institute of Administrative Sciences and the Institute of Public Administration for Turkey and the Middle East.
38. See Beigbeder (1988), pp. 51–56.
39. Doc. A/2533, par. 72.
40. Doc. A/52/488 and Add.1.
41. Doc. ST/SGB/1998/19 of 10 December 1998 includes the revised Regulations and Rules and an explanatory commentary.
42. *UN Staff, the Voice of the Staff Union*, New York, January 1997; *FICSA Newsletter*, November 1997 (FICSA is the Federation of International Civil Servants' Associations, based in Geneva); *International Documents Review*, 24 November 1997.
43. The World Bank Group published in December 1999 its Code of Professional Ethics: see http://www.worldbank.org/ethics. It has also a Professional Ethics Office, and a hotline for fraud and corruption.
44. For details on these bodies and their role, see Beigbeder (1997), chapters 3 and 7.
45. Res. 48/801/Add.2.
46. See http://www.unausa.org/issues/reform/103098conf.htm
47. Doc. A/53/849, 3 March 1999. A reporting facility within OIOS was set up by Administrative Instruction ST/AI/397 of 7 September 1994. It provides for direct confidential access by staff members and other persons engaged in activities under the authority of the Organization who wish to report possible misuse of funds, waste, or abuse of UN facilities or privileges.
48. Doc. A/47/500.
49. See UNAT Judgment no. 358 and no. 479.
50. Res. 48/218 E.

Bibliography

Beigbeder, Y. *Threats to the International Civil Service: Past Pressures and New Trends.* London: Pinter Publishers, 1988.

Beigbeder, Y. *The Internal Management of United Nations Organizations: The Long Quest for Reform.* Basingstoke: Macmillan Press Ltd; New York: St. Martin's Press, Inc., 1997.

Marinelli, L. *Shroud of Secrecy: The Story of Corruption within the Vatican.* Toronto: Key Porter Books, 2000.

PART III

IMPLEMENTATION

The first two parts of this volume deal with international decision making at the strategic level of the organization and more internally focused decision making and management. Of course, these issues partly overlap. This third part turns to implementation issues in what is called "the field." How autonomous is the international organization in the field? Do the management problems change considerably? There are other actors active at the field level than at the strategic level, varying from local NGOs and municipal governments to warmongering criminals. Sometimes tensions arise between headquarters and the field, while donor government demands and policies can become far removed from the local reality. Since program management is such a crucial tool for international organizations, the topic will open this part and set the stage for chapters on the role of human rights organizations, managing CIVPOL, and the development of NGOs and civil society in Bosnia and Herzegovina.

Chapter 7

PROGRAMS AND THE PROBLEMS OF PARTICIPATION

❧

Dennis Dijkzeul

Introduction

Programs are the preferred tool of action at the field level for most international organizations. They are used for many tasks in development cooperation, as well as in human rights promotion and public sanitation, to name just a few. Their popularity is not confined to international organizations alone; most corporations also use programs or projects extensively, for example, in research and development, and in organizational development (Graham and Englund 1997; Kerzner 1998). One of the potential strengths of the program approach is that it allows for the participation of various groups. In general, such participation is necessary to ensure local ownership, follow-up, and sustainability. However, in reality many, if not most, programs fail to foster such participation; as a result, their impact is often minimal or even negative. This chapter studies why this is the case.

The chapter looks at the reasons for the popularity of the program approach. It delineates the different program stages and the criticism on the program approach, as well as techniques for improvement. Further, the chapter reviews some of the related organizational and interorganizational issues. It also asks whether alternatives to the program approach offer a way out of the pathologies associated with the programming approach.

What Is a Program?

Many international organizations use program management as an instrument to structure their activities, in particular, their service delivery. As a consequence, programs have almost become synonymous with service delivery for many managers. In manufacturing terms, this service delivery is known as the primary process of the organization. Hence, understanding program management, or, as it is often called, the program approach, can provide valuable insights into the operational core of the organizations, as well as their interorganizational relationships.

Reasons for Program Management

Organizations generally need to integrate different projects into a concerted program. Wijnen et al. (1990: 30) define a project in the following terms:

- A project has a limited set of separate activities.
- A project is an endeavor in which several parties (persons, groups, or organizations) have a clear interest.
- A project needs to be realized within a set time frame and with limited resources.
- A project focuses on one or more concrete results that often contain one or more completely new elements for the parties involved.

This is a broad definition that highlights the fact that projects contain non-routine tasks. They combine a quest for results in terms of change, while specifying the resources and time allocated. In principle, they are well suited for the development, humanitarian, environmental, and human rights work of international organizations, which often focus on societal change.

With a program, one can combine projects in various functional fields, such as health, education, and agriculture, as well as projects from different organizations that focus on different activities. For example, a program that aims to bring down the Under Five Mortality Rate (U5MR) of children can integrate projects for maternal education, prenatal care, oral rehydration, and breast-feeding, as well as the improvement of local agriculture for better feeding and advocacy to the local governments. Programs are thus sets of related projects. One can see a program as a megaproject involving the same elements, but integrated at a larger scale to achieve synergy among the individual projects.

Within the UN system, most organizations originally focused on individual projects. In many organizations, this project focus has slowly evolved into a broader, more long-term program approach (see UNDP/1990/9). NGOs differ widely in the quality of their programming. Some are still stuck in the individual project mode; others have become leaders in their field and have produced elaborate manuals (see Eade and Williams 1995: 21; Gosling and Edwards 1995).

Definition of Program Management

Programs "can be seen as responses to either perceived or incipient communal problems." Their origin lies in "the recognition of a 'social

problem'—by which we mean a defect in the human and social condition—and a resolve to take purposive, organized action to remedy the
problem" (Rossi and Freeman 1985: 38–39). The basic assumption behind
program (and project) management is that intentionally structured action
can lead to societal improvement. A program provides a procedure in the
sense of ordered steps to achieve results. Like a hammer that does not
determine which nails you need to hit into whatever object is at hand,
program management does not determine by itself which actions or societal improvements need to be realized.

In its simplest form, program management comprises three related
stages: preparation, implementation, and evaluation (see figure 7.1). A
carefully established program should consider the possibilities and provisions for good evaluation research. Evaluation often has a double
meaning: it is seen either as the final assessment of a program (or project),
or as a review of each stage of program management. An evaluation of
the preparation stage is called appraisal; during implementation it is
called monitoring. After the completion of a program, the final evaluation
takes place. All in all, programs become long processes that are subject to
many external variables.

From a positive point of view, the program approach is a powerful tool
to rationalize and ameliorate the process for long-term societal investment. "Its principal advantage lies in providing a ... framework and
sequence within which data can be compiled and analyzed, investment

FIGURE 7.1 Stages of Program Management

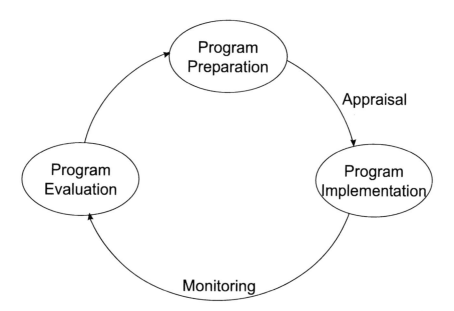

priorities established, project or program alternatives considered, and sector policy issues addressed. It imposes a discipline on planners and decision-makers, and ensures that relevant problems and issues are taken into account and subjected to systematic analysis before decisions are reached and implemented. Correctly applied, it can greatly increase the development impact of ... scarce investment resources" (Baum and Tolbert 1985: 335).[1]

Baum and Tolbert (ibid.: 335) go on to describe the limitations of the program approach. The success of a program also "depends on quantitative inputs of data and can be no more reliable than those data. It ... depends on estimates and forecasts, which are subject to human error. Risks can be assessed but not avoided, and projects must be designed and implemented against a constantly shifting background of political, social, and economic changes." They conclude that "in the last analysis, the effectiveness of the ... approach depends on the skill and judgment of those who use it." In principle, the tools to improve program management come in two groups: first, techniques to improve the activities for each of the program stages and their interaction, and, second, techniques to improve the various substantive aspects of program management. In practice, they are often used together, but for the sake of analysis these two groups will be treated separately.

Program Preparation

During the preparation stage, the perceived problem and the organization's policies are translated into projects that, hopefully, will have a lasting impact on the problem. The program will be the framework in which the projects should fit. Although it is impossible to foresee all future changes, careful program preparation can, to some extent, prevent problems. Program preparation generally results in a "program proposal," sometimes officially called a statute. Conscientious program appraisal can strengthen a program proposal considerably (World Bank 1998: 101). Sabatier and Mazmanian (1980: 544–548) have developed a statutory model that distinguishes seven independent "variables" in a proposal that "together lend direction and coherence to the complicated process of program implementation."

Policy variables
1. Precision of objectives: Does the program statute provide clearly ranked instructions for the agency and show the target group how to conform to program objectives?
2. Validity of causal theory: Does the program statute indicate how the implementing agencies will produce the planned change in the target group?

Instrumental variables
3. Hierarchical integration: Does the program statute create an integrated hierarchical network of implementing agencies? And which organization, department, or person is responsible for which tasks?
4. Stakeholder participation: Does the program statute provide liberal rules of participation in decisions made by stakeholders committed to the program?
5. Decision rules: Does the program statute stipulate how the decision regulations of the participating organizations support the program goal?

Resource variables
6. Financial resources: Does the statute indicate the availability of funds for the program activities?
7. Personnel resources: Does the statute assign program implementation to officials who are strongly committed to program objectives? (see Van de Vall 1991: 47).

Partly overlapping techniques have been developed to assess each of these variables. Since they can be used independently without applying the statutory model for program appraisal, they are treated separately later in this chapter. A program that scores positively on all seven variables is not necessarily successful, as unforeseen problems can arise during the implementation process.

Program Implementation

Politicians and diplomats score headlines with policy initiatives, not with their execution. As a result, the implementation stage often receives scant attention. Nevertheless, such attention can offer opportunities to improve the current program and to lay the groundwork for future programs and more effective policies. Particularly after the early 1970s, business and public administration scholars increasingly focused on the topic of implementation (Berman 1978; Mayer and Greenwood 1980; Pressman and Wildavsky 1984; Sabatier and Mazmanian 1980; Scheirer 1981; Van de Vall 1991b: 41–57; Van Meter and Van Horn 1975). These scholars emphasized the complexity of joint action as one of the crucial characteristics of implementation. Subsequently, they attempted to develop conceptual models to graphically describe and analyze (aspects of) the multiactor program process (Van de Vall 1991a: 5). These models differentiate internal implementation from external, or contextual, implementation (see Berman 1978: 157). Internally, the organization is rather autonomous and can establish its own procedures. Externally, the context of the organization deeply influences program management.

Internal implementation. In daily practice, the programming process is often long and complex. It combines decisions at headquarters with

FIGURE 7.2 The Relationship between Statutory Variables and Program Implementation

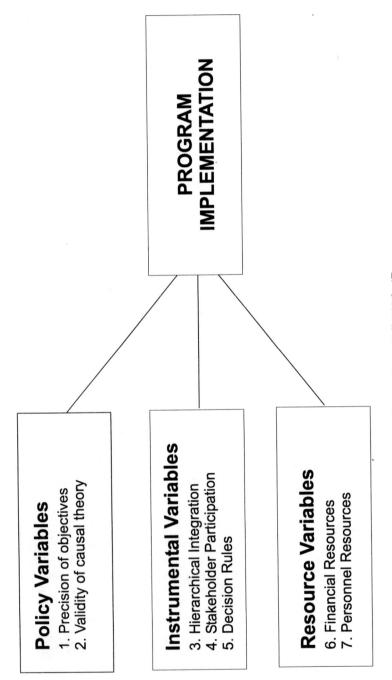

Source: Van de Vall (1991b: 47).

international funding and activities in the field. With a delta flow chart, it is possible to capture the organizational procedures from program conception to completion. Such a flow chart aims specifically at clarifying the internal aspects of program management (Harrel Allen 1978: 107; see also Scholtes et al. 2000). They are frequently used in total quality management and other internal organizational improvement techniques. Figure 7.3 provides an example of the UNICEF programming process.

Contextual implementation. Van de Vall (1991b: 48–50) has elaborated a contextual model (see figure 7.4) that was originally developed by Mayer and Greenwood (1980: 130). This model provides an overview of the entire execution of the program and the variables that impinge on it. The model incorporates nine variables into a causal pattern. Four variables are manipulable, and five other variables are non-manipulable by the management of the organization. "The core of the model is the relationship between the independent variable statute of the program and the dependent variable program impact." In between are two intervening variables: internal program management and the bridging variable. The latter variable indicates the complexity of joint multiparty action in achieving program impact. Various actors involved in the program are so autonomous that they cannot be forced directly to cooperate with the program. Consequently, the "bridging variable is a non-manipulable condition for attaining the program goal" (Van de Vall 1991b: 48). "Understanding the success or failure of policy may often hinge on the decision maker's awareness of a bridging variable" (Mayer and Greenwood 1980: 126). Two other intervening variables, namely, environment of the program and characteristics of the target group, are also difficult to control. The third intervening variable, the adjunct variable, represents additional or related programs that help to bring about the desired change in a synergetic way. Better access to health care, for example, can also lead to an increase in family planning. The collateral and latent consequences can best be viewed as side effects from, respectively, program preparation and program results.[2]

Program Evaluation

Evaluations, sometimes called assessments, can in principle take place at any time during the program cycle. Originally, the term "evaluation" was associated with a focus on the quantitative outcomes of a program, but one can also focus on qualitative appraisal, monitoring, or retrospective evaluation. These quantitative and qualitative methods of evaluation can be combined with each other. Figure 7.5 depicts the resulting possibilities.

Concentrating on the quantitative outcomes of a program implies emphasizing the state of a societal problem *ex ante* and *ex post* of the program. Evaluation research from this more traditional perspective can be defined as "research with a quasi-experimental design which tries to

FIGURE 7.3 Internal Program Management at UNICEF

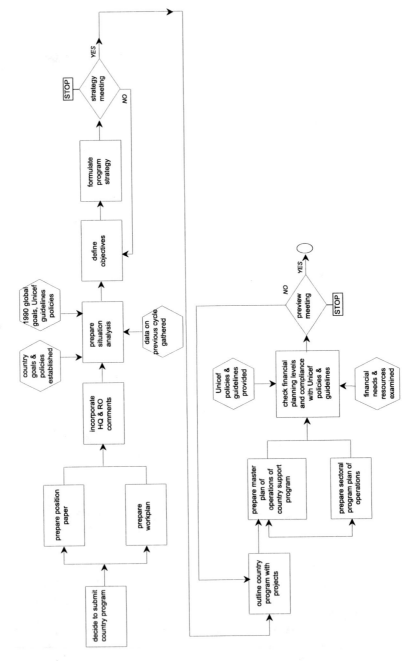

FIGURE 7.3 Internal Program Management at UNICEF (cont.)

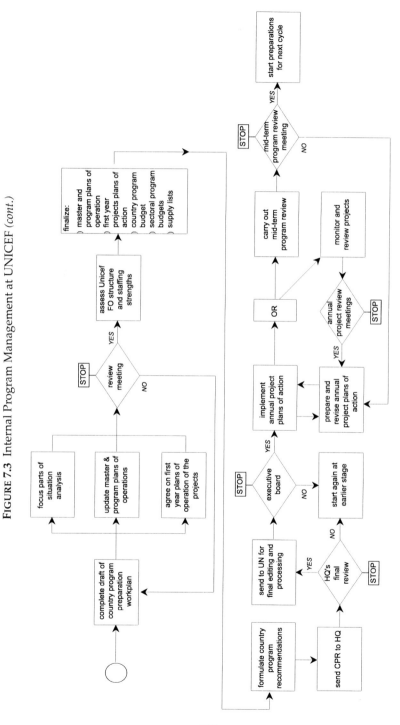

Source: Compiled from UNICEF guidelines, interviews, and field notes, 1992–1993.

FIGURE 7.4 Contextual Model of Program Management

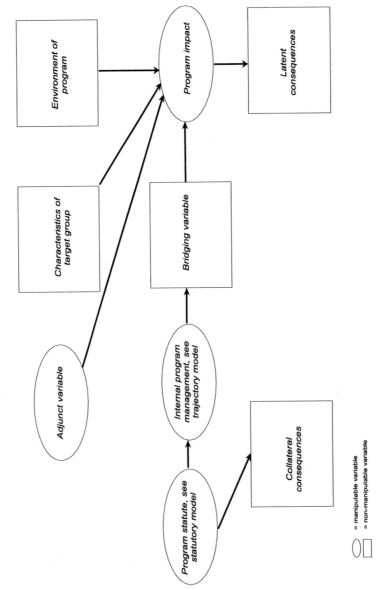

Source: Based on Mayer and Greenwood (1980: 130).

determine to which degree a used policy measure is effective, with pre-established goals and criteria" (Van der Zouwen 1990: 90). Considering the experimental nature of this definition, it becomes evident that evaluation "uses the methods and tools of social research … in an action context that is intrinsically inhospitable to them," for researchers are unable to control the conditions of a real-life situation as they would in an experiment (ibid.: 89). The interests, resources, goals, and priorities of sponsors, stakeholders, and executing agencies will often be in a state of flux. Furthermore, unanticipated problems can arise in the intervention or during the research itself. Finally, preliminary results of evaluation research can lead to alterations during the different stages of a program (Rossi and Freeman 1985: 33). In sum, the continuous changes in both the implementing agency and the program environment give rise to so many intervening variables that it becomes difficult to assess whether the program does in fact cause the change in the policy problem that it set out to address.

Practically, the quantitative focus on the *ex post* and *ex ante* situation can have one important drawback—it can draw attention away from the preparation and implementation of the program. The implementation phase particularly is then treated as a black box, which makes it hard to determine why a program was effective or ineffective. This lack of relevant feedback is a crucial impediment to improving policy analysis and programs (Patton 1978: 151). The program manager or policymaker is left in the dark on the execution and improvement of a program. Consequently, a focus on outcome measurement runs the risk of having a low utility for the daily management of a program.

Another method concentrates more on the different stages of program management. Such evaluation research "is the systematic application of social research procedures in assessing the conceptualization and design, implementation, and utility of social intervention programs" (Rossi and Freeman 1985: 19). This method offers more qualitative guidance to the decision maker. Problems and opportunities are identified, together with pathways for policy and program improvement. The statutory,[3] trajectory, and contextual model are all useful tools in this respect. They can provide a base line for comparison in the final evaluation.[4]

Limited availability of resources may force an organization to choose between the two evaluation methods. The two methods can also be triangulated into a so-called comprehensive evaluation, which combines the strengths of each method. Eventually, knowledge of both outcomes (what are the results?) and the implementation process (how did the results come about?) offers the most beneficial learning experience for the organization. Such a comprehensive evaluation comes close to policy analysis. Hence, evaluation not only leads to changes in the program, but can also contribute to broader policy changes.[5]

FIGURE 7.5 Different Forms of Evaluation during the Program Cycle

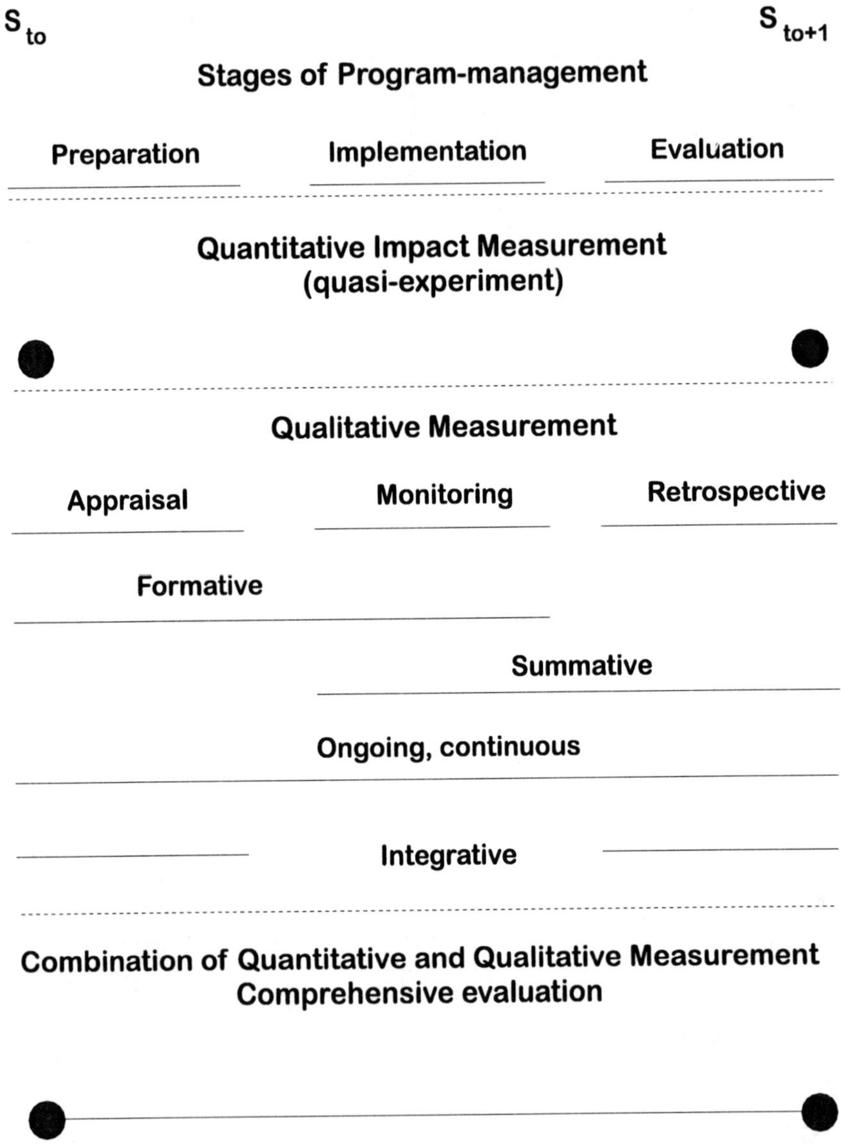

S_{to} S_{to+1}

Stages of Program-management

Preparation   Implementation   Evaluation

Quantitative Impact Measurement
(quasi-experiment)

●   ●

Qualitative Measurement

Appraisal   Monitoring   Retrospective

Formative

Summative

Ongoing, continuous

Integrative

Combination of Quantitative and Qualitative Measurement
Comprehensive evaluation

●━━━━━━━━━━━━━━━━━━━━━━━━━━━━━━━━━━━━●

Source: Based on Pressman and Wildavsky (1984: 181–205) and Rossi and Freeman (1985).

Techniques and Tools for Program Management

In addition to improving the different program stages, a growing set of tools has been developed to cater to the needs of program and project management in various fields of operations. These tools are linked to the specific aspects of the program as well as to the environment in which they are applied. Commonly used techniques include cost-benefit analysis, logical framework analysis, stakeholder analysis, institutional assessment, and participatory rural appraisals. In its own way, each technique can fit into the three stages of program management and the concomitant models discussed above.

What Is a Technique or Tool for Program Management?

The simplest way to clarify the concept of techniques or tools of program management is to explain one of them in detail: Logical Framework Analysis (LFA).

The logical framework—usually called "logframe"—is a clear example of a managerial tool, because it attempts to deal with the specifics of program and project management in the development and relief fields in a well-structured manner. Originally developed by USAID in 1969, LFA was later adopted by other bilateral and multilateral organizations, as well as NGOs. It has been defined as "a tool which provides a structure for specifying the components of [a program] and the logical linkages between a set of means and ends.… It is a means by which a project may be structured and described in a logical fashion."[6] Therefore, it is a way of testing the logic of a plan of action. It consists of a 4x5 matrix that analyzes means and ends. The ends are defined in logical order by the (1) program objective (the ultimate goal), (2) project objectives, (3) outputs, (4) activities, and (5) inputs; and the means are defined by the (1) project structure or narrative summary, (2) indicators by which the project/program can be measured, (3) means of verification and/or the data sources for those indicators, and (4) assumptions and critical factors upon which the program or project was formulated (see table 7.1). These are often concepts or hypotheses about environmental factors outside the control of the program management. For example, after the Asian financial crisis, many development programs had to adjust their activities because there was less funding available. The basic assumption is that logical ordering and clarifying assumptions will facilitate implementation.

Hence, LFA is an organizing device that covers every step from the project formulation to the specific arrangements for implementation. USAID wanted a device "that would lay out the flow of project inputs and anticipated outputs and indicate possible measures for project fulfillment" (Bryant and White 1982: 119). This device is used to structure and describe a project in a logical fashion. If correctly applied, LFA

TABLE 7.1 Outline of Logical Framework for Program Design

Program Structure	Indicators	Means of Verification	Assumptions and Critical Factors
Program Objective	Measures of goal achievement	Examination of records, statistics, and surveys	Assumptions and external factors necessary to sustain objectives in the long run
Project Objective(s)	Conditions that indicate purpose achieved at end of project	Evaluation data	External conditions necessary if achieved project purpose is to contribute to reaching project goal
Outputs	Magnitude of outputs (products from activities)	Measures and observation data	Factors out of project control, which, if present, could restrict progress from outputs to achieving project purpose
Activities	Actions undertaken to produce outputs (what will be done)	Organization's records and documents, financial and observation data	Factors out of project control, which, if present, could restrict progress from activities to achieving project outputs
Inputs	Implementation target	Organization's records and documents	Assumptions on availability of inputs (funds, equipment, human resources, etc.)

Sources: Bryant and White (1982: 120); DFID (1998: 17); Fyfe (1993: 31-42).

focuses on mutual consultation and clarifications fostering dialogue among participants. A widely used variant of LFA is Objective Oriented Intervention Planning (OOIP) or *Ziel Orientierte Projekt Planung* (ZOPP), as it is known in German. OOIP is based on the same concept and structure as LFA, but emphasizes a team approach to project planning. OOIP has also been used as a participatory planning tool, adapting the method to make it locally relevant.

In terms of the statutory model, the logical framework can help to increase the precision of the objectives. As a consequence, logical framework analysis can greatly aid further appraisal, implementation, monitoring, and evaluation. In turn, clear and well-linked objectives can also facilitate the checking of several other variables of the statutory model. Logical framework analysis addresses the hierarchical integration of the different actors in the implementation network; for example, clear objectives help to determine who is responsible for which tasks. This can also provide an input for stakeholder analysis and simplify the decision rules. Internally, the ranking of objectives and discussion of the means can create greater clarity on the necessary financial and personnel resources.

The critique of the logframe approach has focused on its application. Some have argued that it stifles creativity. Instead of thinking through projects and programs anew, managers in the field tend to reuse old logframes; they thus miss out on original new solutions or inappropriately recycle old ones. As a result, the logical framework analysis can defeat its own purpose of clearly thinking through all aspects of the program in advance.

Evolution of Program Management and Its Tools

As mentioned before, program management tools and techniques are linked to and influenced by the specifics of the development or humanitarian program as well as the environment in which they are applied. This section concentrates on the evolution of techniques as a way to exemplify practitioners' receptiveness to critiques of the implementation and outcomes of programs.[7]

As might be anticipated, the evolution and improvement of the specific tools applied in order to reach the objective(s) of the program also reflect the changes in development and humanitarian cooperation. This general evolution in development and humanitarian cooperation has led to the improvement of existing techniques or the creation of new tools to cope with the new objectives that the development and relief industries have envisioned. Similarly, specific critiques relating to the failures of implementation have forced the improvement of existing tools or the creation of new ones.

Changes in the conceptualization of humanitarian and development cooperation also affect program management. This is clearly seen in the "culture of performance," that is, the interest of both donors and practitioners in being able to measure the results and achievements of development and relief programs. This interest in measuring results goes hand in hand with the increasing set of monitoring and evaluation tools that have been redefined and newly formulated in order to facilitate performance analysis. In recent years, large donor agencies have developed manuals for performance monitoring and evaluation for the use of their staff and partners. While some performance analysis guidelines are widely applicable, others are relevant only to specific sectors, elements, or actors. For example, specific tools have been created for institutional and environmental evaluation.[8] Also, the increasing importance given to institutions and the generation of new "capacity building" programs have been reflected in the creation of new management tools for these types of projects, with institutional assessment being one of the best-known means to diagnose the state of institutional development.[9] Similarly, new attention to the role that different stakeholders can play in the design and implementation of programs and projects has given rise to a range of different methodologies, generally known as stakeholder analysis. Stakeholder analysis focuses on the interests a group takes in an issue and the level and types of resources a group can mobilize to affect the outcomes; the purpose is to indicate which interests should be taken into account, and which should not, when making a decision.[10]

Among the multiple general changes, two have had critical repercussions in program management techniques. The first has been the growing awareness about the interrelation of disciplines in development and humanitarian projects. The second has been the shift from a top-down to a bottom-up approach to development, which has been reflected in the attention given to participation in program management. These two developments are crucial because they have changed to a great extent the conceptualization of program management per se. In other words, these changes have forced not only the creation of new tools to meet new needs, but also the "reconceptualization" of existing tools and the inclusion of multidisciplinary and participatory approaches in whatever new tools are created.

Multidisciplinarity

The new paradigm of development as a multidisciplinary discipline,[11] instead of an economic one, has been expressed in critiques of specific techniques that were unable to include social or non-economic issues easily. In other words, such critiques questioned the underlying causal theory of development and humanitarian activities. Besides economics, sociology, anthropology, political science, behavioral psychology, law, and organizational theory, just to name a few, have become integral parts of the multidisciplinary approach to development.[12] In principle, the program approach itself easily allows for a more multidisciplinary approach —one can just add more projects.

A clear example of the criticism on monodisciplinary approaches is the critique of cost-benefit analysis. This form of analysis simply examines the project proposal in terms of its costs compared with its projected financial benefits; all benefits are converted into financial terms for the purpose of the analysis.[13] Therefore, cost-benefit analysis requires economic expertise. It is especially relevant for those programs whose objective is to increase wealth—and this is precisely the focus of the critique. For those development programs that have social objectives instead of financial ones, the technique's appropriateness has been questioned. There were attempts to overcome these critiques while still considering costs and benefits, such as the variation called cost-effectiveness analysis, which has been used to analyze whether or not the objectives can be achieved at a reasonable cost. Although both techniques have been used extensively when trying to compare different programs or when trying to compare different projects that hope to achieve the same objectives, their lack of flexibility to include social or non-economic issues has remained a source of criticism.

The increasing concern about development as a multidisciplinary discipline that is connected not only to economics but also to other social sciences has been reflected in the use of new or improved tools that account for the effects of economic development in the social sphere and vice versa. Hence, the increasing importance that the development field began giving to the environment required management tools to cater to and measure the environmental sustainability of the projects under consideration. Similarly, the increasing importance of gender considerations has required program management tools to include gender components in them. An interesting outcome of this evolution is that these changes have given rise not only to specific tools for gender and the environment but also to the inclusion of these components in other more general tools, echoing the multidisciplinary approach.[14]

In sum, the change toward a more interdisciplinary approach in development has been driven by both critiques in the general policy arena and critiques of programs that failed to deliver the expected results. Indeed, the argument to envision a more multidisciplinary approach can become crucial if critics are able to point precisely to the lack of cross-field analysis as the cause of the failures of one particular program in reaching its objectives. A multitude of recent books and articles have focused on analyzing in depth such failures as infrastructure projects that harmed the natural environment, or projects that did not consider the social implications of a particular action or that were not culturally sensitive. The failures of these programs that lacked crucial aspects for development in both their design and implementation can be more broadly divided into errors of commission and errors of omission.

Most of the techniques discussed so far have implied a broader range of activities for each program. Of course, applying all of these techniques is a logistical impossibility. Resources committed to analysis cannot be used for implementation. One cannot do everything at the same time, and appraisal cannot last forever. In daily practice, only a few techniques are selected for use in actual programming. Sometimes this means that program managers overlook various multidisciplinary aspects of the problems at hand. Other times, the managers apply the techniques in a technocratic or rushed manner, which results in superficial programming. Nevertheless, despite the growing use of multidisciplinary approaches, one crucial omission stands out: the difficulty of dealing with power politics at different levels of society.

In this respect, it is important to note that the current architecture of international laws and institutions is not conducive to success in at least two ways. First, rich countries have not committed themselves to global antipoverty obligations or commitments that extend further than merely providing aid, and even then only on an ad hoc basis. They have insufficiently opened up their markets to Southern exporters, large or small. Too often they still use subsidies, tariffs, and quotas to protect their own producers. Progress with debt relief has been slow. Rich countries have also routinely supported corrupt regimes. In addition, they have not stemmed the international weapons trade and have sometimes supported warring factions for their own short-term economic or geopolitical advantage. Second, the amount of Official Development Assistance (ODA) has been decreasing. Although humanitarian assistance increased over the last decade, it has not offset the decline in ODA; more ODA could help to stabilize and strengthen societies (Development Initiatives 2000: 26). As a consequence, the global economic system often does not facilitate successful program management (Dijkzeul and Danchin 2001: 215). Southern countries and other actors lack the leverage to change this global system.

Naturally, the question of power also comes into play at the national and local levels. In his study of an integrated rural development program in Lesotho, Ferguson (1994) describes its failure and the unexpected political outcomes. By conceptualizing the program as a technocratic, value-free, economic development endeavor for improving agriculture in a poor mountainous area, the designers failed to see the severe shortcomings of their analysis.[15] They did not take into account the oppressive political situation and local culture, with its different traditional property rights and economic values for men and women that prohibited the free trade of cows and some other livestock. Nor did the designers realize that the regional economy had already been monetarized and was fully dependent on migrant labor in the mines of South Africa (which itself suffered under the apartheid regime). Instead, the program unrealistically elevated the role of local agriculture and predicted that better market access and technical improvements would improve the agricultural outputs and local economy considerably. Predictably, all of the efforts in livestock improvement, administrative decentralization, and crop improvement failed. Yet the political side effects of the program were considerable.[16] The program involuntarily extended the oppression of the ruling party by providing access roads, administration, and newly built facilities. Soldiers were also able to reach the region better than before. Failing to reach its goals, the project inadvertently assisted the undemocratic central government in extending its own influence.

In a similar vein, Uvin (1998) provides a critique of the way the development agencies in Rwanda failed to see how their work actually contributed to the genocide. He studies both specific projects and the broader development policies and activities and how they impinged on local society. He argues that racial prejudice among Tutsis and Hutus had been a structural feature of life in Rwanda at least since colonial times. Structural violence and social exclusion characterized Rwandese society and caused "profound popular anger, frustration, cynicism, ignorance, and desire for scapegoating." Parts of the Rwandan elite were able "to mobilize these sentiments against minority groups." Under military, political, and economic threat, this elite instigated the genocide. Uvin (ibid.: 8) summarizes that "[a]t different points in time, and through different processes, the development aid system interacted with the processes of social exclusion, shared many of the humiliating practices [for example, obligatory communal labor, expropriation of patches of land for development project buildings, or income differences and displays of wealth], and closed its eyes to the racist currents in society. Aid was also unwilling and possibly unable to stop the process of radicalization that took place in the 1990s."

In sum, despite the many efforts to broaden the scope and inclusiveness of programs to provide better aid, one problem remains hard to solve: challenging and changing existing power relationships. Often, program management sticks to a technocratic application of procedures and fails to address the wider political and social problems. Ferguson and Uvin both show, in different ways, that the inability to address this problem of power can have extremely dire consequences.

Participation

The second general change identified above is the shift from a top-down to a bottom-up approach to development, which has been reflected in the crucial importance given to participation in program management. Participation and multidisciplinary program approaches interact conceptually. The daily problems that the local population brings to the table through its participation do not follow neat, academic categories. They are linked, and, as a result, they normally require multidisciplinary approaches. Participation can also have a political effect by making the voices of the local population better heard. Finally, it can also lead to demands for greater accountability of political leaders.

Participation "entered the international discourse on development in the 1960s and achieved wider currency in the 1970s" (see Stiefel and Wolfe 1994: 22).[17] "The development community first began experimenting with participatory methodologies … through the application of social anthropology, farming systems research, participatory action research, and others" (Maynard 2000: 1). In the traditional structure of rural projects, decisions were made and resources were allocated by "outside experts"; local people were rarely consulted and even more rarely had any role in decision making.

The shift toward a more bottom-up approach to development also meant that local people were no longer seen as passive beneficiaries, but rather as active agents and partners. The idea that the "outside experts" had the key to solutions was replaced by recognition of the knowledge of local people. Consequently, the role of development professionals has also changed; they tend to be seen less as controllers and more as facilitators. Table 7.2 gives an example of an innovative participatory action-research project.

Participatory Rural Appraisal

The growing trend toward more participation is further illustrated by the conception and use of one of the best-known tools for enhancing participation in program and project management: participatory rural appraisal.

Participatory Rural Appraisals (PRAs), which refer to rural, and increasingly also urban, data-gathering techniques, have their origins in the participatory learning movements in South Asia as well as the increasing dissatisfaction with rural development in the 1980s. PRA is intended to be more than just a tool to learn more about the realities of local people; rather, it emphasizes the process that enables local people to analyze the data and the circumstances that are meaningful to them. PRA has been described as "a growing family of approaches and methods used to enable people to analyze and share their knowledge of life and local conditions. Through PRA, both rural and urban groups are able to identify their own priorities and make their own decisions about the future" (Jones 1996: 11).[18]

Therefore, the participatory approach is not simply a specific technique or methodology. It goes beyond the boundaries of a data-gathering technique to become a new paradigm: action *with* and *by* local people. This includes the creation of methodological approaches to gather more accurate information as well as approaches for joint analysis and planning to ensure meaningful participation.[19] Hence, the specific methods employed tend to use group discussions as well as visuals and diagrams, as opposed to individual interviews and verbal communications that were the norm in the traditional work of development practitioners.

The core of the PRA is a process of sharing and developing ideas within the community where the program is intended to be implemented; this process ideally leads to local analysis, planning, and action as well as monitoring and evaluation. Hence, it includes all of the stages of the program or project cycle, yet it is implemented under a participatory approach. The complete approach would start with a participatory appraisal, local analysis, participatory planning, locally driven action, participatory monitoring, and local evaluation that would then serve as feedback for the next participatory appraisal. Understood as a process, the PRA not only leads to information analysis but also actively involves and engages people, focuses on local capabilities, creates ownership, builds self-reliance, and empowers local people.

TABLE 7.2 Participatory Action Research in Postconflict Contexts

---

**New Research Directions in Postconflict Contexts:
Basing Policy Dialogue on Participatory Action Research**

One specific project, actually, an action-research project, has been the War-Torn Societies Project (WSP). In response to the question as to what social science could contribute to the amelioration of war-affected situations, WSP undertook action-oriented and interactive country projects on a pilot basis, each lasting about two years, in Eritrea, Mozambique, Guatemala, and Somalia.

WSP projects focused on postconflict reconstruction. In each country case, research was initiated on what were perceived to be the key issues in reconstruction, mapping out what was being done and what needed to be done in such areas as demobilization, returnee integration, provision of basic needs, establishment of justice, and so on. The choice of themes was made by a project group, comprising all interested parties, national and international, in the project. Invariably, though, national views were given priority in making these choices. The research was implemented in several successive phases according to a particular common scenario, and was carried out exclusively by teams of well-qualified and well-accepted national researchers.

Around each chosen research theme, a working group of up to 10 to 12 members was formed, consisting of representatives of national and inter-national agencies taking a special interest in the respective theme. On food security, for example, a working group might comprise members from the Ministry of Agriculture, from farmers organizations, from NGOs involved in the provision of food aid and rehabilitation schemes, and from the Food and Agriculture Organization (FAO) or the World Food Programme (WFP) representatives wherever applicable, etc. On refugee resettlement issues, similarly, one would have representatives from the main national organi-zations responsible for returnee programs, the United Nations High Commissioner for Refugees (UNHCR), international and national NGOs engaged in resettlement schemes, the United Nations Population Fund (UNFPA), and others with an involvement or interest in the field. These working groups would meet regularly, approximately once a month, during the course of the research, giving both direction to the research activities and feedback to the field data and results. In this sense, the research was a kind of participatory action research, but here with the active participation of people from various agencies with a stake in the broad policy field, and thus with participation at a macro rather than the more usual micro level (in a village or other local community).

As it turned out in the various pilot projects, the research theme plus associated working group setup became significant in two major ways. First, the research material gathered often constituted the first compilation and stocktaking of relevant and up-to-date information and analysis on the given field in the country in the postwar situation, and thus had a direct relevance to many parties involved. But second, and at least as important, was the dialogue that ensued in most working groups in connection with the

TABLE 7.2 Participatory Action Research in Postconflict Contexts *(cont.)*

research. The dialogue was fed by the research, and in turn dialogue fed into the research, but it was also a research-induced dialogue among various stakeholders in the respective policy area itself, which in several cases turned out to be extremely valuable. Indeed, involvement in informal WSP working groups enabled representatives from different ministries, agencies, political parties, or other organizations to compare notes, to get a better understanding of other members' involvement and perspectives, and to understand the rationale for certain policy positions, or the shortcomings of particular policy measures. While there was an inclination, and perhaps an implicit objective, to try to move toward consensus, it certainly did not mean that participants would yield, or be expected to yield, to other parties' positions. Invariably, the dialogue aspect in all four pilot cases, judging by numerous expressions of interest by participants concerned, has proven a particularly striking feature of the WSP projects.

What made it even more interesting, however, was that in each case a dialogue tended to emerge between different kinds of broadly defined actors. In one case (Eritrea) the basic division would be internal-external, in two others (Guatemala and Somalia) the emphasis was on internal divisions (though of quite different kinds), while in Mozambique the pattern was mixed with both an internal-external and an internal-internal dimension.

In Eritrea, the international organizations and national government originally had a hard time understanding each other. The government strongly stressed its own policy priorities and regularly kept international organizations at bay. WSP provided a way for better information exchange and mutual understanding. The Guatemalan case exhibited strong tensions between the government forces and mainly indigenous, armed liberation fronts, while civil society was also opening up. In Somalia, the problem was getting different local groups to come together and work together during ongoing, low-key civil conflict in the absence of a central government. In Mozambique, WSP offered fact finding and a neutral space between the two different and opposed liberation groups that are now political parties: Frelimo (in government) and Renamo (in opposition).

In a way, these very different kinds of dialogue are to be expected, since each particular social and political context per definition is different and will show a different set of dynamics and key divisions. Launching the same "tool" in different contexts—in particular, if it remains as unspecified as research-driven dialogue or dialogue-driven research—thus means there was every chance it might be taken up in a different way. In all four instances, however, the ensuing dialogue element stood out.

Source: Adapted from Doornbos, M. "New Research Directions in Post-conflict Contexts: The Scope for Action Research Based Policy Dialogue," paper prepared for the workshop "Living in War Times—Living in Post-war Times," University of Hanover History Department, Melsungen, 22–24 January 1999.

Unfortunately, the rapid spread and the increasing demand for PRA has not necessarily meant fostering local participation in either analysis or decision making. Among the main causes of its failure, the most notorious have been: routine and rushed applications, the lack of well-trained practitioners or poor quality training, and the neglect of behavior and attitudes crucial for participatory approaches. These implementation problems have shown that although the rhetoric of PRA was increasingly used, it did not necessarily keep up with the main philosophy and objectives of the participatory approach. Ironically, in some cases, the top-down imposition of PRA by donors has led to the use of the rhetoric over the real practice of PRA. In other cases, participation meant that the local population had to provide labor "voluntarily," without being involved in decision making for the program. In other words, participation became a way for international organizations to obtain cheap labor.

These failures in implementation and the use of only the rhetoric of PRA—with the subsequent decrease in expectations about its applicability—are some of the major obstacles to achieving viable solutions to the inherent problems of program and project management.[20] When participation leads to more local organizing and more vociferous demands for accountability and political change, it can also provoke a counterreaction from undemocratic forces. Hence, one cannot lightheartedly start a participatory approach. International organizations need to think through the possible consequences as much as possible in advance. Taking risks may be necessary, but at times it requires careful tradeoffs.

Management Issues

Given the complexity of the societal problems that most international organizations address, setting up the internal organization geared to facilitate program management poses a considerable challenge. Figure 7.3 of the UNICEF programming process illustrates how intricate the programming process can become.

Setting up an organization for program management leads to a paradox. While the program itself is temporary, program management for the organization is not. There will always be several programs going on simultaneously. Moreover, programs always contain one or more new elements for their participants. Yet for the international organizations, be they UN or non-governmental organizations, program management has become a routine process. When one program cycle ends, it automatically feeds into a new cycle. In other words, the organization applies standard processes to create something new. For the managers at headquarters and in the field, that requires setting up an organization that controls what is happening in the field while remaining flexible.

Likewise, to achieve success managers need a program that is comprehensive in scope and yet targeted enough to make a critical change. Field managers often express that they would like to be more flexible, better able to do contingency planning and grasp opportunities. Whereas they often complain that the programming process is too labor intensive, managers at headquarters often fret about their lack of control: programs last too long, cost too much, and do not deliver sufficient results. Finding a balance between control and flexibility, comprehensiveness and targeting is not easy. Fortunately, organizations can do a lot on their own initiative to facilitate program management.[21] Sometimes such facilitation implies that it is actually better for top management not to interfere in an ongoing program. One can jointly determine deadlines, objectives, and methods in advance, but changing the scope of the program midway or the responsibilities of the people in the field often wreaks havoc.

Not surprisingly, most recommendations for improving the management of programs focus on the relationship between upper management, often at headquarters, and the field.[22]

1. A clear mission for the organization acts as a unifying theme so that everybody knows where the organization is heading. It helps to set priorities and facilitates communication.
2. Ideally this mission informs a strategy for decentralized service delivery for faster response to local needs and capacities. Some important points for attention are:
   - Is it possible to simplify the current program processes to make them more flexible? Review and remove unnecessary documents and meetings; make sure that program staff obtains a good overview of the whole program process; provide good guidelines with clear techniques.
   - Does upper management support the programs well enough? The answer to this question is eminently practical. It focuses on such practices as "negotiating deadlines, supporting the creative process, allowing time for and supporting project planning, choosing not to interfere in project execution, demanding no useless scope changes, and changing the reward system to motivate project work" (Graham and Englund 1997: 6).
   - Should there be a different division of labor between field and headquarters? Think, for example, of creating self-contained tasks for the field offices, in particular, for the execution of the programs. Support this with measures such as higher budget ceilings, local procurement, and local staffing so that headquarters—and regional offices—will fulfill less administrative work and can focus on support, audit, and control.
   - Can the organization create teams that combine upper and field managers? Multidisciplinary approaches always require help

from people with different backgrounds. Is teamwork rewarded or is the organization focusing on departments and divisions that have a hard time working together?

- Can the capacity to process information between headquarters and field be improved? For example, is it possible to use management information systems, in particular, to streamline and speed up budgeting processes? Good program management software should be utilized. When possible, use the information system for obtaining and distributing "compiled evaluation lessons." In addition, the organization can strengthen training, both as an induction into the organization and its programming and as a method for continuous skills improvement, which also leads to a higher degree of professionalization.
- Do programs use clear goal setting—for example, in a logical framework—in order to provide a shared sense of direction and to promote evaluation of the programs? Participation is crucial in setting these goals.
- Is there a need to strengthen evaluation capabilities? This can be accomplished through setting up better organizational structures and better guidelines for explaining the evaluation methodology.

It may seem a paradox, but a clear mission can actually foster local participation. Participation does not mean slavishly following what the local counterparts want; it is more about finding out who wants to address which problems and how to do that effectively. Participation implies openness and mutual adjustment. The organization needs to develop its areas of expertise and have resources available. For this, it needs a mission and a strategy. In response to local initiatives, the organization can work at its edges and over time change its mission, but fostering participation requires in-house expertise, and this takes time to develop.

Many of the recommendations above may seem straightforward, but organizations always struggle with implementing them. For example, participatory approaches and the shift from a project mode to the programming approach have been promoted since the 1960s. Still, after almost four decades, many international organizations still struggle with these approaches. Hence, all organizations need to work continuously on improving their management. But international organizations face an extra hurdle. On the one hand, implementing these programs requires open communication and clear goals; the recommendations are based on a managerial logic that emphasizes the values of authenticity (managers mean what they say) and sincerity (managers really do what they say they will do). Without these values, implementing the recommendations will first take place in a haphazard manner, and slowly implementation will become harder, if not impossible. On the other hand, the political contexts in which these programs are implemented require extremely deft handling. Here managers need to follow a political logic that emphasizes the role of power, ambiguity, feasible steps, and compromise. These two logics are not always in conflict, but they certainly do not automatically function in happy unison. Generally, the managerial logic can be followed within the organization, and the political in cooperation with other parties that have a stake in the program.

Interorganizational Issues

As stated, many parties are involved in programming. At the international level, the donor government or the public at large needs to be satisfied. But catering to these groups does not imply meaningful participation at the field level. It is more common than not that donor organizations do not know what actually happens in the field. Moreover, many donors push their own pet projects and policies, which are often intertwined with other national interests. Through their funding, donor governments have considerable leverage over UN organizations and NGOs. As a result, international organizations need to cater to their donors and local partners at the same time, which limits the autonomy of the programming organization and makes program management difficult.

If international organizations succeed in dealing with the donors smoothly, they need to work under the rules and regulations of the national government of the country where they are active. Officially, UN organizations can only design and carry out programs at the request of the national government. Unofficially, they of course make suggestions to their governmental counterparts. NGOs generally have more leeway, but they still need the cooperation of the government with such issues as accreditation, security, and taxes. Especially during civil conflict or when the government is corrupt, international organizations need to be savvy operators in order to reach and work with the local population without antagonizing those in power. Yet the nature of their programs in development, humanitarian affairs, human rights, and so on, often leads to either tensions or conflicts with the government, other elites, or even local warlords. As a consequence, the international organizations often try to work in a technocratic manner—supposedly value-free and neutral. With such a way of operating, the organization can claim that its autonomy should be safeguarded, which can make life considerably easier in a multiparty context. Nevertheless, technocratic behavior can take the organization only a limited distance; in order to be successful in their program, they can never leave the local political context completely out of consideration.[23]

Even if they succeed in overcoming the hurdles above, they face yet another problem: the other organizations. Although international organizations are non-profits, they can compete fiercely for media and donor attention. In addition, their management systems and procedures may be

incompatible, making coordination difficult. For example, in the Hue-
heutenango department of Guatemala, there were at least five agricultural development organizations active at the same time. They all
professed to support local participation, but their programs were rarely
compatible. In one specific case, one UN organization did not want to
work with an agricultural government agency; instead, it worked with an
independent governmental investment fund. This meant that the older
agricultural organization, in fact, got an additional competitor within the
governmental structure. International support thus complicated local
agricultural improvement and turned two government institutions
against each other. In a somewhat similar vein, one donor government
funded two local organizations that sometimes worked at cross-purposes
(author's field notes, Guatemala 1999).

Governmental institutions are not the only national or local bodies that
international organizations work with. They also cooperate with local
NGOs in the hope of strengthening local civil society. This is a crucial
"make-or-buy" decision for the international organization that deeply
influences the nature of program management. "Farming out" can lead to
long aid chains (see Biekart 1999; Fowler 1996: 169–186). In principle,
supporting and working through a local NGO is already a form of participation, albeit minimal. However, in their funding of these local NGOs,
international organizations make many mistakes. Smillie (1996) observed
in Bosnia, arguably a good case for supporting civil society as an instrument for peace, that international organizations and donor governments
took several common missteps, namely:

1. They did not adequately assess the capacities of the NGOs. As a
   result, the organizations grew rapidly in financial terms, but did
   not yet possess the skills to implement good-quality projects.
2. They often provided only short-term funding, whereas the local
   NGOs needed assurances of long-term funding to strengthen
   themselves. Many of their rebuilding projects also required long-
   term funding.
3. They did not make their payments on time; since the NGOs had
   no liquidity of their own, these delays caused considerable hardship and led to inadequate financial management.
4. They did not pay a reasonable proportion of the overhead costs of
   the organization, but to be viable an NGO also needs to build up
   its own capacity.
5. They wanted local NGOs to take over some of their projects, but
   did not support them to become financially sustainable.
6. They imposed considerable requirements on the NGOs, for example, a deluge of paperwork regarding monitoring, evaluations, and
   budgeting. Even worse, the international organizations used different guidelines and formats to which the local NGOs had to conform.

In addition, donors often promoted their favorite program topics and were insufficiently responsive to the local needs and capacities. They simply did not listen well enough to the proposed initiatives from the local NGOs and population. In this sense, the international organizations need more responsive funding mechanisms (Salomons and Dijkzeul 2001). International organizations focused at different times on infrastructure rebuilding, reconciliation, and psychosocial care. However, local needs differ from place to place and do not follow a straight path in which one works first on infrastructure, then on psychosocial care, and then on the next new thing. Sustained and responsive funding is a necessity. In chapter 10, Smillie and Evenson discuss these problems and recent developments in Bosnia and Herzegovina in more detail.

In general, such popular buzzwords as empowerment, promoting self-reliance, and, yes, participation reflect the assumptions, priorities, and marketing of either donor governments or international organizations. In their actual use of these terms, international organizations rarely reflect on the perspective of the local population, but rather impose their concepts on the local fabric, which in turn hampers meaningful participation and decreases sustainability. Only through actual local participation can the local situation be better understood and updated continuously. Yet, as mentioned, in some cases the elite, the warlords, or the corrupt or weak government may actually oppose such participation, because it weakens its power base.

All in all, international organizations engage in complicated networks of a great variety of actors that carry out their service delivery. At times, they will run into opposition. Working in these networks requires political and tactical acumen, which brings back, or actually intensifies, the problematic tension between the political and the managerial logic.

Critique of the Program Approach

Earlier, this chapter cited Baum and Tolbert by enumerating the advantages of program management, namely, providing a framework for analyzing and compiling data, establishing investment priorities, considering project or program alternatives, and addressing sector policy issues. It imposes discipline on both planners and decision makers. It also ensures that relevant problems and issues are taken into account and analyzed systematically before decisions are reached and implemented. "Correctly applied, it can greatly increase the development impact of ... scarce investment resources" (Baum and Tolbert 1985: 335).

The crux of the criticism on the program approach lies in two words: correctly applied. Is it possible to do so? Program management must inevitably deal with the diversity of a multiparty environment. Depending on their goals, values, and interests, various parties will define the meaning of "correctly applied" differently. But the program approach at least forces the main parties to explicitly consider their value judgments. Baum and Tolbert also stress the importance of good quality data for program design and the difficulty of implementing programs in a constantly changing world. In their final analysis, the quality of the program depends on the skills and judgment of those who apply the program. This chapter illustrates many techniques to improve these skills and judgments, but it also demonstrates that many of these techniques could be ill applied. Almost by definition, international organizations have to tackle difficult development and humanitarian problems. Many things can go wrong.

- The program can be ill conceptualized. There can be problems in analysis as well as with faulty assumptions. Understanding different cultures and perceptions is time consuming but necessary.
- The program can lack critical mass to make a change.
- The program may be insufficiently multidisciplinary and participatory.
- The program may not succeed in taking the political aspects sufficiently into account.
- The program may be set up, funded, or executed by an organization that is not up to par in its program management.
- The program can suffer from too little, too late, or irregular funding.
- The program may take place in a network of organizations that compete with each other for funding and media attention, without considering how different programs in the same region could fit together.

If the program is truly multidisciplinary and participatory, the program managers will almost inevitably have to deal with the tension between the political and managerial logic. Part of the appeal of the programming approach lies in the fact that it is just an open procedural tool for linking sectors and actors through design, implementation, and evaluation. It gives the impression that it can be applied everywhere in a similar manner. By providing objectives, an activity timetable, and a budget, the program approach allows for a high degree of control of the development or humanitarian projects. However, in itself, the program approach does not indicate whose objectives are being taken into account and the degree of cultural sensitivity that will be applied. In some politicized environments, it allows the pretension that this approach involves simply technocratic, value-free work. As a ploy to get work done, this may function well, but when program staff starts to believe that it is actually just carrying out technocratic tasks, then it must think again—seriously. The issue of political control is bound to raise its head. A program helps to control the management of service delivery, but it does not automatically align itself with other actors and broader societal processes.

Alternatives

We should always entertain the possibility that it may be better not to start a program (see Ferguson 1994: 287). Sometimes the local population is better off on its own. Other times, programs can worsen the local situation, as has happened with many structural adjustment programs and humanitarian interventions. In those cases, it is better to stay home and look for the root causes of poverty and conflict that do not lie in the developing countries. What are the decisions and activities in the industrialized world that hamper local development elsewhere? This may often be of greater fundamental importance than program management, because it influences the conditions for overall development. Many international organizations will have a hard time selling this approach, but they probably should do so more often.

Within the South, it is also possible to mention non-program alternatives. They fall into two categories of responsible governance, namely, sound macroeconomic policy and promoting law. To start with the latter, most developing countries have good laws—they are just not implemented well enough. Respecting laws can range from promoting a well-functioning judiciary to fighting corruption to the proper maintenance of land reform law. Land reform can be effective in fighting poverty (Chambers 1983: 151–152). Legal aid to the local population and respecting fair interest rates, especially in extremely poor areas or after disasters, can also bring great benefits.[24]

The effects of macroeconomic policy play out in at least two different ways: first, in prices and terms of trade, and, second, in terms of the national budget and its priorities. According to Chambers, prices are an important weapon in augmenting incomes. Monopoly marketing of cash crops by para-statals creams off surpluses from the local farmers and reallocates these to the bureaucracy and elite behind the para-statal organizations. Similarly, "[a]n overvalued foreign exchange benefits the urban middle classes by keeping down the prices of the imported goods they buy, and discriminates against the rural populations by giving them less for the commodities they produce for export, such as jute, sisal, tea, coffee, cocoa, coconut oil, palm oil, rubber, and cotton" (Chambers 1983: 150–151).

Some governments also have an official exchange rate for international organizations that is higher than the (black) market rates. The banks and/or government institutions responsible for money exchange then pocket the difference between the official and market rates. As a result, this money is not spent on the actual programs, but rather is used to finance the bureaucrats in power.

Closely related to the issue of prices and terms of trade is the issue of sound macroeconomic budgeting by the government. In and of itself, this is a broad and contentious area. Budgetary policies, however, do reflect the actual government priorities and have great influence on economic growth and the possibilities of reduction of poverty and other forms of social exclusion. For programming, it is crucial to note that aid is fungible. Even if aid is focused on a certain sector or program, it still expands the total government budget, so that the government can allocate other parts of its budget differently. For example, if an international organization supports an educational program, then the government can spend its freed-up funds on the military. Program evaluations rarely to never measure these net effects of programming.

In contrast, in countries with sound macroeconomic policy and good public service delivery, the World Bank (1998) has made a case to give aid directly in the form of overall budget support. Such support can considerably simplify administration and lessen overhead for both donor and recipient—something that happens too rarely with programs.

All of these alternatives have a common theme: when a government functions well, the need for outside interventions by international organizations decreases. Respect for the law, fair prices, and sound macroeconomic policy all assume that the government has the interests of the population close to its heart. Hence, it is easy to turn this argument on its head. Whenever national governments fail, it is important for outsiders to step in. In response to the World Bank, the Global Humanitarian Assistance report asked: "If development cooperation is restricted to 'good policy' countries, where does this leave the most vulnerable people and countries where stability, resources, and optimism may be in shortest supply?" (Inter-Agency Standing Committee 2000: 76). It is of course possible to doubt whether national budgets reflect democratic participation. And when they do, it is generally through a convoluted bureaucratic process. In addition, even with sound economic policies, specific groups, such as women, children, and people living in pockets of poverty, will need assistance, which will generally be given in the form of, once again, programs.

Except for doing nothing and turning the focus of action, including advocacy, northwards, the alternatives do not make programming superfluous. It is more that the alternatives place the onus of responsibility on national actors, in particular, the government. In doing so, proponents of the alternatives implicitly claim that the government should be free of corruption and should work for the interests of the people. To put it mildly, this is not always a realistic option, and programming by outside organizations remains necessary. Moreover, the alternatives do not exclude programming. If a government receives direct budget support or promotes the law, it will need programs to carry out its policies. In conclusion, with the alternatives the need for specific programs changes and the actors involved change, but programming itself does not disappear.

Conclusions

International organizations are heavy users of the program approach, which has strong managerial advantages. It is a procedural tool to link activities and actors in a phased manner. It allows for disciplined analysis, execution, and evaluation. Most of all, it can be applied in many different contexts. Still, after more than 30 years of trying, the idea of participation in program management is not terribly effective. The weaknesses of the program approach stem from the assumptions behind it, namely:

1. A program is a procedure that is open and amenable to different kinds of societal problems.
2. A program can divide the problem and the answer to it into stages and (sub)projects, which are limited in time and resources.
3. A program is an intentional tool in the sense that goals and purposively structured action lead to the desired results.
4. A program receives sufficient support to carry out the program.
5. A program is based, adjusted, and evaluated on the basis of correct data.

The irony of programming is that it rarely takes place in an environment in which these assumptions are fully realized. First of all, these assumptions do not elucidate who controls the programming process. By focusing on procedure and leaving out the question of who controls the program, a technocratic approach is implicitly fostered. If the procedure is open and amenable, it does not guarantee that the right societal problem (and root causes) is being addressed. Nor does a program by itself divide the problems into stages and subprojects; societal problems and processes have their own rhythm, and it is not at all certain that the program can tap into that rhythm with its time frame and limited resources. Problems can also differ hugely; the procedures for programs in development and humanitarian work need to be adapted considerably. It is certainly not always true that the programming organizations can collect the right data for their decisions. They often need to play it by ear and work with insufficient information.

Intentional action by international organizations may not be possible or required to alter societal processes. Intentional action in a multiactor environment can lead to opposition. Other actors will have different views and values; they may not care about the problem or might have different priorities. In particular, they may conceptualize the societal problem differently. This also weakens the assumption of sufficient support. Underneath this assumption is the hope that one or more actors—a benign state bureaucracy, a capable UN organization, a wise local leader, an idealistic NGO, and so on—are autonomous enough to pull the program through. Yet, the international organization is often more limited in its autonomy than the programming process assumes. One can argue that this problem of control can be overcome or circumvented if the concepts or interests behind the program are cogent and valuable enough that they unify the actors involved in a common pursuit. This may sometimes be true when there is a strong consensus within a society about a problem and its possible remedies. However, such a consensus is more often absent than not, for international organizations focus on such hard and contested problems as development, humanitarian affairs, human rights, and the environment.

Finally, donor governments and national governments of the countries where the field activities take place often play a dominant role. Even if the governments cooperate well, the self-interest of management can preclude or hamper local inputs. In both cases, a top-down approach prevails and participation suffers. The problem of control often shows the hardships in combining the managerial and political logic of action.

The three models—statutory, contextual, and internal—and the many programming techniques in this chapter are efforts to address these problematic assumptions. To some extent, they can succeed at this, but generally they find ways to deal better with the shortcomings of the assumptions instead of eliminating them. In addition, the actual use of the techniques has its own problems. For example, they can lead to one-sided attention to analysis and goal setting, instead of actual implementation. Moreover, applying them requires tradeoffs between control and flexibility, as well as between comprehensiveness and targeting. Still, the alternatives do not fundamentally exclude the program approach.

In the end, how a program will be carried out depends on the skills and judgment of the actors. As a procedural tool, the program approach has a double nature: it can be used to shove delivery down local throats or to foster a participatory process toward the realization of shared objectives. In other words, the program approach allows for the integration of value judgments of donors, executing agents, and the local population, but it does not do so by itself. Programming is an inevitable tool, but its quality depends on its actual application, in particular, on the participation of other actors. Its pathologies depend on its application. As a result of the assumptions behind programming, most practitioners of the program approach fail to see its double nature and the need for delicate management. All the resources of the world, improved programming techniques, and the right language do not, by themselves, lead to successful participatory programs.

Notes

1. Baum and Tolbert mainly concentrate on project management, but their argument is equally valid for program management.
2. The contextual model also has a disadvantage. As a linear model, it does not display the feedback loops that exist among the various variables.
3. With time and money, it is possible to compare the degree of realization of the statutory variables to infer how they contributed to the program outcomes.
4. Retrospective evaluations and final assessments can take many forms: output measurement, efficiency measurement, effectiveness assessment, societal cost and benefit studies, and sustainability studies. Finally, meta evaluations compare several program evaluations in order to compile the lessons learned from several programs.
5. The next problem, of course, is whether the evaluation will actually be used to improve the current or new programs.
6. Part of this definition is originally from the International Service for National Agricultural Research (ISNAR), and was quoted by Price (1991).
7. But it is beyond the scope of this chapter to enumerate them all, including their applicability, usefulness and failures.
8. For institutional evaluation, see "Participatory Organisational Evaluation Tool" (POET), UNDP (1998); "Assessing Progress Towards Sustainability," IUCN/World Conservation Union (1997); "Institutional Assessment: A Framework for Strengthening Organizational Capacity for IDRC's Research Partners," IDRC (1995); "Institutional Capacity Assessment Guidelines," CARE (1993); "An Evolutionary Approach to Facilitating Organisational Learning: An Experiment by the Christian Commission for Development in Bangladesh," CDS, Swansea (1997); "Discussion-Oriented Organizational Self-Assessment (DOSA)" (http://www.edc.org/INT/CapDev/dosapage.html). For environmental monitoring/evaluation, see "Monitoring Environmental Progress," World Bank; or "Changing Views on Change," IIED Environmental management tools, 1997.
9. It also facilitates assessing all three instrumental variables—hierarchical integration, stakeholder participation, and decision rules—of the statutory model.
10. Obviously, stakeholder analysis is a useful tool for addressing the stakeholder participation of the statutory model.
11. Interdisciplinary development programs are the ultimate ideal as a set of projects that form one "Gestalt" in which the dividing lines between the disciplines are not visible anymore. While this is a great ideal to strive for, it is either rare or impossible in practice that programming participants can seamlessly fit together all of their different backgrounds, approaches, and goals.
12. The validity of the causal theory is an important part of the statutory model.
13. It can also provide a useful input for gauging the resource variables, in particular, the financial resources, of the statutory model.
14. In the 1970s, integrated programming was very popular. It combined different functional sectors and disciplines, for example, better health required better health care and improved diets (see Krishna and Bunch 1997: 137–152).
15. Ferguson lays out in detail how this deficient analysis is based on a broader development discourse. He uses Foucault to criticize the depoliticizing concept of "development."
16. Following Foucault, Ferguson uses the term "instrument effects" for "side effects." Although the contextual model is rather instrumental—an approach that Ferguson criticizes—these side effects comprise the collateral and latent consequences of this model.
17. Stiefel and Wolfe (1994) focus on broader popular participation and its many meanings, such as pluralist democracy, labor unions, peasant movements, and social movements of the poor. These are, of course, broader societal issues than just program management.
18. A variation of the PRA that reduces the time and the monetary resources applied is the Rapid Rural Appraisal (RRA), which is a set of different methodologies to collect accurate information from local people. Qualitative methodologies for acquiring data are

crucial for RRA. The RRA concentrates on generating information, which is then analyzed away from the field. Although local people are consulted, the decision-making process is still rarely done by local people.

19. In his classic *Rural Development: Putting the Last First*, Chambers (1983) illustrates many of the pitfalls in understanding (and neglecting) rural poverty. In addition, he provides many suggestions for better learning from local rural people and suggests improvements for professional behavior and practical action.

20. Also outside PRA, thinking about participation has developed further. In their influential book *Rising from the Ashes*, Anderson and Woodrow (1989) make the simple yet crucial distinction between reducing vulnerabilities and building (on) capacities. They argue that humanitarian organizations have focused too little on building (on) local capacities. After all, participation also means building on local initiatives, which reduces the chance of creating dependency. Anderson and Woodrow also argue to take into account simultaneously the physical and material, the social and organizational, and the motivational and attitudinal aspects of rebuilding. Recently, attention to rights-based programming has increased in humanitarian circles. However, the idea is still ill defined. The main thought behind it seems to be that refugees, internally displaced people, and others affected by conflict have a right to assistance. Moreover, this assistance should fulfill certain quality criteria. People in war-torn societies thus have a claim to assistance; they are not just needy subjects left to the whims of international organizations. Such a rights-based approach would enhance the accountability of international organizations and is in line with other initiatives such as the SPHERE Project *"Humanitarian Charter and Minimum Standards in Disaster Response"* (2000) and the developing ideas for a humanitarian ombudsman and for humanitarian accountability projects.

21. By and large, management literature focuses on the management of projects within the organization. Development and humanitarian literature focuses far more often on the role of the programs and projects in the field.

22. For a broader analysis of these recommendations for management improvement in UN organizations, see Dijkzeul (1997).

23. This problem is especially severe in humanitarian programs.

24. Enforcing law ties into the broader discussion on the relationship between democracy, economic growth, and human rights (see the UNDP *Human Development Report* 2000).

Bibliography

Anderson, M.B., and Woodrow, P.J. *Rising from the Ashes: Development Strategies in Times of Disaster*. Boulder: Lynne Rienner Publishers, 1989.

Anderson, M.B. *Do No Harm: How Aid Can Support Peace—Or War*. Boulder/London: Lynne Rienner, 1999.

Baum, C.W., and Tolbert, S.M. *Investing in Development: Lessons of World Bank Experience*. Oxford: Oxford University Press, 1985.

Berman, P. "The Study of Macro- and Micro-Implementation." *Public Policy*, no. 26 (1978): 157–184.

Biekart, K. *The Politics of Civil Society Building: European Private Aid Agencies and Democratic Transitions in Central America*. Utrecht/Amsterdam: International Books and The Transnational Institute, 1999.

Bryant, C., and White, L.G. *Managing Development in the Third World*. Boulder: Westview Press, 1982.

Buzzard, S., and Edgcomb, E., eds. *Monitoring and Evaluating Small Business Projects: A Step-by-Step Guide for Private Development Organizations*. New York: PACT, 1987.

Chambers, R. *Rural Development: Putting the Last First*. Harlow: Addison Wesley Longman Ltd., 1983.

Crosby, B.L. "Stakeholder Analysis: A Vital Tool for Strategic Managers." *IPC Technical Note No. 2*. USAID's Implementing Policy Change Project, March 1992.

Development Initiatives. *Global Humanitarian Assistance 2000*. An independent report commissioned by the IASC from Development Initiatives. Somerset/Geneva, May 2000.

DFID. *Guidelines for Project Formulation*. London: U.K. Department for International Development, 1998.

Dijkzeul, D. *The Management of Multilateral Organizations*. The Hague/London/Boston: Kluwer Law International, 1997.

Dijkzeul, D. "UNOPS in Guatemala: From Relief to Development." In Mathiason, J. *Managing the World*. New York: New York University, forthcoming.

Dijkzeul, D., and Danchin, P. "Humanitarian Assistance." *A Global Agenda: Issues Before the United Nations 2001–2002*. Lanham: UNA-USA, Rowman and Littlefield, 2001.

Doornbos, M. "New Research Directions in Post-conflict Contexts: The Scope for Action Research Based Policy Dialogue." Paper prepared for the workshop "Living in War Times—Living in Post-war Times." University of Hanover History Department, Melsungen, 22–24 January 1999.

Eade, D., and Williams, S. *The Oxfam Handbook of Development and Relief*. London: Oxfam (UK and Ireland), 1995.

Ferguson, J. *The Anti-politics Machine: "Development," Depoliticization, and Bureaucratic Power in Lesotho*. Minneapolis/London: University of Minnesota Press, 1994.

Fowler, A.F. "Assessing NGO Performance: Difficulties, Dilemmas and a Way Ahead." Pp. 169–186, in Edwards, E., and Hulme E., eds. *Beyond the Magic Bullet: NGO Performance and Accountability in the Post–Cold War*. West Hartford, CT: Kumarian Press, 1996.

Fyfe, A. *Child Labor: A Guide to Project Design*. Geneva: International Labour Organisation, 1993.

Gosling, L., and Edwards, M. *Toolkits: A Practical Guide to Assessment, Monitoring and Evaluation*. London: Save the Children, 1995.

Graham, R.J., and Englund, R.L. *Creating an Environment for Successful Projects: The Quest to Manage Project Management*. San Francisco: Jossey-Bass Publishers, 1997.

Harrel Allen, T. *New Methods in Social Science Research: Policy Sciences and Futures Research*. New York: Preager Publishers, 1978.

Inter-Agency Standing Committee. *Global Humanitarian Assistance 2000*. An independent report commissioned by the IASC from Development Initiatives. Geneva: Office for the Coordination of Humanitarian Affairs, 2000.

Kassam, Y., and Mustafa, K., eds. *Participatory Research: An Emerging Alternative Methodology in Social Science Research*. New Delhi: Society for Participatory Research in Asia, 1992.

Kerzner, H. *In Search of Excellence in Project Management: Successful Practices in High Performance Organizations*. New York: Van Nostrand Reinhold, 1998.

Krishna, A., and Bunch, R. "Farmer-to-Farmer Experimentation and Extension: Integrated Rural Development for Smallholders in Guatemala." Pp. 137–152, in Krishna, A., Uphoff, N., and Esman, M.J., eds. *Reasons for Hope: Instructive Experiences in Rural Development*. West Hartford CT: Kumarian Press, 1997.

Macrae, L., and Leader, N. "Shifting Sands: The Search for 'Coherence' Between Political and Humanitarian Responses to Complex Emergencies," *HPG Report* 8. London: Overseas Development Institute, 2000.

Mayer, R.R., and Greenwood, E. *The Design of Social Policy Research*. Englewood Cliffs, NJ: Prentice Hall, 1980.

Maynard, K. *Post-conflict Community Participation: Using a Development Approach in a Chaotic Environment*. Unpublished paper for UNDP's Emergency Response Division and USAID's Office of Transition Initiatives for the roundtable "Community-Based Reintegration and Rehabilitation in Post-conflict Settings." 30 and 31 October 2000.

Miles, M.B., and Huberman, A.M. *Qualitative Data Analysis: An Expanded Sourcebook.* 2nd ed. Thousand Oaks/London/New Delhi: Sage Publications, 1994.

Patton, M.Q. *Utilization Focused Evaluation.* Beverly Hills: Sage Publications, 1978.

PRA in Central Asia: Coping with Change. Compiled by Carolyn Jones for INTRAC. IDS, 1996.

Pressman, J.L., and Wildavsky, A. *Implementation: How Great Expectations in Washington Are Dashed in Oakland.* 3rd ed. Berkeley: University of California Press, 1984.

Price, N. "The Project Framework Approach to Population Project Planning and Management: A Working Paper of the Sir Davis Owen Population Center." Unpublished paper. Photocopies available from Overseas Information. SCF, 1991.

Rossi, P.H., and Freeman, H.E. *Evaluation: A Systematic Approach.* 3rd ed. Beverly Hills: Sage Publications, 1985.

Sabatier, P., and Mazmanian, D. "The Implementation of Public Policy: A Framework of Analysis." *Policy Studies Journal*, Special Issue, Symposium on Successful Policy Implementation (1980): 538–560.

Salomons, D., and Dijkzeul, D. "The Conjuror's Hat: Financing United Nations Peace-Building in Operations Directed by Special Representatives of the Secretary-General." New York/Oslo: The Center on International Cooperation (NYU) and The Fafo Programme for International Cooperation and Conflict Resolution, 2001.

Scheirer, M.A. *Program Implementation: The Organizational Context.* Beverly Hills: Sage Publications, 1981.

Scholtes, P.R., Joiner, B.L., and Streibel, B.J. *The Team Handbook.* 2nd ed. Madison, WI: Oriel, 2000.

Smillie, I. *Service Delivery or Civil Society? Non-governmental Organizations in Bosnia and Herzegovina.* Discussion paper (in mimeo). December 1996.

The Sphere Project. *Humanitarian Charter and Minimum Standards in Disaster Response.* Oxford: Oxfam Publishing, 2000.

Stiefel, M., and Wolfe, M. *A Voice for the Excluded—Popular Participation in Development: Utopia or Necessity?* London: Zed Books, 1994.

UNDP. "Agency Support Costs." *Report of the Expert Group*, DP/1990/9, 27 December 1989.

UNDP. *Programming Manual.* New York: United Nations Development Program, 1999.

UNDP. *Human Development Report 2000.* Oxford: Oxford University Press, 2000.

Uvin, P. *Aiding Violence: The Development Enterprise in Rwanda.* West Hartford, CT: Kumarian Press, 1998.

Van de Vall, M. "Social Practice: Problems, Theory, and Methods." *Knowledge and Policy: The International Journal of Knowledge Transfer*, no. 3 (1991a): 3–9.

Van de Vall, M. "The Clinical Approach: Triangulated Program Evaluation and Adjustment." *Knowledge and Policy: The International Journal of Knowledge Transfer*, no. 3 (1991b): 41–57.

Van der Zouwen, J. *Grondbegrippen van de Methodologie* [Basic Methodological Concepts]. Amsterdam: Vrije Universiteit, 1990.

Van Meter, D.S., and Van Horn, C.E. "The Policy Implementation Process: A Conceptual Framework." *Administration and Society*, vol. 6, no. 4 (1975): 445–488.

Wijnen, G., Renes, W., and Storm, P. *Projectmatig Werken* [Project Work]. 7th ed. Utrecht: Marka, Uitgeverij Het Spectrum B.V., 1990.

World Bank. *Assessing Aid: What Works, What Doesn't, and Why.* Oxford: Oxford University Press, 1998.

Chapter 8

HUMAN RIGHTS, INSTITUTIONAL WRONGS

Alex de Waal

Introduction

It is frequently embarrassing to be a known as a human rights activist in Africa today.[1] Using the label "human rights" in countries across the continent regularly invites derision. Many ordinary African citizens see that human rights organizations prosper while human rights are routinely violated. Many human rights organizations originally fostered high hopes, but have failed to deliver. There is a sense of betrayal, felt most acutely in the countries where human rights have been most outrageously violated.

Few would disagree that there is a human rights crisis in Africa. It is hard to think of a country in which the promises of the Universal Declaration of Human Rights, now more than half a century old, are being fulfilled. There is plenty of work for those concerned with human rights; the need for human rights organizations appears greater than ever. Yet, this chapter puts forward the argument that the crisis in human rights is also located within the institutions that are supposed to protect human rights, including United Nations institutions, Western governments with human rights components in their foreign policies and aid programs, and nongovernmental human rights organizations (HROs), which played a key role in setting the international human rights agenda in the 1990s. The methods that these institutions have deployed to promote the values of universal human rights have not always been appropriate to the realities of Africa. But the leaders of international HROs rarely, if ever, recognize this problem; they make the error of conflating their own institutional practices with the rights that they, usually sincerely, endeavor to uphold.

The argument emphasizes that it is essential to distinguish between the universal values of human rights and the specific institutions that can be used to further them in particular social and political circumstances.

The formulae for "human rights" that are advanced by most international HROs are, in fact, too often a political illusion. In Africa today, political illusions are dangerous luxuries, and when they explode, as they inevitably do, the damage can be considerable.

Many of those who work in leading positions in international HROs will be somewhat baffled by this critique, and might mistake it for an assault on human rights values themselves. The argument should not be interpreted this way.

Human Rights Traditions in Western Europe and North America

Every culture and society has a concept of human rights. But it is Western human rights traditions originating in Enlightenment Europe that have come to dominate the world. The first section of this chapter gives a very brief overview of four traditions of rights activism in the West. The widespread usage of "human rights" is extremely recent, although philosophers have used comparable terms for many centuries. Until the last few decades, people did not struggle for abstract conceptions of rights but rather for changes that would directly bring benefits to their lives. This we may call the "first generation" of human rights struggle. There were few rights organizations as such, and the aims and methods used in these struggles were extremely varied, sometimes making little or no reference to the concept of rights at all.

Primary Mobilization

Historically, the struggle for civil and political liberties was a struggle against religious intolerance, monarchical absolutism, and heavy taxation. It began in Europe and its North American colonies. People were mobilized to struggle for freedom of religion, freedom of conscience, and social and economic progress. These were highly political struggles. Asserting freedom of conscience in England required a civil war and the execution of a monarch, while establishing the sovereignty of Parliament required the deposition of another king. The American Constitution required a successful rebellion, and the French assertion of the "Rights of Man" needed a revolution. More recently, struggles for rights have often been non-violent, using the freedoms established by revolution or granted by rulers who recognized that autocracy could best be preserved by providing space for civil liberties.

The nineteenth-century campaigns in Britain against the transatlantic slave trade and against child labor in factories ("Yorkshire Slavery," as the campaigners called it) combined a measure of religiously inspired philanthropy with liberal plutocratic self-interest. In India at the turn of the twentieth century, the British Raj recognized that containing the pressures of Indian nationalism required implementing effective policies for preventing famine, because recurrent epidemic starvation was discrediting British rule abroad, and, even more seriously, stirring up unrest in the subcontinent itself. The British policy of making minor concessions worked for almost half a century, until the failure to prevent the eminently preventable 1943 Bengal famine brought shame on British rule. It was a gross violation of basic economic rights, and it stimulated popular pressure for the basic political right of independence, which was duly achieved a few years later (de Waal 1997).

Similarly, throughout the twentieth century and into the twenty-first century in Europe and America, popular mobilization for civil and political rights has been inseparable from the pursuit of social, economic, and cultural rights. To put it more strongly, people have mobilized to protect their own interests, to remove restrictions on their personal lives, and to oppose threats to their personal welfare, aspirations, and dignity. This is the core of human rights, and it is a very hard core indeed. Examples include the women's movement—the campaign first for the right to vote and then for equality under the law. Trade union rights and legislation on employment—indeed, on national economic policies to promote employment—are other cases. Campaigns for nuclear disarmament and the withdrawal of troops from Vietnam and Northern Ireland are additional instances. The recent environmental movements in the developed world have been stimulated by very immediate concerns for preserving people's surroundings. Perhaps the defining example is the American civil liberties movement in the 1960s, a non-violent movement by citizens to claim their right to send their children to schools, to obtain jobs, and to vote for their representatives. Legitimate self-interest set in a universal moral idiom is extremely powerful.

This is politics. This is the slow and often painful struggle by which people establish what is rightfully theirs. This is the practical negotiation of a social contract.

Any attempt to create a definition of these diverse social and political movements would be doomed to failure. But there are some key ingredients that have contributed to success. One essential element is mass mobilization. The physical fact of so many people demanding their rights was instrumental in these movements. A second element is non-violence. Most (though not all) have used non-violent methods, or have used symbolic violence only. This has given them the moral high ground over their oppressors. The discipline of non-violence has also been very important in keeping the moral vision of the movements intact. On the governmental side, these movements have required a certain degree of tolerance to survive. Mahatma Gandhi's Indian independence movement could have been violently crushed by the British government, but in what was arguably its most enlightened step ever, it chose not to try.

When a government is prepared to be utterly ruthless in suppressing its citizens, non-violent resistance may not be an option. The African National Congress was a non-violent movement for the first half of the twentieth century; however, this achieved nothing, and it was pushed to armed struggle. This resort to violent resistance was characteristic of the later struggle against colonialism and racism in Africa (Sutherland and Meyer 2000).

Primary activism is a complicated process. It is not simply a matter of rousing people to action by whipping up their passions. On the contrary, it requires a moral vision and a patient commitment to public education and community assistance. Many of the elements that were to become prominent in "secondary activism," such as research, documentation, publishing, and using the law, were also widely used in primary mobilization. It is important to note that in no sense was this primary mobilization "neutral" or "impartial"—and still less was it "non-political." Quite the reverse. These men and women were pursuing highly controversial political goals that challenged the supremacy of a government or of one section of society.

Legal Aid and Public Interest Litigation

The foundation of protection for human rights is the rule of law. Rights commonly exist in law (provided for by constitutions or common law) that may not be upheld in practice, either through custom and neglect, or through abrogation of rights by governmental institutions. Laws often also need clarification, which can only be obtained through test cases.

Actually using the courts is a classic area in which respect for civil and political rights is dependent on the exercise of social and economic rights. In most countries, access to the courts is expensive, sometimes prohibitively so. In many countries, women, members of ethnic or social minorities, and people living in remote rural areas face enormous obstacles in pursuing their rights through the judicial system. On the other hand, wealthy and powerful people are often able to use the courts in a way that selectively benefits them. The British libel laws are a notorious example of the way in which wealth enables certain individuals to use the courts to intimidate newspapers and individuals, and, in practice, to suppress free speech. In many countries, property and land laws or divorce and inheritance laws often provide instances in which the practice of law favors wealthy and powerful sections of society.

Legal aid and public interest litigation are important traditions of Western legal practice. They have been essential in providing a counterbalance to the use of the judicial system in favor of the privileged, making it possible for less fortunate individuals to enforce their rights. Social action litigation, as developed within some South Asian judicial systems, takes this practice a step further, developing forms of judicial populism

238 | *Alex de Waal*

(Gooneskere 1998). To work, they require some important preconditions to be present, in particular, a strong political tradition of the rule of law. In some of the most authoritarian or autocratic societies, this formal legalism has been present (e.g., in nineteenth-century Britain and Apartheid South Africa), while in some ostensibly more democratic societies, the courts have been much less independent or their judgments have simply been ignored by the executive.

The tradition of legal aid and public interest litigation is bound up, sometimes very closely, with primary mobilization. The law has been one means used by disadvantaged groups to challenge discrimination and systemic violations of rights. Meanwhile, legal aid clinics have been an important means of educating people about their rights and, in turn, prompting them to form associations to protect those rights.

Philanthropy

Philanthropy has played a subsidiary role in rights activism. There is no doubt that in cases such as the campaigns against slavery and child labor or in Henri Dunant's creation of the International Committee of the Red Cross (ICRC) and the first Geneva Convention, the moral activism of individuals who had no direct material interest in the cause for which they struggled was important. A sense of philanthropy among radicals also proved significant in gaining support for some progressive causes, such as Indian decolonization and the struggle against apartheid. Their work of documentation, publishing, arousing public concern and outrage, and lobbying parliamentarians is, in some respects, the precursor of today's "second-generation" activism. Many of their methods also made an important contribution to primary movements.

However, while important crosscurrents in the Western tradition of philanthropy may support rights activism, the trend as a whole is against it. Charity strongly supports the status quo: it is a privilege for the "deserving poor" to receive the benefactions of the rich. Under British law, human rights activities are defined as non-charitable, and organizations such as Amnesty International are denied the tax benefits of being a registered charity.

The Laws of War

The laws of war (in recent decades known as international humanitarian law, or IHL) are arguably the oldest "human rights" tradition of all. The concept of "the warrior's honor" and constraints on warfare in the name of humanity are found in all societies (Best 1994; Ignatieff 1998). In modern times, IHL developed as different and complementary to human rights law, in that the latter is concerned with the relationship between a sovereign state and its citizens, while IHL is applicable where this relationship does not exist or has broken down entirely through armed conflict. Despite much overlap and some convergence, IHL is not human rights law: it recognizes and legitimizes the right of a combatant to kill and commit other acts that in other circumstances would be considered human rights violations. IHL does, of course, contain human rights provisions (such as the right to a trial) and reflects concepts of individual rights (notably in Common Article 3 of the Geneva Conventions), but its philosophy is markedly different from human rights law. Also, save in exceptional circumstances such as the international criminal tribunals of the mid-1940s and mid-1990s, there have been no mechanisms for penal sanctions except those voluntarily imposed by belligerent forces on their own soldiers. IHL is not international law either: it is founded on the distinction between *jus ad bellum* (the right to wage war) and *jus in bello* (the conduct of war), and preserves the latter by refusing to judge the former.

One of the main philosophical and practical reasons for the separation of IHL from human rights law is that if human rights law were applied in conflicts, IHL would instantly be violated and brought into disrepute.

The laws of war are highly significant to this discussion because, among other things, they embody a formal recognition that respect for human rights is specific to the context. In the circumstances of armed conflict, a different set of rules is called for. Moreover, the essence of IHL is practicability, not aspiration; it is an attempt to achieve a workable balance between legitimate military necessity and basic humanity. The concept of "proportionality" is fundamental to IHL: the infliction of death, suffering, and damage should be proportional to the military threat to be faced or advantage to be gained. In addition, each army's adoption of the Geneva Conventions is usually subject to their interpretation of justifiable exceptions to the rules.

Second-Generation Human Rights Organizations

The "second generation" of HROs has come into existence since the late 1970s. Although there have been predecessors as far back as the Anti-Slavery Society (founded in the 1840s, based on older associations), the Save the Children Fund (founded in 1919), the International Federation of Human Rights Leagues (1922), and Amnesty International (established in 1961), it was only at this time that the wider phenomenon of non-governmental human rights organizations became significant (Power 2000). These organizations depend not on mass mobilization, but on the "shortcut" of "mobilizing shame." They use research, documentation, and publication, combined with the skillful use of the media and the lobbying of politicians, to make their concerns known. Their basic premise is that if people know about an abuse, they will be moved to want to stop it.

The origins of second-generation activism lie in the success of many primary movements in the West, particularly the American civil rights movement. Rights, which had previously been marginal concerns, became legitimate subjects for professional work. Politicians were ready to listen. Some of the veterans of these struggles decided to put their efforts into deepening and broadening human rights work, notably, in trying to influence US foreign policy and assist citizens in other countries, such as Latin America and Eastern Europe, to replicate their own successes.

Primary mobilization is very time consuming and difficult. Social changes in the West have made it more so. The generations that came of age in the 1970s and afterward have been noticeably less activist than their parents. This may be a result of greater peace and prosperity, of geographical and social mobility leading to a decline in a sense of "community," of the rise of television or other factors. For whatever reason, it became both more attractive and more possible to undertake "secondary activism."

A particular event was instrumental in creating a rich seam to be mined by second-generation activists. This was the signing of the Helsinki Accords in 1975, which included a "final basket" concerned with human rights. One historian of the Cold War has written: "In retrospect, the Helsinki treaties of 1975 appear as the West's secret weapon, a time bomb planted in the heart of the Soviet Empire. Throughout Eastern Europe and the Soviet Union itself, a handful of brave and determined campaigners used the human rights provisions of the Helsinki 'Final Basket' to insist that their governments live up to the commitments they had signed " (Walker 1994: 237).

Ultimately, and to the total surprise of both superpowers, citizens' mobilization in Eastern Europe to defend the rights enshrined in these Accords became the lever that brought down the Berlin Wall and brought an end to the Cold War. The peaceful end of Central European communism, led by Solidarity in Poland and churches and organizations such as the Helsinki Citizens' Assemblies in various countries, was one of the great victories of primary rights mobilization. Charter 77 in Czechoslovakia was more a movement of intellectuals and artists and less a popular mobilization, but at the key moment in 1989, its leaders were ready to take to the streets themselves. Not only did they help organize the demonstrations that brought down Communist rule, they put themselves at the forefront of those protests. In much of the former Soviet Union, particularly in Transcaucasia, the story is rather different, with the opportunities for successful peaceful opposition being much smaller.

In Western Europe and North America, the most significant response to the human rights provisions of the Helsinki Accords was markedly different. It saw the creation of the seminal institution Helsinki Watch, which was soon to team up with Americas Watch to become Human Rights Watch. This has become the model for innumerable other human rights organizations.

In the 1980s, these second-generation HROs seemed to have discovered a shortcut to achieve respect for human rights. It was no longer necessary to bring the people out onto the streets, or to tramp around small towns speaking to audiences in church halls. Instead, journalists could expose human rights atrocities in the media, professional lobbyists could get congressmen and congresswomen to ask awkward questions and even pass legislation tying US assistance to human rights guarantees, and occasionally lawyers could bring cases to national or international courts. Aryeh Neier, founding director of Human Rights Watch, called it "mobilizing shame." This form of activism constrained the US government—a bit—and heartened the anti-Communist activists in the Eastern bloc. And although primary mobilization was fading—the local roots of the human rights movement were being neglected—the legacy of the civil rights movement left enough of a domestic constituency to legitimize and constrain the second-generation activists.

Along with choosing to focus on research, publishing, and lobbying, the new HROs made a critical decision about their mandates. They decided to confine themselves to violations of fundamental rights, such as torture, arbitrary detention, and execution, along with restrictions on civil and political liberties. Overwhelmingly, they are not concerned with social, economic, and cultural rights, nor with the social and economic obstacles to establishing the rule of law. Some are even opposed to recognizing social and economic rights as true rights at all. The decision has been partly philosophical and partly practical (initially, the HROs' resources and influence were severely limited). But it has had profound consequences, particularly in the post–Cold War era.

What Are Second-Generation HROs?

The main characteristics of second-generation, or secondary, activism include the following. First, human rights activism has become professionalized. A profession has arisen, dominated by lawyers, journalists, and publishers, but without the formal accoutrements of a profession, such as certification or registration. There is a strong sense of a "human rights community," particularly in New York and Washington, D.C. Peer pressures within this community are very important: there is a strong internal conformism. Some of the new human rights professionals have had first-hand experience of primary mobilization (especially the founders of organizations such as Human Rights Watch), and others are themselves former victims of human rights abuses. But an increasing number are college graduates who are drawn to the profession from a combination of seeing it as an attractive career, along with personal moral concerns. There is a simple generational phenomenon at work: most HROs are now staffed by people who did not grow up during the domestic struggle for civil rights and for whom human rights is less a vocation than a profession. Their peer group is in government, academia, law, and commerce, and they do not have the moral reference group of protest marchers that so strongly influenced their predecessors.

Second, a new kind of specialist institution has emerged. Human rights organizations typically have mandates framed by lawyers referring to articles in the Universal Declaration of Human Rights or something similar. They take their funding from philanthropic foundations and corporations (especially in the US), or sometimes from governments or quasi-governmental foundations (especially in Europe). A few, like Amnesty International, have mass membership, but this is growing uncommon. HROs have career structures and administrative hierarchies. Like most institutions, after a while, they give more and more emphasis to preserving their institutional viability. This contrasts with primary movements, whose mandates arise from very specific issues, and for whom institutionalization is developed only as an instrumental strategy for helping to achieve these goals.

Third, arising from the legally defined mandates, there is a universalization or internationalization of concern. Second-generation organizations may work with issue-specific or case-specific organizations, but they do not aim at mobilizing a mass constituency. Rather, they tend to focus on influencing a liberal and educated elite on behalf of people in faraway countries.

Fourth, these organizations focus on documentation, publishing, and using the media. Their essential rationale is that if an abuse is publicized, public opinion and the conscience (and sense of dignity) of policymakers will ensure that action is taken against it. Some human rights organizations have been little more than specialist publishing houses. As other forms of media develop, they have also adapted marketing techniques from commercial companies and relief agencies. For example, they may try to "humanize" their "product" by presenting individual victims whom their "consumers" can identify with, using these as representatives of a much wider problem.

This relates to the focus on high-profile individuals. Some organizations, like Amnesty International, deal almost entirely with individual cases. Others prefer to highlight prominent people. If you are a prisoner, it is very helpful to be a writer, lawyer, Olympic athlete, princess, or of course a prize-winning human rights activist. It's unfortunate if you are a peasant: some Western human rights activists may take up your case, but not many, and not with much vigor.

A particular brand of this approach is the sanctification of prominent individual human rights activists. There are some very brave and determined individuals around the world who have stood up, sometimes almost alone, against tyranny. And these people deserve our support. But it is questionable if the Western HROs' cult of the human rights hero is actually supporting their cause. It worked in the 1980s, but it has arguably become overblown now. The generous and sometimes indiscriminate award of human rights prizes can create more problems than it solves. To elevate one individual from a broader movement risks creating vanities and jealousies among the leaders of the movement, apart from the way in which it can misrepresent the nature of the struggle. Sometimes the search for the appropriate individual can become absurd: I have been rung up a number of times by mainly American HROs looking for a character reference for some supposedly prominent human rights activist in northeast Africa, whose name I have never heard before. And of course there is the problem that the definition of "human rights activist" has an element of subjectivity, compounded by the danger that these people may not always follow the approved "human rights" career after getting their awards. The Roman Catholic Church prefers to elevate people to the sainthood only after they have died: it might be prudent for HROs to follow this model. The award of human rights prizes actually has more to do with publicizing the HROs back home—and providing a focus for fundraising events—than in promoting human rights in other countries. When the two aims harmonize, it is fortunate.

Fifth, many of these organizations focus much effort on influencing the policies of their national governments, particularly the US government. The lobbyists' charm, pragmatism, and inside knowledge are indispensable tools in this work. Some have become so adept at this that it appears to be their prime justification—almost an end in itself. The "influence trap," whereby principles are incrementally abandoned in order to maintain an "in" with the government, is an ever present danger.

Secondary activism in the United States began in the early 1980s in an adversarial confrontation with the government. That Republican decade was an ideal opportunity for pioneering secondary activism; most HROs were staffed by Democrats. The US had a global reach and with the globalization of anti-Communist containment, there was no part of the world, however small or faraway, that did not have some US "angle" to it. The American government was either propping up a pro-Western regime or trying to undermine a pro-Soviet one, or at the very least had a significant influence on policy. At the same time, the ideology of freedom meant that there was moral leverage on US foreign policy. The gap between rhetoric and reality was relentlessly and brilliantly exploited.

In the 1990s, this changed. Years had passed and staff had changed. There was a Democratic administration. Along with the institutionalization of HROs as lobbying organizations, a revolving door emerged between HROs, legal firms, academia, think tanks, the UN, and, above all, the US administration. This happens at various levels, from HRO board members who take senior government posts to interns who work for members of Congress and then switch to HROs, or vice versa. It follows that this elite governmental stratum is the peer group for these "international" HROs. They share the same world-views.

Sixth, the HROs' relationship with foreign (formerly Eastern bloc, now predominantly Third World) governments responsible for abuses has, by contrast, remained largely adversarial. In the 1980s, Communist countries were remarkably vulnerable to the moral challenge based on human rights. Under pressure, they released political prisoners, let Jews emigrate, and allowed dissidents to organize. Most of the time, they played by the rules. Meanwhile, pro-American governments (notably in Latin America, where the human rights movement has focused much of its energies) had to respond to pressure from the US administration. They could not unduly embarrass their patron, and had to show that "authoritarian" pro-Western regimes were more law abiding than "totalitarian" Communists.

In the 1990s and into the millennium, the adversarial stance has not changed. In dealing with governments in Africa, Asia, and Latin America, principle counts more than influence, to the extent that some HROs appear to be dogmatic, insisting on operating in their standard manner even when it is obviously not the best strategy for producing practical results. Thus, the idea of a Western HRO becoming engaged in helping an African government set up its legal system, or collaborating with a legal aid scheme, might be rejected on the grounds that it would compromise the "independence" (or, by implication, the ethical purity) of the HRO. Similarly, HROs will be ready to recommend cutting aid or trade links to an abusive government, but will be reluctant to press for expanding aid to a government committed to human rights.

Many Western HROs also criticize their national governments. Human Rights Watch criticizes the US administration and Amnesty International criticizes the British government. But the power relations here are markedly different, and these organizations are part of democratic, national political processes.

Lastly, and especially in the post–Cold War era, many of the HROs' concerns have converged with those of international humanitarian organizations, such as UNICEF, CARE, Oxfam, and others. Many of the places where human rights violations are most acute are no longer authoritarian states, but so-called "complex emergencies"—otherwise known as civil wars—that have unleashed mass human displacement and hunger. In such cases, HROs have begun to tread on uncertain ground. Where there are no effective governments (e.g., Somalia), conventional human rights activism cannot work. Monitoring the laws of war remains a valid exercise, but recent years have seen strong pressures to revise these laws. Along with international humanitarian agencies, HROs have participated in the attempts to develop novel legal doctrines, such as humanitarian intervention and the privileging of humanitarian agencies under IHL and its offspring "humanitarian principles." A critique of these initiatives falls outside the scope of this chapter.

Successes of Second-Generation HROs

Following the triumph of Eastern Europe in 1989, second-generation HROs succeeded in setting the human rights agenda for the 1990s. They are the model for how to do it; theirs was a tremendous success. But their success was also a product of historical circumstance. As argued above, Human Rights Watch was a child of the last decade of the Cold War. The zenith of the second-generation organizations' power was, ironically, the moment at which their project began to unravel. When the Cold War ended, realities became much more complicated.

It is notoriously difficult for HROs to measure their successes and failures. But there are two unquestionable successes. First, massive abuses cannot occur in secret any more. It is extremely unlikely that large-scale abuses, such as the massacres perpetrated by the Khmer Rouge in Cambodia, the Government of Burundi in 1972, or the USSR's Gulag, would occur again without being widely known around the world.

Secondly, human rights concerns have become an internationally legitimate subject. No dictator can refuse to acknowledge the legitimacy of international concern over his treatment of his own citizens. This is reflected in the passing of much human rights legislation at the UN and the European Parliament. In turn, it also legitimizes the international search to uncover human rights abuses in faraway places. There has been enough determination among HROs and journalists to expose, for example, the Sudan government's secret attempts to destroy the Nuba people or the Indonesian government's wars in East Timor and Irian Jaya.

But these successes are not without their problems. Human rights activism is not a science in which one can predict cause and effect with total confidence. There is some evidence that the tools have become blunted.

Possible Failures of Second-Generation HROs

Perhaps the most serious challenge to the work that HROs do is the question, posed by two very experienced human rights activists, as to whether the exposure of abuses actually leads to genuine pressure to stop them. The entire second-generation HRO project is premised on this assumption.

Since the UN signed its historic declaration half a century ago, the underlying supposition has been that if people knew enough, if the quality of research and reporting was good enough, if the information reached the right people, then action was bound to follow. That is turning out to be false. In any other field of human endeavor, such meager results to show for such an enormous amount of effort would not be tolerated (Moorhead and Owen 1996: 55).

The context of this criticism was Rwanda—the first unmistakable case of genocide since the adoption of the Convention on the Prevention and Punishment of the Crime of Genocide in 1948. The killings were televised. And the world did nothing.

One of the reasons for the decline in effectiveness is "overkill." There is simply so much human rights information around, and so little attempt to calibrate and prioritize it, that it is difficult for the public or policymakers to discern a case of genocide amid all the "noise" of detentions and extra-judicial executions. The way in which humanitarian relief agencies have also entered the picture—presenting wars, massacres, and genocides as crises needing charitable relief—has also complicated the picture.

It is likely that the professional standards of human rights investigations have also slipped. The proliferation of HROs and their reliance on American and European staff members, some of whom have little or no experience of the countries they are "covering," and the use of interns who are wholly new to the business have led to a number of cases of poor research and unsubstantiated allegations. The HROs rarely admit to this, but it is becoming a question of credibility. Serious though these cases are, it would be a mistake to see them as the disease; rather, they are the symptom of a deeper problem.

A second and related failing has been that much new human rights legislation has been adopted, but to uncertain effect. The numerous new instruments of human rights have been ignored more often than they have been followed. As I shall argue below, this is only partly a problem of governments cynically abusing rights. Partly, it is a problem of HROs being unrealistic, and therefore not in practice serving their aims.

A third failing has been that many abusers have found creative new ways of circumventing the system. Human rights activism works according to certain well-known formulae, for example, Amnesty International's "prisoners of conscience." To avoid the difficulties of holding known prisoners of conscience, governments have adopted various tactics. One, used for a while by the Sudan government, was to arrest political opponents for a very brief time in non-regular detention centers, and then—just as word was reaching the London offices of Amnesty International (AI)—release them, but ask them to report on a daily basis to a security office. And then perhaps rearrest them, but rapidly release them. The effect was basically the same as imprisonment of the political opponent, but the Sudan government could claim that it held no political prisoners. Another, more disturbing response appears to be the way in which some Latin American dictatorships have simply made their opponents "disappear," partly as a way of circumventing the problems that the governments would encounter with AI. Even discussing this possibility has caused very severe consternation at AI. There are many other ways for abusive governments to achieve their goals while avoiding censure by HROs. Another example is to create ethnic unrest and use ethnic militias to carry out the government's will.

A fourth failing is that while it has proved possible for second-generation HROs to influence Western government policy, this has rarely been the case when there are vested interests at work in the opposite direction. One example is the Clinton administration's award of most-favored-nation status to China, prioritizing commercial interests over the pressures of HROs. A second example is the failure of the land mines campaign in the US to get support from the administration to ban antipersonnel mines. By contrast, the European, East Asian, and Southern African mines campaigns, which involved mobilizing numerous citizens' groups in a form of primary mobilization, did successfully change governments' policies, overriding the vested interests of mines manufacturers. The neglect of the roots of the human rights movement has paid a price.

Perhaps the most important failing, however, has been political hubris. "International" HROs based in Western capitals have assumed that because human rights are universal, their model of work is universal. This has led to a cultural and political insensitivity that is at times almost funny, for example, when Human Rights Watch's headquarters moved to the Empire State Building in New York City. In New York terms, this is not a prestigious address, but it sends a certain message to the rest of the world, particularly those countries with direct experience of being part of other countries' empires. If HRW was not aware of this, it was a sign of insensitivity, at the least. If HRW *was* aware, it is perhaps even more revealing.

Human Rights Organizations as an Exportable Commodity

The historical reality is that respect for human rights has developed in countries through popular mobilization and the use of the legal system by citizens themselves. Where these political and institutional preconditions do not exist, human rights work is more akin to trying to protect civilians using IHL: exhortation, persuasion, and pressure are required from an external source. In short, negotiation is needed, not preaching. However, what has happened is that the model of second-generation HROs has been uncritically exported from the liberal democracies to other countries with very different historical experiences. In some places this has worked, and in others it has not. In addition, the model has even been applied to conflicts, merging the formerly distinct traditions of human rights law and IHL.

The second-generation HRO arose from particular historical circumstances, which made it effective in that context (the last decade of the Cold War). The times have changed, but the institutional context for preserving these institutions has persisted. The institutional donors are still there, the media are still interested, and Western governments are still highly receptive to the information and analysis (though the results of activism in terms of policy changes have been in sharp decline). Above all, this model of HRO has become institutionalized, and those within the system can see no other. It is self-perpetuating and self-legitimizing. The same institutional context that has maintained the Western HRO in its current form has also encouraged the creation of African, Asian, and Latin American HROs on the same model. In countries where there is a strong tradition of popular mobilization, liberal government, and the rule of law, this can work reasonably well. Where there is not, it is deeply problematic.

There are a number of characteristic syndromes that rights-watching HROs tend to be vulnerable to, especially in Africa. This is not a universal rule, though, and many of the organizations are in fact well aware of these problems and strive to avoid them. One problem is "donorism": the African HRO's institutional survival depends upon getting funding from foreign donors who work according to a standard bureaucratic format. Much of the energy of the organization is devoted to writing project proposals, negotiating with donors, and preparing the right kinds of reports. Along with financial dependence on donors, this creates accountability oriented toward external interests. These interests may appear to be institutional rather than overtly political, but the tendency is there. It also means that the organization is obliged to adopt a certain model of activities—a professionalization rather than democratization.

A second problem is commercial opportunism. Running an HRO can become a means of earning a living. With the decline in state-provided professional employment, many capable professionals need to find niches for themselves, and this is one.

The third, and perhaps the most serious, problem is that involvement in a local HRO can become a means of political opportunism. It is common to have a revolving door between political office and human rights monitoring and activism. Criticizing the human rights record of a government is perhaps the most legitimate means of criticizing it, and can become a cover for smuggling in many other non-human rights criticisms as well. Involvement in an HRO can afford a politician a higher profile and more publicity, as well as moral protection and an income. A number of presidential and parliamentary hopefuls in Kenya have human rights prizes on their office walls.

The current attempts to develop a UN declaration on human rights defenders, while an intrinsically laudable exercise, may run into the danger of overprivileging the second-generation HRO. It is questionable whether human rights law is the best mechanism for protecting human rights defenders. In countries where human rights defenders are most needed, states are least likely to be respectful of the more arcane pieces of human rights legislation. There is also the problem that if one tries to define human rights activities, one may end up restricting them. A universalistic definition of human rights, for example, might exclude or marginalize groups campaigning for minority rights or those promoting social and economic rights. But failing to define the term "human rights defender" might also open the door to an abuse of the declaration: any opposition political activist could claim to be a "human rights defender," thus jeopardizing all human rights work. Even worse, singling out HROs for privileged treatment runs the risk of focusing human rights concern on HROs rather than on ordinary people. While this is not the legislators' intention, it might be the result. In short, the process is colored by the concerns of second-generation HROs and the lawyers who tend to dominate them.

Many human rights activists in Africa are unhappy with the way in which the second-generation model is open to abuse and has discredited their profession in the eyes of citizens and governments—and even some donors. Some activists are making strenuous efforts to avoid these pitfalls, but the constraints and dangers remain.

The organizations that work best tend to be those that are organically linked to the material interests of a community or profession. Their concern is commonly to use civil and political liberties to advance their material well-being—the practical integration of civil and political rights with social and economic ones. These groups include self-help groups, such as revolving credit organizations or marketing cooperatives; professional associations; and legal aid organizations.

One of the reasons why human rights institutions do not export very well from the US and Europe is their sole focus on civil and political rights, excluding social and economic ones. In the West, this has enabled human rights to be adopted into governments' aid and economic policies in a deeply problematic way.

Human Rights as a Foreign Policy Tool for Western Governments

One of the successes of Western HROs has been the adoption of "human rights" and "ethics" into the foreign policies of their governments. But this has proved to be a double-edged sword. Governments have been ready to use human rights rhetoric in foreign policy statements and (less often) to act in ways consonant with those policies. They have also been more amenable to pressure from HROs. But they have also appropriated the concept of human rights and have bent it to serve other ends.

Aid Conditionalities

The imposition of conditionalities on aid provision has been one of the most common elements of Western governments' human rights policies. This began when domestic HROs objected to their aid being sullied by being used for human rights violations, for example, when US-supplied weaponry or US-trained military personnel were implicated in atrocities in El Salvador. It broadened to a much wider range of conditions on any form of aid, sometimes to an absurd degree. For example, US aid for UN population control programs in Kenya was held up because, according to US law, the US (where abortion is legal) cannot support population control in Kenya (where abortion is illegal) through an organization that does not oppose abortion.

Such cases aside, there are fundamental problems with aid conditionalities on human rights. To start with, there are double standards. Strategically or commercially important aid recipients are routinely exempted from this conditionality, for the simple and good reason that they would just reject the aid and not change their behavior. Hence Israel, China, and Indonesia, to name but three examples, have almost entirely escaped any effective conditioning of aid to human rights. By contrast, poor and aid-dependent countries tend not to have much strategic or commercial significance for aid donors, so aid conditionality is both domestically possible and could, in theory, actually work. Poorer countries thus face tougher conditions.

Because the leading Western HROs have deliberately blinded themselves to social and economic rights—insisting that poverty is no excuse for rights violations—they do not see this systematic double standard. Rather, they are just upset that countries like China and Indonesia escape the "proper" sanctions.

A second problem is the regular shifting of the goal posts. In the last decade, the focus of donor conditionality has, broadly speaking, changed from tying aid to basic human rights, to tying it to multiparty electoral systems, and, more recently, to tying it to fighting corruption. None of these conditionalities has been implemented long enough or consistently enough across donors and across different kinds of aid provision to provide any real incentive for recipients to change their behavior. Concerted action—for example, in the case of the Paris Club toward Kenya in 1991— has occasionally produced dramatic changes in a recipient's political strategies, but these have tended to be superficial or short-lived. Meanwhile, economic conditionalities imposed by the International Monetary Fund (IMF) have proved much more enduring and powerful, with the result that determined governments, however poor, have been able to attract foreign aid by agreeing to structural adjustment programs while ignoring the then-current human rights or democracy conditionalities of aid. Uganda is a case in point.

A third problem with human rights conditions is that they are almost entirely negative. Aid is cut off when there is a perceived violation, but those who conform to the requirements rarely get a positive reward. Punitive sanctions are by far the most popular instrument that donors use to link aid and human rights, and it is easy to see why. As a powerful gesture to the domestic human rights lobbies that are so influential, sanctions are not only cheap, they actually save the donor money. By contrast, programs to support police forces or prisons are expensive, long term, and unlikely to gain much domestic approval; on the contrary, as all police forces and prison services have a tendency to commit abuses sooner or later, they are virtually guaranteed to garner criticism from HROs.

The fourth problem is conditionality overload. Many Western governments—particularly the US—have proliferated the number of human rights preconditions on assistance. If all of these preconditions were enforced, it would be all but impossible for the US to have a foreign assistance program at all, so complicated and far-reaching are they. So they are not enforced except in an ad hoc manner when a particularly persistent NGO demands it or when a desk officer wants to make a point to a recipient country, which often treats the exercise in a pragmatic or even cynical manner.

A fifth problem with human rights conditionality is that the most common instrument, punitive conditionality, is an arbitrary measure without due process. While the entire aid process is notoriously lacking in transparency and democratic accountability, the sudden withdrawal of aid is perhaps the most arbitrary and opaque of all measures. In response to an alleged abuse, the donor makes a diplomatic representation and immediately suspends aid. The recipient has no right of appeal. There is no independent means of assessing whether the allegation was justified, whether the abuse has been rectified, or whether the sanctions have had the desired effect. The whole exercise is in fact likely to generate cynicism among the sanctioned recipient. It is a simple but valid truism that democracy and human rights cannot be promoted by methods that are themselves arbitrary and lack due process.

This points to the final and fundamental problem with aid and human rights. An aid process that is itself not democratized or transparent will be incapable of making a systematic contribution to human rights and democracy in the recipient country. This is a complex subject, yet it is remarkable that most donor and NGO assistance programs are closed to any form of public scrutiny. Ironically, it is the World Bank, the most regularly demonized of all aid institutions, that has led the way in opening itself up for public scrutiny and consultation. While aid negotiations remain secretive, a very large part of the governmental apparatus in poor and aid-dependent countries will remain undemocratic. It is only by making the aid encounter more open and more democratic than the other aspects of domestic politics in the recipient country that there will be a real chance for aid to sustain democratic processes and structures.

Free Enterprise as a Fundamental Right

One of the most significant elements in Western donor policy on human rights in the 1980s and 1990s was the systematic delinking of civil and political rights from social and economic rights. Western HROs have, for the most part, gone along with this or even encouraged it. This has allowed Western donors to follow policies that, on the one hand, promote democratization and, on the other hand, enforce economic policies on poor countries. The result is that the electorate is forbidden from having any say at all in economic policy.

The ideological rationale for this belief is that any form of state intrusion into economic life is a violation of liberty. Political liberty must be conterminous with economic liberty. This is a doctrine that no Western government would dare enforce at home, where elections are most often contested over governments' economic policies, and special interest pressure groups ensure that subsidies are granted to agriculture and industry. No Western electorate would consider democracy worthwhile if the next government's economic policies had been completely determined in advance by the IMF.

Structural adjustment programs have another profound effect on human rights. Governments' public spending is squeezed so hard that they cannot train and pay enough police officers and judges, or provide enough prisons. Lawyers command high salaries, as the accounts of any American HRO will demonstrate. It is simply not true to say that human rights are free, unless one is prepared to tolerate "people's justice," such as some liberation fronts have developed while in the field, for all levels of justice, including enforcing the commercial code.

In the early 1990s, it was fashionable for international financial institutions (and some others) to predict and welcome the near-total demise of the state in Africa and the former Communist countries. More recently, the role of the state has been acknowledged as a prerequisite for a market economy. The following statement, referring to the former Eastern bloc, is equally valid for Africa: "The post-Communist challenge is to restore the authority of states without re-collectivizing societies. State repair is the main condition of market-based prosperity, on which, in turn, depends our ability to tame, if not solve, the 'post-Communist' problems of nations, races and borders" (Skidelsky 1995:164).

The strongest and most legitimate states in Eastern Europe have been those best able to survive the "shock therapy" of instant economic liberalization and manage the transition to a market economy. Only the fact that the market economy has in fact delivered a modicum of prosperity has averted a major crisis of legitimacy in these countries. But it is notable that a number of former Communist parties have been voted back into power.

As argued above, historically, the protection of civil and political liberties has been intimately tied with the promotion of social and economic rights. If the latter are delegitimized by externally enforced economic policies, then the former are in danger of losing their credibility, too.

Have Human Rights Instruments Become "Overinflated"?

In important respects, international second-generation human rights activism is more akin to the ICRC's attempts to gain belligerents' compliance with the laws of war than citizens' attempts to guarantee their rights vis-à-vis their governments under the law. The HROs can exhort and embarrass and occasionally enforce punitive sanctions, but their ability to mobilize the people or develop the law is very limited. This is an illuminating parallel because a number of scholars believe that in recent years, IHL has become too complex and demanding, and thus impractical.

This process can be dated from 1977 when the Additional Protocols were added to the Geneva Conventions. Written in a legalistic manner that made them more remote from the realities of war, the Additional Protocols filled some important gaps left by their predecessors, but also blurred some important distinctions. One authoritative commentator has concluded that their impact was to make IHL "overinflated" (Best 1994: 419). His argument was that the introduction of some external political considerations into the drafting of the laws, in particular, the characterization of wars of national liberation as "international," undermined the clarity and practicability of the Geneva Conventions. In addition, the insistence on giving all civilians the same degree of protection—irrespective of whether they were small children or guerrillas out of uniform or munitions workers—challenges the law's foundation in a military commander's sense of a legitimate military objective. The fear is that if the law is too demanding, commanders will simply ignore it, and thus bring the entire edifice of IHL into disrepute.

If "overinflation" was a problem in 1977, it has become a crisis since then. In the last two decades, human rights law and IHL have increasingly overlapped and have even fused together. There has been an elaboration of IHL along several paths. One of these paths is the refinement of the concept of "customary international humanitarian law," which usually takes the strongest restrictions on the conduct of war to be found in any document and then applies them across the board.

A second path is the development of "humanitarian principles" by discussion among aid agencies. These are statements of high principle that have the effect of further restraining belligerents while lifting the hitherto strict conditions imposed on relief agencies in conflict, instead giving them what amounts to blanket protection, come what may. For example, the Red Cross's 10-point "Code of Conduct," drawn up in 1994 and "approved" by governments and NGOs in 1995, consists principally of abstract statements about the aims of humanitarian relief, counterposed by far-reaching concrete demands from host governments and belligerents to respect and privilege relief agencies. A professor of international relations commented: "Not one of the ten points addressed in any way the critical issue of how to protect vulnerable populations and aid activities, nor how impartial relief work could be combined with human-rights advocacy, sanctions or other coercive measures. [Donor] governments and NGOs appeared to be addressing humanitarian issues in a pious and abstract manner far removed from the harsh dilemmas resulting from wars" (Roberts 1996: 60–61).

A third path has been the activism of the UN Security Council in developing, in an ad hoc way, doctrines of humanitarian intervention and the privileges of humanitarian organizations as well as the widening mandate of agencies such as UNHCR.

In these processes of attempted lawmaking, soldiers—particularly those actually fighting the wars in question—are notable by their absence.

The foundation of IHL, in practicability and acceptance by soldiers, has been abandoned in favor of the lawmaking privileges of lawyers and humanitarian officials.

The "overinflation" of IHL reached a crisis point in the Great Lakes region of Central Africa during and after the genocide in Rwanda. This point will be returned to later. Arguably, a similar process of inflating human rights standards and demands has taken place in international human rights law and practice. The case of the proposed UN declaration on human rights defenders is one case among others. High standards are to be welcomed. Sovereign states should respect their citizens, and their citizens should demand and enforce that respect through the law. But the object of any *international* exercise in promoting human rights should be more pragmatic.

The multiplication of HROs and their activities has both contributed to and been partly driven by a plethora of new human rights instruments. United Nations bureaucracies produce these because it is their job to do so, and governments sign them because it is unbecoming not to. All of these human rights instruments—on the rights of children, women, minorities, displaced people, relief workers, etc.—are all laudable. But they are all "soft" law, that is, aspirations rather than justiciable instruments.

This proliferation of laws is a problem. Many are impractical. Some cannot realistically be implemented. Others have been signed by governments that do not have the capacity or the will to implement them. This is actually a sign of disrespect for the rule of law. In many cases, the signatory governments do not take them seriously because they know that the laws are not justiciable. Thus, the Sudan government has signed the 1989 Convention on the Rights of the Child but continues to violate it flagrantly. In other cases, laws are signed by countries that have functioning legal systems, but in some cases they are so overjusticiable—due to the court procedures being so elaborate, protracted, and open to innumerable appeals—that it is unlikely that they will be taken seriously. In the US, for example, there are few professions held in such public contempt as lawyers. In addition, the proliferation of human rights law, reflecting the proliferation of institutions developing it, coincides with the weakening of states' sovereign power to enforce these laws, due to economic globalization and the dominance of neoliberal economic doctrine that reduces the state's economic reach.

The rather indiscriminate proliferation of human rights instruments opens the door to challenges based on "Asian values" to the core of liberal human rights or the prioritization of economic rights. In their more legitimate forms, these challenges identify the social and economic preconditions for effective institutions to protect human rights (i.e., national security, the rule of law, a measure of economic prosperity) and seek to prioritize these alongside liberal human rights. In a less legitimate manner, these challenges can also be a means of distracting attention from inexcusable abuses. It is important to reclaim human rights from over-control by lawyers and lawyerly institutions.

The Genocide in Rwanda and the Routinization of Human Rights

The most insidious effect of the growth of HROs has been to make the protection of human rights into a business that is removed from the basic material and political struggles of ordinary citizens. If it becomes the responsibility of a special brand of professionals to promote human rights, then citizens can be subtly disqualified from engaging in rights work. Similarly, if HROs are responsible for preventing or protesting against abuses, then other citizens can rest content that the work is being done and they need not worry.

The way in which human rights work has become a routine and a con-cern for a professional elite has, arguably, contributed to the worst-ever crisis for the human rights movement—that is, Rwanda. In 1993–1994, Rwanda was a model for second-generation human rights activism. There were seven local organizations active, supported by a range of vig-orous Western organizations that were unusually collaborative. Western donors were deeply concerned. Even the UN force in the country (UNAMIR) had a mandate for promoting human rights. Thus, there was an illusion that Rwandan human rights activists had international pro-tection and could work with bravery in the face of an authoritarian state and its agents, apparently safe in the knowledge that the "international community" had undertaken to protect them.

When the Rwandese human rights community was wiped out, there was nothing that the international HROs could do, and the UN chose to do nothing. Under extreme pressure, at least one former human rights activist, along with a number of priests, journalists, and aid workers, themselves joined in the killings. Among the others, some went to great lengths to conceal the culpability of some of their friends and relations. These were, of course, exceptional circumstances, and human rights activists are no more nor less human than anyone else. But the cult of cel-ebrating the human rights hero did not stand Rwanda—nor the cause of human rights—in good stead. Neither did the institutionalized, routine cataloguing of human rights abuses on a day-to-day basis.

International HROs proved extremely defensive when the facts came out that a former human rights activist in Rwanda had submitted to the genocidaires' demands and had become a killer. This discomfort reflects the way in which the second-generation HROs have fetishized them-selves: they cannot distinguish between human rights values and the actually existing human rights institutions, which are inevitably flawed like all human institutions. This is going to prove a profound crisis for this form of activism. Whether it is able to acknowledge this crisis, apologize for its errors, and learn from them will be a major test of its maturity.

Even before the crisis of human rights activists who became involved in genocide emerged, another profound problem had arisen. Let me illustrate with the case of Amnesty International, though there are other organizations in broadly the same situation. The genocide of the Rwandese Tutsis lasted something less than one hundred days. Up to one million people were murdered. This was a short, confusing, and dangerous period in which to do human rights research. It was possible, as proved by Rakiya Omaar, who produced a 750-page document during this period and the following month (African Rights 1994), but she is an exceptional individual. Amnesty International succeeded in putting out a 14-page statement on the genocide. In the aftermath, which was also a confused period in which some survivors and some Tutsi soldiers distraught with grief and anger took revenge on suspected killers—some of them guilty, some of them probably not guilty—Amnesty International did succeed in sending a mission to Rwanda. It produced a second report, also 14 pages long, concerned with some 100 or so revenge killings. Some of these allegations were refuted by a delegation from Physicians for Human Rights (UK), which also happened to be in Rwanda at the time and was in the places at the times when incidents were supposed to have happened. What they saw was very different. Over the subsequent months and years, numerous human rights organizations, including a UN human rights monitoring program, have meticulously documented many abuses by the new government. Some have been substantiated; others have not. In contrast, their efforts to investigate the genocide have been rather meager. The UN Special Rapporteur, Rene Degni-Segui, gave UN human rights activities an encouraging start in June 1994, reaching a clear conclusion that genocide was being committed, but hopes were disappointed over the succeeding months. The UN's efforts to document the murder of survivors and witnesses—in fact, the renewed attempt at committing genocide by the same extremist forces—were also belated and minor, at best.

It is striking that the UN Special Rapporteur also issued a report warning of genocide in eastern Zaire in early 1996. He was speaking of the Interahamwe, in exile in Zaire, and some Zairean forces killing local Zairean Tutsis. The human rights community did not take this up. But the alleged mass killings of Hutu civilians and militia by the Rwandese Patriotic Army and Zairean rebel forces became a cause célèbre of the human rights movement.

These mass killings, if substantiated, are grave violations of international humanitarian law. Relief agencies and HROs have been vociferous in condemning these alleged violations of the Geneva Conventions. But there is a very important sense in which the relief agencies and HROs themselves brought IHL into disrepute, by both overinflating it and violating its requirements by their own actions.

This is a complex story, and a summary will have to suffice. The humanitarians' violations of IHL fall into three categories. First, the humanitarians insisted on awarding refugee status to people who were fugitives from justice, namely, the Interahamwe and the former Rwandese army that took the civilian population hostage. They also violated refugee law by not demilitarizing the "refugee" camps. UNHCR's presence in these camps was probably unlawful. Second, IHL has rigorous preconditions on humanitarian assistance if it is to be considered neutral and impartial. These include not allowing aid to be diverted or to support a war effort. These conditions were not met, yet the relief agencies who did not meet them still claimed protected status under IHL. Third, the agencies interpreted IHL—and their own elaboration of it, called "humanitarian principles"—to mean that it was not legitimate for one belligerent (the Rwandese Patriotic Army and its allied Zairean rebel forces) to attack another (the Interahamwe and former Rwandese army) simply because the former were based in a populated area receiving relief aid. This is absurd. They compounded this error by calling for an international military intervention to protect their aid programs and, by extension, not only the civilian population but the Interahamwe too. Thus, some humanitarian agencies tried to abolish the foundations of IHL—namely, the concepts of proportionality in the use of military force and the legitimacy of military objectives—and to immunize themselves from any obligations under IHL. The entire structure of IHL has been jeopardized by these actions, which turn IHL from a practicable reality into a naive and unrealizable aim.

The issue is partly one of political bias and double standards. But there is also a question of the apparent incapacity of the HROs to grapple with the enormity of genocide and the challenges it poses. Genocide cannot be dealt with simply by means of routine human rights reporting, and then, when it is over, by regarding it as a "past abuse" requiring straightforward judicial action, albeit by a special international criminal tribunal. Genocide is more than just a multiple killing. It is a crime that destroys the capacity of a society in incalculable ways. It is so profoundly demoralizing—in the sense of creating despair among survivors and a moral crisis and vacuity among killers and those complicit—that much more far-reaching measures are required. The men and women who wrote the 1948 Genocide Convention, who had seen the death camps of Nazi Germany, knew this, which is why they drafted the simplest and most ambitious of all international treaties.

This is not to excuse the new government of Rwanda for its mistakes and abuses. But it is necessary to begin to understand some of what has happened, and to appreciate that it is completely inappropriate for the UN or HROs to continue with "business as usual" in Rwanda. Still less do the HROs and relief agencies have the moral authority to dictate the actions of the survivors of the genocide and those who are trying to rebuild the country. Human rights is founded upon justice, and justice is a much more powerful and deeply rooted concept than any of the practices of the foreign HROs and relief agencies.

It is as though HROs were astronomers who have developed powerful telescopes for watching the stars. When the sun comes out, astronomers can still see the stars through their telescopes. But these astronomers have become blind to the sun: they are still following their tiny little stars.

A Human Rights Agenda for Africa

Rwanda is, thank goodness, exceptional, though not unique. There are parallels with other experiences that are recognizable, such as Cambodia under the Khmer Rouge and Europe in the 1940s. Later in the 1940s, the foundations of the modern human rights order were laid.

Probably the greatest human rights outrages of the twentieth century were those of Nazi Germany, and arguably the greatest citizens' mobilization of all time was the Allied effort during World War II. Though not a human rights movement as such, this did result in the historic watershed of the postwar human rights and humanitarian legislation of the United Nations. The 1948 Universal Declaration of Human Rights reflects not only the victorious governments' horror at what the world had just undergone, but also the popular democratic pressures on them. The Universal Declaration and the other great pieces of humanitarian law, such as the 1948 Genocide Convention, the 1949 Geneva Conventions, and the 1951 UN Refugee Convention, are both products of their times and documents of enduring, universal validity. Among other things, the Universal Declaration clearly asserts that civil and political rights are indistinguishable from social, economic, and cultural rights, while the Charter of the United Nations links respect for human rights to peace between nations.

These basic instruments speak particularly strongly to Africa, a continent emerging from genocide, total war, and economic disaster in which political extremism and continuing economic problems, such as unemployment and painfully slow reconstruction, pose a threat to democratic aspirations. For the international context in Africa today, I believe that a return to these fundamentals is very important. They can be seen as a triangle of three sets of balancing principles.

The first set is composed of realism and idealism. In the Geneva Conventions, we see realistic practicability. There is nothing in there that a humane but professional military commander would disagree with. Yet when we turn to the Genocide Convention, we have the simplest and starkest of all international treaties. It lays an absolute and non-negotiable obligation on states to prevent and punish genocide. Let us recall that the men and women who drafted these two conventions, within a year of each other, had seen both war and genocide. They saw the first as a regrettable reality, the second as absolutely unacceptable.

The principles in the second set are statehood and citizenship. The UN is an association of sovereign states. The prerequisite of being an accepted member is agreeing to be a "peace-loving" state, to which the condition of respecting the rights of one's citizens should be added. Citizenship is itself a right and carries with it associated rights. But states remain the foundation of both the international system and the system of human rights. Many of the states were, of course, new. The process of decolonization, beginning in India, was one important legacy of the war.

The third pairing is civil and political liberties, on the one side, and social and economic rights on the other. While the shattered states of Western Europe and Japan were painfully and slowly reconstructing their civil and political institutions, they were also rebuilding their economies. The United States' Marshall Plan provided much of the financing for ambitious, state-centered reconstruction programs. This is the sort of international legal, political, and economic framework that would be extremely positive in enabling the pursuit and protection of human rights in African countries.

Internally within African states, I believe that there are lessons that follow from the general analysis of this chapter. There is the importance of primary mobilization. This is up to citizens. It is also up to governments to allow it to happen and to succeed. But if primary mobilization is to be focused on social and economic rights, as historically much of it has been in Europe and the US, then there must be some capacity for citizens to decide over the basics of economic and social policy.

The rule of law is of course paramount. This goes beyond the formalities of having an independent judiciary and judges with security of tenure, though those are important. It is also a question of having a judicial system that has the confidence of the people, and is accessible to the people. This cannot be decreed. It is a long struggle—for government institutions such as the office of an Ombudsman or a Human Rights Commissioner, for lawyers and legal aid programs, and for the citizens themselves.

Lastly, for all their problems, second-generation HROs are here to stay. There is a role for private HROs in monitoring human rights abuses. National HROs can do it well in their own countries; indeed, it is their right to do so. But theirs is a heavy responsibility, too, to avoid some of the dangers to which I have alluded. Rather than springing from rooted primary organizations, HROs in Africa should develop popular constituencies. One of the means to accomplish this is to focus on social and economic rights, using civil and political liberties to press for them.

Note

1. An earlier version of this chapter was presented as a paper at the Conference on the Human Rights Commission and Office of the Ombudsman, Ethiopia, in May 1998.

Bibliography

African Rights. "Rwanda: Death, Despair and Defiance," London: African Rights, September 1994.

Best, G. *War and Law since 1945*. Oxford: Clarendon Press, 1994.

Gooneskere, S. *Children, Law and Justice: A South Asian Perspective*. New Delhi: Sage Publications, 1998.

Ignatieff, M. *The Warrior's Honor*. London: Chatto and Windus, 1998.

Moorhead, C., and Owen, U. "Time to Think Again." *Index on Censorship* (January 1996): 55.

Power, J. *Like Water on a Stone: The Story of Amnesty International*. Hamondsworth: Penguin, 2000.

Roberts, A. "Humanitarian Action in War: Aid, Protection, and Impartiality in a Policy Vacuum." London: IISS, *Adelphi Paper*, no. 305 (1996): 60–61.

Skidelsky, R. *The World After Communism: A Polemic for Our Times*. London: Macmillan, 1995.

Sutherland, B., and Meyer, M. *Guns and Gandhi in Africa: Pan African Insights on Nonviolence, Armed Struggle and Liberation in Africa*. Trenton, NJ: Africa World Press, 2000.

Waal, A. de. *Famine Crimes: Politics and the Disaster Relief Industry in Africa*. Oxford: James Currey, 1997.

Walker, M. *The Cold War*. London: Vintage, 1994.

— Chapter 9 —

MANAGING CIVPOL

The Potential of Performance Management
in International Public Services

❧

Dennis Smith

Introduction

During the past two decades, the United Nations has undergone an organizational transformation that in some ways resembles the proverbial frog
in gradually warmed water: the largely undetected change has produced
no significant reaction in the Organization or in the world of scholarship
relating to it. While research and policy debates about the UN have remained focused on global security and diplomacy, the United Nations had
become an important service-delivering agency. The extraordinary management challenge of using a global organization to deliver public goods
and services has been largely unremarked and unstudied.[1] The premise
of this chapter is that the performance of the UN in critical areas of public service can be enhanced by applying the tools of policy analysis and
public management to the study of the UN.[2]

This chapter examines a relatively new but rapidly growing area of UN
action, the use of civilian police (CIVPOL) to carry out complex missions
related to peacekeeping. The case of CIVPOL both illustrates the "mission
creep" that the UN has experienced and validates, beyond any doubt, the
central contention that managing the delivery of global services occupies
the outer limit of organizational and managerial complexity, thus posing
great challenges. It will also examine the relevance of police management
reform experience in New York to this complex area of international policing. In particular, the chapter examines the potential use of a police management reform known as COMPSTAT, which has produced significant
performance improvement in New York and elsewhere.

The Case of CIVPOL

For the past decade, the United Nations has assembled police officers from countries around the world to serve as an international force in places as diverse as Cambodia, Haiti, Kosovo, and East Timor, with a mandate that has varied in specific terms but has always aimed to restore law and order. In one of the most recent and largest deployments of United Nations organized police, in Kosovo, the operation is significantly different from previous UN civilian police missions. Whereas previously, training police and monitoring local police behavior were the dominant charges, in Kosovo the UN police force *is* the law enforcement unit—the *only* law enforcement unit.[3] Its strategic goals are two: provide temporary law enforcement, and establish and develop a professional, impartial, and independent local police, called Kosovo Police Service (KPS). The current activities of the UN police, drawn from 47 countries, include the following:

- patrolling and maintaining public order,
- investigation of crimes,
- preventing crime,
- field training of KPS,
- collection of criminal intelligence,
- border immigration control, and
- traffic control.

A recent *New York Times* article by McNeil (29 October 2000) chronicled the work of the UN police in Kosovo. His excerpts from the UN police daily record clearly show the public safety challenges facing this international law enforcement effort (see table 9.1). The level and diversity of violent crime, in a concentrated area, exceed in seriousness the threats faced by the police in many inner cities of modern Western democracies.

In one form or another, the UN has been in the police service "business" at least since its peacekeeping mission in the Congo in the early 1960s. At the end of 2000, there were almost 4,000 officers serving in Kosovo alone, 1,500 in Bosnia and Herzegovina, and 1,300 in East Timor (see table 9.2). The scope of CIVPOL responsibilities seemed to go far beyond previous assignments, but it was quickly matched, and perhaps eclipsed, by a similar broad scope for UN police in East Timor (Traub 2000).

In 1984, the International Peace Academy published a *Peacekeeper's Handbook*, which included a detailed chapter on CIVPOL. It built on the "lessons learned from civilian police involvement in UN missions in the Congo, Indonesia, and Cyprus. While the Peace Academy's review of early operations showed that there are many inherent difficulties, it foresaw the substantial expansion in the deployment of civilian police under UN auspices.[4]

TABLE 9.1 Excerpts from UN Mission in Kosovo

Excerpts from UN Mission in Kosovo (UNMIK)
Police Blotters from a 10-Day Period

Oct. 15

Mitrovica North—1800 hrs. A Turkish female reported that three K-Albanians went to her residence in the Serb area and threatened to bomb her flat because she was living with K-Serbs.

Janina Voda Village, Kosovo Polje—1945 hrs. A K-Serb male was instantly killed and another seriously injured when the tractor they were driving ran over and detonated an anti tank mine....

Oct. 16

Croklez Village, Istok—2200 hrs. The bones of a 28-year-old K-Albanian male, who was reported missing since 25/08/00, were discovered in a field approximately 300 meters away from his residence. Investigation is continuing.

Oct. 17

Gnjilane—1000 hrs. A K-Albanian male, employed by Unmik as a pump attendant, was noticed entering inflated records on several occasions, thus creating surplus fuel for stealing. Investigation is continuing.

Shurdhan Village, Vitina—1200 hrs. Four K-Albanian males reported that a K-Albanian male assaulted them by throwing two grenades at them. While Unmik police officers were investigating the case, another K-Albanian male shot at the officers and the victims with an automatic rifle without hitting or injuring someone. Two K-Albanian male suspects were arrested by Unmik police.

Oct. 18

Ramoc Village, Djakovica—1400 hrs. A K-Albanian male, who went off to cut trees in the woods, was found shot and killed in a wooded area. The family removed the body prior to reporting the incident to Unmik police.... The circumstances of the crime are under investigation.

Vucitrn—1425 hrs. A K-Albanian male reported that while driving with his family two known K-Albanian males pursued him with their vehicle. After he dropped off his family the chase continued and one of the suspects shot at him, hitting only the car. No injuries were reported. The suspects were arrested by Unmik police.

Stimlje Village, Lipljan—1900 hrs. An unknown person threw a grenade at a K-Roma house, injuring two females. Both victims were taken to hospital in Pristina with serious injuries.

Prizren—2030 hrs. A K-Albanian female reported that as she was walking on Ring Road a vehicle pulled up and an unknown male tried to drag her into the vehicle. The victim managed to escape unharmed. Investigation continuing.

TABLE 9.1 Excerpts from UN Mission in Kosovo *(cont.)*

Oct. 19

Pristina—0115 hrs. Two unknown persons attacked an employee of a local gas station by spraying a chemical in his face and then taking away a wallet containing cash. A co-worker found his colleague lying unconscious on the floor. Investigation continuing.

Pristina—0155 hrs. Five masked suspects entered the Norwegian Red Cross premises, tied up the guard and forced him to surrender his keys. They took a safe containing cash from the building. The guard received minor injuries and was treated at the hospital.

Pristina—1215 hrs. A K-Albanian male was arrested after he fired several times in the air with a pistol outside the Dardania Economic School.... No injuries were reported.

Mirace Village, Vucitrn—1700 hrs. A K-Serbian male was found under a tree in an open field. The body was transported to Pristina hospital for an autopsy to determine the cause of death. Investigation continuing.

Kosovo Polje Town—1830 hrs. A 37-year-old gypsy male was arrested when a hand grenade was discovered in his vehicle during a routine vehicle stop.

Oct. 21

Vukac Village, Glogovac—1115 hrs. A ... search operation resulted in the recovery and confiscation of two rifles, three grenades, one pistol, three AK-47 magazines, two flak jackets, one cocking lever, mortar sight, periscope, binoculars, radio charger, and 107 various types of ammunition.

Pristina—1420 hrs. A K-Albanian male was arrested after his vehicle was stopped at a checkpoint.... The suspect was found to be in possession of a 7.65-millimeter machine gun and two magazines containing 31 rounds of ammunition, one 7.62-caliber pistol with two magazines containing thirteen rounds, and one Sig-Sauer 9-millimeter pistol with one magazine containing nine rounds of ammunition. The suspect was arrested and the weapons were seized.

Radavac Village, Pec—2115 hrs. A K-Albanian male was arrested for attempting to smuggle two tons of cheese. Unmik police intercepted his truck after observing it trying to avoid a customs checkpoint. The truck and contents were seized.

Oct. 22

Dakovica Town—0130 hrs. A K-Albanian reported that an unknown person threw a hand grenade at his home damaging the door and telephone box. No injuries were reported. Investigation continuing.

Dakovica Town—0230 hrs. A K-Albanian member of the LDK party reported that an unknown person threw a hand grenade at his home. Minor damage to the windows was reported. There were no injuries to the victim. Investigation continuing.

TABLE 9.1 Excerpts from UN Mission in Kosovo *(cont.)*

Dakovica Town—0230 hrs. A local leader of the LDK party found an unexploded hand grenade in the rear garden of his home. The device was defused.... Investigation continuing.

Dakovica Town—0920 hrs. A hand grenade was located by a local resident after he reported seeing it in a street drain. The device was defused....

Vitina Town—1100 hrs. A K-Albanian male reported that he went with his brother into the forest to collect some wood. The brothers met two unidentified men armed with rifles, who fired some shots and caused them to flee the scene. There were no injuries. Investigation continuing.

Oct. 25
Vitina Town—0600 hrs. A K-Serbian home was damaged by a grenade attack and gunfire. No injuries were reported and only minor damage was done to the home.... Investigation continuing.

Urosevac Town—0745 hrs. An inhabited K-Albanian residence was the target of a grenade attack. Unmik police responded to the scene and found a male victim unharmed. The home suffered extensive damage. The suspect is a known K-Albanian male. Investigation continuing.

Pristina—1246 hrs. An anonymous Albanian-speaking male called the emergency telephone system and stated there were eight kilos of explosives in four different locations inside the Pristina sports stadium.... No explosives were found. Investigation continuing.

Source: McNeil (2000).

TABLE 9.2 Police Officers Representing the United Nations

Police officers representing the United Nations are serving in countries in conflict:

The International Police Task Force in:	*Number of Officers*
Bosnia and Herzegovina (UNMIBH)	1,572
Kosovo (UNMIK)	3,954
East Timor (UNTAET)	1,303
Cyprus (UNCYP)	31
Sierra Leone (UNMASIL)	34
Recent missions:	
Eastern Slavonia	450
Haiti	300
Angola	300
Macedonia	25

Source: Office of the Police Advisor, CIVPOL, http://www.un.org/Depts/dpko/dpko/home_bottom.htm, July 2000.

It is probably necessary to state explicitly that the international policing referred to here is not the role referred to in the question "Is the UN the world's policeman?" In every reference in the literature to "world police-men," the issue is who will make nations law abiding in their conduct toward each other. Our focus is on the official[5] institutions that maintain law and order within states and, more specifically, on the use of interna-tional organizations to support, guide, monitor, temporarily replace, and create the local provision of police services by states in trouble. UN in-volvement in the organization and provision of the local public safety of Member States is a vivid illustration of the extent to which it is now en-gaged in delivering public service.

CIVPOL is a separate unit in UN Peacekeeping. When deployed, it is under the command of a Police Commissioner who reports to the Special Representative of the Secretary-General (SRSG). It is expected to coordi-nate its efforts with all other UN units in the field and with humanitarian non-governmental organizations (NGOs). Depending on the nature of the overall UN mission, CIVPOL works especially closely with the military and human rights components. Its function varies with the mission, but recurring roles include monitoring the local police and protecting human rights. It is often involved in the training of local police and, when elec-tions are involved, in helping to protect the security of the electorate and the integrity of the electoral process. In general, until Kosovo, CIVPOL did not directly enforce the law and did not have powers of arrest;[6] instead, it was expected by its presence, training, and encouragement of the local force—who *do* have those responsibilities and powers—to influ-ence their use in constructive ways. Since the Cyprus mission in the 1960s, CIVPOL forces have been noted for using their contact with the local pop-ulation to play an informal role in ameliorating communal conflict.

As part of a general effort to learn formally from experience, the United Nations Peacekeeping's Lessons Learned Unit has addressed the experience of CIVPOL in its reports on a number of UN missions. In 1995, the UN also conducted a seminar in Singapore on civilian police that brought together officials who had participated in a number of missions. In his address to the seminar, Brigadier-General Ghani, the Deputy Mili-tary Adviser who as Chief of Planning for the UN Department of Peace-keeping Operations (DPKO) supervised the Civilian Police Adviser, noted the context in which the rise of CIVPOL has occurred (Ghani 1995).

We know now that with the end of the Cold War a tremendous level of insta-bility was generated in the world, and with superpowers no longer playing their traditional role in the resolution of these conflicts the task of resolving these issues has fallen to the United Nations. The nature of the conflicts had changed too, with many of them being intrastate rather than interstate, and the UN missions have had to adapt. Of the five operations active in early 1988, four were related to interstate wars with only one to intrastate conflict. Of the 21 operations since 1988 [in 1995], only eight have related to interstate conflict, whereas 14 have related to intrastate conflicts. Of the 11 operations started since 1992, all but two relate to intrastate conflicts. Thus last year [1994], the UN found itself with over 73,000 troops deployed in more than 20 operations. This included more than 2000 Civilian Policemen. I must add that at the height of the Cambodia operation this was even greater. There are still more than 1700 civilian police deployed.[7]

While the basic patterns observed by Brigadier-General Ghani have not changed since his comments in 1995, with Bosnia, Kosovo, and East Timor, the number of CIVPOL deployed has risen to 8,500.[8]

The dual points that are crucial to understanding CIVPOL are highlighted by the General's observations: "[I]nternational civilian police are being deployed in growing numbers in intrastate conflicts in states that are somewhere between unstable and complete chaos." Learning from the experience of the UN, it seems advisable to ask, in this early stage of its development, what can reasonably be expected from CIVPOL.[9]

The Police Function and Complex Organizations

Early studies of organizations assumed that there are principles of organization that are universally valid. Modern organization theory has been largely devoted to elaborating themes first articulated in the 1960s that argued that the relationship between organizational design and performance is contingent on the organization's domain (what it does, for whom, and how it does it) and its task environment (the simplicity or complexity, including the stability or dynamism, of the suppliers, consumers, regulators, and competitors that matter to the organization, given its domain).[10]

The bottom line of this approach to understanding organizations is that organizations doing routine tasks using reliable technologies in simple and stable environments are less complex and easier to design and manage than organizations doing non-routine work without a reliable technology in a multidimensional and dynamic environment. Studies of urban police organizations, not surprisingly, have come to the conclusion that policing services—notwithstanding their symbolic use of paramilitary bureaucratic trappings—are at the far end of the complex-simple organization continuum. Police departments in urban areas of developed nations[11] deploy staff around the clock, seven days a week, to spatially dispersed locations (thus difficult to supervise) and confront unpredictable, often conflicted, and sporadically violent situations with tools far less developed in terms of their proven effectiveness than those used by many other professionals, and with staff whose education and training is typically far less extensive than that of other professions. Police work is at the intersection of a number of multifaceted service systems (health, mental health, and other social services), not just the criminal justice system, which is quite complex in its own right. Also, it matters whether the political system in which policing is done is democratic or not (Bayley 1994).

What do these observations imply for the likely challenges facing the management of CIVPOL? The most systematic way to address that question is to place this management problem in the context of a conceptual model of policy implementation.

CIVPOL and the Implementation Process

To attempt to assess prospectively the international provision of police services in nations in conflict, we propose to use a general model developed to illuminate the process of public policy implementation. The model identifies major factors that affect the likelihood of successful policy implementation.[12] The Van Meter and Van Horn model of the policy implementation process treats implementation as a major problematic. Successful implementation (in this case, high CIVPOL performance) cannot be assumed; it depends on, in particular, the six clusters of variables arrayed in figure 9.1.

If we view a CIVPOL mandate as a public policy and apply this model to examine implementation prospects for CIVPOL, the problems are obvious.

1. *Standards and objectives.* Policies vary in their clarity, the scope of values affected, and the scale of change they intend to bring about. Policies that attempt small, clearly articulated, incremental, and non-controversial change are, other things being equal, much more likely to be implemented than changes that are large, vague, comprehensive, and hotly contested.

In an early review of CIVPOL, Chappell and Evans (1997: 75) wrote:

[A]ny UNCIVPOL component in a peacekeeping operation must be viewed within the context of the politics [that] give rise to that operation. Although clearly defined mandates are highly desirable, the realities of the political situation may produce unanticipated confusion and operational dilemmas. To minimize these dilemmas UNCIVPOL representatives should be involved from the outset in any political negotiations about a proposed peacekeeping mandate in order to advise on what is possible and feasible. It should be noted that no representatives of UNCIVPOL were involved in this way in ONUC, UNFICYP, or UNTAC.[13]

Chappell and Evans's review focuses on CIVPOL in the Congo, Cyprus, and Cambodia, as well as the United Nations Protection Force (UNPROFOR) in Bosnia. The authors continue: "Clear guidelines are required from those establishing any UNCIVPOL component regarding how such a component will operate. Despite nearly four decades of experience with CIVPOL, no such guideline exists" (Chappell and Evans 1997: 76).[14] The police mandate in general is complex ("dilemmas" is the frequently used

FIGURE 9.1 Implementation Model

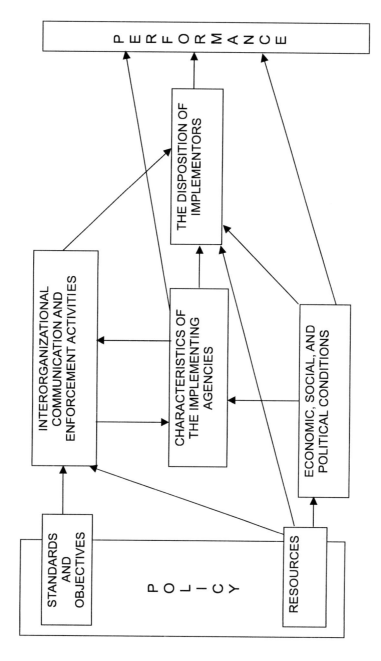

Source: Van Meter and Van Horn (1975: 463).

term), for example, combining service with enforcement and being a servant to those whom you have the authority to control. In the context of CIVPOL assignments, international police observers are expected simultaneously to monitor and report local police misconduct, and to persuade those same police officials to follow their lead in providing police services to the community. On another level, CIVPOL must convince a skeptical community that it is effectively monitoring the local police adherence to human rights, where there is often a history of police abusing human rights, while at the same time being seen as routinely helping the police control the population. In another example of mandate confusion that CIVPOL faced in Cambodia, its mandate included being police observers in a place where the previously operating police had abandoned the field, and there was no local policing to observe.[15]

2. *Resources.* While the term "resources" immediately conjures the variable "funding," it may also include such factors as reliable technology, trained personnel needed for achieving desired policy outputs, and legitimacy of the auspices of the policy. Well-funded efforts that are authorized by respected institutions and that can depend on a proven technology operated by appropriately trained staff have enhanced implementation prospects.

Human resources are the most important resource for any police organization. CIVPOL gets its personnel from Member States, which agree to provide them at the request of the Secretary-General. In contrast to the Congo mission—in which first a single contingent of police from Ghana and subsequently another from Nigeria patrolled the streets of Kinshasa (then Leopoldville)—it is now common for police officers from 20, 30, or even 40 nations to be part of a CIVPOL mission. Obviously, given the diversity of police systems around the world, these officers will not all follow the same standards. However, the UN has learned that it has to set standards. Nevertheless, as Chappell notes: "[T]he UN set guidelines for the selection of personnel for these missions which were clearly being ignored by many member states." In UNPROFOR, the standards require police monitors who have at least five years of "regular police service" experience, who can speak and write English fluently, and who are experienced, licensed drivers.

A UNPROFOR Station Commander, in reporting to Chappell the wide disparity between the standards and the reality, offered his assessment so that "a better appreciation will be gained of the unique challenges associated with delivering a multi-national police monitoring service." While he based his assessment on the 14 officers in his unit, he asserted that his experience could be generalized throughout the mission area. Most disturbing is his contention that only four of the 14 met the requirement of having had five years of "regular police service."[16]

Given the widely covered failure of some nations, especially the United States, to pay fully their UN assessment and the attendant financial strain on the Organization, it will come as no surprise that another challenge to successful CIVPOL implementation is scarce finances. While some of the problems could be attributed to excessive bureaucratic process ("blue tape"), there is every reason to believe that the combination of expanded demand for UN action and budgetary retrenchment are taking a toll on the functioning of support services. While most "lessons learned" reports include some evidence of equipment failures and shortages, few official accounts capture the point as well as that of a police manager in Haiti, who made this statement to Chappell and Evans (1997: 72):

> We're to the point where our people are actually not given the proper supplies that we need to get the mission done. Communications are very inadequate, and it goes on and on. If you want CIVPOL to do a good job then you should reflect it in the type of equipment that you give them. If you give them sub-standard equipment ... well, we're pretty low on the totem pole here. And so basically if I were going to say something to the UN I would say simply this, "If you want CIVPOL and you want quality CIVPOL, you'd better give them the attention that they really need to get the job done." And it goes beyond just transportation and communications. It includes other types of equipment that they need to get the job done, like computers, and clothing, a proper hat and headgear, and things like that. They really feel that they are playing second, third, fourth fiddle to not only the military but to the [civilian UN] people. There is a lot of frustration....

Another resource is proven technology. In general, policing lacks a proven technology for accomplishing some of its most important functions.[17] In the case of CIVPOL, there are major debates on basic issues of production strategy, such as whether police observers should be armed, and whether it is better to deploy police in national units (to achieve coherence) or international units (to achieve "global representation"). The *Peacekeeper's Handbook* describes one of the tasks of CIVPOL as "a matter of winning the hearts and minds" of people in the community. But one wonders which tools available to the international police monitors in a rural Haitian village would enable them to compete with the local practitioners of voodoo for the hearts and minds of the villagers.[18]

3. *Interorganizational communication and enforcement context.* Few policies are so simple as to be the exclusive province of a single organization or answerable to one authority. This variable refers to the number of organizations that must work together to produce the intended product and raises the question as to how many are in a position to direct or assess authoritatively the work being done. The more complex the communication and enforcement, the greater the obstacles to coordinated effort and the more uncertain the outcome of implementation efforts.

It is a commonplace to describe emerging patterns of UN peacekeeping operations as "multidimensional," "multiprofessional," or "multidisciplinary." It has always been multilateral. The multiplicity of actors participating in decision making and action has consequences for policy implementation.[19] CIVPOL must be coordinated with military, political, humanitarian, development, and human rights agencies, and with multiple specialized units of the UN Secretariat. It must also be responsive to the Permanent Representatives of all countries participating in a mission. CIVPOL's mission to monitor and assist local police forces sometimes involves more than one local force (sometimes, as in Cyprus, antagonistic local police forces) and other governmental agencies as well. An international police monitoring organization concerned about both building local law enforcement capacity and protecting human rights cannot escape dealing with other organizations comprising the criminal justice system. For example, in Cambodia CIVPOL had to create a special UN prosecutor's office; in Haiti judges and jails were either non-functioning or were themselves major separate threats to basic human rights; and in Bosnia and Herzegovina observing and inspecting judicial organizations is an explicit function of the International Police Task Force.

For all of these reasons, one can safely place CIVPOL on the complex far end of the scale of interorganizational communication and enforcement complexity.

4. *Political and economic conditions.* Is policy direction stable, or chaotic, or something in between? Is there feast or famine? Stability and munificence in the environment increase the likelihood of successful implementation.

The import of this variable for CIVPOL implementation is almost too obvious to require elaboration. Nations with stable political and economic conditions do not require UN peacekeeping operations. The only point worth stating is the extremity of this limiting condition. Writing about UNPROFOR conditions, Chappell states: "While by no means all members of the CIVPOL contingent attached to UNPROFOR were located directly in an immediate war zone, the effects of the conflict were manifest throughout the mission area with large flows of refugees and massive requirements for humanitarian aid and assistance. In sectors where armed conflict continued, the unarmed and largely unprotected CIVPOL members were confronted with the same dangers and privations, [that] affected the lives of so many civilians caught up in the war" (Chappell 1996). He goes on to assert:

> It remains a debatable question whether in conditions like these it makes sense at all to deploy unarmed civilian police. Quite apart from the personal risks involved to their general safety and well-being, their ability to perform the types of monitoring and allied tasks assigned by the UNPROFOR mandate was clearly compromised by the continued fighting. As is well known, the much larger and armed military contingents attached to UNPROFOR were largely powerless and ineffective in their efforts to alleviate the conflicts in former Yugoslavia. Only when the conflict ended with the Peace Accords brokered at Dayton in late 1995 were the conditions appropriate, in the view of those critical of earlier CIVPOL deployment, for the injection of a civilian police presence. (Chappell 1996)

Of course, no threat to policy implementation could be greater than the decision not to try—the decision that conditions are so inimical that the effort should be withdrawn.

5. *Characteristics of implementing agency.* Is the structure of the primary organization responsible for implementing the policy appropriate to the specific policy-assigned task? Does it have the requisite managerial capacity? Is the policy that it is to implement consistent with its traditional role? Is the task a priority of the organizations? To the extent that the answer to these questions is yes, the prospects for successful implementation increase.

The implementing agency—a specific CIVPOL mission—is a classic ad hoc, or temporary, organization. Even the "main office" of CIVPOL in New York, which was created in 1993 with the appointment of a Civilian Police Adviser, is only marginally more stable than an "adhocracy": in 1998, according to UN term limits and given the staff in place, following the rule would have resulted in a total changeover in leadership.

Until recently, all (four) senior staff members in the main office were on loan from member governments. The posts are formally limited to two-year assignments.[20] The leaders of CIVPOL field missions, the UN Police Commissioners, are police officials selected from Member States typically for two-year terms. Their terms may or may not be coordinated with the terms of other senior staff. The Commissioner of the very large and complex CIVPOL mission in Cambodia met his senior staff for the first time at the last stopover on his flight en route to Phnom Penh.

The staff of CIVPOL is assembled, often over a period of months and behind schedule, specifically for a mission; staff members are "contributions"[21] from UN Member States. They remain employees of the contributing states, typically holding rank[22] based on their home police agency, and are paid by them. A CIVPOL mission may have officers from 30 or more states; for example, the International Police Task Force (IPTF) in Bosnia now includes representatives of 34 nations, while Kosovo has more than 40. As noted before, they are supposed to (but not infrequently fail to) meet certain minimum requirements, and they receive very brief basic training on the UN, CIVPOL, and the specific mission at the start. With rare exceptions, until recently UN civilian police monitors were not armed, and were not deployed with others from their country but rather in multinational units, which typically have not had police powers of arrest. While one of the requirements is fluency in English, it is not unusual for officers to need interpreters—not just for the local language, but also for English. Most CIVPOL missions are divided into regions or districts and stations, and are housed in borrowed or rented space. A shortage of vehicles and communication equipment is commonly reported in CIVPOL missions.

Given the mode of recruitment of CIVPOL staff, to the extent that a mission requires specialized police skills beyond "regular police experience" or even "community policing," acquiring personnel with those skills is a function of luck and the scale of the mission. If a mission is large enough, the chances of the needed skills being included in the pool increases. Limited personnel records and retrieval capacity makes it harder for CIVPOL managers to make full use of this potential.

The CIVPOL missions are not and cannot be the locus of CIVPOL police officers' careers, so many elements of organizational control and customary organizational incentive structures are missing. Sanctions available for police commanders to use in cases of officer misconduct, which have on occasion been needed, are limited; sending the offending officer home is the most common outcome.

The officers assembled in a CIVPOL mission come from diverse countries and have had diverse jobs in diverse police organizations. In addition, they are personally diverse in terms of religion, culture, and primary language. They did not necessarily know, prior to the mission, the other officers from their own country, and it is virtually certain that they did not previously know any of the officers from the other countries. Finally, they all know that this is a temporary assignment.[23]

What is the glue that holds this organization together? The answer that they are all police professionals is probably the best available, but it does not offer a lot of reassurance because, as already noted, police service around the world manifests considerable diversity. In any case, the unity of purpose of members of the same police department anywhere in the world is by no means guaranteed in a CIVPOL mission.

If the CIVPOL organization just described were given a simple assignment, with plenty of resources and no interference from outside political forces or other organizations, making it a highly productive unit would still be a management challenge. The problem is the uncertain disposition toward the job of the individual officers, that is, the implementers.

6. *Disposition of implementers.* In the final analysis, the implementation of policies or programs depends on individual action. All of the preceding variables ultimately matter only to the extent that they register on and influence decisions and actions of individual actors who must participate in implementing the policy. Organizational control systems, cultures, incentive structures, socialization, and training all are intended to dispose workers to carry out particular policies, but their success is variable.

In addition to the multiple aspects of diversity in the organization just described, the participants in a CIVPOL mission have many different reasons for being there. All are supposed to be "volunteers," but some participants come from countries where volunteerism is underdeveloped in the extreme; in effect, they are ordered to serve in CIVPOL. Among those who volunteer, the reasons can range from the pursuit of professional service or development norms to adventure seeking by would-be soldiers of fortune. Some seek a career opportunity in leaving their home country, and some will in fact gain financially from the per diem allowance, if they come from a country whose police pay is at the bottom of the scale. In earlier missions, some may have felt that being a police observer meant not having to work very hard, which has been the case when some missions have been stalled, sidetracked, or poorly managed.

Given a choice, any manager of a complex organization trying to assemble a staff to do high-quality professional work would want to recruit a sizable pool of candidates for the available jobs, then carefully screen, check references, and interview the candidates to select only those both qualified and motivated to do the best work. With CIVPOL, these rudimentary tasks are not carried out.

7. Performance. Successful implementation means that an assigned job gets done as intended. Yet it does not necessarily have the impact that it is expected to. While results different from intended effects may occur because the premises on which the policy is based are flawed, even the best policies do not exist in a vacuum. Other, sometimes powerful factors come into play. Consequently, even if the operation is a success (implementation), the patient may die (impact).

In sum, this exploration of a model of the factors affecting the policy implementation process shows the improbability of a high degree of implementation success of CIVPOL missions. In fact, the remarkable part of the CIVPOL record to date is the amount that has in fact been accomplished. Part of the explanation is that the UN has been fortunate to recruit as CIVPOL Commissioners some very knowledgeable, dedicated, and charismatic police managers.[24] Second, because the job to be done is so huge, and in some cases the CIVPOL contingent sufficiently large, even if only some of the officers are constructive and productive, and even if only some of the needed work gets done, it is a valuable and important contribution. Of course, this is another way of saying that, under the circumstances, the performance standards are rather low and that, under the circumstances, performance measurement is very difficult to achieve.

This point opens up an important alternative line of implementation analysis. The Van Meter and Van Horn model used here is arguably a top-down conception of the process. Other bottom-up approaches, such as Lipsky's "street-level bureaucracy" model, could provide insights into how CIVPOL, through adaptive behavior of police officers on the ground, actually solves some of the problems identified above. Unfortunately, the bottom-up model requires detailed data about actual CIVPOL practice and performance that have not so far been collected.

Until recently, the now growing literature on CIVPOL, such as traditional public administration texts, hardly mentioned outcome measurement, focused almost exclusively on such inputs as staffing and structure, and paid little systematic attention to CIVPOL behavior and outputs. The exception to that pattern, at least in terms of interest, is the May 2001 Report of the Office of Internal Oversight Services (OIOS), which cites the "absence of clearly defined milestones and performance indicators" as an important deficiency.

Reinventing CIVPOL?

With respect to performance measurement, the field of public administration has been substantially reinvented in the past 20 years. As just stated, traditional texts in the field focused on organizational designs and processes and hardly mentioned performance measurement or program evaluation. If mentioned at all, the discussion usually explained the enormous obstacles to measuring public goods and services. When governments began to measure public services production, they tended to dwell on counts of inputs (expenditures, personnel) or activities (miles patrolled, responses to calls) or, to some extent, outputs (arrests made, summonses issued), but almost never on the desired outcomes of public services (crime reduction or safety improvement). In the mid-1970s, in the wake of a fiscal crisis that revealed that New York City had been essentially "flying blind" in terms of tracking money spent and services delivered, the New York City government introduced a system of performance targeting and measuring called the Mayor's Management Planning and Reporting System (MMPRS). A study of the MMPRS at the end of the 1980s found that in the voluminous agency statistics reported to the public twice a year there were almost no measures of outcomes or "results" (Smith 1993).

At the heart of the "reinventing government" movement that flourished in the past decade is the idea of "managing for results." In New York City, the agency that pioneered "managing for results" was the police department. The NYPD's development of the COMPSTAT (computer statistics) system of police management in New York City focused not only on outcome measurement, but also, more importantly, on managing for improved outcomes. Since the introduction of COMPSTAT by Police Commissioner William Bratton in 1994, crime (defined as "outcomes of policing") has gone down—in some cases, including homicide—to 1960s levels.

From 1993 to fiscal 1999, major declines were reported in all categories of crime in New York City and in all precincts. New York City outperformed the nation in all categories, often by a wide margin, and was an early and leading contributor to the crime reductions reported nationally. New York City's relative crime rate ranking among the nearly 200 US cities with populations of 100,000 or more has improved from 88th place to 165th since COMPSTAT was introduced. More specifically, from 1993 to 1999 in New York City:

- Murder declined 67 percent (in the United States as a whole, only 29 percent).
- Grand larceny motor vehicle was down 61 percent (19 percent).
- Burglary was down 53 percent (18 percent).
- Robbery declined 54 percent (30 percent).

- Grand larceny decreased 37 percent (6 percent).
- Felony assaults dropped 30 percent (14 percent).
- Forcible rape declined 27 percent (13 percent).

COMPSTAT departed from both the traditional model of a highly centralized, reactive bureaucracy and from the new model of community policing. Commissioner Bratton's model differs in philosophy, structure, and management process from its predecessors. COMPSTAT is based on a complex set of interrelated assumptions about cause and effect in the production of public safety. Figure 9.2 presents the conceptual logic of COMPSTAT.

To oversimplify, the philosophical change involved the belief that police action can affect crime and levels of public safety. The structural change involved empowering precinct commanders and equipping them technologically to track problems and patterns of performance. The key management innovation was the introduction of a performance review process that provided much greater opportunities for learning on the part of managers, and also much more accountability for performance. Many observers of COMPSTAT have emphasized the implementation of modern technology—for example, computers in every precinct with programs to provide geographic information system maps—as a contributing factor. The most important transformation, however, has been the development of systematic thinking about performance by management. The designers of COMPSTAT claim that its strength lies in four basic principles:

1. Accurate and timely intelligence
2. Effective tactics
3. Rapid deployment of personnel resources
4. Relentless follow-up and assessment

While all of these factors are facilitated by the availability of extensive empirical data and computer-aided statistical analysis, their power comes more from the way they structure thinking about the work to be done. New York City's 20-year history of collecting and reporting voluminous numbers, agency by agency, for the Mayor's Management Report, without a focus on performance management, shows that numbers and statistical analysis are secondary to having a clear vision of performance, having a management strategy that identifies clearly to all which numbers are important (because they inform managers about performance), focusing on obtaining quickly and distributing strategically the numbers that matter, and helping managers to perform, while holding them accountable for performance.

The detailed tracking process casts a much wider net to include more than just index crimes. It includes indicators believed to be warning markers, such as shooting incidents, shooting victims, and gun arrests, all displayed in geographically pinpointed detail.

FIGURE 9.2 Conceptual Model of COMPSTAT

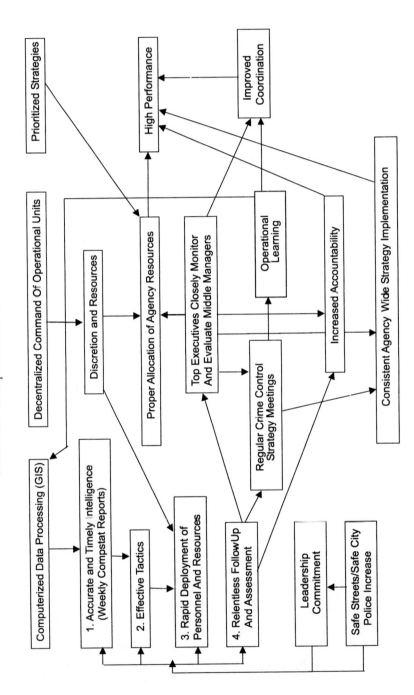

Several other New York City agencies have adapted COMPSTAT principles to their own performance agendas with dramatic positive results. The Corrections Department cut prison violence by more than 60 percent, and the Parks Department doubled the number of park facilities rated clean and safe (from 40 to 80 percent). The question remains as to whether the lessons learned in police management reform in New York City can be applied to the complex challenges facing CIVPOL.

In the COMPSTAT model, "accurate and timely intelligence" includes the idea of ascertaining the public safety concerns of the public and responding to those concerns, even if they do not involve "serious crimes." Successful policing, whether in Brooklyn, New York, or Pristina, Kosovo, depends on citizen participation and public support. To gain those, the police have to be viewed as public servants, not just public authorities.

Clearly, the settings in which CIVPOL is called upon to function vary widely. Bosnia had been part of a relatively modern industrial state with an educated populace, whereas East Timor was much less economically developed even before the devastating destruction wrought by the conflict there. Nevertheless, in both of these settings the basic ideas of COMPSTAT, if applied to CIVPOL operations, by placing a focus on outcomes and on the role and process of management in producing intended outcomes, would introduce a level of rigor and coherence that would both serve the immediate mission and lay the foundation for learning from experience. Under traditional modes of operation, the UN "lessons learned" reports produced after missions do not show the relationship between the inputs, activities, and outputs of the police, nor their mission accomplishments (or lack thereof), because they are not outcomes oriented.

For those cynics who reply that CIVPOL does not focus on, measure, or use outcomes to manage because little accomplishment can be expected from police, COMPSTAT's answer is perhaps the biggest departure from traditional thinking about policing. Commissioner Bratton addressed that point in 1995 in a seminar entitled "Measuring What Matters," which was organized by the National Institute of Justice:

I have been asked to write on the question: Should we expect police activities to impact on measures of crime, disorder and fear and how will we know? I'd like to begin by turning the question around: If we don't expect police activities and police departments to have an impact on crime, disorder, and fear, they almost certainly won't. By accepting the prevailing image of police departments as slow moving and relatively ineffectual bureaucracies and by assuming that nothing can be done to change them, we are, in effect, making a self-fulfilling prophecy. No organization, whether it's a police department or private business, is going to achieve high performance results in an atmosphere of such low expectations.

I am a police manager not a criminologist. I tend to think about crime not as a sociological problem but as a management problem. The scholarship about the underlying causes of crime is very interesting, but it is of limited utility to someone charged, as I am, with public safety in a large city. The fact that many criminologists have argued that police don't have much impact on crime just adds to my management problem. My job is to direct police resources and to motivate 38,000 police personnel. I literally cannot afford to subscribe to a system of belief that tells me that the police can't accomplish our primary mission of controlling and preventing crime. (Bratton and Knobler 1998)

Conclusions and Recommendations

It is impossible to read the descriptions of the field conditions from Cambodia to Bosnia and from Haiti to Angola and have any doubt that if the UN had not created CIVPOL, it would now have to invent it. Unlike the marketplace, in which inventions tend to precede the creation of enterprises to produce them—and sellers may decide that a locality is inhospitable to business and withdraw or not enter—public sector organizations tend to go where the problems are. The decision is often to make public investments in areas of public problems even if nobody has invented a solution. The collapse of law and order in human communities around the world is just such a case. The UN is to be applauded for responding to the crises around the world and especially for its recent attempts to identify the "lessons learned" from the places in the world where CIVPOL has been deployed. But a lesson is demonstrably "learned" when it alters behavior or at least produces clear evidence that alternatives are being explored.

In the case of CIVPOL, evidence of progress can be seen in the development of new training curricula and materials for CIVPOL, and, equally importantly, a plan for ensuring that those sent into a mission receive the necessary training. As the Police Adviser's office learned from its discovery that material about recruitment and training that they distributed in New York to Permanent Representatives was not reaching the field where it was suppose to be used, plans for training are now more firmly grounded. Similarly, the dispatch of Selection Assistance Units to countries scheduled to send sizable contingents to a mission—so that testing and verification of minimum qualifications can be done before the UN goes to the expense and copes with the delay of sending unqualified personnel back home—is a clear example of learning from experience. Both these developments originated in the Police Adviser's Office of DPKO, an innovation in UN structure which, though small, should be seen as an example of institutional learning rather than bureaucratic expansion. Without excusing bureaucratic excesses, it is important to remember that when recurring problems require institutional memory and tested procedures, bureaucracy as a form of organization can be an efficient response.

Another sign of progress is that a number of scholars have begun to examine the experience of countries whose police officers have been deployed in CIVPOL operations. Analysts have begun to look for "lessons learned" from the perspective of participating countries and to make recommendations for improvements at the country level.[25] [26]

The reform agenda around CIVPOL must be far more ambitious. While there may not be agreement on answers, the questions need to be confronted and placed high on the agenda of UN reform. The first question to address is whether the mission given to CIVPOL can be effectively carried out by an ad hoc organization. Without remotely suggesting a standing UN police force, it no longer makes sense to wonder if another CIVPOL mission will arise. The only question is when—and will the UN be more ready than it has been in the past. Here is one scenario. Following roughly the model of military reserve organizations in the US, Israel, and elsewhere, the UN should carefully assess the feasibility of creating an international police reserve force, in which police officers from the nations of the world serve for three or four years, during which time they participate in language and skills training, more than likely organized by region, and under some circumstances, doing non-traditional CIVPOL work, such as disaster relief, in order to develop an organizational structure and esprit, and to develop a record that can be used in classifying strengths and weaknesses before being placed in the crucible of a CIVPOL mission. If done properly, the service in the CIVPOL Reserve Force should provide tangible benefits to the police forces that contribute personnel. Reservists would be expected to do one CIVPOL mission (one year) or complete the multiyear reserve period, whichever came first. Obviously, this proposal should be subjected to a cost/benefit analysis, but we should not ignore that there are significant costs and losses of potential benefits associated with the current ad hoc organizing and staffing of CIVPOL.

In the same vein, there should be a CIVPOL Command Academy somewhere in the world where candidates to be CIVPOL Commissioners or mission senior staff would participate in training that would include debriefing the experience of CIVPOL commissioners. This pool of potential senior commanders could use their time together to address key recurring questions of CIVPOL management, such as issues of logistics and supply, and the problems of divergent national rank structure. This senior police command group would constitute an advisory body to the Office of Police Adviser, and would have the experience to confront the UN as an organization before police are in the field in crisis situations. The scale, length of program, location (rotating, most likely), and other details of this proposed Command Academy are not spelled out here, but the details could easily be provided by veterans of earlier missions reflecting on what would have helped them.

There are major policy issues that should be addressed directly by the UN rather than allowed to drag on as they have in the growing "lessons learned" literature. Whether the CIVPOL forces should be grouped by nationality or totally dispersed is a difficult question with strong proponents on either side, just as is the case with the question of whether or when (if ever) CIVPOL officers should be armed. These policy questions cannot be resolved without debate, and the debates should be informed by the rigorous examination of evidence of performance, commissioned by the UN.

Even if CIVPOL could develop a more stable organizational base, and could recruit and train more qualified personnel, led by better prepared commanders, there would still be a question about what can reasonably be expected from a CIVPOL mission. In order for CIVPOL to perform well on a particular mission—and to improve its performance over time—I believe it needs to adapt the approach of performance management that was pioneered in policing in New York City. This approach may have a direct positive impact on CIVPOL performance, but its greatest promise—and the strongest argument for its introduction—is the contribution of a performance management approach to organizational learning. Making the logic of policing strategies explicit and measuring the component parts of the model, especially outcomes, would dramatically increase the opportunities to learn about the implementation of policies that can enhance CIVPOL in the long run. Since the likelihood is great that CIVPOL will be needed often in the future, learning about and improving its capacity and performance level should be high on the list of priorities.

The growth of CIVPOL as an institutionalized and integral part of UN peacekeeping operations over the past decade illustrates the movement within that international organization from a focus on just intergovernmental affairs to intragovernmental issues, such as the delivery of everyday, local police services in states with admittedly extreme problems. Using a model developed for analyzing the domestic US policy implementation process, this chapter has examined the growing literature on CIVPOL missions to discover the challenges facing international public management. Given the factors arrayed against CIVPOL operations, the absence of documented dramatic failures is remarkable. The recommendations in this chapter hold promise for a better functioning of CIVPOL in the future.

Notes

1. By way of contrast, during that period, business schools all over the world were in the process of retooling and restyling themselves to prepare professionals to manage in the "global marketplace."

2. In a working paper, "Delivering Global Services: A Public Management Perspective on Reform at the United Nations," which we wrote for the NYU symposium "Managing Global Services" in 1986, John Mathiason and I reported findings from a detailed empirical examination of the work done by the United Nations that documented the

shift in the "domain of the organization"—what it does, for whom and how it does it. See also Mathiason and Smith (1987).

3. See "The Criminal Crucible that is Kosovo" (*The Economist*, 17 February 2001: 36): "With his blackthorn stick, formal bearing and tough talk of 'zero tolerance,' Christopher Albiston is a policeman's policeman. But the UN's new chief in Kosovo, a 48-year-old veteran of the Royal Ulster Constabulary, may soon feel the problems of Northern Ireland are simple compared to the devil's brew he has now taken on."

4. In 1995, the United Nations Department of Peacekeeping Operations first published the *United Nations Civilian Police Handbook*, an illustrated, pocket-sized manual that includes basic descriptions of UN agency structure, terminology, procedures, and forms. This highly practical document includes as appendices an English/French picture dictionary, including illustration of automobile parts, office stationary, and military weapons, as well as the United Nations standards for peacekeeping police, prepared by the Crime Prevention and Criminal Justice Branch of the UN Office in Geneva, that covers laws of arrest, the use of force, human rights, the treatment of victims, prisoners, torture and cruel treatment, illegal executions, and genocide, among other topics.

5. It is necessary to distinguish "official" public safety producers from others because of the growing recognition that much public safety is produced by non-state, non-official actors and institutions. See Baillargeon and Smith (1980) and Shearing (1992).

6. By now the number of CIVPOL missions is large enough and the diversity of situations in the field they have faced great enough that almost no generalization can be absolute. On at least one other mission (Cambodia), "when it had to," CIVPOL officers have made arrests and in some cases have felt that they have had to enforce the law rather than merely observe its enforcement.

7. Ghani went on to predict correctly that in the former Yugoslavia "there will be greater requirement for civilian police. In fact, there will be exponential growth in this area because of the devastation associated with internal civil strife and the implications that it has for governmental control and the failure of judicial structures" (Ghani 1995).

8. Report of the Office of Internal Oversight Services on the Management Audit of United Nations Civilian Police Operations, May 2001.

9. Stabilizing expectations is an important part of the effective management of organizations. In *United Nations, Divided World* (1988), Evan Luard summed up the contemporary assessment of the UN this way: "The role currently fulfilled by the UN, therefore, falls far short of what was hoped in 1945.... It can plausibly be argued that the type of system that is set out in the Charter could never have come about, whatever the character of the member states, since it bore no relationship to the reality of international relations and state power. Was it ever reasonable to believe, for example, that the permanent members, which themselves wielded dominant power, would be able to agree both on the creation of a collectively controlled international force which could decisively influence events, and on the way such a force should be authorized and controlled? Was it realistic to believe that Member States would always be willing submissively to obey, as they undertook to do, the 'decisions' of a small and not very representative body calling on them to send their forces to the far side of the world to meet some crisis which might appear of no immediate importance to them? Would states which disagree so fundamentally on so many vital political issues really be able to form a common view on the many acute political conflicts of the age and work together to maintain the peace?" In summary, were altogether excessive expectations focused on an institution that had been founded in the first place on overly optimistic premises?

10. Scott (1987). For an early exposition, see Thompson (1967).

11. The literature on policing in the US is by far the most extensive, but studies in other industrialized countries present similar conclusions. See Bayley (1994).

12. Van Meter and Van Horn (1975); also, see an application in Van Horn and Baumer (1985).

13. ONUC (United Nations Observer Force in the Congo), UNFICYP (United Nations Peacekeeping Force in Cyprus), and UNTAC (United Nations Transitional Authority in Cambodia).

14. The need for this clear mandate was foreshadowed in the *Peacekeeper's Handbook* (International Peace Academy 1984) and recognized by the UN: "There must be clearly defined common goals and objectives which provide all components of a peacekeeping operation—military, humanitarian, civilian police (CIVPOL), human rights, political, administrative—with a coherent framework for their activities. This framework must be drawn from the mandate of the mission." Lessons Learned Unit, DPKO, "Multidisciplinary Peacekeeping: Lessons from Recent Experience," December 1996. Unfortunately, such exhortations abound in the "lessons learned" reports. See, for example, the discussion of the need for "clear and achievable goals so as to avoid unrealistic or ill-founded expectations" learned from the Cambodia mission in IPS/UNITAR (1994).

15. This situation was described by the UNTAC Police Commissioner, Klaas Roos, at the Singapore conference in December 1995 (see Chappell 1996). This is in sharp contrast to the same objective situation in the Congo, where the UN police force was sent in explicitly to fill the void. The issue is partly the content of the assignment but also the clarity. See International Peace Academy (1984: 299).

16. In the "lessons learned" literature, the lack of language and driving skills is more frequently cited as a problem. In some cases, officers were sent home after arriving at the mission because they were determined to be unable to pass a basic driving or English-language test. In other cases, such as UNPROFOR, Commissioner M.F. O'Reilly describes the elaborate steps taken to cope with gaps between the presenting officers and the promised (required) skills. See Chappell (1996). The problem was sufficiently recurring that the CIVPOL office in New York has adopted the practice of sending staff (Selection Assistance Units) to countries offering officers, to test them before they are dispatched and to avoid the dilemma of deploying them despite their deficiencies, or incurring the cost of sending them home without serving. These may be more often cited because the standard is less ambiguous. An operational definition of "regular police service" has been hard to establish. It is hard to see how the solution proposed by the IPS/UNITAR report on the Cambodia mission, that is, requiring a number of years of "community policing" (1995: 21), would reduce the problem.

17. The original formulation of this point is in Wilson (1968). Technology is used very broadly to mean knowledge of the cause-and-effect relationships needed to produce the desired output.

18. The problem was described in an interview with a senior American police officer who served in the US organized international police monitor group that preceded CIVPOL deployment.

19. The classic exposition of this point is Pressman and Wildavsky (1973). The authors used Rube Goldberg illustrations to convey "the complexity of joint action," that is, federal policy implementation.

20. As a former Deputy Director explained, there was pressure to end the practice of staffing the main office of CIVPOL with "loaned officials"—not because it was unstable, but because it biased the selection of police leadership. Only wealthy Member States can afford to contribute the services of senior police officials.

21. Each country is supposed to be paid a flat fee for each officer provided, but the UN has frequently been unable to pay contributing countries in a timely manner.

22. Rank, like other aspects of policing, means different things in different countries. Some countries have attempted to manipulate the ranks of their officers in an attempt to influence assignments or other aspects of their service in CIVPOL, rather than it being based on their role or merit in their home department. Since US officers are typically no longer in active service, having resigned or retired, and are working under contract, and since their service can be in departments of very diverse sizes, their rank is also an issue.

23. While the United Nations General Assembly (2001) for the most part identified the same litany of problems I had noted, it did add the negative impact on institutional memory in the field of the temporary nature of CIVPOL organization.

24. For a discussion of different approaches to implementation analysis, see Parsons (1995: 463–490).
25. See Holm and Eide (1999).
26. An especially lurid version of the self-scrutiny by individual nations—in this case, by the news media—of participation in CIVPOL missions is the *Washington Post* article (Lynch 2001) entitled "Misconduct, Corruption by U.S. Police Mar Bosnia UN Mission: Europeans Query Push to Bring in More Officers." While there are some anecdotal references to problems of managing a CIVPOL, including a quoted assessment from Ambassador Richard Holbrooke that the civilian police are the "weakest component," the focus of the study is on allegations of sexual misconduct, such as frequenting brothels or statutory rape, by individual US police officers. The article reports questions raised about the recruitment and screening done by a Dallas-based corporation, DynCorps, which has a multimillion-dollar State Department contract to supply American police officers to CIVPOL missions, because the US has no national police force from which to deploy officers. It also notes the limited sanctions that are available to managers when individual US contract officers misbehave. The "Query" in the headline refers to the Bush administration's stated interest in replacing the US military presence in Bosnia with civilian police.

Bibliography

Baillargeon, D., and Smith D.C. "In Pursuit of Safety: Alternative Patterns of Police Production in Three Metropolitan Areas." *Journal of Social Issues*, vol. 36, no. 4 (1980): 35–58.
Bayley, D. *Police for the Future*. London: Oxford University Press, 1994.
Bayley, D. "Who Are We Kidding? Or Developing Democracy Through Police Reform." Paper presented at Conference on Policing in Emerging Democracies, October 1995.
Bratton, W., and Knobler, P. *Turnaround*. New York: Random House, 1998.
Chappell, D. "The Role, Preparation and Performance of Civilian Police in United Nations Peacekeeping Operations." Unpublished report. UNCIVPOL Headquarters, New York, 1996.
Chappell, D., and Evans, J. "The Role, Preparation, and Performance of Civilian Police in United Nations Peacekeeping Operations: A Reference Document." Working draft, at http://www.dfait-maeci.gc.ca/ni-ka/peace/peacekeeping-e.asp, January 1997.
Ghani, Brigadier-General. "Role and Function of Civilian Police in Peacekeeping Operations: Debriefing and Lessons." Singapore, UNITAR/IPS/NIRA, 11–13 December 1995.
Goldstein, H. *Problem-Oriented Policing*. Philadelphia: Temple University Press, 1990.
Greene, J.R., and Mastrofski, S.D. *Community Policing: Rhetoric or Reality*. New York/Westport, CT/London: Praeger, 1986.
Hill, S.M., and Malik, S.P. *Peacekeeping and the United Nations*. Brookfield, VT: Dartmouth Publishing Company, 1996.
Holm, T.T., and Eide, E.B., eds. "Special Issue: Peace Building and Police Reform." *International Peacekeeping*, vol. 6, no. 4 (Winter 1999).
International Peace Academy. *Peacekeeper's Handbook*. London: Pergamon Press, 1984.
Luard, E. "Conclusion: The Contemporary Role of the United Nations." In Roberts, A., and Kingsbury, B., eds. *United Nations, Divided World: The UN's Roles in International Relations*. London: Oxford University Press, 1988.
Lynch, C. "Misconduct, Corruption by U.S. Police Mar Bosnia UN Mission: Europeans Query Push to Bring in More Officers." *Washington Post*, 29 May 2001.
Maple, J., and Mitchell, C. *The Crime Fighter: Putting the Bad Guys Out of Business*. New York: Doubleday, 1999.

Mathiason, J.R., and Smith, D.C. "Delivering Global Services: A Public Management Perspective on Reform at the United Nations." Working paper for the symposium on Managing Global Services: An Overview of the United Nations, September 1986.

Mathiason, J.R., and Smith, D.C. "The Diagnostic of Reform: The Evolving Tasks and Functions of the United Nations." *Public Administration and Development*, vol. 7, no. 2 (1987): 166–199.

McNeil, Jr., D.G. "Word for Word/Kosovo Police Blotter: The War Is Over. Now Violence Is Daily Routine." *New York Times Magazine*, 29 October 2000.

Oakley, R.B., Dziedzic, M.J., and Goldberg, E.M., eds. *Policing the New World Disorder: Peace Operations and Public Safety*. Washington, D.C.: National Defense University Press, 1998.

Parsons, W. *Public Policy: An Introduction to the Theory and Practice of Policy Analysis*. Cheltenham: Edward Elgar, 1995.

Pressman, J.L., and Wildavsky, A. *Implementation: How Great Hopes in Washington Are Dashed in Oakland; or, Why It's Amazing that Federal Programs Work at All*. Berkeley: University of California Press, 1973.

Scott, R.W. *Organizations: Rational, Natural and Open Systems*. 2nd ed. Englewood Cliffs, NJ: Prentice-Hall, 1987.

Shearing, C. "The Relations between Public and Private Policing." In Tonry, M., and Morris, N., eds. *Modern Policing*. Chicago: University of Chicago Press, 1992.

Smith, D.C. "Performance Management in New York City: The Mayor's Management Planning and Reporting System in the Koch Administration." Paper prepared for the annual meeting of the Association of Public Policy and Management, Washington, D.C., November 1993.

Smith, D.C. "What Can Public Managers Learn from Police Reform in New York? COMPSTAT and the Promise of Performance Management." Paper prepared for the annual meeting of the Association of Public Policy and Management, Washington, D.C., November 1997.

Smith, D.C., and Barnes, R. "Making Management Count: Toward Theory-Based Performance Management." Paper prepared for the annual research conference of the Association of Public Policy and Management, New York City, October 1998.

Smith, D.C., and Bratton, W. "Performance Management in New York City Police: COMPSTAT and the Revolution in Police Management." In Nathan, R., and Forsythe, D., eds. *Quicker, Better, Cheaper? Managing Performance in American Government*. Albany: SUNY Press, 2001.

Thompson, J.D. *Organizations in Action*. New York: McGraw-Hill, 1967.

Traub, J. "Inventing East Timor." *Foreign Affairs* (August 2000): 74–89.

IPS/UNITAR. International Conference on "The United Nations Transitional Authority in Cambodia Debriefing and Lessons." Singapore 1994. Geneva: UNITAR, 1995.

UNITAR/IPS/NIRA. International conference on "The Role and Function of Civilian Police in Peacekeeping Operations: Debriefing and Lessons: Executive Summary," Singapore 1995.

United Nations General Assembly. "Management Audit of United Nations Civilian Police Operations." *Report of the Secretary-General on activities of the Office of Internal Oversight Services*. March 2001 (A/55/812).

Van Horn, C., and Baumer, D. "CETA: The Politics of Unemployment." *CQ Press* (1985).

Van Meter, D.S., and Van Horn, C.E. "The Policy Implementation Process: A Conceptual Approach." *Administration and Society*, vol. 6, no. 4 (February 1975): 445–488.

Wilson, J.Q. *Varieties of Police Behavior*. Cambridge, MA: Harvard University Press, 1968.

— *Chapter 10* —

SUSTAINABLE CIVIL SOCIETY OR SERVICE DELIVERY AGENCIES?

The Evolution of Non-governmental
Organizations in Bosnia and Herzegovina

Ian Smillie and Kristie Evenson

Introduction

In 1996, Ian Smillie, a long-time NGO-watcher, visited Bosnia on behalf of CARE International, and subsequently wrote a paper entitled "Service Delivery or Civil Society? NGOs in Bosnia and Herzegovina." The paper was highly critical of what Smillie saw as short-sightedness among donor agencies and international non-governmental organizations (NGOs), in creating and fostering a community of organizations with short life expectancies, even shorter attention spans, and agendas based largely on serving the needs of their foreign benefactors. While "building civil society" was the donor watchword, short-term service delivery was mostly what they paid for. "Capacity building" was undoubtedly a common feature among the donor community, but this too was limited, focusing mainly on training local NGOs in proposal and report writing—essentially, how to conform better to the administrative needs of their benefactors. Translated into Bosnian, "Service Delivery or Civil Society?" was widely circulated among NGOs, and struck a resonant chord at the time.

In 2001, Kristie Evenson returned to the region to see what had changed. This chapter, the product of a collaboration between Smillie and Evenson, uses 1996 as a kind of benchmark, and looks at how the issues, the donors, and the non-governmental community changed in the subsequent five years.[1]

Background and Recent History of
Bosnia and Herzegovina

The 1995 Dayton Peace Accords were the first official step toward normalization in Bosnia and Herzegovina (BiH). With the creation of two "entities" within BiH, the Republika Srpska (RS) and the Federation, political and administrative structures were established and strategies were developed to build a new, modern state. What quickly became apparent was that the new state existed more in the minds of international facilitators and donors than in those of the leaders of Bosnia's political factions and state institutions. Polls in 1997 and 1998 resulted in the reelection of nationalist politicians who continued to engage in ethnic, rather than state-building, politics.

Subsequent elections in 2000 signaled a turn to more moderate politics in some parts of the country. However, hardliners in all three representative ethnic groups continued to impede the functioning of the central government. Most dramatically, hard-line Bosnian Croat leaders refused to recognize moderate Bosnian Croats as their representatives, and began to demand a third entity in Bosnia, threatening to nullify the Dayton Peace Agreement.

In 2001, this high-level political drama played against a backdrop in which the average citizen struggled with many of the same issues that had persisted since the end of hostilities. The return of refugees (known colloquially among aid agencies simply as "return") had improved in many areas, and much housing had been rebuilt. But beyond these basic conditions, little had changed. The economic cloud over the future of Bosnia had not disappeared, nor had the threat of renewed fighting. Economic survival and the long-term tasks of rebuilding society were being discussed, but little real progress had been made. Major infrastructure projects had been completed, but the return of minorities was slow, infrastructure upkeep was poor (International Crisis Group 1999), general unemployment continued at more than 35 percent (US Government 2001),[2] and economic investment had brought few new jobs. In essence, the existence of a fully functioning democratic state was still more de jure than de facto.

The Third Sector in Perspective

It is widely agreed that democratization requires a transparent and accountable set of governing institutions in electoral practices, governance, and civil society. While multiparty elections contribute to better and more accountable government, democracy is more than elections. It is the interaction between all of these components, embracing as well the principles of legitimacy, accountability, and participation, and the notion of competence.

- *Legitimacy*—a system of government that relies on the consent of the governed; whereby the means exist to change governments and policies; whereby government has respect for and can enforce constitutional order and the rule of law; whereby the judiciary is independent of the political process.[3]
- *Accountability*—a government that is accountable to the citizenry for its policies and actions between elections, ensured through freedom of association, freedom of the press, and freedom to dissent.
- *Participation*—a government that permits and encourages citizens to take advantage of opportunities and rights; pluralism and tolerance for diversity are encouraged, and the means exist to solve conflict peacefully; participation and accountability are developed through the encouragement of a robust and independent civil society, including non-governmental associations based upon public rather than private goals.
- *Competence*—a government with effective, honest, and transparent civilian institutions that have the ability to formulate and implement policy and to deliver essential services effectively.

Civil society thus plays a key role in the overall process of democratization. Or as Stubbs (2000: 1–4) suggests, civil society meshes the formal and everyday politics of life in a manner that provides a rich environment of linkages, and an arena for ideas. There are implications for civil society in each of these categories.

Linking Civil Society and Democracy

Concern about civil society and its connection to democracy grew among donors by leaps and bounds in the early 1990s, as many began working in a variety of countries experiencing "democratic transitions." Fueled as much by changes in Eastern Europe as by experience in developing countries, the expression "civil society" had by 1995 found its way into major policy papers of almost every donor agency, and had become a topic of concern among civil society organizations and non-governmental organizations (NGOs) in legitimizing their role.

"Simply stated," wrote one donor agency, "civil society is, together with the state and market, one of the three 'spheres' that interface in the making of democratic societies. Civil society is the sphere in which social movements become organized. The organizations of civil society, which represent many diverse and sometimes contradictory social interests ... include church-related groups, trade unions, co-operatives, service organizations, community groups and youth organizations, as well as academic institutions and others...." (UNDP 1993).

So much time has been devoted to defining civil society, however, that sight of its importance is sometimes lost. Legitimacy, accountability, participation, and governmental competence are all given as reasons for encouraging it, but empirical evidence of the link between traditions of association on the one hand and development on the other is generally weak. Of theory there is no lack, but evidence of correlation and causality tends to be patchy and contradictory, and sometimes seems like wishful thinking.[4]

In a 20-year study of civic traditions in modern Italy, Putnam (1993) approached the topic more scientifically. In an effort to discover the reasons behind the great differences in government effectiveness, economic performance, and social development between regions in the north and the south of the country, he and his colleagues conducted several waves of investigation between 1970 and 1989. They surveyed regional councilors and community leaders, they conducted institutional case studies and mass surveys, they analyzed all regional legislation over a 14-year period, and they sifted 10 centuries of regional history. What they found was striking. The strong associational life in several northern regions was clearly and unambiguously responsible for good government, and was a factor in the development of a strong economy. Its historical and present-day absence in southern regions led to weak government and to societies based on paternalism, exploitation, corruption, and poverty.

The Putnam study bears out what Ignatieff says about civil society:

> It is in the institutions of civil society ... that the leadership of a democratic society is trained and recruited.... It is civil society in tandem with the state that tames the market. Without a strong civil society, there cannot be a debate about what kind of market to have, what portion of its surplus should be put to the use of present and future generations.... Without a free and robust civil society, market capitalism must inevitably turn into mafia capitalism.... Without civil society, democracy remains an empty shell. (Ignatieff 1995)

Democratization in Bosnia and Herzegovina

Writing about the former Yugoslavia, Ignatieff is more specific. He explains why the state began to disintegrate after the death of Tito. "Because states whose legitimacy depends on the personal charisma of individuals can only fall apart with their deaths. Because Communist regimes everywhere have shown no capacity to sustain electoral or political legitimacy once they lose the capacity to intimidate their populations. What other principle of legitimacy is there in the post-communist world except for nationalism? What other language exists to mobilize people around a common project?" (Ignatieff 1995).

The nationalist dream, Ignatieff says, of uniting or reuniting people into a single entity provides the (former) Communist elite with a diversion: "It is a politics of fantasy, leading the population away from 'real' issues ... it is a fantasy at another level: reunifying Serbs, or Croats or Muslims, for that matter, into a single national state can only be achieved by forcible population transfer, by ethnic cleansing." In three short years, therefore, Yugoslavians were transported from interethnic tolerance and accommodation to barbarism. The collapse of the state and the economy came first, followed by nationalist paranoia fueled by elite manipulation. "Nationalism did not destroy Yugoslavia from the bottom up; it was the elites who destroyed Yugoslavia from the top down" (Ignatieff 1995).

Post-Dayton Bosnia and Herzegovina is, in essence, an ethnic microcosm of the old Yugoslavia. It is an attempt to rebuild the tolerance that disappeared so quickly in the early 1990s. Much of the emphasis, however, is still on economic recovery. Understandably, people still need jobs, and there are massive reconstruction requirements. As stated in a World Bank discussion paper published soon after Dayton: "The Government of the Republic of Bosnia and Herzegovina has expressed its firm determination to rebuild the country as fast as it can. There is equal determination to achieve this goal, not through a system of command and control, but as far as possible through the initiative of private individuals, organized in a modern market economy. It is hoped that in this process of reconstruction and reform, the critical elements of a pluralistic, multi-ethnic society will be re-established and strengthened" (World Bank 1996).

Like many other donors and investors after the Dayton Peace Accords, the World Bank placed a great deal of faith in the idea that a revived and prosperous market economy would lead to peace and security. Ignatieff (1995) is more than a little dismissive of this as the key to change. "Speaking as a liberal," he writes, "I would say that it is time to jettison the traditional liberal fiction—enunciated since the days of Adam Smith—that global commerce will pacify the world, that everyone's objective interest in prosperity gives everyone an interest in social peace. Yugoslavia demonstrates that when ethnic groups feel their identity, culture and survival are at stake, they are willing to lay waste to what was one of Eastern Europe's most prosperous economies."

By 2000, the Bosnian economy had grown,[5] but as Ignatieff had suggested several years before, peace and security did not follow. This was partly due to the fact that much of the growth remained in the hands of ethnic elites who continue to work against a unified and pluralistic Bosnia. It was also partly due to the fact that the forces that tore Yugoslavia apart were also present throughout the society.

Civil society, for example, can be more than a force for good. Civil society can harbor or come to exhibit some of a country's most exclusive tendencies. As Rieff writes about Bosnian Serbs: "Karadzic represented the aspirations of ordinary Serbs in that extraordinary time all too faithfully, and could rightly lay just as great a claim to being an exemplar of civil society as Václav Havel" (in Carothers 1999: 19–21). And as Stubbs (2000) has pointed out in a study of Croatia, many of the most active organizations in the third sector were actually those that preached the most nationalist exclusion. Accordingly, the role played by civil society in the overall development of society should not be taken for granted as a priori positive. Rather, it should be seen as a force that has positive *potential* for democratization and stability, if properly supported and developed.

In the years after Dayton, more observers are acknowledging the implications of civil society as they shift their focus from the economy and formal political structures to other "softer" components of "democratization." Recent studies by the World Bank (1996) and the EastWest Institute (EWI) and the European Stability Initiative (ESI) (2000: 1–5) have found that a key impediment to the realization of a more stable and democratic state in Bosnia and Herzegovina has been the "lack of effective and accountable state institutions." The strengthening of weak institutions is emphasized again and again as the key to reaching a consolidated democracy.[6] Snyder (1995) suggests that "getting the sequencing right" means the establishment of a transparent and stable set of state institutions based on the overall good governance tenets of legitimacy, accountability, participation, and competence. A key to developing such good governance, accordingly, is the presence of a dynamic civil society.

Supporting the Third Sector

These concepts and conclusions are less than earth shattering. For example, most donors working in the component parts of the former Yugoslavia in recent years point to the absence of good governance as a main hindrance in achieving project goals. While major infrastructure projects such as roads and bridges have been completed, they are often not maintained.[7] One reason lies in the fact that accountability for normal road and bridge maintenance requires the functioning and coordination of several layers of bureaucracy, and, perhaps even more importantly, transparency in funding and managerial competency. While the international donor community uses carrots and sticks to cajole local leaders, its patience is often less resolute than that of the politicians who impede the process.[8]

Where civil society is concerned, most donors have not connected their intellectual acceptance of its importance with their strategic planning or their budgets.[9] A look at donor realities in 1996 provides a useful benchmark against which to analyze the lack of donor "return" on investment at the end of 2000.

Realities of 1996

In 1996, many donors and INGOs characterized their interest in supporting local NGOs as an investment in a strong, pluralist, and socially integrated civil society. Yet in Bosnia, donors essentially sought—and found in local NGOs—cheap service delivery. Channeling money through local organizations, they could implement discrete projects with set goals, and get a lot done with a little money. But this worked against the creation of an environment for long-term civil society sustainability.

This service delivery relationship was characterized by the tendency to fund some NGOs far beyond their capacity for good management. Examples of organizations less than a year old charged with managing a project portfolio in excess of $1 million were not uncommon. At the other extreme, donors often failed to make their payments on time, leading to inappropriate financial management and great hardship on the part of the organizations they were "supporting." Little funding—sometimes none—was allocated for administration and overheads, even though good management was high on the list of donor expectations. Disappointed with the results, donors would then pull the plug on the grounds of mismanagement or incompetence.

A common problem for Bosnian NGOs was the short-term nature of funding. It was not uncommon to wait six months for a decision on a three-month allotment. Short bursts of funding for psychosocial projects in the immediate post-Dayton period highlighted a donor tendency to jump from project to project without allowing for long-term effects to be realized. Many international NGOs, ready to "move on," set up local NGOs to "take over" their projects without providing much in the way of resources. "Capacity building" focused mainly on training programs, and training programs focused mainly on proposal and report writing. When the subject of cold, hard cash arose in the context of long-term capacity building, most donors were nowhere to be found. These policies within the context of a weak NGO legal structure and a general local government antagonism toward NGOs created little possibility for significant third sector development.

One response to the problem in 1996—promoted by an unusual coalition made up of CARE, World Vision, Catholic Relief Services, the International Rescue Committee, and the Geneva-based INGO umbrella organization ICVA—was the creation of a multiethnic foundation of Bosnian NGOs. Established in 1997 and tasked with increasing the capacity and effectiveness of the non-profit sector in physical and social reconstruction for long-term development, the Bosnian NGO Foundation sought support from donors for an endowment that would provide it with core funding after the country was back on its feet. Its proposed programming included raising public awareness of civil society, contributing to the sector's financial sustainability through the development of a national fund, and, perhaps most importantly, assisting NGOs in their own professional development.

Realities of 2000

Many of the problems of 1996 persisted at the end of 2000. Donor-sponsored capacity building still focused on operational rather than conceptual goals, and remained uncoordinated. Donors continued to manage their relationships with local NGOs in ways that encouraged very little real development, coordination, or ownership. With regard to the systemic problems of funding priorities, timelines, and long-term sustainability, the donor community remained unable or unwilling to change. The Bosnian NGO Foundation had failed to attract any funding for its endowment, and survived on the same project treadmill as its member organizations. In essence, while the worst aspects of buying cheap service delivery had declined, the lack of fundamental change in funding strategies meant that the trend continued and long-term capacity building could not take off. To better understand the enduring challenges, some background on the development of Bosnia's third sector is in order.

Civil Society in Bosnia and Herzegovina

The NGO Scene in 2001

Non-governmental organizations continue to be a popular alternative forum of ideas, services, and community for people across Bosnia and Herzegovina. While the proliferation of NGOs has declined since the first burst of donor funds and the hasty exit strategies of the mid-1990s, the range of organizations—from simple sports clubs to refugee return groups—continues to change and develop.

In September 1996, the International Council of Voluntary Agencies (ICVA) estimated that there were 98 local NGOs working on reconstruction, infrastructure development, human rights, and women's issues. Most, if not all, had been established since 1993. Many worked within a restricted geographic area, clustering around Sarajevo and Tuzla. Few, if any, had a cross-Entity identity, and there was very slow NGO growth in the Republika Srpska.

By the end of 2000, the number of NGOs had grown by a factor of as much as five,[10] but the major distinctions remained the same. The majority was still clustered in urban areas, although there had been some progress in establishing organizations in rural and isolated locations. NGO growth had also been significant in the Republika Srpska, although numbers remained low, particularly in the eastern portion of the Entity, where the general population's distrust of civil society initiatives ran high, and resources had been especially scarce for political and economic reasons.

Between 1996 and 2001, many service delivery organizations had formed spontaneously to deal with local problems and to take advantage of donor funding. Few, however, had developed out of community spirit, and many operated without boards of directors or anything resembling the sort of "constituency" that Western NGOs take for granted. Apart, perhaps, from human rights NGOs, many of these organizations had developed little understanding of their place in "civil society"—their potential for advocacy and for work beyond simple service delivery. Like the international NGOs they emulated, many had been quick to fall into competition with each other, vying for donor attention and funding. In essence, these organizations were not so much indigenous NGOs as local organizations based on the aspirations of their financial benefactors.

Localizing the International, Preserving the Indigenous

Although the expression "NGO community" is frequently used to describe the totality of its civil society organizations, BiH, it still far from being a *community* with coherence or any particular sense of solidarity and common purpose. Rather, the NGO scene can be broken down into two major groups—what might be called the "local" and the "indigenous."

Local organizations may focus on political or ethnic advocacy issues, or they may be service providers. Many formed as conversions of projects started by international NGOs. Some have been formed to build the capacities of others—local and regional NGO resource centers, for example, and the Bosnian NGO Foundation.

Preconflict "indigenous organizations" are often associations based on the concepts of self-help or self-interest that were created within the context of the erstwhile socialist system. Or they may be locally based sports and entertainment associations. These groups operate in much the way that they did during Yugoslavian times. Many village and rural areas have more of this preconflict, community-based type of organization than the other. And these organizations are often the ones that respond best to the needs of the community, whether in terms of additional services or of social and recreation activities. As the value of these preconflict associations is better understood by the donor community, such organizations are becoming more and more a focal point of donor-driven initiatives.

Underlying Legal Structure and Challenges

The unfavorable regulatory environment for NGOs has changed little since 1996. Despite strong international pressure, legal and structural reforms concerning civil society have been slow to evolve in BiH because of the country's complex political and legal environment. While the international community has pushed for the adoption of new NGO laws based on international standards (CARE 2000: 2–3)[11] in both the Federation and the Republika Srpska, only the Federation had done so by the beginning of 2001. The 1991 Citizens Association Law was still operating in the Republika Srpska.

However, the current law still does not distinguish between a service provider, a political party, and other types of for-profit or non-profit associations. This makes NGOs taxable bodies, essentially applying the same heavy burden of business salary taxes also to NGOs. Payroll taxes and social security serve to increase basic salaries by 100 percent or more, and the tax exemptions that are common in other countries are not always available for local organizations. Income generation and NGO microenterprise efforts are similarly susceptible to heavy rates of taxation. Such financial realities discourage NGOs from drawing attention to their work for fear of the financial authorities.[12]

The new law does seek to define NGOs as non-profit, thereby partially solving financial uncertainties. It also allows for freedom of movement and inter-Entity registration, which may encourage the expansion of inter-Entity NGOs beyond those promoted by donors. However, since the Republika Srpska had yet to pass the law at the beginning of 2001, inter-Entity registration had been slow.

Capacity Building as a Cottage Industry

In recognition of the relative fragility of the NGO sector, capacity-building programs of one sort or another have been widely implemented since 1996 by various international donors, either through umbrella grants to humanitarian service delivery NGOs, or through international organizations such as ICVA. Capacity building and interorganizational coordination programs have increased, but few significant results had been achieved in either coordination or anything more than superficial capacity building. Some of the most prominent initiatives are described below.

On the coordination front, ICVA's main purpose has been "to foster communication and cooperation among the NGOs and to facilitate a coherent NGO interface with the representation of common issues to SFOR [NATO's Stabilization Force], multinational institutions, the Governments, and the cantonal and municipal governments." ICVA continues to provide information and networking services to international and local NGOs, and, through various initiatives, has worked on the promotion of appropriate NGO legislation within BiH and the establishment of an informal "NGO Council" aimed at coordinating the efforts of some international and local NGOs. This overall coordination function is important, but it fails to fully engage those NGOs that are simpler, locally based associations.

On the intergovernmental level, the Organization for Security and Cooperation in Europe (OSCE) started a program in 1997 that facilitates and hosts meetings, and provides training and logistical support, with an emphasis on legal and human rights training. While the program took time to engage with indigenous legal practitioners, it has become a useful link in the overall reform and revitalization of the legal system throughout Bosnia and Herzegovina.

The Reconstruction and Return Task Force (RRTF) was created in 1997 in order to coordinate "return" initiatives among international and intergovernmental organizations and NATO's peacekeeping force, SFOR. The

RRTF got off to a slow start since many organizations did not understand the need for yet another coordinating body. In time, however, the mechanism became more streamlined, but it rarely incorporated indigenous NGOs into its network.

Finally, the creation of the Bosnian NGO Foundation in 1997 was an attempt to provide an indigenous umbrella organization for the NGO community and a sustainable basis of support for the third sector. The Foundation initially focused on capacity building among nine local NGOs while it developed its own organizational capacity. The results have been mixed, but generally the Foundation's impact has been limited because of its (unsuccessful) efforts to build an endowment.

Given these international and indigenous initiatives to strengthen Bosnian NGOs, it would seem only a matter of time before the sector would bloom. But most of the programs remained relentlessly fixed on microdevelopment challenges, too often equating "capacity building" with "training" rather than institutional development.

Even in basic training, there was little coordination among those providing this form of training, and, as in 1996, needs identification tended to favor the interests and perceptions of donors, rather than those of NGOs. "What Is an NGO," "Strategic Planning," "How to Develop a Mission Statement," and "Project Design and Reporting" were all common topics in the range of courses provided. While these are no doubt useful for some NGOs, many attendees complain that they have been through the same thing many times—that much of it is very general and has little relevance to existing realities. For many, the problem is not "how to write a report," despite demanding donor complexities; the problem is how to ensure relevance and how to get *cash*.

Capacity Building beyond the Third Sector

Many hoped that when the new law was enacted, it would assist NGOs in building better relationships with their local governments, since many NGOs feel that local and cantonal officials do not understand their work. While the relationship between NGOs and government officials has improved from one of outright hostility to one of greater cooperation, misinformation still persists, and many non-governmental organizations are considered to be simply "antigovernment." Most NGOs have done little to engage officials or to develop community legitimacy, and image problems continue to hinder the potential for complementarity between NGOs and resource-strapped government institutions. Given that many government departments and social service centers receive very little donor attention compared to NGOs, competition for funds remains a problem.[13]

Donors such as the UNHCR-funded Independent Bureau for Humanitarian Issues (IBHI) and the EU began focusing on capacity-building initiatives between indigenous NGOs and their local governments several years ago, with moderate success; however, refinement of such programs is necessary for countrywide replication.[14] IBHI has been one of the key links in local government capacity building, assisting various institutions to become more accountable and efficient. Of particular note is its role in a UNHCR "Open Cities" project, which aimed to hold local municipal governments responsible for agreements dealing with the return of refugees and internally displaced people.

While IBHI has now incorporated other areas of institution building into its portfolio, its overall impact has remained small due to its scattered presence around BiH and the inherently slow nature of capacity building in local government institutions.[15] IBHI, like its counterpart, the Bosnian NGO Foundation, has yet to become fully operational. In essence, large-scale capacity-building programs have yet to be thought through and implemented. Instead, a continuation of the traditional capacity-building initiatives, such as training in proposal writing, has been the norm.

Donor-Driven Rather Than Mission-Driven

While the growth of an NGO community could be reflective of the larger political context at any given moment, the reality in Bosnia has related more to a combination of donor politics and local opportunism. Since the reckless days of 1996, many donors have learned that local NGOs must become more than cheap service delivery mechanisms and that donor exit strategies must be realistic in both timing and in what they leave behind. However, there are still too many organizations with good programming reputations fighting for their financial lives.

This is partly because donors continue to be "topic" driven, ignoring the capacities and priorities of local organizations. Immediately after the Dayton Accords, the priorities were emergency care and psychosocial assistance, and, understandably, many welfare-type organizations sprang up. Then came reconstruction, and many turned to house building and renovation. Microcredit was the next wave, and welfare organizations scrambled to understand interest rates. Since about 1998, the big donor money has been on "return," and the result was predictable: a huge growth in refugee and return-based associations.

The growth of such groups could validate a badly needed and larger political space for citizen-based groups to argue their rights in front of governmental institutions, but it is not clear which came first—the financial backing for such groups, or the forming of associations to make this happen. As in other parts of the region, politics-by-donor is not a new concept. Funding for targeted minority return and "community revitalization" in Croatia was an extension of efforts in which diplomacy and high politics had failed.[16] However, whether politics-by-donor contributes to an enlarged and beneficial public debate or to further entrenchment of retrograde positions is far from clear.

Donor funding for the ideals of "public space" is not a priori a negative concept. Many in Bosnia would say that without donor money, their activities would be dominated by the ethnic-laden politics of the formalized political arena. For instance, Open Society Institute (OSI) funding of media initiatives and school curricula is a critical element in the long-term democratization process. Given the still shaky foundation for this public space, indigenous NGOs understandably feel a need for more than just financial support.

However, it is clear that donor initiatives do not always appreciate the complexity of the local situation. In 2001, some prominent international NGOs[17] believed that many donors would fund anything involving "return" programming, particularly for the Republika Srpska. These donors may have learned the need to allow NGOs to develop programming to fit their capacity and the context; however, the bottom line is "return," rather than what local NGOs may see as their own or their community's priorities. While some donors may also have learned the price of giving large sums to weak NGOs, the drive for "return" has once again resulted in fast disbursement, without long-term thought as to the consequences.

Donors want program evaluations, but they seldom incorporate the views of the stakeholders or local NGOs in the process. Usually prepared by international consultants and rarely touching on the institutional issues described in this chapter, reports tend to focus on whether things were done right, rather than whether the right thing was done. Most evaluations remain confidential, thereby reducing the opportunity for learning and probably serving as silent indictments of "the locals" for not having the capacity to do things the way the donor had anticipated.

Peace Building in Cycles

As noted above, donor interests change. For a time in Bosnia, it was economic revitalization and small credit schemes; before that, it was the reconstruction of houses and public infrastructures such as schools and clinics; and before that, it was funding of psychosocial assistance. The linear progression may seem logical, yet it fails to capture the less than linear postconflict situation and the consequent need for a less than linear "hot topic" funding strategy.

Much has been written in recent years about how "the continuum" from relief to reconstruction to development, popular in the 1980s, was wrong-headed. Based on the idea of reconstruction after a natural disaster, it ignored the reality of protracted emergencies and the possibility that even in the direst of situations, some developmental work is possible—parents can teach children in refugee camps, people can be trained in new life skills, public health workers can be trained, and so on. While most relief agencies and most development agencies have accepted this idea, the reality of compartmentalized donor funding is that relief money comes out of one cash machine and development money comes from another. Both are influenced by the flavor of the month, and the two forms have little interest in, or communication with, each other. So funding in Bosnia did move on a continuum-like assembly line, and even though traumatized widows still needed psychosocial assistance, they were one day made to see that what they were going to get was either microcredit or nothing. The interesting lesson in Bosnia might be that while it is right and possible to do development work in an emergency situation, it may also be right to continue with welfare-type work even in a situation where the emergency appears to be over.[18]

Time Lines and Overheads

In addition to the problem of donor-driven objectives, Bosnian NGOs continue to live with short-term donor funding and a pervasive donor reluctance to pay for recurrent costs and overheads. These must be squeezed, sometimes surreptitiously, out of projects. And because of the faddish nature of funding, there is little time or opportunity for NGOs to develop their own priorities and programming. The Bosnian NGO Foundation conducted an interesting survey of NGOs in 1999 and came up with a number of almost touching findings. For example, over half the NGOs surveyed suggested that the ideal funding cycle would run for more than a year: where rebuilding can actually take generations. A further 70 percent of the 109 NGO respondents said that lack of donor understanding, especially on issues relating to core costs and administrative expenses, was the major organizational obstacle they faced. And given the fact that more than 80 percent of their funding was being provided by international supporters, this was a formidable problem indeed.

Donors, including international NGOs that suffer from the same problems themselves, were—even at the beginning of 2001—keeping their "partners" on such tight financial leashes that most had little choice but to stay on the project treadmill and hope for the best if they wanted to survive. Donors, of course, cannot be expected to prop up unsustainable organizations forever. Or even for a little while. Or so the argument goes. But how—in a country with no philanthropic tradition, a hostile legal climate, and great dollops of donor funding for what donors want—can independent, sustainable NGOs be developed? And if this is a problem for individual NGOs, how is the kind of civil society described in the opening pages of this chapter ever to develop?

The sad observation about Bosnia is that although much was accomplished between the time of the Dayton Accords and the turn of the century, a great deal more could have been done to build local capacities at all levels of society—not just improved capacities to write and report on proposals or to deliver services on behalf of donors, but improved capacities within civil society to determine what Bosnians see as *their* developmental priorities. The results might have included improved capacities to work on those priorities, and maybe even improved capacities to raise the funds to pay for them in Bosnia.

Regional Challenges

International donors do regard democratization as a major priority in Bosnia. The programming manifestation of the priority, however, is as varied as the multitude of agencies at work in the country. One aspect of democratization is its regional dimension, and a recognition that building civil society cannot be done in a Bosnian vacuum. This view is shared by NGOs throughout the region, and although regional programming resources are limited, there are interesting initiatives.

Refugee associations working with international NGOs on issues of "return" have had to develop a regional perspective and regional strategies on group return and rights. Such initiatives have become more commonplace as practitioners realize the value of informal return networks. For example, "Go and See" visits, such as those sponsored by the American Refugee Committee (ARC) throughout Bosnia and Herzegovina, Croatia, and parts of the Federal Republic of Yugoslavia (FRY), connect individuals and their local refugee associations with their former places of residence. Interaction through these visits has increased the confidence of potential returnees, who can physically visit their homes, and talk with people like themselves who have already returned, or who are going through similar decision-making processes. Such programs strengthen both individual and associational relationships, and are worthy of support and replication.

Regional linkages on other issues are also useful. For instance, legal professionals around BiH have attempted to understand each other better through specific local NGO initiatives, such as the International LEX Center for Human Rights in Banja Luka. Such initiatives allow for the reestablishment of preconflict professional associations, and also support professionals in their attempt to work in what remains a highly partisan environment. In the case of legal professionals, the ability to contact their colleagues on housing issues in other parts of the Federation and the Republika Srpska has allowed them to be more effective in handling housing cases. The ability to contact former colleagues in other republics of the former Yugoslavia has allowed legal professionals to share similar experiences and to rebuild bridges.[19]

While some regional funding has been offered for several years by OSI and the Institute for the Transition to Democracy (TOD), these programs focus primarily on professional and advocacy-based NGOs rather than those based in local communities. This allows for a sharing of ideas, but it may serve to reinforce the growing number of elite NGOs, which seem increasingly removed from average citizens and the issues that confront them on a daily basis. A further problem is the continuing donor reliance on constant rounds of new expatriate advisers, brought in to give sermons on democratization while regional experts and the local specialists who have emerged in recent years watch from the sidelines.

Conclusion: Greener Pastures?

By 2001, democratization in Bosnia had dropped down on the donor agenda because of increased attention to Kosovo and the Federal Republic of Yugoslavia (FRY), especially after the fall of Slobodan Milosevic. Building civil societies there had become a new focus of donor attention.[20] The result was what Bosnian NGOs had feared in the mid-1990s when they had asked in vain for endowments and other forms of long-term financial assistance: a gradual shifting of resources to Kosovo and FRY, creating a financial vacuum and a sense of abandonment in Bosnia. While projects were still being funded in Bosnia, there were clear indications that "donor fatigue" had set in. In reviewing the limited results of five years of effort, donors seemed ready to move on to new opportunities—not to new ways of doing things, but to new pastures where the same mistakes were likely to be repeated. After Kosovo and the Federal Republic of Yugoslavia, Afghanistan has become the next stop.

Where Bosnia is concerned, however, all is not lost. Valuable lessons have been learned, and those donors and international NGOs that remain will operate in a field less cluttered with amateurish do-gooders and more populated with experienced Bosnian organizations that are able to articulate a Bosnian way forward. This Bosnian "way forward," given a chance, may well be compatible with the ideas of the "civil" and democratic society that decorate international donor brochures and annual reports. But real change will not happen overnight, and if productive partnerships are to develop, serious operational and conceptual issues must be addressed in a way that does not repeat past pathologies. The main issues are illustrated in tables 10.1 and 10.2.

Regardless of what donors do, a viable and vibrant civil society will remain essential to genuine democratization in Bosnia and Herzegovina, and NGOs, as part of civil society, have the potential to contribute immensely to the process. Although the phrase "building civil society" has become a sort of shorthand for addressing the country's absence of good governance, donor capacity-building strategies remain confused. Ironically, the characteristics of good governance sought by donors—legitimacy, accountability, participation, and competence—are largely

TABLE **10.1** Conceptual Issues for Donors

1. There is a need to understand that capacity building is more than "training." Building the capacity of a type of organization (women, child rights, microcredit) or even of the entire NGO community (laws, financial stability, support groups) is very complex and time-consuming. It cannot be treated as a sidebar; it cannot be done by people without experience; it cannot be done by a single donor working in isolation from others. Mistakes will reverberate for decades.
2. There is a need to reassess donor-led agendas on advocacy, public space, and "return." Dealing with local priorities and utilizing indigenous expertise has always been the first tactic in reaching bigger issues. Listen. Make "participation" mean something through real participatory evaluation and programming.
3. There is a need to reward proaction and relevancy.
4. There is a need to encourage regional linkages and sustained regional programming.
5. There is a need for the IBHI concept to be expanded and strengthened.

TABLE **10.2** Operational Issues for Donors

1. There is a need for expanded and more imaginative capacity building (such as strengthening the Bosnian NGO Foundation).
2. There is a need for adequate funding for real institutional development of the third sector.
3. There is a need for more interaction and coordination between international and local organizations.
4. There is a need for realistic (i.e., longer) funding cycles that fit local needs and capacities.
5. There is a need for an understanding of how and why "overhead" costs should be funded. Ignoring this issue only makes the problem of sustainability worse.
6. There is a need for support in the development of long-term funding sources.

absent from Bosnian political and institutional life, and appear to be in short supply among the very donors professing their virtues.

The advent of a viable civil society in Bosnia and Herzegovina remains a distant goal. The use of NGOs for cheap service delivery has diminished but has far from disappeared in the years following Dayton, and few lessons about what builds local capacities have been learned, while many more have been forgotten. At both conceptual and operational levels, donor behavior continues to work against the achievements of stated goals. There is a lack of continuity in the day-to-day management of programs, people, and partners. Attempts at capacity building have not been well thought out; patience and staying power have been weak. Resources, although plentiful, have shied away from difficult or unknown territory, such as the creation of endowments and other instruments of financial sustainability. After five years and billions of aid dollars, the state remains fragile and the concept of a civil society remains elusive. Bridges have been built, but institutions have not. The truth is that peace building rarely conforms to international donor blueprints, time lines, and exit strategies. Building real institutions and genuine democratization takes years, and it will take many more years in Bosnia and Herzegovina. Civil society is a pillar of this democratization, and it cannot flourish without continued, appropriate support. The opportunity is passing, but it is still there.

Notes

1. The 1996 study included interviews and discussions with 17 donor agencies and international NGOs in Zagreb, Bihac, Sarajevo, and Tuzla. Discussions were also held with 13 local NGOs, with Bosnian government officials, and with several individuals with broad experience of the NGO sector. Follow-up discussions in early 2001 were held with key donor agencies and field practitioners. Additional observations were based on Evenson's fieldwork in the region between 1996–2000.
2. Most recent data available is from 1999 estimates.
3. This essentially liberal-democratic definition of legitimacy is not all there is to say on the subject. Historically, the legitimacy of the leader or the government was an outcome of several things. Values, tradition, and ideology—such as belief in the divine right of kings—were one factor. This was reinforced or undermined by the quality of the leader's "product"—patronage, peace, and a healthy economy. And a third was the threat of force, required in increasing proportions as the quality of values and product declined.
4. A detailed account of the genealogy, usage, and contradictory interpretations of "civil society," from Hegel, Locke, and de Tocqueville to recent World Bank documents, can be found in Fierlbeck (1997).
5. Republika Srpska and Federation Statistical Offices, as reported by the Office of the High Representative (OHR), showed a continuing increase in GDP between 1996 and 1999.
6. The term "consolidated democracy" is described by political scientist Snyder (1995) as a country exhibiting key characteristics that ensure a range of institutions being in place, which allow the functioning of a modern state that is subject to its citizens.
7. Thomas L. Friedman (2001) used a similar example in discussing the future of Bosnia and Herzegovina.
8. An example of carrot-and-stick politics could be found near Travnik in 1998, when a critical bridge on the Livno-Sarajevo road was slated for reconstruction. Donor funds had somehow been misplaced by the local government. SFOR (NATO's Stabilisation Force) finally decided that the strategic location of the bridge was more important than holding the government accountable for "lost" funds, and a compromise was worked out.

9. After the Sarajevo and Cologne summits of the Southeast European Stability Pact in 1999, Western donors pledged an additional $2.4 billion for the region (Southeast Europe Stability Pact documents).

10. ICVA estimated in 2001 that there were 365 local NGOs registered throughout the Federation and the Republika Srpska. This estimate corresponds with 1999 USAID figures suggesting between 250 and 500 local NGOs active in BiH. Since most funding goes only to registered associations, there is an incentive to be included in such lists.

11. A new law has been drafted in accordance with Article 11 of the European Convention for the Protection of Human Rights and Fundamental Freedoms (OHR).

12. Over 30 percent (30.27) of NGOS surveyed stated that inadequate legal regulations have had a negative impact on their work (Bosnian NGO Foundation 1999).

13. Municipal institutions, such as the pharmacy and cantonal hospital in Travnik, felt that they could not compete for funds with local NGOs during the first year of an NGO grant scheme offered by UNDP in 1997–1998. Only after several visits by UNDP staff did the representatives begin to see the complementary potential of the other associations.

14. For example, IBHI Travnik (formerly with different names) served in such a capacity-building role for the local municipal government Office of Housing and Return, and has worked with the Social/Welfare Center in Travnik and other cities in BiH.

15. Evenson's field observations (1999), IBHI literature, and follow-up interviews with former IBHI staff in Bosnia and Herzegovina, February 2001.

16. Evenson's work during 1998–1999 with CRS and the PRM/UNHCR funding patterns in the former UN Sector South of Croatia highlighted this linkage.

17. Representatives of CARE and IOCC responding to semistructured interview questions by Evenson (2001).

18. For more on "the continuum," see Anderson (1999) and Smillie (1999).

19. One example of regional networking is the Dalmatian Committee for Solidarity (DOS) in Croatia, which worked on issues of "return" throughout the region, interacting informally with other legal professionals to solve social and legal issues. DOS was particularly active from 1996 through late 1999.

20. The EU and other Western donors made clear to the FRY that the fall of Milosevic would bring needed donor funds into the country. Within weeks of his downfall and subsequent arrest, strategic donor funds began to flow in.

Bibliography

Anderson, M.B. *Report/Thoughts on ICVA Sponsored Mission to Bosnia-Herzegovina.* Cambridge, MA: The Collaborative for Development Action Inc., March 1996.

Anderson, M.B. *Do No Harm: How Aid Can Support Peace—or War.* Boulder: Lynne Rienner, 1999.

Bosnian NGO Foundation. *The Third Sector in Bosnia-Herzegovina.* Sarajevo: Bosnian NGO Foundation, October 1999.

CARE. "Challenges in Civil Society Development in Bosnia and Herzegovina (BiH) Today." Internal paper, 1999.

Carothers, T. "Civil Society." *Foreign Policy* (Winter 1999): 18–29.

Clark, K., and Stubbs, P. "The Civil Society Initiatives Fund (CSIF) in Croatia." *A Review for the Department for International Development* (DFID). June 2000.

Duffield, M. *Social Reconstruction in Croatia and Bosnia: An Exploratory Report for SIDA.* Birmingham: Centre for Urban and Regional Studies, University of Birmingham, November 1996.

EastWest Institute and the European Stability Initiative. "Stability, Institutions and European Integration." Brussels discussion paper, October 2000.

Fierlbeck, K. *Globalizing Democracy: Power, Legitimacy and the Interpretation of Democratic Ideas*. Manchester: Manchester University Press, 1997.

Friedman, T.L. "Bosnia, Sort Of." *New York Times*, editorial, 26 January 2001.

Government of Republic of Bosnia and Herzegovina, Federation of Bosnia and Herzegovina, Ministry of Social Policy, Displaced Persons and Refugees. "Draft Law on Humanitarian Activities and Humanitarian Organizations." September 1996.

Ignatieff, M. "Nationalism and the Narcissism of Minor Differences." *Queen's Quarterly* (Spring 1995).

Independent Bureau for Humanitarian Issues. *The Local NGO Sector within Bosnia-Herzegovina—Problems, Analysis and Recommendations*. Sarajevo: IBHI, October 1998.

International Centre for Not-for-Profit Law. *Comments on Draft Law on Humanitarian Activity and Humanitarian Organizations*. Sarajevo: International Centre for Not-for-Profit Law, July 1996.

International Crisis Group. *Preventing Minority Return in Bosnia and Herzegovina: The Anatomy of Hate and Fear*. Brussels: ICG, 1999.

Jackson, S., and Walker, P. "Depolarising the 'Broadened' and 'Back-to-basics' Relief Models." *Disasters*, vol. 23, no. 2 (1999): 93–114.

Maas, P. "Bosnia's Ground Zero." From *Love Thy Neighbour*, excerpted in *Vanity Fair*, March 1996.

Mansfield, E., and Snyder, J. "Democratization and War." *Foreign Affairs*, vol. 74, no. 3 (May/June 1995): 79–98.

Putnam, R.D. *Making Democracy Work: Civic Traditions in Modern Italy*. Princeton: Princeton University Press, 1993.

Rieff, D. *Slaughterhouse: Bosnia and the Failure of the West*. New York: Touchstone, 1996.

Shimkus, D. *Development of the Non-Governmental Sector in Croatia*. Zagreb: IRC, 1996.

Smillie, I. *The Alms Bazaar—Altruism Under Fire: Non-Profit Organizations and International Development*. London: IT Publications, 1995.

Smillie, I. "Relief and Development: The Struggle for Synergy." *Occasional Paper of the Watson Institute, no. 33*, Humanitarianism and War Project. Thomas J. Watson Jr. Institute for International Studies, Brown University, 1999.

Snyder, J. "Nationalism and the Crisis of the Post-Soviet State." *Survival*, vol. 20, no. 1 (Summer 1995).

Stubbs, P. "Social Reconstruction and Social Development in Croatia and Slovenia: The Role of the NGO Sector." *Research Report R6274*. Zagreb: Overseas Development Authority, 1995.

Stubbs, P. "Towards a Political Economy of 'Civil Society' in a Contemporary Croatia." In *Croatia after Tudjman*. Zagreb, Croatia, 2000.

UNDP and Independent Bureau for Humanitarian Issues (IBHI). "Bosnia and Herzegovina: Youth 2000." *Human Development Report*. New York: United Nations Development Programme, 2000.

USAID. "Bosnia: When Customers Tell Us What We Don't Want to Hear." *The Participation Forum*, no. 20 (January 1997).

USAID. *Lessons in Implementation: The NGO Story*. Washington, D.C.: USAID, October 1999.

USAID. *The 1999 NGO Sustainability Index*. 3rd ed. Washington, D.C.: USAID, January 2000.

US Government. *World Fact Book: Bosnia and Herzegovina*. At http://www.odci.gov/cia/publications/factbook/geos/bk.html, 2001.

World Bank. *Bosnia and Herzegovina: Priorities for Recovery and Growth*. Washington, D.C.: World Bank, September 1996.

Miscellaneous reports and working papers prepared by CARE, the EU, ICVA, the OHR, the OSCE, SEE, UNHCR, USAID, World Bank, and others.

PART IV

TOWARD THEORY

The setup of this book has gone from decision making—first strategically and externally oriented and later more internally oriented—to action at the field level. Now, in the final part of our book, we will evaluate the pathologies and promises from preceding chapters in the light of their possible contribution to a theory, or at least a conceptualization, of international organizations that helps to understand their functioning better. Are there some characteristics that they all share? Evaluating an organization, let alone an international one, is always a hard task. For example, in 1988, UN peacekeeping received the Nobel Peace Prize; that was only a few years before Somalia, Rwanda, and Srebrenica. The Nobel Peace Prize to Médicins Sans Frontières (MSF) in 1999 was probably most useful for improving its fundraising capacity. The 2001 Nobel Peace Prize to the United Nations and Secretary-General Kofi Annan says more about the international stature that Kofi Annan has acquired than about the actual functioning of the Organization. In many ways, Nobel Peace Prizes have become instruments to cheer on developments that the awarding committee wants to foster. If the suddenly rediscovered need for multilateral action, in the wake of September 2001, materializes further and reinforces the UN, then the prize will have been timely. But this rediscovery can also be a temporary hiccup in international unilateralism by powerful states. This brings us back to the questions of how autonomous international organizations and states actually are and whether we can improve the functioning of international organizations. Are there cures for the diseases?

— *Chapter 11* —

CURES AND CONCLUSIONS

Dennis Dijkzeul and Leon Gordenker

Introduction

Searching for the answer to the question "Why is it that the high-minded decisions and ideals for international organizations so often lead to mediocre or counterproductive results?" the contributors to this book have highlighted both pathologies and promises of international organizations. They have accordingly assembled a broad array of relevant empirical examples of the functioning and impact of international organizations. This chapter takes the analysis of the authors a step further. It asks whether a theory or model that explains the behavior of international organizations is possible. In order to develop such a model, the problems in the study of international organizations as noted in the introduction serve as a starting point.

Pathologies and Promises of International Organizations

The general perception of international organizations comprises cycles of high hopes and bitter disillusionment. Many parties—the press, the public, Member States, and scholars—are highly critical. The main complaint is that expectations are not being fulfilled. The ideals and goals of these organizations in fact often fail to be translated into fruitful action.

That this so often happens suggests a systemic problem: goals and ideals are too far from the results of implementation and evaluation. Does this point to problems of organizational design? The answer, we believe, is yes. However, such systemic design problems cannot be resolved easily. In particular, sometimes major, and sometimes minor, parts of the UN system seem moribund; yet death is always delayed indefinitely, and resuscitation is avoided. From critical observers, NGOs have generally received a more positive press, but they also increasingly arouse strong doubts. Nevertheless, the academic study of international organizations seldom proposes remedies for the pathologies that lead to disillusionment. As noted in the introduction, the conventional type of study is hampered by four general shortcomings, namely:

1. A lack of empirical material on, as well as insufficiently appropriate theory about, the actual functioning of international organizations. It is therefore hard to make generalizations about their behavior that would deepen the basis for either positive or negative criticism.
2. A lack of interaction among scholars from the disciplines of international relations, business administration, and public administration. Disciplinary myopia often persists.
3. A choice of units of analysis, concepts, and research methodology that blocks attention to such issues as implementation, internal functioning, and deviations from mandate, but emphasizes such issues as decision making and the role of states. This has led to a distorted focus and ultimately an oversimplified view of international organizations.
4. A lack of attention to Southern perspectives and experiences. The ideals of building on local capacities, empowerment, and participation may be strong, but their implementation is not. The organizations, as well as their media and scholarly critics, are often based in and dominated by preferences of the rich, industrialized North. In this respect, these organizations are too often outside intervenors that share a Northern bias that may be subconscious.

By combining empirical material with analysis based on different disciplines, the authors in this book have closely examined these issues. In addition, several chapters focus on the implementation of either field operations or organizational change. Some common themes have emerged that simultaneously show pathologies and promising trends. The chapters on financing the UN, diplomacy, and Sustainable Human Development (SHD) emphasize the influence of governments on international organizations; yet these organizations are also perceived as actors in their own right. The chapters on UN personnel policies, UNCTAD's reform, and fraud and corruption show how organizational strategy and policy—and concomitant implementation—are only slowly changing. Improvement is slow, hampered by ideological North-South conflict, old organizational habits and procedures, and Member State governments' reluctance to take responsibility for the better functioning of these organizations. And yet, some improvements are being made. The chapters on program management, human rights promotion, CIVPOL, and capacity building for local NGOs show that international organizations have a hard time working at the field level. In terms of implementation, international organizations are generally outsiders that need to keep an eye on their donors' procedures and demands and often poorly understand the local needs and capacities. As a result, they sometimes conceptualize and evaluate their activities badly. The organizations often need to improve their management instruments. Several chapters suggested public administration and private enterprise tools, yet applying these tools is not easy.

While the chapters illustrate many of the problems that international organizations confront, yet more topics as diverse as coordination and population control could have received attention. This abundance results mainly from the growing role of international organizations over the last half century. During the late 1940s and the 1950s, international organizations concentrated on negotiating international rules and standards, while functioning as clearing-houses and forums for information exchange and debate through their intergovernmental machinery. Several UN Specialized Agencies served mainly as expert centers for policy research and development. Hence, they functioned as instruments controlled by the Member States.

Decolonization and its aftermath provided a powerful impetus for taking on operational work, so that more international organizations have become active in relief and development. In essence, they supported the new, nominally sovereign states in their efforts to achieve fuller political and social-economic independence, as well as stability. By taking on operational work, UN organizations increasingly became actors in their own right, in addition to their traditional role as intergovernmental instruments.

Over the years, the growing operational work has posed a dilemma to international organizations. On the one hand, it has allowed them to grow, prosper, and gain global influence. Supporters of international organizations have viewed policy work and building expertise as insufficiently practical. On the other, operational work also entails a pact with the devil; these organizations supposedly can pick up the pieces in ill-functioning states where other governments neither want nor dare to tread. As a result, they are often active in places and on issues that are economically or geostrategically marginalized. Working in these areas is extremely frustrating.

In some regions, international organizations have even taken over or replaced central or local government tasks. This has increased responsibility, and, as Rwanda and Somalia showed, failures can have a horrendous impact on the survival and livelihoods of local people. As a result, international organizations function in political quagmires at both the international and national levels. In particular, humanitarianism will "always be as much an emblem of political failure as it is an expression of human decency" (Rieff 1999: 39).[1] Other situations may be less extreme, but the organizations often face similar conditions of political failure and governmental neglect. Lack of consensus among governments on international policy intensifies the predicament of international organizations.

With the decline of the belief in the welfare state and government intervention from the 1970s on, the NGOs became much stronger in structure and in initiating action, as well as more numerous. They were also presumed to be more flexible in their actor role than international governmental organizations, especially those of the UN system. In addition, the precarious financial position of the UN did not leave much space for improving its functioning. This partly explains the rise of NGOs; they could grow and take on tasks, while the UN could not escape its difficult financial position. Yet many of the most active NGOs have also become financially more dependent on donor government contributions, while taking on extremely difficult, complex, long-term operational work in areas such as relief, rebuilding, human rights, and development. In the end, they also gain and suffer simultaneously from the combination of political and governmental neglect. They gain because their role is to carry out work that states either cannot do or do not want to do on their own. They suffer because they get insufficient international support, be it financial or political.

This predicament is not likely to change. Forms of globalization (migration, transport, trade, telecommunication, tourism, but also crime and arms trade) influence or affect more people at different places simultaneously. Some observers advocate giving international organizations a broader role. The shift from the emphasis on sovereignty to universal human rights, and a concomitant emphasis on social and economic rights mirrors the broadening of peacekeeping that took place in the 1990s. Traditional peacekeeping, which essentially meant placing Blue Helmets between warring factions—generally, two states—after a cessation of fighting while peace negotiations intensified, has increasingly been replaced by "second-generation" peacekeeping operations. These peacekeeping operations work in ongoing, usually civil conflicts with the explicit aim of fostering rebuilding and restarting development. Yet rebuilding and development often remain lofty ideals that are insufficiently realized at ground level. International organizations are thus caught in a double bind of increasingly ambitious agendas and insufficient support. This results in pathologies and simultaneous promises that can better be understood by examining the design of international organizations.

The Origin of International Organizations: The Myth of Autonomy

In essence, international organizations are based on a simple premise: states are interdependent—linked across many issue areas. In this section, an ideal-typical lens is trained on the concepts underlying this interdependence. These determine the design or setup of the international system and, as a corollary, of the international organizations in it. Schematically, the origins and necessity of this interdependence lie in the multilevel processes of societal differentiation and integration that characterize many societies but have become especially dominant since the Industrial Revolution. For international organizations, these processes take place in four related ways, namely:

1. division of peoples and territories into states with governments and, in principle, territorial integrity and political independence;
2. functional differentiation among organizations (mandates, demarcating governance issues);
3. division of labor among organizations, organizational units, and employees;
4. separation of decision making and policymaking from execution.

Functional differentiation generally offers the economic benefits of specialization. As early as 1789, Adam Smith (1978: 109) described these benefits in his famous pin factory example. Through specialization the actors can achieve a higher combined output than by working alone. In principle, the actors also possess more knowledge and control over localized and specialized tasks. The negative sides of differentiation comprise long chains of decision making and action that create such problems as overly complicated manufacturing or policy processes, alienation of workers, and a lack of contact with citizens, customers, or beneficiaries.

Differentiation also requires control, which is achieved through the design of self-contained tasks. The basic assumption is that by specializing and localizing tasks, actors—either as a unit or individually—gain greater autonomy to carry out that task without interference by another actor. Autonomy would be complete if these tasks did not require any inputs or other forms of cooperation from other actors. In such an extreme situation, there is no reason to interfere in each other's business: you take care of yourself, I take care of my own business. Autonomy and non-interference are thus based on the design principle of self-contained tasks.

Normally, however, tasks are almost never completely self-contained. Autonomy is thus always limited. For example, in manufacturing, one task leads to another: one person makes a perfect needle head, another puts these heads together with other components, yet another person packs the needles, and so on. In this way, limited autonomy combines independence with interdependence.[2] Moreover, even the manufacturing process itself is embedded in broader systems. A manufacturing process presumes administrative control processes, be they a traditional hierarchy, budgeting, or total quality management. As a consequence, the assumption of autonomy always breaks down in three related ways, which reflect the shortcomings of self-containment, namely:

1. Some tasks need integration because the actor or unit cannot solve common problems, for example, cross-departmental or cross-border ones, alone.
2. The unit or actor breaks down. This always brings up the question as to who is then responsible and who should intercede.
3. Another unit or actor does not respect the autonomy of other actors.

With the first issue, most actors can still get away with some mutual adjustment and joint decision making. Yet over time, most actors and their units develop their own interests, which can hamper integration. In general, the second issue is very complicated, because when an actor breaks down, outside actors need to step in and cooperate to address the consequences of this breakdown. The third issue spells deep and intense conflict.

In sum, the processes of differentiation separate the actors from each other, yet they generally remain to some extent dependent on each other. Autonomy and non-interference reduce interdependence by trying to limit interaction, but this relates to conceptual design, not to operational reality. Hence, the process of differentiation needs, in addition to autonomy, forms of integration. Through differentiation and integration, however, different actors also develop different interests and perceptions. At times, this can foster cooperation; at other times, it can lead to antagonism.[3] In addition, even in this ideal-typical world there is always the problem of dealing with the breakdown of other actors and units.

Looking at the first form of differentiation from an ideal-typical design perspective, the state can be seen as an attempt to reduce interdependence by creating independent, autonomous systems. Ideally, states can concentrate on solving their problems internally and do not need to interfere in each other's business. The constituencies of these states build up one—or more—political, economic, social, and cultural systems, and they formulate foreign policy.[4] Along this line, as long as states respect each other's territorial integrity and political independence, the international system would not run into problems. Discussing development discourse about Lesotho, Ferguson (1994: 64) calls this the principle of governmentality: "'Development' discourse does not usually assume that the government has absolute and total control, of course, but it does systematically tend to produce analyses which suggest that that which is under state control is determinant, while that which lies beyond its control is secondary."

Governmentality results from a focus on self-contained tasks. And indeed, when such containment shows its shortcomings, from the Rhine Commission to the World Trade Organization (WTO), states institutionalize issues of the environment, development, economics, and cultural ties—as well as migration and other cross-border activities—through setting up international organizations. To a very large extent, these issues can be dealt with through the decisions and norm setting of the intergovernmental machinery. But when there is a breakdown, for example, a Sierra Leone in conflict or economic underdevelopment, other actors have to step in. In any case, for many developing states, sovereign autonomy is more a design principle than a reality. Sovereignty never describes the actuality; striving for self-containment would be a more apt description.[5]

The second form of differentiation, into organizations, also leads to incomplete autonomy and interdependence. In principle, an organization focuses on a few tasks for which it can become self-contained. Public organizations traditionally focus on one (or only a few) functional areas. Private organizations generally focus on core businesses. Yet even as officially independent legal persons, organizations need to exchange goods and services to survive. In this way, the tasks of an organization are never fully self-contained; as a consequence, the organization is always embedded in a broader system of competing and cooperating organizations. Functional organizations in particular encounter challenges with multifunctional—in other words, multidisciplinary—issues.

The third form of differentiation, within organizations, implies that while different departments, divisions, or strategic business units may be good at their core tasks, they always need cooperation, if not integration, with other parts of the organization. Meeting this need becomes the task of the organizational management, by means of, for example, setting a strategy.

Finally, the last form of differentiation, separating decision making and policymaking from implementation, sharply profiles the limits of autonomy. Rare is the situation in which decision making or policy processes are self-contained tasks separated from their implementation. It may be designed this way, but such design assumes stable, predictable environments. In more rapidly changing environments, these processes require feedback and reaction from each other.

In sum, differentiation can be addressed by designing self-contained tasks, which grants a higher degree of autonomy to the specific actor involved. Structuring self-contained tasks is a form of design, in other words, a form of organizing. As a design principle, it may seem perfect and a satisfactory guide to human action, but the reality may be quite different. Some forms of self-contained tasks contradict each other. The strong distinction between decision making and implementation as separate, self-contained tasks, moreover, does not facilitate action at the field level but helps to maintain the myth of sovereign, independent—largely self-contained—states. In a similar vein, international organizations are an acknowledgment that states are interdependent and that these cannot go it alone. This leads to the paradoxical situation that interdependent states control international governmental organizations in order to safeguard as much as possible their independence.

Too much attention to the self-containment of one type of actor leads to a twisted understanding of the relative autonomy of another. International relations theory too often argues that sovereign states dominate international organizations. Business and public administration theories generally focus on organizations as autonomous units fighting for survival and describe the integration of organizational subunits, such as departments and divisions, into the overall organization. In particular, in business administration, governments and politics tend to be seen as nuisances. Further, development theorists frequently argue that the local population cannot participate enough and that both donor states and international organizations are too imperious. These three strands of theory cannot all be right at the same time. Sovereignty and autonomy are always limited. The question then becomes: To what extent are the differently organized tasks self-contained and where and how is self-containment limited? The answer makes it possible to assess which actor controls another.

Differentiation and Integration in Practice

When international organizations confine themselves to helping states negotiate binding or recommended international rules and standards, and if they act as forums for information exchange and debate, they generally avoid serious friction with governments. States either adjust unaided to each other or else make decisions jointly in the intergovernmental machinery—for example, in the G7 or the UN General Assembly—and effectuate these with or without support from an international organization as an expert center.

When, however, international organizations start operational tasks in the diverse fields of development, relief, human rights, environment, and security, conflicts of interest may emerge at both the international and national level. States may disagree with each other on the proper roles and tasks of the international organizations, as with SHD; or one or more states may quarrel with, withdraw support from, or even abandon an international organization, as has happened with UNCTAD.

Operational tasks also inevitably add managerial complexity. In their operations, international organizations not only deal with the central government, but also need to cooperate with subnational governmental institutions, as well as with segments of civil society, such as the private sector and the local population. When parts of society promote different interests, which can reach extreme levels during armed conflict or deep corruption, the functioning of international organizations suffers or even collapses. In severe and increasingly evident cases, international organizations nevertheless address the problems of state failure, as during the complex emergency in Somalia.

Internally, international organizations also confront the twin processes of differentiation and integration. For most, this takes place as functional differentiation into several sectors, such as health and agriculture. Many

UN organizations were set up to resemble national functionally based bureaucracies, such as the ministries of health and agriculture. Many NGOs have also established similar specific sectors of expertise. Still, the problems in the field do not necessarily follow this sectoral setup. For example, the differentiation of international organizations into security, development, and humanitarian organizations and divisions reflects the design of these organizations; it does not reflect the situation on the ground in, say, Kosovo.

The crucial operational question centers on determining when an international organization takes over the tasks of the state. This question implicitly acknowledges that the design principle of governmentality confuses self-containment with autonomy. It poses a spate of new operational questions: When should an international organization intervene in a nominally sovereign—so-called autonomous—state? Does the international organization have sufficient expertise in its mandated areas of interest and others related to it? Consequently, it becomes crucial to determine how other actors operate and how they can be coordinated to offer the multisectoral action that allows sustainable, peaceful development.

In the actuality of daily practice, the presumed self-contained character of an organization guides its actions in the field. It is designed to look at most problems through the lens of its expertise, generally in a functional sector. Its perspective gains reinforcement from the impetus of organizational survival, which discourages giving up autonomy through cooperation. Most international organizations confront the same paradox: they need to cooperate or coordinate at the field level because of weighty political problems and the need to spend limited resources efficiently, yet they also need to compete in order to acquire as much of the limited resources as possible.

Within organizations, a related process of differentiation takes place. International governmental organizations officially function on behalf of the Member States. These states provide funding, set mandates, determine policies, approve programs, and appoint senior management. NGOs also have to be accountable to their donors, generally the same donor governments that finance the UN system (compare Biekart 1999: 61; Duffield 1994: 59). As argued above, decision making and policymaking tend to become separated from implementation. Cultural differences and geographical distances further aggravate this separation. In particular, the distinction between the cultures of headquarters and the field for both international non-governmental organizations and governmental organizations is notorious. Likewise, huge differences usually exist between the final decision documents of international conferences and the actual follow-up actions in the field. As a result, many UN organizations and NGOs have internal command and control problems. In addition, they often work parallel or complementary to state structures, which opens up yet another set of coordination problems.

Differentiation and integration lead to widely different procedures among organizations, as well as to very different organizational forms. When organizations can work independently, procedural differences may not be significant, but when they must cooperate, conflicts may flare. Moreover, together all of these organizations form erratically grown systems in which ad hoc solutions among individual organizations and states linger on. These systems only adapt incrementally (see Smillie 1998: 81–82). Indeed, nobody with a sane mind would have designed the humanitarian relief system as it exists today. Often the local population gets lost in such complicated systems.

In sum, the processes of differentiation and integration operate in different parts of our world at different societal levels and have led to many different types of international organizations. These organizations address issues that states alone cannot or will not address. When they do operational work, they actually take over tasks that would be done by the government in a well-functioning state. Given the important role of states, international organizations have to steer clear between the Scylla of donor dependence and the Charybdis of maintaining autonomy purely for organizational survival. In both cases, the local population can go astray in the maze of international politics and bureaucracy.

What the Model Explains

This section focuses on the operational management of international organizations. These organizations are, in principle, set up to address societal issues; they rely on the assumption that they can ultimately transfer resources and knowledge to people who need them. They operate simultaneously in two arenas: a strategic arena, in which goals are set and decisions are being made; and an implementing arena, in which these goals and decisions should be translated into action in order to help people.[6] Ideally, the latter happens in close cooperation with these people. International organizations form the link between those two arenas; they are intermediary organizations.[7]

As occupants of two arenas, their different functions usually give international organizations the status of outsiders. They are able to transfer resources and knowledge that they can acquire from the rich industrialized countries. Still, they remain dependent on the collectivity of providers of resources, who often also shape the decisions in the strategic arena. Those groups with whom they work in the implementing arena rarely provide sufficient resources and do not always have a voice in the international organization itself. Consequently, neither the arenas nor the international organization are fully self-contained, and they have only limited autonomy.[8]

Knowledge of the intermediary characteristics of international organizations is a prerequisite to understanding their management. Practically,

FIGURE 11.1 The Humanitarian System

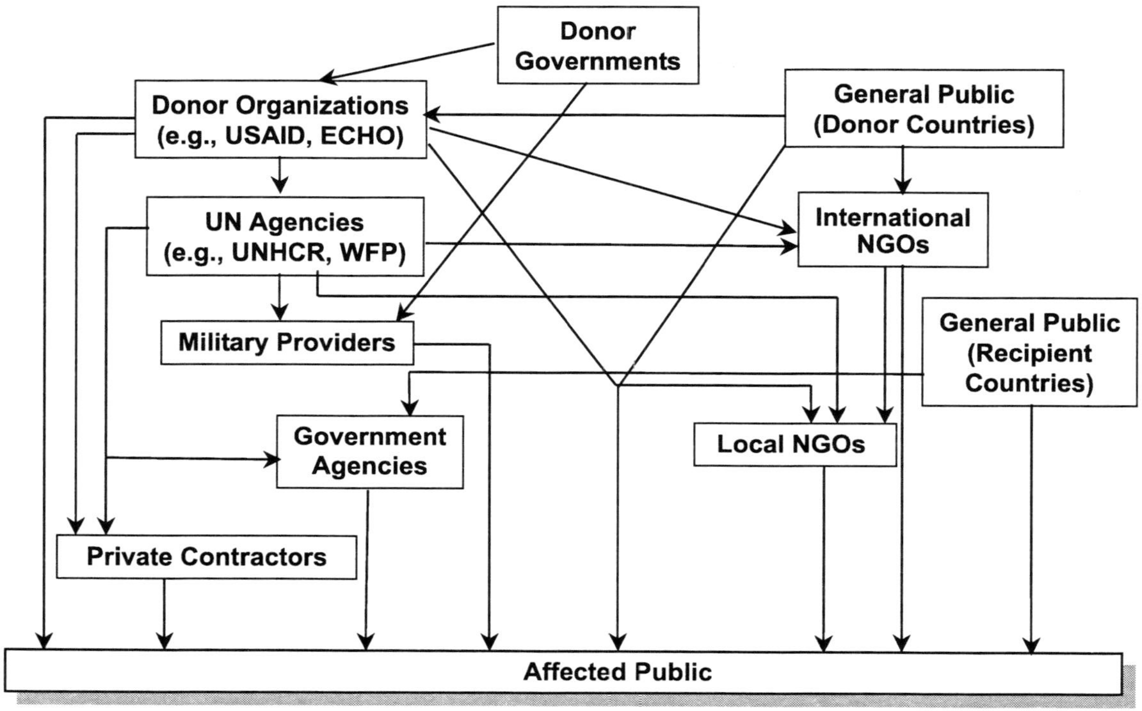

Source: Based on International Federation of Red Cross and Red Crescent Societies (1996: 59).

FIGURE 11.2 The International Organization between Two Different Arenas

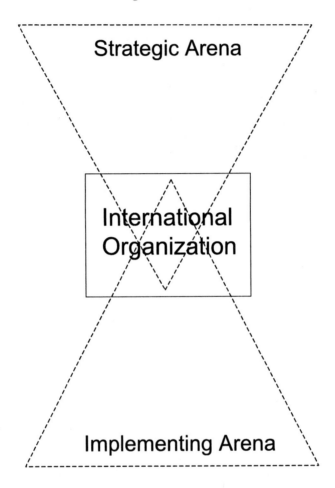

this requires insight in both arenas, as well as an understanding of the internal management processes of individual organizations. Furthermore, the actual complexity and diversity of management reflects the several implementing and strategic arenas in which these organizations need to operate simultaneously.

In the strategic arena, the donor governments set the goals and policies of the international organizations, generally through an assembly or executive board. Each donor may pursue its own ends. In different ways, the chapters by Hüfner and Fomerand in this volume detail the consequences of donor behavior for the financial position of the UN and its relation to North-South antagonism. Recipient governments and other actors may also affect decisions. Moreover, the issues that play in the strategic arena can be highly contentious, including not merely financing, but also forms of intervention, power relations between states, and the nationality of political appointees. Although NGOs and UN organizations can differ widely in their specific arenas, they generally have to deal with an overriding tone setting from the strategic arena.[9]

In coping with the strategic arena, managers of international organizations need diplomatic skills. Often they can promote ambiguity in the debates and decisions, and so facilitate compromise, accommodation, and cooperation among actors with different interests. At least, they should be able to lessen political tensions and avoid dysfunctional directives. Once decisions, mandates, recommendations, and wishes are set out, international organizations have to translate them into the implementing arena by such means as program management and advocacy.

Such action in the implementing arena can be difficult indeed. Possible obstacles range from competing demands from local parties, to corruption, to a lack of competence on the part of recipient governments and of other counterparts. The latter may include other international organizations, NGOs, and local administrations. Sometimes, geographical distances, cultural sensitivities, or something as simple as a faulty phone line can obstruct implementation. Generally, implementation requires patience and persistence.

In short, the international organization needs a political logic in both arenas. This logic raises the question as to whether it is possible to solve collective problems, preferably in a more or less democratic manner (Finger 2001). Understanding power relationships is a crucial part of the political logic.

In the implementing arena, an organization has to obtain official permission from the relevant national government before setting to work. This formal requirement can sometimes become an obstacle and can in some cases simply be ignored. In South Sudan, for instance, some NGOs go in directly without permission. The implementing arena also requires a political logic, but the actual political tactics differ from country to country and from the political logic in the strategic arena. In the latter, a semblance of democracy lingers in the formal rules. In many implementing arenas, special complexity may emerge from the need to deal with such local factors as a corrupt elite or a contentious religious movement. The chapters by Dijkzeul (program management), Smith (CIVPOL), de Waal (human rights organizations), and Smillie and Evenson (capacity building and democratization in Bosnia and Herzegovina) all describe both characteristic complexities in the implementing arena and the strong impact of the strategic arena.

Internally, however, the operational tasks of the international organization are far more straightforward. These tasks are based on a managerial logic that centers on providing goods and services efficiently and effectively (Finger 2001). For international organizations, this means programming for delivering services, training, technology transfer, and advocacy, with the ultimate aim of building national and local capacities for self-reliance. To be successful in these operational tasks, management has to eschew ambiguity. Directness, as well as clear guidance and goals from the actors in the strategic arena, facilitate program management, but this occurs only infrequently. Internally, accountability requires explicit goals, clear lines of authority, and unambiguous delineation of responsibility, as well as strong evaluation and follow-up. This is based on a managerial logic that emphasizes the values of authenticity (managers mean what they say) and sincerity (managers really do what they say they will do). Without these values, implementing organizational change or programs will at first be haphazard and later will become harder, if not impossible.

These, then, are the two central management problems of international organizations. First, they need to be able to use a political logic in both the strategic arena and the implementing arena in order to avoid political pitfalls in resolving collective issues. Only in rare cases will complete clarity carry the day. Second, international organizations nevertheless need a managerial logic in their internal management to achieve results in delivering goods and services in the implementing arena. Integrating the two logics and arenas is difficult.

The implementing arena needs to be understood on its own terms. The perceptions in the strategic arena, which is removed from the field, are not necessarily valid in this arena. The main problem that the international organization faces in the implementing arena is that it comes in as an outsider equipped with resources, knowledge, and often good intentions into local situations that can be very hard to understand. The power relationships, social exclusion, and political volatility of complex emergencies are a case in point. More generally, the needs and capacities of the local population are often ill understood. Hence, management needs political astuteness and often ambiguity in both arenas. International organizations use at least three political approaches, depending on the local circumstances.

1. They use ambiguity and compromise, which allows them to achieve at least part of their goals.
2. They are confrontational, as, for example, some international NGOs are in South Sudan.
3. They become technocratic, which allows the organization to carry out its tasks by pretending that its operational work is value-free and definitely not political.

Actors in both arenas generally do not know each other well enough for meaningful interaction or understanding. After all, not many district midwives address the UN Security Council. In sum, international organizations display several typical management problems that result from the myth of sovereignty (autonomy) of states.

1. International organizations are outsiders. At times they will not understand the local situation, or they are limited in their responsiveness. Building up local capacity takes time. Applying the political logic astutely is difficult.
2. International organizations generally come in when a problem— underdevelopment, overpopulation, pollution, or conflict—is already playing out in full force. So they are almost always late; prevention does not get sufficient attention.
3. They tend to be or become donor-driven.
4. International organizations have an implicit top-down perspective. As outsiders, they bring in intellectual, political, and financial resources that local actors often lack. By focusing on local needs instead of capacities, international organizations start from the assumption that they provide and local actors receive.

Relevant managerial logic is necessary to identify and overcome the related problems of originally being an outsider, being late, being donor-driven, and having an implicit top-down perspective. Addressing these four general problems requires clear and fast procedures, responsiveness, and accountability. Without clarity—or, more specifically, authenticity and sincerity—this is impossible to achieve. Frequently, the concurrence of the political logic and the managerial logic creates a tension between ambiguity that is directed externally and clarity that is required for internal management.

Most managers are not able to carry on this balancing act, because it poses contradictory demands. Overcoming the problems of being a late-coming outsider is challenging enough, but the political pressures, especially those from the strategic arena, are even harder. For example, the staff available to an executive head may be unable to maintain this continuous balancing act. In addition, occasionally an appointee will be pushed—sometimes openly so, but most often only informally—by an interested government. Especially if the candidate is not up to the job or dissatisfies other donors, the appointment of such a person will likely frustrate his or her new colleagues. Yet declining to accept the political appointee will also dissatisfy the appointee's supporters. In addition, other organizations, NGOs and UN, that compete for funding or other resources often benefit when the other party performs badly. Over time, the executive head is likely to err internally with too much ambiguity or externally with too much clarity at the wrong moment. As a result, most organizations become politicized after several years, which in turn leads to a lack of effectiveness in the field.

The manager's job is further complicated by the fact that some strategic arenas pose different politicized issues, such as abortion or free world trade, or because of imperfect technocratic solutions, as is the case with tropical illnesses such as malaria. If the strategic arena is highly politicized—that is, posing controversial social choices—the international organization will also become politicized. This effect deepens the complexity of managing. It can, for example, prevent necessary decentralization to the field, as central management strives to prevent political clashes.[10]

Yet such a tendency to centralization can obstruct work in the implementing arena. For example, as a result of its mandate in population, which automatically touches on political issues such as abortion, premarital sex, the position of women, and the possible use of forced population polices, the United Nations Population Fund (UNFPA) management was under pressure to avoid scandals and other unwelcome attention. It thus was under pressure to centralize; yet effectiveness at the field level required decentralization. UNFPA management thus found itself in a bind from which it was hard to escape.

An organization can sometimes find advantages in operating in several strategic arenas simultaneously. OXFAM, CARE, MSF, and other organizations have established their own national offices within donor countries. By doing this, they can tailor their activities to specific partners, whether national or subnational governments, private enterprise, or the general public. Although this decentralization in the strategic arena facilitates fundraising and international advocacy, it can also lead attention away from other national offices and field operations. At times, it also causes tensions among the management of different national organizations that can permeate their field operations. For example, MSF France sometimes has a tense working relationship with MSF Belgium or MSF Holland. The well-known friction between the ICRC and IFRC also illustrates this fraught relationship.

As with the strategic arena, some implementing arenas are harder to cope with than others. Complex emergencies present the most severe problems. The organizations need considerable political acumen to understand the volatile and violent local power relationships without getting caught up in them. Conventional development cooperation also presents difficulties: it is essentially an attempt to change the behavior of other actors. Success is therefore always indirect and dependent on these others, whether a local community or the central bank.

NGOs often can choose to engage different countries and thus differing strategic arenas. As for implementing arenas, any particular organization rarely wants to act in only one country. UN organizations pride themselves in their universality. Most NGOs try to apply their trade in different areas. This increases opportunities for obtaining resources and motivates many employees. Yet implementing arenas do differ: The Gambia is not Bangladesh; eradicating polio differs from building roads. And the organization will at least initially be an outsider in an unfamiliar implementing arena.

The next problem is that not all organizations fulfill the same kinds of tasks. Other issues for management reflect the differences in the tasks

FIGURE 11.3 The Multiplication of Arenas

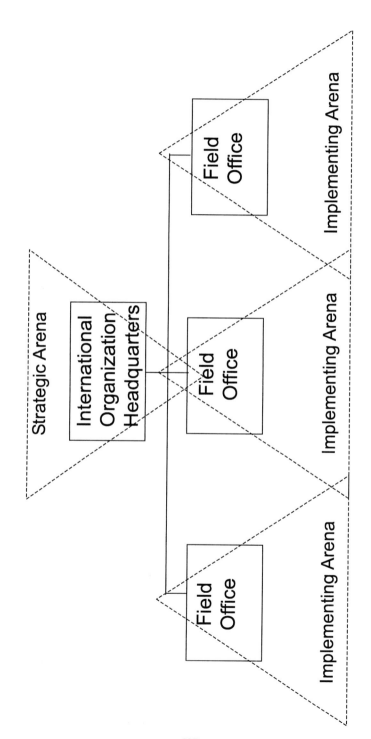

undertaken by international organizations. Some are essentially funding organizations, that distribute their resources to other organizations. Subsequently, they check and support management, program delivery, and outcomes. For example, a Northern NGO helps a Southern NGO, or UNFPA helps fund population activities in an African country through the local Ministry of Health and Social Work. The chapter by Smillie and Evenson on Bosnia and Herzegovina indicates the many problems that result from such cooperation.

Furthermore, the local organization sometimes subcontracts to other national or local organizations. These further forms of differentiation lead to elaborate chains of action, complex interorganizational networks, and unclear accountability.[11] Ad hoc solutions, as noted earlier, linger on. Vested interests and the desire to maintain some organizational autonomy create and maintain these unwieldy networks.

Shortcomings and Strengths of the Model

Like all models, this model is a simplification of actuality. It lacks, for example, the dynamic capacity to show how different concepts in development theory and public administration have shaped the actual functioning of organizations.[12] Nevertheless, the model does highlight the main characteristics of the management of international organizations.

The model draws its main strength from the empirical comparisons in the preceding chapters, which show that despite the influence of governments, international organizations strive to maintain autonomy. Both state sovereignty and organizational autonomy are limited in application as a result of the design principle of self-contained tasks. At the same time, the model explains the lack of bottom-up initiative, the absence of which many development scholars lament. It also explains the similarities in the shortcomings of both international NGOs and IGOs. The specific organizations and arenas may be different, but all international organizations have to deal with the central problems of intermediary organizations: two different arenas and a double political and managerial logic. Monodisciplinary explanations often fail to take into account the complexity of international organizations as intermediary organizations. Hence, scholars and practitioners applying the model can also encourage cross-fertilization among the disciplines of international relations, business administration, and public administration.

Cures

The Individual Organization

After reading the chapters in this book, one might conclude that international organizations are either so complex or pathological that their management cannot be improved. That conclusion would be mistaken. An analysis of the double balancing act of two arenas and two logics leads to the identification of possible cures.

1. *Acknowledge the problems.* Despite the cycles of high hopes for and disillusionment with international organizations and the vociferous criticism they receive, their management hardly receives full or continuous attention in either academia or media (see the introduction). Acknowledging the difficulties with the double arenas and dual logics would forestall some of the high hopes and should thus prevent some of the disillusionment. It would also lead to a better understanding of the limitations of international organizations.

The principal causes for the malfunctioning of international organizations lie with the actors in the strategic arena—in particular, the national governments when they fail to provide sufficient support. The specific problems in the implementing arena further explain a lack of results. In both cases, these problems are part and parcel of the daily functioning of these organizations, but are hardly caused exclusively by them. For governments, international organizations fulfill a positive function whether they fail or succeed. If they fail, they are convenient scapegoats. If they succeed, the governments can continue to hand over tasks in those regions where they do not want to interfere. In any case, our indelible question concerns how to address these problems. International organizations are limited by design; looking beyond those givens will uncover complementary cures.

2. *Build consensus.* Since international organizations are intermediary organizations, it follows that the more aligned the two arenas of their concern may be, the easier their functioning becomes. Some strategic arenas are notoriously difficult, such as the population field, with its issues of abortion, premarital sex, and reproductive health rights. How to align the two arenas? A basic answer is by fostering consensus, which underlines the importance of advocacy for these organizations. Consensus ideally consists of two components:

- *Agreement on a basic substantive issue.* In contrast to the population field, improving the lot of children often gains widespread support; at the very least, there is not much vocal opposition. This popular consensus makes the work of UNICEF and Save the Children easier. It helps with fundraising and implementation.
- *Technocratic approaches.* Without instruments, action becomes difficult or even impossible. Without a medicine, an illness cannot be cured. The availability of such technocratic solutions can help to depoliticize issues. UNICEF, for example, was extremely successful in the late 1980s and early 1990s, with its GOBI measures, which supported Growth Monitoring, Oral Rehydration, Breastfeeding, and Immunization. With these technologically rather simple measures, it has

been possible to reduce child mortality rates dramatically in many countries. In contrast, managing AIDS is still difficult, because there is no cure. UNCTAD's difficulties show that it lacks agreement on its basic substantive issue and possesses only weak technocratic means to carry out its mandate. SHD advocates and human rights organizations have to cope with similar problems. Performance measurement—or actually, the philosophy behind it—offers a technocratic approach to improve UNCIVPOL.

3. *Strengthen management*. International organizations can use innovative general management techniques, varying from strategic management to total quality management and benchmarking. Many of them try the latest management fads and are prone to the same management mistakes as other organizations. In addition, most management techniques stem from profit-making enterprises and are not geared toward working with the double arena and both logics that characterize international organizations. Frequently, these techniques stress only the managerial logic. As a consequence, international organizations apply management tools that are imperfectly suited to their tasks. Although these organizations have the whole regular management tool kit at their disposal, the application of these tools requires adaptation to both logics and arenas. No magic formula exists to solve the contradictory demands inherent to this adaptation. On the positive side, when a managerial technique works well under the adverse conditions of an international organization, then it is likely to function well for other organizations, too.

4. *Rotate staff*. The more staff members learn about both arenas and logics, the better they and their organizations can function. Staff rotation provides a simple tool to achieve this. Many UN organizations and NGOs employ rotation schemes. Yet many staff members dislike moving from one country to another, and many prefer to stay at headquarters. Most organizations, unfortunately, fail to reap the benefits of rotation because they have not (yet) incorporated the information it generates into regular learning and evaluation mechanisms.

5. *Encourage upward accountability*. On all levels of their management and in all stages of their programming, international organizations should dilute their implicit outsider, top-down approaches with far more attention to the local populations. In some cases, this will mean reforming organizational procedures in order to become a better "listener," as the World Bank claims to have done. At the very least, programming and evaluation techniques should always be participatory. This can result in heavy demands on managers, but it is necessary to ensure sustainability. Local capacities should be identified better and used more often. Ombudsman procedures, possibilities for complaint, and so on should also be instituted to a far greater degree. Ideally, local NGOs and communities should carry out evaluations of the quality of their donors and providers of technical

support, but this happens too rarely. The central problem will always be how to get information from the implementing arena to the strategic arena. Such upward accountability is difficult, but not impossible.

6. *Aim for transparency.* Finally, transparency of decisional and administrative processes is crucial. When politicization carries the day, people forget that carefully improving and analyzing management data often offers keys for improvement. Internally, linking budgeting and performance measurement (see Smith's chapter) can be taken much further. Externally, ameliorating the quality of advocacy remains crucial. Some of Kappeler's optimism on information technology can be shared not only with regard to diplomacy, but also for all work of international organizations. It is indeed easier nowadays to link work in the implementing arena with the strategic arena. Yet this is only one step in the long process of ensuring greater transparency and upward accountability.

All six strategies discussed here share two characteristics. They link the strategic and implementing arenas closer to each other, and they acknowledge and counteract the usual shortcomings of self-contained tasks. Their application, especially in a joint manner, would align the two arenas and further their overlapping. This would improve the management of international organizations. Without waiting for states to take action, organizations could strengthen their function by adopting these strategies.

Relationships among Organizations

The six strategies for improving management mentioned above can also help with bettering interorganizational relationships. First of all, when one organization puts its own house in order, it facilitates cooperation with other organizations. Good quality information or the mere absence of delays can already have a great impact. Second, the same strategies can be applied jointly by several organizations.

1. *Acknowledge the problem.* Just being able to state the problem is even more important. Messy international structures and networks cannot be cleaned up easily, which is in a sense acknowledged by slight attempts to do so. Open acknowledgment of the stubborn difficulties would perhaps prevent the cycle of high hopes and subsequent disillusionment, but it alone would not lead to real improvement in effectiveness. For that, the other strategies are required.

2. *Build consensus.* Building consensus is even harder among organizations than among colleagues within an organization. Normally, one organization will have to take the lead. Modern mass media offer new opportunities for either building international consensus or destroying it. The recent campaign to ban landmines provides a successful example of consensus building.[13]

3. *Strengthen management.* Sound interorganizational management requires considerable training and takes time. Most academic education

and organization training falls short in this respect. As earlier noted, the suitability of general management techniques is limited. The main contribution that an individual organization can make to interorganizational cooperation is to have its own house in order.

4. *Rotate staff.* Rotation of staff members among different organizations has been institutionalized only to a very limited extent, mainly by UN organizations. It would be useful if bilateral organizations, NGOs, and UN organizations could exchange staff more frequently among each other. However, different human resources management practices and outdated procedures tend to prevent this. Such rotation could be used as a learning tool, if organizations were prepared to build on the experience and criticism of the exchange staff.

5. *Encourage upward accountability.* Organizations need to take into account the impact of their own work on that of others. If they fail to incorporate an assessment of this impact into their regular procedures, improvement will depend only on ad hoc initiatives by well-meaning individuals.[14] Performance measurement and information technology, as Smith and Kappeler describe in their chapters, also have the potential to improve upward accountability.[15] Ultimately, the local population, or their representatives, should be enabled to evaluate the role and cooperation of donors and international organizations.

6. *Aim for transparency.* The way in which international organizations combine the political and managerial logics against and with each other receives too little attention. Simultaneous competition, cooperation, and coordination require more attention. It would greatly help everyone if international organizations were allowed to go bankrupt more often. The international development and humanitarian systems do not punish malfunctioning organizations strongly enough. This immunity could be defended as long as the causes of malfunctioning lie outside the international organization with the donor governments in the strategic arena, as with funding the UN system. When organizations malfunction in the field, they should either improve or go out of existence. Establishing the legal, managerial, and economic incentives to create such a system needs far more attention than is currently available.[16]

Just as UNCTAD was largely bypassed by WTO, it is highly likely that intermediary organizations will face a hard time when donors directly fund the activities of their Southern counterparts, which is currently starting to happen. Ultimately, such bypasses may force some international organizations, including those of the UN, out of business. At the very least, they will have to shape up their management considerably.

At the interorganizational level of analysis, the limitations of creating self-contained tasks become immediately visible, because interorganizational relationships by definition transcend self-containment. For improving the situation, the onus is on the governments as the main players of the strategic arena. In all likelihood, improvements to the haphazardly designed interorganizational relationships will only be incremental. In any case, reforming one organization is more readily achieved than reforming an interorganizational system.

Conclusions

International organizations are subject to widespread criticism. In order to promote better understanding of them, the authors of this volume have assembled more empirical material than usually underpins critical treatment of the management of international agencies. They have indicated pathologies in many different areas, namely:

- limited funding, and withholding funding to exert influence;
- antiquated personnel management;
- incomplete organizational adaptation to changing circumstances and ideologies;
- North-South antagonism and its impact on sustainable human development;
- uncritical application of program procedures, which hampers local participation;
- fraud, nepotism, and corruption;
- difficult implementation and measurement of activities of civilian police forces;
- too narrow interpretation of human rights by international organizations;
- haphazard and ill-directed funding of civil society in order to promote democracy.

At various points, the authors have used theories and insights from the disciplines of international relations, business administration, and public administration. They have also paid considerable attention to problems of implementation and internal functioning. Finally, they have pointed out the importance of Southern perspectives and experiences. The fact that goals and ideals of international organizations seemingly remain beyond reach suggests a systemic design fault. We posit that self-contained tasks were confused with organizational autonomy and national sovereignty. This has led us to develop an alternative model of international organizations as intermediary organizations that are active in both the implementing and strategic arenas to explain the functioning of these organizations.

In most international relations literature, the assumption prevails that international organizations are largely dependent on states. But it is more accurate to state that they have to carry out a difficult double balancing act of two arenas (implementing and strategic) and two logics (political and managerial) that combine in manifold ways and that contradict the design principle of self-contained, autonomous entities at different levels of society.

Strategies for improvement exist. As intermediaries, international organizations can align the arenas through the six strategies for improvement set out here. While these strategies are no magic eraser to rub out all faults, together they alleviate politicking, conflicts of interest, low-quality media attention, and substandard scholarship. Pathologies are not an immutable given. They can be understood as opportunities for strategic choices to bring promises closer to performance.

Notes

1. Rieff (1999: 39) continues "humanitarians occupy the central role in these crises precisely because they are otherwise of so little geo-strategic or economic importance to the powers that could intervene militarily, or use their diplomatic clout to change the situation on the ground for the better far more effectively than the most dedicated humanitarian can ever hope to. To put it starkly, MSF has a place at the table about Rwanda because so few institutions care about Rwanda."

2. Hence, such limited autonomy only assumes that the actor or unit is generally able to take care of itself, and that it keeps its own house in order in relation to a specific set of self-contained tasks.

3. The classic study of interdependence, which takes a much broader perspective than this paragraph, has been written by Keohane and Nye (1989). The world has changed considerably since they wrote their book.

4. See Ratner (1997: 33–34) for a more elaborate discussion of sovereignty as an amorphous concept.

5. Strictly speaking, sovereignty is a legal concept and points to absolute control by each state of its own affairs, that is, a solute self-containment. In application in the actual world, sovereignty describes only the aspiration of the law. In actuality, it describes nothing at all outside the legal textbooks.

6. Putnam's (1988) article on the logic of two-level games theory is somewhat similar, but it essentially deals with the interplay between diplomatic negotiations at the interstate level and domestic politics. Negotiators have to reach agreement in international negotiations, while they also need acceptance of decisions nationally. In contrast, international organizations possess less autonomy than the politicians and government officials in this theory. Their life is more complicated; even if they are in total alignment with the strategic arena, they still have to work in the implementing arena with many different actors at various level of society. Especially taking into account the role of the different national governments, one can speak of a multilevel theory for international organizations. The two arenas summarize these levels.

7. The intermediary position comes close to the double principal-agent relationship that Eliassen and Kooiman (1993: 1) posit for all public organizations.

8. Weiss et al. (2001: 312) speak of "'two United Nations': the first, where governments meet and make decisions, and the second, comprising the various secretariats, officials, and soldiers who implement these decisions." This perspective offers an interesting similarity with the two arenas, although the authors do not work out this distinction from a management perspective.

9. The actual way in which states control international organizations depends largely on the setup of these organizations. UN organizations have Member States that make

decisions and provide (too little) funding. By following the concept of sovereignty, many international organizations, in particular, those of the UN system, are actually designed to have decisions made by an intergovernmental machinery far removed from implementation in the field. Supposedly, states have a more indirect relationship with NGOs. These NGOs should then have greater autonomy to act on their own volition. In practice, however, governments do have a big influence through funding, national laws, and other legal obligations.

10. It can be argued that the nature of most international organizations, especially UN organizations, is political from inception, and therefore the point about the politicization of international organizations is described more negatively than should be the case. The fact that staff is often politically inept is then more an indictment of the personnel recruitment/selection process than of the organization and its design. In other words, the complexity of politics within and among international organizations is a given. Therefore, the managers of international organizations should be both technically and politically competent no matter in which arena they find themselves. If they are incompetent in one or both capacities, they share some of the responsibility for the malfunctioning of international organizations. However, while this argument is valid about the recruitment process, its conclusion does insufficiently acknowledge that the management of international organizations continuously has to juggle contradictory demands from both the strategic and implementing arenas, as well as both logics. It is near impossible to do this successfully over long periods of time.

11. Biekart (1999) provides a clear description of the elaborate aid chains in Central America.

12. Other factors that deserve attention include short-term interests and ethical aspects of the decision making and actions of states and organizations.

13. At a more operational level, the joint evaluations and studies of the Active Learning Network for Accountability and Performance in Humanitarian Assistance (ALNAP) illustrate practical opportunities for improving humanitarian assistance.

14. For an overview of coordination issues from a managerial perspective, see Dijkzeul (1997).

15. In the humanitarian field, recent initiatives to strengthen accountability include the Ombudsman Project and the Sphere Project on the formulation of a humanitarian charter and minimum standards in disaster response.

16. In this respect, Maynard (1999: 149) argues that "the NGO community as a whole has had few institutional mechanisms for establishing and accepting standards of self-regulation" (see also note 15).

Bibliography

Biekart, K. *The Politics of Civil Society Building: European Private Aid Agencies and Democratic Transitions in Central America.* Utrecht/Amsterdam: International Books and The Transnational Institute, 1999.

Dijkzeul, D. *The Management of Multilateral Organizations.* The Hague/London/Boston: Kluwer Law International, 1997.

Duffield, M. "The Political Economy of Internal War: Asset Transfer, Complex Emergencies and International Aid." Pp. 50–69, in Macrae, J., and Zwi, A., eds. *War and Hunger: Rethinking International Responses to Complex Emergencies.* London: Zed Books with Save The Children Fund (UK), 1994.

Eliassen, K.J., and Kooiman, J., eds. *Managing Public Organizations: Lessons from Contemporary European Experience.* London/Thousand Oaks/New Delhi: Sage Publications, 1993.

Ferguson, J. *The Anti-Politics Machine: "Development," Depoliticization, and Bureaucratic Power in Lesotho.* Minneapolis/London: University of Minneapolis, 1994.

Finger, M. *College Notes 2001 of Guest Lecture at SIPA.* New York: Columbia University, 2001.

International Federation of Red Cross and Red Crescent Societies. *World Disasters Report 1996.* Oxford: Oxford University Press, 1996.

Keohane, R.O., and Nye, J.S. *Power and Interdependence.* 2nd ed. New York: HarperCollins Publishers, 1989.

Maynard, K.A. *Healing Communities in Conflict: International Assistance in Complex Emergencies.* New York: Columbia University Press, 1999.

Putnam, R.D. "Diplomacy and Domestic Politics: The Logic of Two-Level Games." *International Organization*, no. 42 (1988): 427–460.

Ratner, S. *The New UN Peacekeeping: Building Peace in Lands of Conflict After the Cold War.* London: MacMillan Press, 1997.

Rieff, D. "Moral Imperatives and Political Realities: Response to 'Principles, Politics, and Humanitarian Action.'" *Ethics and International Affairs*, vol. 13 (1999): 35–42.

Smillie, I. "Relief and Development: The Struggle for Synergy." *Occasional Paper of the Watson Institute*, no. 33. Providence: Brown University, Thomas J. Watson Jr. Institute for International Studies, 1998.

Smith, A. *An Inquiry into the Nature and Causes of the Wealth of Nations, Books I–III.* London: Penguin Classic Books, 1978 [1776].

Weiss, T.G., Forsythe, P.D., and Coate, R.A. *The United Nations and Changing World Politics.* Boulder: Westview Press, 2001.

CONTRIBUTORS

Yves Beigbeder (ybeigbed@easynet.fr) started his professional career as an intern at the Nuremberg trials. He earned an M.Sc.Ed in 1948 and a Ph.D. in Public Law in 1973. He was Personnel Officer at FAO and WHO (1951–1984). He now works as a Senior Fellow of UNITAR and as Chairman of the Conciliation Board, ESA. He is also a Board Member of the Union of International Associations, and a lecturer in international organization and administration at universities in Paris, Geneva, and North America. Finally, he is also legal counsel to international civil servants. He has written several books and articles on international organization and administration, and on international criminal justice. His latest books include *New Challenges for UNICEF, Children, Women and Human Rights* (Palgrave, 2001), and *Judging War Criminals: The Politics of International Justice* (Macmillan/St. Martin's Press, 1999).

Dennis Dijkzeul (dd459@columbia.edu) is the director of the Program for Humanitarian Affairs at the School for International and Public Affairs of Columbia University in New York. He is also a corresponding member of the Institute for International Law of Peace and Armed Conflict at the Ruhr Universität in Bochum, Germany. He has been working as a consultant for international organizations in Africa, Central America, Europe, and the US. His main interests concern the management of international organizations and the (non-)participation of local populations in development and humanitarian programs. His latest books are *Reforming for Result in the UN System: A Study of UNOPS* (Macmillan/St. Martin's Press, 2000) and together with Dirk Salomons *The Conjuror's Hat: Financing United Nations' Peace-building in Operations Directed by Special Representatives of the Secretary General* (FAFO, CIC, 2001).

Kristie Evenson (kdedor@yahoo.com) specializes in sustainable security issues. With extensive experience in countries of the former Yugoslavia, she has worked at the village level in the local language, designing and implementing projects focused on issues of political/social reconstruction and return with such agencies as UNDP, OSCE, CRS, and BPT. She has also worked closely with local legal and human rights activists as a capacity builder for NGO and legal rights networks. She received a post-graduate certificate in peace studies from the European University of Peace Studies and has a master's degree in International Affairs at Columbia University's School for International and Public Affairs, where she served as a teaching assistant to the former US ambassador to Yugoslavia, Warren Zimmermann. She is currently working as a political analyst for Southeast Europe on a project that analyzes state stability in global emerging markets.

Matthias Finger (mfinger@isp.fr) has a Ph.D in Political Science and a Ph.D. in Adult Education (both at the University of Geneva). He is interested in public sector reform and transformation, and has written numerous articles and books on this subject. He consults with public enterprises in the postal, energy, communications, and water sectors, as well as with public administrations and political authorities in Switzerland and internationally. He is currently a professor of public management at the Swiss Graduate School of Public Administration and a managing partner of The Praxis Group, Ltd.

Jacques Fomerand (fomerand@aol.com) is director of the United Nations University Office in New York. He studied law and graduated in political science from the Institut d'Etudes Politiques in Aix en Provence, and earned a Ph.D. degree at the City University of New York. He has taught at CUNY, SAIS, Long Island University, and Seton Hall University. At the UN, he followed economic and social questions in the Office of the Under-Secretary-General for International Economic and Social Affairs. He has written on matters related to the functioning of the UN, and is currently completing a book on US development cooperation policies in the United Nations.

Leon Gordenker (gordenke@princeton.edu) is a veteran scholar of multinational affairs and a specialist on the United Nations system, which he has followed since its earliest days. Born in Detroit in 1923, Gordenker earned his bachelor's degree at the University of Michigan and his master's and doctor's degrees at Columbia University. He is now Research Associate at the Center of International Studies at Princeton University and Professor Emeritus of Politics there. Both a participant and an observer, he has worked as a member of the UN Secretariat, has represented a non-governmental organization, and has been a consultant for the United Nations, the UN Institute for Training and Research, and currently for the UN University. He has taught in universities in Africa and Europe as well as the United States. Leon Gordenker is the author or editor of numerous articles and books. Among his recent books are *NGOs, the UN and Global Governance* (Lynne Rienner, 1996), *The United Nations at the End of the 1990s* (St. Martin's Press/Macmillan, 1999), and *International Cooperation in Response to AIDS* (Pinter, 1995).

Klaus Hüfner (huefner@wiwiss.fu-berlin.de) is a professor at the Freie Universität in Berlin and Honorary President of the World Federation of United Nations Associations (WFUNA), Geneva/New York. He is also president of the German Commission for UNESCO in Bonn, and chairman of the Advisory Board of the European Centre for Higher Education (UNESCO-CEPES) in Bucharest. In addition, he is a member of the Governing Board of the International Institute for Educational Planning (UNESCO-IIEP) in Paris.

Dietrich Kappeler (kappelerblonay@bluewin.ch) holds a doctorate in international law from the University of Bern. He served in the Swiss diplomatic service from 1958 to 1965. From 1965 to 1975 he was a consultant to the Carnegie Endowment for International Peace for diplomatic training. In 1975, he became associated as professor with the Graduate Institute of International Studies and seconded to the Centre for Graduate International Studies at the University of Tehran from 1975 to 1977. From 1977 to 1990 he was seconded to the University of Nairobi, Diplomacy Training Program and Faculty of Law. He was founding director of the Mediterranean Academy of Diplomatic Studies from 1990 to 1993, and remained its chairman until 1998. In 1993 he was recalled to Geneva to serve as director of the Diplomatic Studies Programs at the Graduate Institute of International Studies. In this capacity he became a member of the International Forum of Diplomatic Training. He served as its rapporteur from 1996 to 1998, and retired in October 1998.

Bérangère Magarinos-Ruchat (magarinos@itcilo.it) works at the United Nations System Staff College in Turin, Italy. She develops training and learning activities on the themes of trisectoral partnerships and global governance networks. Her program targets both UN country teams in the field and UN staff at headquarters level. The concern at the core of her work is how UN staff can adapt to the challenges of globalization. Her work focuses more specifically on the nature of the relations between the UN and the business community. She has a master's degree in Public Administration from the Graduate Institute for Public Administration in Lausanne, Switzerland, and a Ph.D. degree in International Relations from the Maxwell School for Citizenship and Public Affairs at Syracuse University, New York.

Dirk Salomons (dirksal@aol.com) is managing partner of The Praxis Group, Ltd., an international change management-consulting firm based in the US and Switzerland. Praxis works mainly with public service entities, and its collaborators have expertise in humanitarian assistance, peacekeeping, and postconflict recovery, as well as in human resources and privatization. He holds appointments as Adjunct Professor of Public Administration at both Columbia University and New York University. Earlier in his career, he served in a wide range of management, peace building, and policy advisory functions in organizations of the UN system, including FAO, UNDP, UNAIDS, UNOPS, and the UN Secretariat. His most cherished assignment was as executive director of the United Nations peacekeeping operation in Mozambique. He holds a *kandidaats* degree and a *doctoraal* in comparative literature and sociology from the University of Amsterdam.

Ian Smillie (ismillie@magmacom.com) is an Ottawa-based development consultant and writer. He has lived and worked in Sierra Leone, Nigeria, and Bangladesh. He was a founder of the Canadian development organization, Inter Pares, and was executive director of CUSO from 1979 to 1983. He is an associate of the Humanitarianism and War Project at Tufts University in Boston, and is an Adjunct Professor of International Development Studies at Tulane University in New Orleans. During 2000 he served on a UN Security Council panel investigating the links between illicit weapons and the diamond trade in Sierra Leone. His latest books are *Mastering the Machine Revisited: Poverty, Aid and Technology* (IT Publications, 2000) and *Managing for Change: Leadership, Strategy and Management in Asian NGOs* (with John Hailey, Earthscan/OUP, 2001).

Dennis Smith (dcs2@nyu.edu), a political scientist with a Ph.D. from Indiana University, is a member of the faculty and director of the Office of International Programs at Robert F. Wagner Graduate School of Public Service at NYU, which includes a master of science program in the Management of International Public Service Organizations. In recent years, he has studied the problems of measuring the success of reforms in public sector organizations, especially "problem-solving community policing." His article on police reform in New York City, coauthored with former NYC Police Commissioner William Bratton, was published in the fall of 2001. He is a board member of the Institute of Public Administration and a senior consultant on performance management at SEEDCO in New York City.

Alex de Waal (Alex_de_Waal@compuserve.com), a writer and an activist, has worked for 17 years on questions of war, famine, and human rights in North East Africa. He was educated at Oxford, where he obtained a D.Phil. in social anthropology. He is a director of Justice Africa, a London-based organization that supports human rights, peace, and democracy in Africa, and director of programs at the International African Institute. Formerly, he has worked for African Rights, InterAfrica Group, and Human Rights Watch, as well as being chairman of the Mines Advisory Group. He is also a consultant to the UN Economic Commission for Africa on the New African Initiative. He is author of six books and numerous articles, including: *Famine that Kills: Darfur, Sudan, 1984–1985* (Clarendon Press, 1989), *Facing Genocide: The Nuba of Sudan* (African Rights, 1995), *Food and Power in Sudan* (African Rights, 1997), and *Famine Crimes: Politics and the Disaster Relief Industry in Africa* (James Currey, 1997).

AUTHORS INDEX

Gouillart, F., 142
Graham, R.J., 197, 220
Greenwood, E., 201, 203, 206
Grüning, G., 10

Haas, E.B., 7, 14, 18
Hanan, N., 124
Handler Chayes, A., 8
Harrel Allen, T., 203
Holloway, S., 50
Holm, T.T., 285
Hulme, D., 8

Ignatieff, M., 238, 290–291

Jacobson, H.K., 5
James, R.R., 124
Jervis, R., 5
Jolly, R., 104
Jönsson, C., 7, 9
Jordan, R.S., 102, 125
Judge, A., 4, 74, 187, 239

Kelly, J., 142
Keohane, R.O., 9, 14, 16, 334
Kerzner, H., 197
Kingsbury, B., 13, 18
Klingebiel, S., 7, 8, 18
Knight, W.A., 10
Kooiman, J., 10, 334
Kottler, J.P., 142
Krasner, S.D., 7, 14
Kratochwil, F., 5, 19
Krishna, A., 230
Kristinsson, G.H., 118

Langrod, G., 117–118
Lanting, B., 19
Laurenti, J., 33
Lindenberg, M., ix, 4, 11, 19
Loewenheim, F.L., 72
Luard, E., 283
Lynch, C., 285
Lyons, G.M., 50

Malone, D.M., 18
Maren, M., 8
Marinelli, L., 192
Mathiason, J.R., 282–283
Mayer, R.R., 201, 203, 206
Maynard, K.A., 215, 335

Maynes, C.W., 74
Mazmanian, D., 200–201
McNeil, D.G., 262, 265
Mearsheimer, J.J., 19, 20
Mercier, J.-Y., 142
Messick, F.M., 72
Meyer, M., 237
Miles, R., 142, 276
Minear, L., 19
Mintzberg, H., 142
Moeller, S.D., 19
Moorhead, C., 245
Morales Nieto, J., 8
Muldoon, J.P., 104

Ness, G.D., 7
Nicholls, L., 77
Nienhaus, V., 19
Nye, J.S., 334

Omaar, R., 256
Osborne, D., 10
Owen, U., 245

Parry, S.B., 134
Parsons, W., 285
Pasic, A., 8
Pasmore, W.A., 9
Patrick, S., 18
Patton, M.Q., 208
Pollitt, C., 142
Power, J., 239
Pressman, J.L., 7, 201, 207, 284
Price, N., 230
Putnam, R.D., 290, 334

Rapley, J., 101
Ratner, S., 334
Reinicke, W.H., 10
Rey, J-N., 142
Rieff, D., 291, 313, 334
Roberts, A., 13, 18, 253
Robles, A.C., 14
Rochester, J.M., 5
Rosenau, J.N., 10
Rossi, P.H., 199, 207–208
Ruchat (Magarinos-Ruchat), B., 83, 141
Ruggie, J.G., 5, 7, 19

Sabatier, P., 200–201
Salomons, D., 224

KEYWORDS INDEX

WATER FOR PEOPLE – WATER FOR LIFE
The UN World Water Development Report

Published in Association with **UNESCO**

The world's freshwater resources are coming under growing pressure through such environmental hazards as human waste, urbanization, industrialization, and pesticides. The problems are exacerbated through drought in many parts of the world. The improvement of the water quality itself and access to it have been major concerns for politicians and development agencies for over a decade. First officially formulated at the Rio Earth Summit of 1992, they have been restated or expanded since then.

The UN Millennium Declaration of 2000 transformed general guidelines into specific targets. The international community pledged "to halve by 2015 the proportion of people who are unable to reach, or to afford, safe drinking water" and "to stop the unsustainable exploitation of water resources, by developing water management strategies at the regional, national and local levels, which promote both equitable access and adequate supplies." Thus, ten years after Rio it is time to take stock.

Based on the collective inputs of 23 United Nations agencies and convention secretariats, this Report offers a global overview of the state of the world's freshwater resources. It is part of an ongoing assessment process to develop policies and help with their implementation as well as to measure any progress toward achieving sustainable use of water resources.

Generously illustrated with more than 25 full-color global maps and numerous figures, the report reviews progress and trends and presents seven pilot case studies of river basins representing various social, economic, and environmental settings: Lake Titicaca (Bolivia, Peru); Senegal river basin (Senegal, Mali, Mauritania, Guinea); Seine Normandy (France); Lake Peipsi/Chudskoe (Estonia, Russia); Ruhuna basin (Sri Lanka); Greater Tokyo region (Japan); and Chao Phraya (Thailand). It assesses progress in 11 challenge areas, including health, food, environment, shared water resources, cities, industry, energy, risk management, knowledge, valuing water, and governance. Proposing methodologies and indicators for measuring sustainability, it lays the foundations for regular, system-wide monitoring and reporting by the UN, together with the development of standardized methodologies and data.

With its comprehensive maps, glossary, references, and coverage of a broad range of themes and examples of real-world river basins, the UN World Water Development Report will no doubt prove to be a most valuable reference work.

Spring 2003, ca. 500 pages, 25 maps, figs., tables.
ISBN 1-57181-627-5 hardback
ISBN 1-57181-628-3 paperback

Related Titles by *Berghahn Books*

TIBETANS IN NEPAL
The Dynamics of International Assistance among a Community in Exile

Ann Frechette

Based on eighteen months of field research conducted in exile carpet factories, settlement camps, monasteries, and schools in the Kathmandu Valley of Nepal, as well as in Dhara-msala, India, and Lhasa, Tibet, this book offers an important contribution to the debate on the impact of international assistance on migrant communities. The author explores the ways in which Tibetan exiles in Nepal negotiate their norms and values as they interact with the many international organizations that assist them, and comes to the conclusion that, as beneficial as aid agency assistance often is, it also complicates the Tibetans' efforts to define themselves as a community.

"This is a detailed and unsentimental book. It examines and explains the remarkable financial success of the Tibetan refugees in Nepal, by exploring the effects of powerful foreign assistance and lively Tibetan cooperation. The agendas of the political patrons of the Tibetans and the motives of the Tibetans themselves are inspected in a global framework of engineered transformations and organized responses. This is mandatory reading for anyone interested in international affairs and the newest achievements in anthropological fieldwork."
—**Sally Falk Moore,** Harvard University

"Frechette explicates the social and institutional conditions of Tibetan success in exile in a global-izing world.… A stimulating ethnographic excursion into the landscape of globalization."
—**Levent Soysal,** Free University, Berlin

"[The] really terrific chapter, Friends of Tibet, [is] by far the best example of transnational iden-tity around."
—**Henry Rutz,** Hamilton College

Ann Frechette is Luce Junior Professor of Asian Studies in the Department of Anthropology at Hamilton College.

Fall 2002, 256 pages, 12 ills., 6 tables, 5 figs., 3 maps, index
ISBN 1-57181-157-5 hardback
Volume 11, *Studies in Forced Migration*

Related Titles by *Berghahn Books*

CONSERVATION AND MOBILE INDIGENOUS PEOPLES
Displacement, Forced Settlement and Sustainable Development

Edited by **Dawn Chatty** and **Marcus Colchester**

Wildlife conservation and other environmental protection projects can have tremendous impact on the lives and livelihood of the often mobile, difficult-to-reach, and marginal peoples who inhabit the same territory. The contributors to this collection of case studies, social scientists as well as natural scientists, are concerned with this human element in biodiversity. They examine the interface between conservation and indigenous communities forced to move or to settle elsewhere in order to accommodate environmental policies and biodiversity concerns.

The case studies investigate successful and not so successful community-managed, as well as local participatory, conservation projects in Africa, the Middle East, South and South Eastern Asia, Australia, and Latin America. There are lessons to be learned from recent efforts in community-managed conservation, and this volume significantly contributes to that discussion.

Dawn Chatty is General Editor of Studies in Forced Migration and teaches at the Center for Refugee Studies of the University of Oxford.

Marcus Colchester works for the Forest Peoples Programme.

Fall 2002, 416 pages, bibliog., index
ISBN 1-57181-841-3 hardback
ISBN 1-57181-842-1 paperback
ISBN 1-57181-843-X e-book
Volume 10, *Studies in Forced Migration*

Related Titles by *Berghahn Books*

THE POLICING OF POLITICS IN THE TWENTIETH CENTURY
Historical Perspectives

Edited by **Mark Mazower**

The role of the police has, from its beginnings, been ambiguous, even Janus-faced. This volume focuses on one of its controversial aspects by showing how the police have been utilized in the past by regimes in Europe, the United States, and the British Empire to check political dissent and social unrest.

Ideologies such as anti-communism emerge as significant influences in both democracies and dictatorships. And by shedding new light on policing continuities in twentieth-century Germany and Italy, as well as Interpol, this volume questions the compatibility of democratic government and political policing.

Contents: Introduction: Political Police and the European Nation-State in the Nineteenth Century, *Clive Emsley;* A Republican Political Police? Political Policing in France under the Third Republic, 1875–1940, *Jean-Marc Berlière;* Continuity in Policing Politics in Italy, 1920–1960, *Jonathan Dunnage;* Policing Politics in Germany from Weimar to the Stasi, *Herbert Reinke;* The International Criminal Police Commission and the Fight against Communism, 1923–1945, *Cyrille Fijnaut;* Policing the Anti-Communist State in Greece, 1922–1974, *Mark Mazower;* Police and Government in Northern Ireland, 1922–1969, *Keith Jeffery;* Securing the British Empire: Policing and Colonial Order, 1920–1960, *David Killingray;* Political Policing in the United States: The Evolution of the FBI, 1917–1956, *Athan G. Theoharis;* The Tokko and Political Police in Japan, 1911–1945, *Elise K. Tipton;* Conclusion: The Policing of Politics in Historical Perspective, *Mark Mazower*

Mark Mazower received his D. Phil. in Modern History from Oxford University. He taught History at Princeton University and International Relations at the University of Sussex, and currently he is Professor of History at Birkbeck College, University of London.

1997. 272 pages, index
ISBN 1-57181-873-1 hardback

www.berghahnbooks.com